C

T3-BPX-371

DISCARDED
FROM
UNIVERSITY OF DAYTON
ROESCH LIBRARY

PROLEGOMENA TO LIBRARY CLASSIFICATION

PROLEGOMENA TO LIBRARY CLASSIFICATION

by

S. R. RANGANATHAN

With a Preface by
W. C. BERWICK SAYERS

LONDON
THE LIBRARY ASSOCIATION
CHAUCER HOUSE, MALET PLACE
1957

MARIAN LIBRARY

SHIYALI RAMAMRITA **RANGANATHAN**, 1892–

Edition 1:   1937
Edition 2:   1957

2 : 51
N 57

Z
69
R2
57

Made and printed in Great Britain by
THE GARDEN CITY PRESS LIMITED, LETCHWORTH, HERTFORDSHIRE

TO

CHIRANJIVI
TRIPLICANE RANGANATHAN YOGESWARAN
B.Sc.(Hons.), Diplom Ingenieur(ETH)

3-26-65 B. H. Blackwell £ 2 - 5

ACKNOWLEDGEMENTS

The Author acknowledges his indebtedness to the following institutions and persons:

1. The Library Association, London, for its taking up the publication of this book;
2. Messrs. J. Mills, B. I. Palmer and B. C. Vickery, for their help in preparing the press-copy of the book;
3. Mr. D. J. Foskett for relieving the author totally of all the work involved in seeing the book through the press;
4. The Garden City Press Ltd., for the excellent style in which the book has been produced.

23239

CONTENTS

PART 1

General Theory of Classification

PART 2

Theory of Knowledge Classification
First Approximation. Enumerative Classification

Contents

PART 3

Theory of Knowledge Classification. Second Approximation. Analytico-Synthetic Classification

PART 4

Theory of Knowledge Classification
Third Approximation. Depth Classification

PART 5

Theory of Knowledge Classification
Demonstration

Contents

PART 6

Theory of Book Classification

PART 7

Schemes of Library Classification
Looking Back

PART 8

Theory of Abstract Classification
Looking Forwards

Contents

Chapter		Page

PREFACE

It is a special pleasure to be invited to preface this remarkable book with a few words. For thirty years, since its author, then Librarian of Madras University, came to the School of Librarianship at University College in London, and listened patiently to my own tentative lectures on library classification, I have watched his career with increasing interest and something akin to wonder. There were librarians in India before Ranganathan, but this new one brought new qualities. Our courses were too elementary for him and he wisely directed himself to the mastery of our librarianship literature, to a stay in a public library, and visits to schools and cultural institutions, and so became convinced that in libraries was a field of immense importance to the new India coming to independence. As is known, he first reviewed that field in his first significant book, *The Five Laws of Library Science,* 1931 (new edition 1957), a work of great simplicity which conceals depths and yet reveals what may be called the spiritual but intensely practical springs of his activity.

Early he told me that his mind was intent upon a new scheme of classification for India. I demurred that this meant a life work, but he was not deterred. *Colon* emerged, and the call for five more editions since, is one measure of his success. It was while immersed in the problems of *Colon* that he " forged," to use a strong verb of which he is fond, his *Prolegomena* which came to us in 1937. A most precise, theoretical, practical and comparative exposition of library classification theory that, while it acknowledged the influence of Bliss's two well-known books on *The Organisation of Knowledge,* was still intensely original. It is not within my space here to say in what ways it over-rode many of the obstacles to real understanding of the art of analysing and assembling books; that the student will discover by the rewarding study of the book itself.

All through the years, in spite of his occupation in India and in both hemispheres with other general and special problems of librarianship, his work on classification has continued, so that now there is hardly a classifier who has not felt his influence. He has recorded in many places the developments that followed and a glance at his own copy, interwritten for this edition of *Prolegomena,* would show that the book has been practically recast. Its arrangement is masterly, its scope enormous; its contribution invaluable. When Earl Mountbatten, India's Governor-General, as Chancellor, bestowed the University of Delhi's degree of Master of Letters on Shiyali Ramamrita Ranganathan, its then Professor of Library Science, the Vice-Chancellor, Sir Maurice Gwyer, presented him with the words " He is the father of library science in India. . . . His reputation as a Librarian extends far beyond the borders of his own country and his opinion and advice are valued in all lands where libraries are held in honour." A view now generally accepted.

The work of setting Dr. Ranganathan's formidable manuscript in order and preparing it for the press has been the labour of love of Mr. D. J. Foskett, one of his most gifted English disciples. He has fulfilled his task skilfully.

The Library Association does honour to a pioneer in publishing this edition and gives privilege to itself. I may add that all the profit of his many books Dr. Ranganathan has devoted to the establishment of a Chair of Librarianship, at his own University of Madras, the consummation of a devoted life.

W. C. BERWICK SAYERS

LISTS OF CANONS, PRINCIPLES AND DEVICES

1 CANONS OF CLASSIFICATION

21

4 POSTULATES

Note: The figure in brackets, against each postulate, is the number of the section dealing with it.

(1) Time, Space, Energy, Matter, and Personality are postulated as Five Fundamental Categories (3501).

(2) Every characteristic can be assigned to one and only one fundamental category (3502).

(3) Whole, Part, Portion, Organ, and Constituent are postulated as useful concepts (3503).

(4) Division of a universe on the basis of a characteristic may yield classes containing only wholes, portions, organs or constituents respectively (3504).

(5) The physiographical features of the surface of the earth are analogous to the organs of a person, from the point of view of levels in classification (3522).

(6) The first manifestation of energy in a basic class is its First Round Energy Facet; the second manifestation, the Second Round Energy Facet; and so on (3532).

(7) An Energy Facet can have only one array (3535).

(8) The first round is started by the basic class (3561).

(9) Energy can start a new round (3561).

(10) In any round, any number of levels of personality may occur consecutively (3561).

(11) In any round, any number of levels of matter may occur consecutively (3561).

(12) There is no level for energy (3561).

(13) In any round, the fundamental categories occur in the sequence —Personality, Matter and Energy (3561).

(14) Space and Time can occur only in the last round (3561).

(15) Space and Time stand arranged in the sequence—Space and Time (3561).

(16) A common personality or matter isolate may start a round (3561).

(17) A common personality or matter isolate may be after-space or after-time (3561).

(18) The round preceding a common isolate round may end with a space facet or with a time facet, according to the nature of the common isolate initiating it (3561).

(19) An actand facet should precede and an actor or an instrument facet should succeed the energy (action) isolate concerned, when the result of the action is not an ultimate commodity (4611).

(20) The product facet should precede and the instrument facet

should succeed the energy (action) isolate concerned, when the product is an ultimate commodity (4612).

(21) Starter should be omitted if either (1) the subject device number starts a phase, or (2) all the foci in an array are got by subject device; Arrester should be omitted if the subject device number is not followed by a facet belonging to the whole of the class number ending with the subject device number (36144).

LIST OF NORMATIVE PRINCIPLES

THE FIVE LAWS OF LIBRARY SCIENCE

1. Books are for use.
2. Books are for all; or Every reader his book.
3. Every book its reader.
4. Save the time of the reader.
5. A library is a growing organism.

CHAPTER o

CONSPECTUS

01 SUDDEN IDEA

WHEN ONE IS ENGAGED on a problem, the most useful ideas occur suddenly. They seem at once to cast a flood of light over murky tracts of half-formed thought, and promise reward to further exploitation. This has been my experience, and it is doubtless shared by many others. These surprise ideas present themselves as ready-made wholes, coming at the oddest moments. They seldom come if they are sought, and delight in choosing moments when pen and paper cannot be used to impede their flight. They come and whisper in our ears as we lie sleepily in bed, or as we mechanically repeat a long-drawn-out hymn as part of the daily routine of worship. To sit at the study table, with note-book and pencil, with the intention of meditating on one's problem, invariably produces only sleep.

011 Sense of Assurance

There is one notable feature of these ideas: they always seem at first inspired. We think them quite original. But before long, there comes awakening, usually even before we have developed our first notes. Somebody else is found to have thought of the same thing before, and has expressed it all in some well-known work! One's feelings at this discovery are mixed. First there is dismay at being deprived—nay, robbed—of well-deserved priority. Then there is relief that one is spared the labour of cudgelling one's brains over the pioneer work involved. Further, there is satisfaction in the thought that if other, cleverer, men have trodden this way before, then one is probably on the right path, and not wandering hopelessly in the wilderness. A sense of assurance emerges.

012 Enjoyable Journey

Finally, one is buoyed up by the hope that if one continues long enough on this path, one will in the end have climbed the crests of the known and be looking forward to undiscovered country. Would that it were possible that in this book the distant peaks should be visible through the wreaths of mist! One can hope for no more than this, and yet one is conscious of a thoroughly enjoyable journey, which has recalled again and again the sentiment expressed by R. L. Stevenson, " To travel hopefully is a better thing than to arrive."

02 POSITIVISTIC PREPARATION

This book has its roots running into:

(1) Thirty years' work in forging and polishing the Colon Classification;

(2) Twenty-seven years' work in teaching the Colon Classification and the Decimal Classification;

(3) Seven years' work in teaching and critical study of the Universal Decimal Classification and the Colon Classification.

Much of the teaching was to mixed classes composed of some highly disciplined minds and a few bewildered but willing ones in need of being led step by step with explanations and illustrations even of the obvious. In teaching such classes, the exposition given in existing textbooks was sometimes found inadequate. This experience gave a positivistic preparation for the sprouting of new ideas.

03 HIDDEN POTENTIALITIES

It is now thirty years since the Colon Classification was forged. During this period the scheme has been applied to more than 200,000 volumes and articles, some of which covered the wave-front of nascent thought on all the most important subjects. It afforded a good test, which disclosed hidden potentialities in the scheme. These had not been consciously sensed at the time of the first forging.

04 HIDDEN FAULTS

It also disclosed some maladjustments. These could no doubt have been avoided if I had been working on the basis of a well-tested theory of classification. But the process was reversed in my case. My theory had to be developed later to discover the cause of such hidden faults, and to set them right. The first edition of the Colon Classification (1933) was rapidly becoming exhausted by 1936, and so I decided that it would be advantageous to work out the theory of classification before preparing the second.

05 INCUBATION

Thus it became a personal necessity and did not seem a useless labour to collect my thoughts bearing on the theory of classification, and record them in exact terms. These thoughts had been incubating in extra-conscious regions of my mind during the preceding twelve years, in a way which seemed to me exactly expressed in this passage from John Drinkwater's *Loyalties*:

> " Haunting the lucidities of life
> That are my daily beauty, moves a theme
> Beating along my undiscovered mind."

06 **PRECIPITATION**

These were the general predisposing causes. But the book was actually precipitated in June, 1936, in an attempt to expound to the class the full import of Hospitality in reference to Book Classification. The experience in the class-room had activated the latent thought-mass at all levels. The catalyst was Ramanathan, a member of the class. He was well versed in the traditional logic (*Nyaya*) of Indian thought, and he, too, felt intrigued. He stayed in the library till 8 p.m., the closing hour. Then we walked down the sea beach till 10 p.m., discussing Hospitality. When I came home I found sleep impossible. Seeing my restlessness, and probably disturbed by it, a relative sleeping in my room gave an innocent piece of advice. " Why don't you take up a book and read for a while? " he said. " That will bring you sleep." No doubt he was not aware of Schopenhauer's observation, " To put away one's own original thoughts in order to take up a book is to sin against the Holy Ghost." However, this suggestion recalled two books which I had set aside for later study, when at the first attempt I had found them unmanageable. They were the books of Bliss on Classification: *The Organisation of knowledge and the system of the sciences* (1929), and *The Organisation of knowledge in libraries* (1933).

061 **Mould Effect**

My mind was by this time so saturated with the theory of classification that so far from these two books proving difficult and causing sleep, before midnight, in a single movement, I had forged through their entire range of 740 pages. My mind was pressed through these pages in so intimate and critical a way that my own book emerged clear cut as from a mould. All that remained was to fill in details and provide illustrations.

07 **SLOW FORGING OF EDITION 2**

Unlike Edition 1, Edition 2 has been taking shape slowly during the last eight years. It has been built section by section, chapter by chapter, and part by part. It is not the result of the sudden uprush of the whole result from the trans-intellectual region. On the contrary, it is the result of slow intellectual grind—sometimes in solitude, and sometimes in company with others. Five factors favoured this.

071 **Teaching M.Lib.Sc. Class**

The first factor was the institution of a Master's and a Doctorate degree in Library Science in the University of Delhi. This was in 1948, and was, no doubt, at my suggestion. But it was the vision of Sir Maurice Gwyer, the Vice-Chancellor, his desire to make the University of Delhi the hub of research activities in India, and his faith in the full potentiality of library science in the rebuilding of renascent India, that made the Department of Library Science and these advanced courses actualities. This provided a splendid opportunity to teach General Theory of Classification at an advanced level. This demanded a systematic and detailed comparative study of the Colon Classification and the Universal Decimal Classification.

072   Contact with F.I.D.

The invitation of Donker Duyvis and his enterprise, with the help of E. J. Carter, brought me into contact with the International Federation for Documentation (F.I.D.), also in 1948. It started with a paper on *Classification and international documentation*, prepared at the request of Donker Duyvis and published by the F.I.D. Experience of the annual meetings of the F.I.D. and of its long series of documents gave me an insight into the difficulties of fitting the U.D.C. and C.C. to face the outpouring of micro-thought. In 1950, the F.I.D. felt the need for examining the foundations of classification, and accordingly formed its Committee F.I.D./C.A. on the General Theory of Classification. I was asked to be its Rapporteur-General, which turned me virtually into a whole-timer on the subject. Each of the five *Annual reports* made to the F.I.D. marks a stage in the slow forging of the matter now being incorporated into this second edition of the *Prolegomena*.

073   Contact with Unesco

J. B. Reid established contact with the Science Wing of Unesco in 1950. It engaged me for a few weeks to examine the connection between classification and machinery for bibliographical searching. The results were published by Unesco in *Classification, coding, and machinery for search* (1950).

074   Medium for Exchange

The *Abgila* was started as an organ of the Indian Library Association in 1949, when I was President of the Association. Its *Annals* part was reserved for high-level articles based on research. This served as a medium for the international exchange of nascent thought, and proved a great stimulus; many potential original thinkers in branches of library science became actual thinkers. Many of them contributed to the series *Optional facets* appearing in the *Annals* part from 1949 to 1952, and to the series on *Critique of the U.D.C.* and on *Dialectics of the U.D.C.* I withdrew from the Presidency of the Association in 1953. There was then no sign of the *Abgila* being continued, but the demand for a high-level medium was appreciable, and, in particular, colleagues in India, Japan, England, Holland and the U.S.A. promised support for such a medium. Accordingly, the *Annals of library science* was started as a private venture in 1954, and was taken over in 1955 by a public body, the Indian Science Documentation Centre. This body has to classify everyday nascent micro-thought in hundreds of articles, and thus it is a fitting laboratory to carry forward researches on the foundation of library classification, with a background of reality. The articles on the subject appear in the *Annals* in the series entitled *Depth classification.*

075 Contact with Industries

In 1950, the Rockefeller Foundation invited me to the U.S.A. Its president told me that one of the reasons for inviting me was to give me facilities to forge the foundations of library classification as a language of ordinal numbers, so as to make it serve, if possible, as an international language of communication, free from folk-modifications and the fuzziness usually caused in national languages by folk-modifications, emotional undertones, and the association of ideas. This question was examined in my *Classification and communication* (1951). The Foundation provided facilities to contact many industries, where I observed the manufacturing processes and the organisation of documentation in several industrial and specialised research libraries. These observations disclosed many faults in the foundation of classification. A preliminary analysis was made at the Conference on Bibliographic Organisation held by the Graduate School of Library Science at the University of Chicago in July, 1950. The mode of formation of micro-thought in industry and in the departments of administration in commerce, industry and government pointed a way for reconstructing the foundations of classification, so as to take the load of micro-thought, now becoming more and more atomised.

076 Library Research Circle

Further pursuit needed collective thinking among peers, and to supply this want a Library Research Circle was formed in Delhi, also in 1950. It gave stimulating opportunities to dig deeper and deeper into the foundations of classification until the primordial rock was struck. Sunday after Sunday, the circle met at my residence, C6 Maurice Nagar, for nearly six hours, from 2 till 8 p.m. This went on for about four years.

077 Classification Research Group

In this pursuit, ideas became clarified by contact with the Classification Research Group in London, through occasional visits and correspondence.

078 Preliminary Consolidation

In 1953 my students, past and present, co-operated splendidly in collecting together and consolidating in a preliminary way the results obtained between 1947 and 1953. These results were presented to the Tenth All-India Library Conference held at Hyderabad in the form of the book *Depth classification* (1953).

079 **Endless Vistas**

Discussion with all these colleagues—many of them old students accustomed to scientific method—led to considerable reconstruction. The substance of this second edition of the *Prolegomena* has been forged slowly, laboriously and quantum by quantum, in this manner. Endless vistas needing continued investigation are laid bare as we move forward in this enchanting, though laborious, pursuit. The postulational approach suggested in this book has great potency. Incidentally, it suggests a test to decide when a scheme of classification is essentially different from another or is essentially new.

08 **LAYOUT**

The layout has been changed drastically in this edition. The progress made in the work since the publication of the first edition in 1937 has made this change necessary. In place of the original nine chapters grouped into two parts, this edition has sixty-four chapters grouped into eight parts. Part 8 is new; it looks forward, and suggests the need for the formation and pursuit of a new discipline—Abstract Classification.

The contents of the several chapters in the several parts are displayed in detail in the " Contents " given in pages 7 to 17. But an important change should be mentioned here. Part 5 reproduces a part of the matter of chapters 7 and 8 of the first edition. In that edition, the Decimal Classification was one of the schemes compared. But a full comparison of the D.C. and C.C. was made by diverse hands in 1944, and the results were published in the *Proceedings* of the Sixth All-India Library Conference held at Jaipur in 1944. The D.C. has therefore been replaced by the U.D.C. in this second edition, and the Bibliographic Classification has also been brought into the comparative study.

PART I

GENERAL THEORY OF CLASSIFICATION

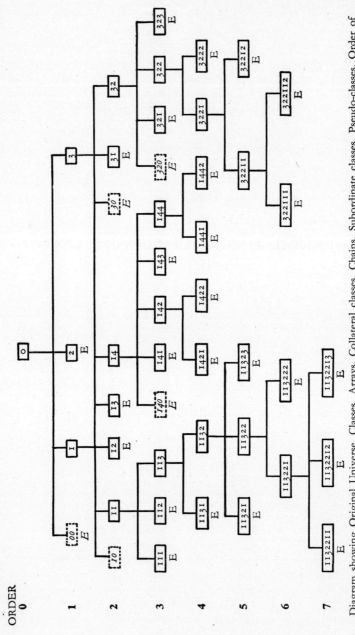

ORDER
0

1

2

3

4

5

6

7

Diagram showing Original Universe, Classes, Arrays, Collateral classes, Chains, Subordinate classes, Pseudo-classes, Order of classes and arrays, Division, Assortment and Filiatory arrangement

The numbers in the rectangles are Decimal Fractions. A decimal point should be understood to the left of each number

34

CHAPTER 11

DIAGRAMMATIC APPROACH

110 Introduction

To APPRECIATE THE STRENGTH and weakness of a scheme of classification, to compare the relative merits of two or more schemes and to do the day-to-day work of classification in a library consistently and in conformity to the chosen scheme, it is necessary and helpful to enunciate a set of tests and to lay down some systematic procedure. To arrive at the tests, to lay down a system of procedure, and to study schemes of classification in precise and concise terms, it is necessary and helpful to have the fundamental concepts and terms associated with the discipline of classification examined and defined as a preliminary measure. This part is devoted to the last-mentioned problem. This chapter will deal with it diagrammatically and concretely, and the second chapter will make an analytical approach in an abstract manner.

111 Original Universe

The diagram on the left-hand page is the basis of exposition. In the diagram there are forty rectangles, excluding the dotted ones; they are all marked with numbers. They all represent classes, hanging, as it were, from the class o. This class will be called the Original Universe.

112 Unitary Class

There are twenty-five rectangles marked E, excluding the dotted ones. These rectangles will be taken to contain *one* and *only one* Entity, and each such class is a Unitary Class. These entities will be named by the numbers contained in their respective rectangles, and these numbers will be used to denote their respective entities.

These numbers are 111, 112, 1131, 11321, 1132211, 1132212, 1132213, 113222, 11323, 12, 13, 141, 1421, 1422, 143, 1441, 1442, 2, 31, 321, 322111, 322112, 32212, 3222, 323.

This will look like a mess, if the numbers are integers; but they are all decimal fractions. A decimal point should be taken as understood to the left of each number, and then it can be seen that these decimal fractions are arranged strictly in ascending order of magnitude.

35

113 Complete Assortment

Let us consider the twenty-five entities contained in the twenty-five unitary classes. These twenty-five entities lie isolated from each other. Proceeding from left to right, they are arranged in a definite sequence, namely the ascending sequence of the decimal fraction numbers denoting them. An arrangement like this, of unitary classes in a definite sequence, is a Complete Assortment of the entities.

Let us think of the starting-point. Then, all these twenty-five entities were huddled together in the rectangle at the top, marked o. We have already agreed to call this aggregate of the twenty-five entities the Original Universe. Now we shall trace the successive stages by which the entities may be isolated.

114 Class

Let us imagine that the aggregate of these twenty-five entities in the original universe o is divided into the three sub-aggregates or Groups marked 1, 2 and 3, on the basis of some Characteristic or Attribute determining them as those assignable to group 1 or group 2 or group 3. Let us further assume, as actually appears on the diagram, that these groups are arranged in the ascending sequence of the numbers 1, 2, 3 denoting them. Then the groups are arranged in a definite sequence; in other words, each group is assigned a rank, or, to put it more simply, each group is Ranked. A ranked group is a Class. Thus the rectangles 1, 2, 3 are classes. The twenty-five entities of the original universe o have been at this stage Assorted into the classes 1, 2 and 3. Each of these classes is of Order One.

115 Array of Classes

1151 First Order

These classes form an Array. They have been derived from the original universe by one process of assortment. Therefore, we call their array an Array of Order One.

Now the class 2 is marked E, and it is therefore a unitary class, that is, it contains one and only one entity; it has isolated one entity. But the classes 1 and 3 are not marked E, and therefore they are not unitary classes. Therefore, they must be Multiple Classes, and each one of them has more than one entity. In fact, the remaining twenty-four entities of the original universe have been shared among them. A little counting in the diagram will show the number of entities shared by each of them: class 1 should contain seventeen entities, and class 3 should contain seven entities.

1152 Second Order

Let us follow the diagram further. At the second stage, class 1 would be subdivided into the four classes 11, 12, 13, 14. These four classes are of Order Two, and their array is an Array of Order Two. Similarly, Class 3 would be subdivided into its two classes 31 and 32. These two classes form another Array of Order Two, and the classes are also of Order Two.

Now of the six classes of Order Two, the classes 12, 13 and 31 are marked E, and they are therefore unitary classes. The remaining three classes 11, 14 and 32 are multiple classes, sharing between themselves the twenty-one entities not yet isolated. A little counting in the diagram will show the number of entities shared by each of them: the multiple class 11 should have nine, the multiple class 14 six, and the multiple class 32 six entities.

<h3 align="center">1153 Higher Order</h3>

At the third stage, class 11 would be subdivided into the three classes 111, 112 and 113. Each of these is of Order Three. Similarly, class 14 would be subdivided into the Third Order Classes 141, 142, 143 and 144; so also the class 32 would be subdivided into the Third Order Classes 321, 322, and 323. These ten third order classes arrange themselves into three Arrays of Order Three. Of the ten third order classes, six are marked E, and are thus unitary classes. The remaining four, 113, 142, 144 and 322, are multiple classes. These four multiple classes should share among themselves the fifteen entities not yet isolated.

In this way, classes of orders four, five, six and seven are formed at successive stages as shown in the diagram. All the classes of the seventh order are marked E, and therefore no further division is possible.

The diagram shows that fourteen multiple classes, other than the Original Universe, are formed in the process of the Complete Assortment of the twenty-five entities of the original universe.

<h2 align="center">116 Filiatory Arrangement</h2>

Let us arrange all the classes and all the entities (unitary classes), numbering forty in all, in the ascending sequence of the decimal fractions denoting them. We get, 0, 1, 11, 111, 112, 113, 1131, 1132, 11321, 11322, 113221, 1132211, 1132212, 1132213, 113222, 11323, 12, 13, 14, 141, 142, 1421, 1422, 143, 144, 1441, 1442, 2, 3, 31, 32, 321, 322, 3221, 32211, 322111, 322112, 32212, 3222, 323.

This arrangement has given a special sequence. It arranges together all the twenty-five entities of the original universe and all the fifteen classes, including the original universe, formed in the course of the complete assortment of the original universe of the twenty-five entities. This is Filiatory Arrangement.

The resemblance of the diagram to a genealogical tree is obvious. The above arrangement is like that which has the ancestor at the head with line after line of descendants coming thereafter in succession in the best order of filiation. The arrangement is called a filiatory arrangement because of this resemblance.

37

The arrangement of the entities alone, that is, the result of knocking away from the filiatory arrangement all the classes, has already been named a Complete Assortment.

117 Scheme of Classification

A third alternative is to consider the arrangement of the fifteen classes alone, that is, knocking away from the filiatory arrangement all the entities. Thus we get the following arrangement of classes: 0, 1, 11, 113, 1132, 11322, 113221, 14, 142, 144, 3, 32, 322, 3221, 32211. This arrangement of the classes alone is a Scheme of Classification. It is not a random arrangement; on the contrary, it is a filiatory arrangement of the classes.

118 Chain of Classes

A few more terms and concepts may now be introduced:

A set of classes such as 3, 32, 322, 3221, having lineal kinship, so to speak, is a Chain of Classes. Class 3 is the First Link of the chain, class 3221 is its Last Link.

The chain 0, 32, 322, 3221, has the original universe for the first link; such a chain is a Primary Chain.

In the chain 32, 322, 3221, 32212, the last link 32212 is a unitary class; such a chain is a Loose Chain.

The chain 0, 3, 32, 322, 3221, 32212, is both primary and loose; such a chain is a Complete Chain.

The next chapter gives a formal and abstract treatment of the question, and also precise definitions of the various terms. Illustrations may be taken from the diagram on the page facing this chapter and also from the diagrammatic approach of this chapter.

CHAPTER 12

ANALYTICAL APPROACH

120 Postulated Terms

WE START WITH SOME postulated terms. These are substantial terms in the Theory of Classification; some of them are given some explanation, some are defined by being linked together in a statement. Some auxiliary terms also will be assumed in the course of development. These always form the common apparatus of any thinking. Certain terms receive a formal definition.

An Entity is any existent, concrete or conceptual, that is a thing or an idea.

Examples

1 a boy	3 redness	5 a system of philosophy
2 a book	4 sweetness	6 a subject of study

An Attribute is any property or quality of an entity.

Examples

(1) In the case of a boy, the following are some attributes:

11 height	193 character
12 colour (of the skin)	194 date of birth
13 possession of face	195 age
14 mother tongue	196 horoscope (the position of
15 intelligence	planets at the time of birth)
16 extent of knowledge	197 mode of dressing of hair
17 handwriting	198 nature of clothing
18 physical strength	
191 ancestry	
192 wealth	

(2) In the case of a book, the following are some attributes:

21 subject-matter	23 colour of the covering material
22 form in which the subject-matter is expounded (say as a catechism, a dictionary, a skeleton, or a continuous narrative)	24 quality of the paper
	25 author
	26 language
	27 year of publication
	28 printer

(3) In the case of redness, the various degrees of it and their wave-lengths are some attributes.

(4) In the case of sweetness also, the various degrees of it are some attributes.

(5) In the case of a system of philosophy, the following are some attributes:

51 number of ultimate principles assumed (e.g. monism, dualism, pluralism)	52 attitude towards reality (or otherwise) of things
	53 founder of the school
	54 country of origin

(6) In the case of a subject of study, the following are some attributes:
61 field comprehended
62 extent to which books or documents have been written on it

An Aggregate is a collection of entities, without any special arrangement among them.
A Universe is an aggregate under consideration.

121 Division
1211 LIKE AND UNLIKE

Two entities sharing a given attribute equally in measure, intensity, extent or on any other basis are Like with reference to that attribute.

Two entities not sharing a given attribute equally in measure, intensity, extent or on any other basis are Unlike with reference to that attribute.

Examples

(1) Two boys, each five feet high, but born in 1926 and 1927 respectively, are Like with reference to their *height*, but Unlike with reference to their *age*.

(2) Basu's *Algebra* and Radhakrishna Ayyar's *Algebra* are Like with reference to their *subject-matter*, but Unlike with reference to their *author*.

It must be noted that the terms Like and Unlike have no significance (1) except with reference to an attribute, and (2) unless there are two or more entities with that attribute.

1212 CHARACTERISTIC

A Characteristic is any attribute or any complex of attributes with reference to which the likeness or unlikeness of entities can be determined and at least two of them are unlike.

Examples

(1) Height is a characteristic of boys, but possession of face is not, although both of them are attributes. Possession of face is an attribute shared equally by all boys, and hence with reference to it all the boys are Like. Thus it is not a characteristic of boys considered as entities.

(2) If we are considering boys-of-equal-height as entities, height will not be a characteristic.

1213   PROCESS AND RESULT OF DIVISION

Division of a universe is the process of sorting its entities into sub-aggregates with reference to a chosen characteristic, putting like entities into the same sub-aggregate and unlike entities into different sub-aggregates.

Division will also be used to denote the result of division, i.e. a group of sub-aggregates formed by a division of the entities of a universe.

The chosen characteristic is the Division Characteristic.

Example: The aggregate of boys in a class-room is a Universe. Sort them with reference to their height. Then the Division Characteristic is height; and boys of the same height form a sub-aggregate. Division denotes the state of having been sorted as well as the process of sorting.

Divisions of the same universe based on Concomitant Characteristics will not be different.

Divisions of the same universe based on Independent Characteristics will, in general, be different.

Example: Height and age are independent characteristics; they will, in general, divide the boys into two different sets of sub-aggregates. But age and year of birth are concomitant characteristics; they will divide them into the same set of sub-aggregates.

The number of possible different divisions (considered as processes) of a universe cannot be greater than the number of independent characteristics of the entities of that universe.

1214   GROUP

Any sub-aggregate of a universe is a Group.
A Unitary Group is a group containing one and only one entity.
A Multiple Group is a group containing two or more entities.

1215   PROCESS OF COMPLETE DIVISION

Complete Division of a universe is the process of continuing its division on the basis of a sequence of characteristics until no multiple group is left.

At the first stage of division, some groups may be unitary, and some may be multiple. Each multiple group may, in its turn, be considered a universe, and may be divided on the basis of a further characteristic. Each multiple group will, then, give rise to a number of groups; some of these may be unitary, and some may be multiple. If the process of division is continued with each resulting multiple group, and if the number of entities is finite, a stage will be reached when there will be no multiple group left, and the universe will then have been sorted into unitary groups. This means that the entities of the original universe will have been isolated.

12151   Result of Complete Division

Complete Division will also be used to denote the result of complete division, which is the completely isolated state of the entities of the universe.

It is obvious that in the second sense of the term, there can be one and only one Complete Division of a universe, whatever may be the initial characteristic and the further characteristics used, and whatever may be their sequence of succession.

Example: If the universe of boys in a class-room is divided on the basis of their height, the first multiple group so formed may be divided by age, the second by weight, the third by colour, the fourth by age, and so on. Again, we may further subdivide the multiple groups that still remain by appropriate characteristics, so that ultimately all the boys will be separated. The result would be the same even if we had divided first by colour, and then by age, and so on.

122   **Assortment**

Assortment of a universe is the process of its division into groups *plus* that of arranging the groups in a definite sequence (i.e. of ranking or assigning a rank to each group that arises).

Assortment will also be used to denote the result of assortment (i.e. the groups so formed and ranked).

12201   Assortment Characteristic

The Assortment Characteristic is the characteristic on the basis of which (or by which) the universe is assorted.

Example: Consider the universe of the boys in a class-room. Use height as the characteristic of assortment. Let us assume that the height of each boy is between 50 and 65 inches. Put into one group all the boys above 50 but not above 51. Put into another group those above 51 but not above 52, and so on. Then the number of groups will be fifteen or less. Let us assume that there are fifteen groups.

These fifteen groups can be arranged among themselves (ranked) in several ways, such as, in ascending sequence of height, in descending sequence of height, or so that the group having the greatest height is in the centre and those on either side of it in descending sequence as we proceed away from it, and so on. Let us assume that the groups are arranged in ascending sequence of height. Then each group is ranked.

Now there are fifteen! (factorial $15 = 1 \times 2 \times 3 \times 4 \times 5 \times 6 \times 7 \times 8 \times 9 \times 10 \times 11 \times 12 \times 13 \times 14 \times 15$) possible ways of arranging the groups among themselves. Thus, while only one *division* by height is possible, there are fifteen! ($= 1,307,674,368,000$) possible *assortments* by height.

In general, every different division of a universe will give rise to several assortments of it.

1221   CLASS

A Class is a ranked group.
A Unitary Class is a class comprising one and only one entity.
A Multiple Class is a class comprising two or more entities.

1222   ARRAY

An Array is the sequence of the classes of a universe, derived from it on the basis of a single characteristic and arranged among themselves according to their ranks.

1223   COMPLETE ASSORTMENT

Complete Assortment of a universe is the process of continuing its assortment on the basis of a sequence of characteristics until no multiple class is left.

At the first stage of assortment, some classes may be unitary, and some may be multiple. Each multiple class may, in its turn, be considered a universe, and so may be assorted on the basis of a further characteristic. Each multiple class will then give rise to an array of classes, some of which may be unitary, and some multiple. The process of assortment may be continued with each resulting multiple class and, if the number of entities is finite, a stage will ultimately be reached when there is no multiple class. Then the universe will have been assorted into unitary classes, that is, the entities of the original universe will all have been isolated and ranked.

Complete Assortment will also be used to denote the result of complete assortment.

12231   Individualise

To Individualise the entities of a universe is to separate them and rank them, that is, to arrange them in a sequence.

A complete assortment of a universe individualises its entities.

1224   SCHEME OF ASSORTMENT

A Scheme of Assortment means a statement of
  (1) the characteristics used; in conjunction with
  (2) their sequence; and
  (3) the mode of ranking of classes in each array arising in the progress towards a complete assortment of a universe.

12241   Associated Complete Assortment

The complete assortment resulting from the implementing of a scheme of assortment is the Associated Complete Assortment.

By varying the scheme of assortment, it may be possible to vary the complete assortment.

The number of complete assortments of a universe is limited. It is $n!$ if the universe contains n entities. The number of schemes of assortment may be far greater, and thus it is possible for two or more different schemes of assortment to give one and the same complete assortment.

12242   Associated Scheme

An Associated Scheme of Assortment of a given complete assortment is any of the schemes of assortment giving the complete assortment in question.

Example: Let us consider the simple case of a class-room of four boys; twenty-four complete assortments of these boys are possible. Let us take their names to be Gopu, Ramu, Seenu and Yogi.

Let us also assume that

Gopu is short, fair and light (in weight);
Ramu is tall, fair and heavy (in weight);
Seenu is tall, dark and very heavy; and
Yogi is short, dark and very light.

Now there are four characteristics available for arriving at a complete assortment of the four boys. Let us consider a few of the possible schemes of assortments and the associated complete assortments.

Scheme 1. Characteristic: name. Ranking: alphabetical. The associated complete assortment: Gopu, Ramu, Seenu, Yogi.

Scheme 2. Characteristic: weight. Ranking: descending sequence of weight. The associated complete assortment: Seenu, Ramu, Gopu, Yogi.

Scheme 3. Characteristic: weight. Ranking: very light, very heavy, heavy, light. The associated complete assortment: Yogi, Seenu, Ramu, Gopu.

Scheme 4

(1) Characteristic: height. Ranking: descending sequence of height.
(2) Characteristic: colour. Ranking: dark and fair for the tall, and fair and dark for the short.

The associated complete assortment: Seenu, Ramu, Gopu, Yogi.

Scheme 5

(1) Characteristic: colour. Ranking: fair, dark.
(2) Characteristic: name. Ranking: alphabetical.

The associated complete assortment: Gopu, Ramu, Seenu, Yogi.

Scheme 6

(1) Characteristic: height. Ranking: descending sequence of height.
(2) (*a*) For the tall:

Characteristic: colour. Ranking: dark, fair.

(*b*) For the short:

Characteristic: name. Ranking: alphabetical.

The associated complete assortment: Seenu, Ramu, Gopu, Yogi.

We can improvise several other schemes with the given attributes by varying the succession of characteristics and the ranking in each array. We can also increase the number of schemes by introducing other independent characteristics.

In the examples given, Schemes 1 and 5 give the same complete assortment, Schemes 2, 4 and 6 give the same complete assortment, different from that of schemes 1 and 5, and scheme 3 gives a third kind of complete assortment.

123 Order

The Order of a Class is the number of successive characteristics or complexes of characteristics used to derive it from an original universe.

The Order of an Array is the same as that of the classes forming it.

The classes belonging to one and the same Array are Co-ordinate. See the diagram facing chapter 11.

The Immediate Universe of a class is that class of the next smaller order, from which it has been derived; the Immediate Universe of an array is also that class of the next smaller order, from which it has been derived.

Any class of any order may be considered a class of the first order of its immediate universe. The immediate universe may in its turn be considered a class of the first order of its own immediate universe. This latter immediate universe is the universe of the second remove of the class with which we started. In the same way, we can define the universe of the third remove, the fourth remove, and so on, until we reach the original universe.

Classes of the same order but not co-ordinate are Collateral Classes.

Arrays of the same order are Collateral Arrays.

A class is Subordinate to its immediate universe, and also to its universes of all removes. Similarly, an array is Subordinate to its immediate universe and to its universes of all removes. See the diagram facing chapter 11.

The original universe is the only class of Zero Order.

124 Chain of Classes

A Chain is a sequence of classes made up of any given class, its immediate universe, and its universes of the second remove, third remove and so on. A chain may be arrested at any stage short of the original universe.

Example: In the diagram facing chapter 11, the classes marked 11, 113, 1132, 11322 and 113221 form a chain.

It is obvious that no two classes of a chain can be of the same order.

Each class in the chain is a Link in the chain.

The First Link of a chain is the class of the lowest order comprised in it.

The Last Link of a chain is the class of the highest order comprised in it.

Example: In the example of a chain cited above, class 11 is the first link and class 113221 is the last link.

The Order of a chain is the order of its first link.

Example: In our example, the order of the chain is 2, because the order of class 11, its first link, is 2.

A Primary Chain is a chain of zero order, that is, a chain with the original universe as its first link.

Example: In the diagram facing chapter 11, the chain whose successive classes are 0, 3 and 32 is a primary chain. It can be seen that there are many other primary chains in the diagram.

A Loose Chain is a chain with a unitary class as its last link.

Example: In the diagram facing chapter 11, the unitary classes are marked E, since each of them contains only one entity. The classes marked 3, 32, 322 form a loose chain.

A Complete Chain is a loose primary chain.

Example: In the diagram facing chapter 11, the classes 0, 3, 32, 322 and 3222 form a complete chain.

It is obvious that there is only one class (the original universe) that can be the first link of a complete chain. But any one of the entities may be the last link of a chain, so that the number of complete chains possible is the same as the number of entities in a universe.

1241   Measure of Rank
12411   Class

Consider a class of the nth order with rank a_n in its array. Consider the successive classes in its primary chain, beginning from the original universe. Suppose that the class of the first order in the chain has rank a_1 in its array, the class of the second order in the chain has rank a_2 in its array and so on, the class of the $(n-1)$th order in the chain has rank a_{n-1} in its array. Then the class of the nth order in question may be said to have, in the assortment as a whole, rank a_1 of the first order, rank a_2 of the second order ... rank a_{n-1} of the $(n-1)$th order and rank a_n of the nth order. To be more compact, $(a_1a_2a_3 \dots a_n)$ may be taken to be the Measure of its Rank. This number may be considered a pure decimal fraction (i.e. as if there were a decimal point before a_1).

12412   Entity

Consider a complete assortment. Consider the last links of the complete chains, that is, the individual entities of a universe. They will stand arranged according to the measures of their ranks. Take an entity a. Suppose it is of order m. Suppose it has rank a_1 of the first order, a_2 of the second order, and so on, and a_m of the mth order. Then the decimal fraction $(a_1a_2a_3 \dots a_m)$ may be taken as the measure of the rank of the entity a in the complete assortment.

Obviously, no two classes or entities can have equal measures of rank, and the measures of rank of all the entities taken among themselves will have a definite ordinal relation among themselves.

125   Filiatory Sequence
1251   Pseudo-Entity

Consider any array and its immediate universe. Each class of the array will contain one or more entities. Before their assortment, they will all have been comprised in their common immediate universe. Into this immediate universe, introduce the immediate universe

46

itself as an additional entity. This additional entity is its Pseudo-Entity.

We shall assume that it possesses no attribute in common with any other entity of its class.

1252 AMPLIFIED CLASS

A class enriched by the addition of its pseudo-entity is an Amplified Class.

In the assortment of such an amplified class, its pseudo-entity will form a unitary class. Make its rank smaller than that of any other class in the array produced by the assortment; this may be done by making the rank of the pseudo-class zero.

Example: In the diagram facing chapter 11, a few pseudo-classes, oo, 140, 30, 320, are shown by dotted lines.

1253 PSEUDO-CHAIN

Any loose chain with a pseudo-entity as its last link is a Pseudo-Chain.

Any complete chain with a pseudo-entity as its last link is a Complete Pseudo-Chain.

1254 COMPLETELY AMPLIFIED UNIVERSE

Amplify each multiple class in each array by the addition of its pseudo-entity, and amplify the original universe also by its pseudo-entity; then the result will be as if the original universe were amplified with as many pseudo-entities as there are multiple main classes. The original universe so amplified is a Completely Amplified Universe.

1255 COMPLETELY AMPLIFIED CLASS

Obviously, every multiple class arising in the process of assortment of a completely amplified universe will comprise all the pseudo-classes possible to it. It is a Completely Amplified Class.

1256 FILIATORY ARRANGEMENT

A Filiatory Arrangement of the entities of a universe is a complete assortment of that universe completely amplified.

A complete assortment merely separates the entities of a universe and ranks each of them—arranges them in a definite sequence, while the corresponding filiatory arrangement introduces into the sequence the different *classes* formed in the process of complete assortment. These classes are not interpolated among the entities at random, but each has a unique filiatory position.

126 **Analogies**

The peculiarities of this filiatory positioning of the classes may be visualised by two analogies.

1261 FAMILY OF SIDDHAS

First, let the original universe (the class of zero order) be the ancestor of a family of beings known as *Siddhas* in India; several generations of these are believed to be alive at the same time with him. Then a chain of classes corresponds to the beings in one line of descent —a set of lineal kinsmen. An array is a set of brothers—a fraternity. The immediate universe of the array is the father of the fraternity.

Assume that every being has either no son or more than one son. Call a being with no son a *non-father*. Assume also that the brothers in any fraternity are ranked in descending sequence of age. Then an entity or a unitary class or a loose link of a chain—which are the same— corresponds to the members of the family who are *non-fathers*. The order of classes corresponds to the order of generations.

Suppose the members of the family are to be arranged in a line according to their degree of relationship. To put each father close to his sons and the sons together would be ideal, but obviously we cannot do so for all fraternities, because the members of some fraternities have their own children, and in remaining with them they are necessarily separated from their brothers.

Now it will be assumed that persons have more attachment to their own lineal descendants than to their brothers, or to the lineal descend-ants of their brothers. Then a reasonable compromise will be that the degree to which we satisfy the wish of any father and his immediate family to be together, with the sons arranged according to age, is made to vary with the generation to which the family belongs. The later the generation, the more willing should the brothers be to be separated from each other by their descendants. In other words, it should be secured that no two lineal groups get intermingled. Also, if we ignore for the moment the presence of the descendants of the members of any fraternity, the members of that fraternity themselves should be in order of age with their father at their head. The ancestor will of course be at the head of all the members of the family.

Such an arrangement is the best arrangement of the ancestor in relation to all his descendants, or the Filiatory Arrangement of the family. In this arrangement, it will be seen that the *ancestor* represents the *original universe,* and the *fathers* represent the various *classes.*

1262 SORTING BOXES

Alternatively, each multiple class of any array of any order, including the original universe, may be considered as a sorting box. The multiple classes constitute the different sorting boxes used in the complete assortment of the universe, and each entity of the universe has to pass through one or more of them in its progress towards attaining its rank in the final arrangement.

Mark the boxes with distinctive symbols; whenever an entity is put into a box, let it acquire the symbol of that box.

12621   Related and Stranger

An entity is said to be a Related Entity with reference to a given box if it passes through that box in the course of complete assortment.

An entity which is not a related entity is a Stranger Entity with reference to a given box.

Similarly, a box is said to be a Related Box with reference to a given entity if that entity passes through it in the process of complete assortment.

A box which is not a related box is a Stranger Box with reference to a given entity.

Two boxes are said to be Related Boxes if they have a common related entity, and Stranger Boxes if they have not.

12622   Relations among Boxes

It is obvious that (1) the box corresponding to an original universe will have no stranger entity or stranger box; and (2) an entity and a box, or a box and a box, will be related if they lie on a chain, i.e. if they have *lineal kinship*.

Assume that (1) all the entities are equal in size, and (2) the size of each sorting box is just that which is necessary and sufficient to hold all the entities that it must receive during sorting of the entities of an original universe.

When the entities are completely assorted, all the sorting boxes will be empty. It will be seen that the empty boxes correspond with pseudo-entities.

Arrange all the entities in a line in accordance with their final rank in the complete assortment. Let the empty boxes be arranged among the entities in the following way. Consider any box. It will be seen that the entities related to it will be contiguous. In other words, no entity which is stranger to it will lie between the entities related to it. Place the box just before the first of its related entities. When every box has been so placed, it may happen that two or more boxes lie side by side. Then they will necessarily be of different capacity. Arrange them in descending order of capacity. When all the boxes are so ranked, each entity acquires a new rank.

This arrangement implies that

(1) no box will be posterior in rank to any of its related entities;
(2) no box will be posterior in rank to any related smaller box;
(3) the box corresponding to the original universe will rank first;
(4) the last place will be occupied by an entity and not by a box; and
(5) if we start from a box and proceed along the line, we shall meet with no box or entity stranger to it until we have passed the last of its related entities.

There is also a sixth implication, which the following may make clear.

49

12623   Collecting the Entities

Collect all the entities into the biggest box at the head of the line, proceeding systematically as follows. Locate the last box in the line; pick out in their order each of the entities posterior to it, and put them in the box until it is full. The number of entities posterior to it will be just enough to fill it, or more than enough, but never less than enough.

Then take the empty box prior to the last; pick out, in their sequence, each of the entities posterior to it, and put them into it until it is full. If the box first filled is reached before the second box is full, there will be enough space in the second to empty into it the whole content of the other. Further, there will be posterior to the second box either enough or more than enough entities (either stray or in a filled-up box) to fill that second box.

Again take the next prior empty box. Fill it up as before with the entities posterior to it. If a filled box is reached before this third box is full, there will be enough space in it to receive the whole content of the filled box.

If this is done with every box, at the penultimate stage the first box will be empty and the line will contain some filled and some empty boxes and some stray entities.

12624   The Ultimate Stage

At the ultimate stage, all the boxes but the first will be empty, the first will be full, and there will be no stray entity. In other words, all the entities will have been collected into the first box, which is the biggest, and which corresponds to the original universe.

The arrangement proposed implies that

(1) no entity will pass through a stranger box;
(2) every box when it is full will contain all its related entities;
(3) no box will receive a stranger entity;
(4) no filled box will be emptied into a smaller or a stranger box;
(5) no box will receive the contents of a bigger or stranger box; and
(6) when a box is full, all its related smaller boxes will be empty.

This arrangement of entities and boxes (pseudo-entities or the classes arising in the process of complete assortment) shows the kind of coherence implied by *filiatory arrangement*.

127 **Scheme of Classes**

Considerations of symmetry lead us to a new concept. This can be seen by a comparison of the following three statements.

(1) Filiatory Arrangement of a universe arranges together, in a single coherent or filiatory sequence:

(*a*) the entities of the universe; and
(*b*) the classes arising in the process of its complete assortment.

50

(2) Complete Assortment masks the classes in the filiatory arrangement. It concerns itself only with the sequence of the entities.

(3) The Scheme of Classes masks the entities in the filiatory arrangement, and concerns itself only with the sequence of the classes.

Considerations of symmetry suggest the concept of Scheme of Classes to balance the concept of Complete Assortment.

Each Scheme of Assortment gives rise to (1) an Associated Complete Assortment, and (2) an Associated Scheme of Classes. By varying the scheme of assortment, we can get different schemes of classes.

The number of different complete assortments of a universe of n entities is only $n!$ But the number of different schemes of classes associated with the universe will be far greater. It will be a function of n, the number of entities in the universe, and also of m, the number of characteristics used in the process of assortment.

1271 DEFINITION

A Scheme of Classes is a statement showing a *coherent* or *filiatory arrangement* of the classes that arise in the course of the complete assortment of a given universe.

1272 IMPLICATION

A scheme of classes, therefore, implies:

(1) that there is an associated scheme of assortment, i.e.:

    (*a*) a statement of the succession of characteristics used in the course of the complete assortment; and

    (*b*) a scheme of ranking adopted for the classes in any array arising in the course of the complete assortment;

(2) that the classes belonging to any array lie ranked continuously with their common immediate universe (if we ignore the presence of the classes of the lower order which are lineally related to them); and

(3) that any class in the statement has, immediately next to it, all the classes belonging to all the chains of which it is the first link, with no class belonging to any other chain intervening;

or in other words

that any class has, immediately next to it, all the classes of later order which are lineally related to it, with no class of a later order not lineally related to it nor any class or the same or earlier order intervening.

1273 ELIMINATION OF ENTITY

We started with *entities*; and we used successively the ideas of *universe, complete division, complete assortment, class* and *filiatory arrangement* of the universe before reaching the idea of a *scheme of classes*.

A scheme of classes states explicitly only classes; the definition of a scheme of classes refers only to classes, characteristics and the ranks in each array of classes. Neither refers explicitly to the entities or the number of entities in the universe. The advantages of thus eliminating entities and their number will be seen when we come to deal with the theory of knowledge classification.

128 Concepts in Classification
1281 FOUR INHERENT CONCEPTS

A scheme of classes involves four inherent concepts:

    (1) characteristics;
    (2) array of classes;
    (3) chain of classes; and
    (4) filiatory arrangement.

1282 TWO ADDITIONAL CONCEPTS

Certain aids are necessary in order to work with a scheme of classes, and they correspond to the facts that (1) there are classes in the scheme, and (2) the classes fall into a unique sequence; in other words, their ordinal arrangement is unique.

The first fact suggests the need to have a set of names to denote the classes; the second fact suggests the need to have a set of ordinal numbers to represent the classes, and, in fact, naming each class by an ordinal number will *mechanise* the ordinal arrangement of any random sample of the classes in the scheme. To " mechanise " means to eliminate the need to remember or consider the exact connotation or denotation of the classes in their mutual relation.

Thus two additional concepts are thus necessary in a scheme of classes:

    (1) the terminology of the scheme; and
    (2) its notation.

1283 SCHEME OF CLASSIFICATION

A Scheme of Classification is a scheme of classes fitted with terminology and notation.

12831 Terminology

The Terminology of a scheme of classification is the system of terms in a language denoting or naming the classes of the scheme.

A Term may be in a natural language or in the jargon of a profession or trade.

12832 Notation

The Notation of a scheme of classification is the system of ordinal numbers representing the classes of the scheme.

The Class Number of a class is the ordinal number representing it in a scheme of classification. A class number should be unique, meaning that it should represent one and only one class.

The class number of a class may be taken as its Ordinal Name.

A system of class numbers forms an artificial language of ordinal numbers, designed to mechanise the arrangement of classes. It is a Classificatory Language.

A classificatory language of class numbers should have no synonyms or homonyms. This is an essential characteristic in a classificatory language.

1284 SCHEDULE OF CLASSIFICATION

The Schedule of a scheme of classification is a vocabulary (or dictionary) giving the meaning of each class number (or each constituent of a class number) in a natural language or a jargon.

A schedule of classification is arranged by class numbers (or their constituents).

1285 INDEX TO CLASSIFICATION

The Index to a scheme of classification is a dictionary giving the class number (or its constituents) representing a term in a natural language or a jargon.

The index to a scheme of classification is arranged alphabetically.

1286 CLASSIFICATIONIST AND CLASSIFIER

A Classificationist is one who designs a scheme of classification.

A Classifier is one who classifies a universe in accordance with a preferred scheme of classification.

1287 CLASSIFYING

Classifying the entities of a universe ordinarily implies:

(1) the existence of a scheme of classification applicable to the universe;

(2) the implicit or explicit indication of the associated succession of characteristics;

(3) the adoption of a scheme of classification;

(4) the assignment of each entity to the appropriate class of the scheme of classification by ascertaining the way in which each of the characteristics of the scheme is shared by it;

(5) the assignment of the appropriate class number to each entity; and

(6) the creation of a new class, when necessary, in accordance with prescribed rules.

It will be seen later that, when the universe is one of knowledge or books, classifying may also imply the creation of new classes in accordance with set rules of practice, and the location of these new classes in appropriate places in the scheme of classification, before the assignment of some of the entities to their appropriate classes.

CHAPTER 13

CANONS FOR CHARACTERISTICS

130 Seven Canons

THE ASSOCIATED SCHEME of characteristics and each characteristic of the scheme should satisfy the following seven canons:

(1) Canon of Differentiation.
(2) Canon of Concomitance.
(3) Canon of Relevance.
(4) Canon of Ascertainability.
(5) Canon of Permanence.
(6) Canon of Relevant Sequence.
(7) Canon of Consistency.

These are commonsense canons; no scheme of classification worth considering will violate them.

131 Differentiation

Each characteristic used should differentiate, that is, it should give rise to at least two classes. This is the **Canon of Differentiation.**

This has been made the actual definition of characteristic in section 1212, and the necessary examples were given in that section.

132 Concomitance

No two characteristics should be concomitant. This is the **Canon of Concomitance.**

Obviously, the use of a concomitant characteristic is futile, and this has also been pointed out already, in section 1213.

133 Relevance

Each characteristic should be relevant to the purpose of the classification. This is the **Canon of Relevance.**

Examples

(1) Let us take the universe as the boys in a class-room.

(*a*) Let the purpose of classification be to divide the boys into convenient graded groups for tutorial work. Then mother tongue, intelligence and extent of knowledge may be relevant characteristics; but height, colour, handwriting, physical strength, wealth, mode of dressing hair and nature of clothing may not be relevant characteristics.

(*b*) Let the purpose of classification be to divide the boys into convenient graded groups for physical games. Then height, physical strength and age may be relevant characteristics; but colour, extent of knowledge, handwriting, ancestry, wealth, mode of dressing hair and nature of clothing may not be relevant characteristics.

(*c*) Let the purpose of classification be to divide the boys into convenient graded groups for answering matrimonial queries from outside. Then colour, mother tongue, ancestry, wealth, age and horoscope may be relevant characteristics; but handwriting, mode of dressing hair and nature of clothing may not be relevant characteristics.

(2) Let us take the universe of books.

(*a*) Let the purpose of classification be to suit the needs of binders. Then thread and tape used for stitching, style of stitching, boards used, covering material and tooling may be relevant characteristics.

(*b*) Let the purpose of classification be to suit the needs of printers. Then typography, leading, margin, illustrations and paper may be relevant characteristics.

(*c*) Let the purpose of classification be to suit the needs of the readers in a library. Then subject-matter, language, date of publication and author may be relevant characteristics.

1331 Too Many Relevant Characteristics

The characteristics relevant to the purpose of classification are usually many. Practical considerations, however, will restrict us to the inclusion of only a few of them in the Associated Scheme of Characteristics. Further, it may also happen that the scheme of classification becomes as efficient as it can be even without giving us an opportunity to use all the relevant characteristics. If then there is need for a selection of only a few of the possible relevant characteristics, it follows that we can construct different schemes of characteristics, and they may produce different associated schemes of classification for one and the same universe. All these schemes of classification may not be equally helpful to the purpose in view.

1332 Genius and Flair

This naturally raises the question, how to select just those relevant characteristics for the construction of the associated scheme of characteristics that is likely to give us the most helpful scheme of classification. There can be no definite answer to this question, as obviously there can be no *a priori* rules for hitting upon the most helpful characteristics. Generally it depends on genius; but, other things being equal, those with more knowledge and experience are more likely to have the flair to reject the less helpful characteristics.

134 Ascertainability

Each characteristic should be definitely ascertainable. This is the **Canon of Ascertainability.**

Unless this test is satisfied, it will be difficult to use the characteristic. To give a ridiculous example, the date of death is a characteristic of the persons in a group, as there is next to no probability that *all* the persons will die on the same day. But it may not be definitely ascertainable, even with the aid of astrologers and palmistry specialists.

135 Permanence

Each characteristic should continue to be both ascertainable and unchanged, so long as there is no change in the purpose of the classification. This is the **Canon of Permanence.**

Unless this test is satisfied, confusion will be caused whenever a characteristic undergoes a change in an entity. Such a change may lead to the shifting of the entity to a new class, and consequently the classes themselves will undergo a change.

Imagine the result of using colour as a characteristic for classifying chameleons! We often experience a similar difficulty in classifying politicians by their political complexion or their party affinity! Here are two further examples.

1351 PERIODICALS

It has been the tradition to divide periodicals into two classes—those that are published by learned societies being put into one class, and those that are not into another. This has led to not a little difficulty in libraries. As has been fully discussed in chapter 8 of my *Classified catalogue code* (1952), periodicals undergo frequent changes in the authority or agency publishing them.

For instance, the periodical *Medical library*, which had been running its course from 1883 without a learned " godfather," was taken over in 1890 as its official organ by the American Electrotherapeutic Association, just then founded. In 1926 it took as a joint foster-father the International Association of Climatologists.

Here is another example, from India. The *Journal of Indian botany* was launched as a private concern in Madras in September, 1919. It was the property of a private individual, Mr. T. R. D. Bell, then Chief Conservator of Forests, Bombay. In 1920 the Indian Botanical Society came into existence, and at a meeting held on February 3rd, 1922, it decided to take over the *Journal* as the property and official organ of the Society. Accordingly, with the second issue of Volume 3 of the *Journal* it became the official organ of that learned body.

Here is a third example, from the universe of periodicals in physics. The following extract from the first page of the first volume of the second series of the *Physical review* will make clear how the characteristic under consideration underwent a change in January, 1913: " With the present number the American Physical Society takes over the *Physical review. . . .* In so doing the Society wishes to give expression to its deep appreciation of the great service done to physics and physicists in America by the editors who in July-August, 1893, put forth the first number of a new journal. . . . During nearly twenty years the original editors have carried on the arduous task of maintaining this journal on a high standard. . . . The former editors have now thought best to complete their task by transferring their control to the American Physical Society, and the *Physical review* now becomes the Journal of that Society."

The Madras University had about 1,600 periodicals in 1930, and even then the difficulty caused by such cases of change of characteristic was pronounced; the library therefore decided to give up this characteristic of classification, and to put both kinds of periodicals in one and the same class.

1352 POETRY

Here is another example from the universe of books, belonging to the category of poetry. Form is one of the commonest attributes used in the classification of literature. Poetry is, in fact, a form division of literature. Let us consider the further division of poetry on the basis of the same characteristic of form. Here is a typical pronouncement. With regard to poetry, form is used in ways not only divergent but also contradictory. And all the ways are in turn justifiable, as W. P. Ker puts it on page 95 of his *Form and style in poetry* (1928). He adds (page 159) that in English poetry the forms change through different causes, and (page 286) that form in poetry is often merely an aspect, something one takes for convenience of understanding, and then lets go. Opinion changes frequently regarding the forms of poetry, such as lyric, narrative, ode, elegy, sonnet, epic and so on. To his own *Tintern Abbey*, Wordsworth added the note, "I have not ventured to call this Poem an Ode." Probably he thought of it as nearer to lyric.

The result of this lack of definability of the form-characteristic is that, in most of the schemes of classification, no attempt is made to classify poems into different forms. In other words, "form" is not used as a characteristic to divide or classify the universe of poems. This practice is in conformity with Canon 5 for characteristics, the Canon of Permanence.

136 Relevant Sequence

The characteristics of the scheme are to be used in a sequence relevant to the purpose of the classification. This is the **Canon of Relevant Sequence.**

Examples

(1) Take the problem of classifying the boys in a class-room for matrimonial purposes. Let us assume, for definiteness, that they are

all Hindu boys. Then the following sequence of the relevant characteristics may be considered relevant:

Mother tongue, Ancestry, Horoscope, Wealth, Age and Colour.

Suppose that the families with mother tongue B give more weight
to wealth than to horoscope and more weight to horoscope than to
ancestry, and that in language C colour is ignored but otherwise the
same sequence as B is preferred, then the relevant succession of
characteristics will have to be stated as follows:

First characteristic: Mother tongue.

Further characteristics:

(*a*) For mother tongues other than B and C, ancestry, horoscope,
wealth, age and colour.

(*b*) For mother tongue B, wealth, horoscope, ancestry, age and
colour.

(*c*) For mother tongue C, wealth, horoscope, ancestry and age.

(2) In the Decimal Classification, Language, Form, Period and
Author are the four characteristics used in classifying Literature. There
are twenty-four different sequences in which these four characteristics
can be used. But the D.C. has rightly chosen the sequence Language,
Form, Period, Author, as most relevant to the purpose of the classification of books, which is the convenience of the readers.

(3) Similarly, in the Colon Classification, Language, Form, Author,
Work, are the four characteristics used in classifying Literature. Out
of the twenty-four different sequences possible, the C.C. has fixed the
sequence Language, Form, Author, Work, as the most relevant. The
implications of the choice, in self-arrangement, are fully discussed in
section 6111 of *Colon classification*, ed. 4, 1952.

137 Consistency

The sequence of applying the chosen characteristics should be consistently adhered to. This is the **Canon of Consistency**.

Obviously, lack of consistency will lead to chaos, and defeat the
purpose of classification. Once a decision is made about the sequence
for the application of the chosen characteristics, we should not deviate
from it—otherwise chaos will result.

Examples

(1) For the universe of books in history, the D.C. has chosen the
Geographical and the Period characteristics as the only necessary ones.
It has also decided their sequence as Geographical, Period. Those who
use the D.C. should not change this decision from time to time; they
should adhere to it consistently—otherwise chaos will result.

(2) For the same universe, the C.C. has chosen four characteristics
instead of two. They are the Community, Part, Problem, Period. In
Rule VO, it has also decided that this is the most relevant sequence.
Those who use the C.C. should adhere to this decision consistently—
otherwise chaos will result.

CHAPTER 14

CANONS FOR ARRAY

140 Four Canons

EACH ARRAY OF CLASSES in a scheme of classification should satisfy the following four canons:

  (1) Canon of Exhaustiveness.
  (2) Canon of Exclusiveness.
  (3) Canon of Helpful Sequence.
  (4) Canon of Consistent Sequence.

141 Exhaustiveness

The classes in any array of classes should be totally exhaustive of their common immediate universe. This is the **Canon of Exhaustiveness.**

According to this canon, every entity comprised in the immediate universe should find a place in one of the classes in the array derived from the immediate universe. This is always possible. The real value of the canon consists in drawing our attention to the need for examining if the enumeration of classes in the array has been correctly completed.

(1) To take an example, let us consider the universe of rational numbers. Let the characteristic used be the remainder left by dividing a number of the universe by 2. Obviously, the remainder may be 0 or 1 or a fraction. If we enumerate the classes of the array merely as " odd numbers " and " even numbers "—as one is likely to be tempted to do on account of their intimate association with division by 2—the classes in the array will not be totally exhaustive of the universe in question. The least that should be done to make them totally exhaustive is to introduce at least one more class into the array under the name " Mixed or pure fractional numbers."

(2) As another example, we may cite a practice of the D.C. Throughout the class Literature, a class entitled " Minor poets " or " Minor dramatists " or " Minor writers " comes after the enumeration of certain individual authors. Such a provision of residual classes under the caption " other " is found scattered throughout the D.C.

(3) The C.C. employs the concepts of " open arrays " and " octave notation " to meet this canon. This will be explained in chapter 25.

142 Exclusiveness

The classes in an array of classes should be mutually exclusive. This is the **Canon of Exclusiveness.**

According to this canon, no entity comprised in the immediate universe can belong to more than one class of the array. In other words, no two classes of the array can overlap or have an entity in common. This condition will be automatically satisfied if we follow the instruction that the classes of an array are to be derived from its immediate universe on the basis of a single characteristic.

To show that it is possible to construct an array without adhering to a single characteristic, an example may be given. We may divide the universe of professors into the array comprising the classes " mathematicians," " physicists," etc., and " dull lecturers," " brilliant lecturers," etc. The earlier set of classes are formed by using their subject as the characteristic. The later classes are formed on the basis of their rhetorical ability as the characteristic. Obviously, each professor will fall into two classes of the array so formed, and thus the canon will be violated.

143 Helpful Sequence

The sequence of the classes in any array should be helpful. It should be according to some convenient principle, and not arbitrary, wherever insistence on one principle does not violate other more important requirements. This is the **Canon of Helpful Sequence.**

Various principles may be available for fixing the sequence of classes. Some of them are arranged here in order of preference:

(1) Principle of Increasing Quantity.
(2) Principle of Later-in-Time.
(3) Principle of Later-in-Evolution.
(4) Principle of Spatial Contiguity.
(5) Principle of Increasing Complexity.
(6) Principle of Canonical Sequence.
(7) Principle of Favoured Category.
(8) Principle of Alphabetical Sequence.

1431 INCREASING QUANTITY

If the characteristic used admits of quantitative measurement, the sequence of the classes may be in the ascending sequence of the measure in which the classes share the characteristic. This is the **Principle of Increasing Quantity.**

Examples

(1) If the universe under consideration comprises the boys in a class-room and the classification characteristic is age, it is convenient to arrange the age-classes in ascending sequence of age rather than in any random sequence.

(2) In classifying the universe " Geometry " on the basis of the dimension of the space under consideration, the C.C. arranges the classes in the sequence Plane, Three Dimensions, Four Dimensions, Five Dimensions, n Dimensions. This is the ascending sequence of the dimensions of the spaces.

1432   LATER-IN-TIME

If the classes in an array have originated in different times, they may be arranged in a parallel progressive time-sequence. This is the **Principle of Later-in-Time.**

Examples

(1) In classifying the universe " Religion," the C.C. arranges the religions in the sequence Vedic, Post-Vedic (Hinduism), Jainism, Buddhism, Judaism, Christianity, Islam. This is more or less the commonly accepted time-sequence.

(2) In classifying the universe " Poets " in any particular language, the C.C. uses the " year of birth " as the characteristic, so that the individual poets are arranged in the increasing sequence of their years of birth.

(3) In classifying the systems of psychology, the C.C. arranges them in the increasing sequence of their years of formulation.

1433   LATER-IN-EVOLUTION

If the characteristic is of an evolutionary nature, the sequence of the classess may be parallel to the course of evolution. This is the **Principle of Later-in-Evolution.**

Examples

(1) In classifying the universe " Zoology " on the basis of the Natural Group as characteristic, the D.C., C.C. and Library of Congress Classification arrange the resulting classes in evolutionary sequence, beginning with Protozoa and ending with Mammalia.

(2) In classifying the universe " Linguistics " on the basis of the " Element " of study as characteristic, the C.C. arranges the resulting classes in the sequence Isolated Sounds, Syllables, Words, Phrases, Clauses, Sentences, Pieces of Composition, Readers as Practising Materials. This is the correct evolutionary sequence.

(3) In classifying the universe " Geography " on the basis of the " Subject of study " as the characteristic, the C.C. sets down the classes in the sequence Mathematical Geography, Physical Geography, Bio-Geography, Anthropogeography, Political Geography, Economic Geography. This is an acceptable evolutionary sequence for the entities forming the subjects of study.

1434   SPATIAL CONTIGUITY

If the classes of an array occur contiguously in space, they may be arranged in a parallel spatial sequence. This is the **Principle of Spatial Contiguity.**

Examples

(1) In classifying the members of the Solar System, the L.C. Classification uses the sequence Sun, Mercury, Venus, Earth, Mars,

Jupiter, Saturn, Uranus, Neptune. This is their correct spatial sequence.

(2) In classifying the parts of the human body on a basis different from regional and functional, the C.C. arranges the classes in the sequence Bones, Muscles, Connective Tissues, Skin, Hair, etc. This is acceptable as a convenient spatial sequence.

(3) In classifying " Stratigraphy," the D.C., C.C. and L.C. Classification arrange the classes in the sequence Archaen, Primary or Palaeozoic, Secondary or Mesozoic, Tertiary or Cainozoic, Quaternary or Glacial, Recent. This at one and the same time agrees with the sequences numerical, developmental, spatial, time.

1435   INCREASING COMPLEXITY

If the classes in an array show different degrees of complexity, they are arranged in the sequence of increasing complexity. This is the **Principle of Increasing Complexity.**

For example, the sequence of Natural Groups in Zoology, mentioned in section 1433, satisfies this principle also.

1436   CANONICAL SEQUENCE

If the classes are traditionally referred to in a specific sequence, although no underlying principle is discoverable, it will be convenient to conform to this traditional sequence. This is the **Principle of Canonical Sequence.**

It may even happen that no specific characteristic can be isolated as forming the basis of the derivation of the classes, except that they are simply those into which their immediate universe has been traditionally divided. In the C.C., such classes are known as *canonical classes*.

The classes of many arrays in almost all schemes of classification are arranged only in canonical sequence. The reason is that the classification characteristic does not lead to classes admitting of quantitative, temporal, spatial, evolutionary or any other relational sequence. Examples are given from two schemes.

14361   Colon Classification

In the C.C., the classes in the following arrays are in canonical sequence:

(1) The classes in the first order array of " Mathematics," viz. Arithmetic, Algebra, Analysis, Other methods, Trigonometry, Geometry, Mechanics, Potentials, Astronomy.

(2) The classes in the first order array of " Physics," viz. Properties of matter, Sound, Heat, Light, Electricity, Magnetism, Cosmic hypotheses.

(3) The classes in the first order array of " Geology," viz. Mineralogy, Petrology, Structural geology, Dynamic geology, Stratigraphy, Palaeontology, Economic geology, Cosmic hypotheses.

(4) The classes of precious stones given under " Mineralogy," viz. Diamond, Ruby, Sapphire, Opal, Topaz, Spinel, Pearl.

(5) The classes of physical characters of minerals given under " Mineralogy," viz. Density, Hardness, Touch, Taste, Smell, Thermal characteristics, Optical properties, Electrical properties, Magnetic properties, Etching.

(6) The form classes of " Literature," viz. Poetry, Drama, Fiction (including short stories), Letters (literature written in the form of letters), Orations, Other forms of prose, *Campu.*

14362 Decimal Classification

In the D.C., the classes in the following arrays are in canonical sequence:

(1) The classes of fruits in " Agriculture," viz. Pome fruits, Stone fruits, Citrus fruits, Minor fruits, Nut fruits, Palmaceous fruits and Small fruits.

(2) The classes showing the departments of the United States Government, in the subject " Administration," viz. State department, Treasury department, Interior department, Post office department, Justice department, War department and Navy department.

(3) The classes in the first order array derived from " Law," viz. International law, Constitutional law, Criminal law, Martial law, Private law and Church law.

1437 FAVOURED CATEGORY

The classes in an array may be arranged in the sequence of the decreasing quantity of published documents on them. This is the **Principle of Favoured Category.** This may also be called the Principle of Literary Warrant, a term introduced by Wyndham Hulme about half a century ago. For example, the classes in the universe of seed-food-crop plants in the main class " Agriculture " are arranged by this principle in the C.C.

1438 ALPHABETICAL SEQUENCE

When no other sequence of the classes in an array is more helpful, they are arranged alphabetically by their names current in international usage. This is the **Principle of Alphabetical Sequence.**

144 Consistent Sequence

Whenever similar classes occur in different arrays, their sequences should be parallel in all such arrays, wherever insistence on such a parallel does not run counter to other more important requirements. This is the **Canon of Consistent Sequence.**

Conformity to this canon will be conducive to economy of time and of attention or mental energy. It will minimise the load on the memory both for the classifier and for the user, and is responsible for certain practices in some of the schemes of classification.

1441   SUBJECT CLASSIFICATION

The Categorical Table of the Subject Classification is an example. In introducing this concept, Duff Brown says, " In the absence of a more expressive portmanteau word, ' Categorical ' is used to denote a table of forms, phases, standpoints, qualifications, etc., which apply more or less to every subject or subdivision of a subject. It was thought unwise to load the Classification Tables themselves with repetitions of such categories." The construction of such a Categorical Table has automatically secured the fulfilment of this canon to a large extent.

1442   EXPANSIVE CLASSIFICATION

Similarly, we find in Cutter's Expansive Classification two auxiliary tables of classes that secure automatic conformity to this canon: (1) the Local List, arranging the geographical divisions in a definite sequence; and (2) the table of Common Subdivisions.

1443   DECIMAL CLASSIFICATION

In the D.C., the geographical classes, the classes of industries and the common subdivisions are arranged in exactly the same sequence wherever they occur.

The prototype for the sequence of geographical classes is given in the History Schedule covering the numbers 940-999. Wherever classification on that basis is warranted, instruction is given to divide like 940-999.

Examples

(1) Under the class " 376.9 Education of women in special countries," we find the following note: " Subdivided like 940-999, e.g. 376.943 Education of women in Germany."

(2) Under the class " 325.2 Emigrants," we find the following note, " Divided by country of origin like 940-999, e.g. Chinese emigrants 325.251."

The prototype for the sequence of industries is given in the schedule of Useful Arts covered by the numbers 620 to 699. Wherever classification on the basis of industries is warranted, instruction is given to divide like 620-699.

Examples

(1) Under the class " 331.8928 Strikes—By industry," we find the note, " 82-89 divided like 620-699."

(2) Under the class " 658.9 Sales and salesmanship in specific industries," we find the note, " 92-.999 Special material. May be subdivided like 620-699, e.g. Dry goods stores 658.977."

The common subdivisions are always given in the same sequence under each class; an alphabetical index of the common subdivisions is given separately in " Table 2, Form divisions," at the end of the later editions.

14431   Further Parallels

(1) Here is one set of parallels from the D.C.:

In Medicine	In Psychology
Eye	Vision
Ear	Hearing
Organs of smell	Smell
Organs of taste	Taste
Organs of touch	Touch

(2) Here is another set of parallels:

In Physics	In Chemistry	In Therapeutics
Mechanics	Solid state	Mechanical rendering
Liquids	Liquid state	Imponderable rendering
Gases	Gaseous state	
Light	Photo-chemistry	Light
Heat	Thermo-chemistry	Heat
Electricity	Electro-chemistry	Electro-therapeutics
Magnetism	Magneto-chemistry	
	Radio-chemistry	Radio-therapy

1444   COLON CLASSIFICATION

In the C.C., this practice of automatically securing conformity to the canon of consistent sequence is developed to a much larger extent, resulting in great economy in the length of the schedules.

14441   Common Isolates

Chapter 2 of Part II of the C.C. gives schedules of common isolates. The application of these automatically secures that all common isolates, in whatever array they may be found, fall into a parallel sequence.

14442   Geographical Device

Chapter 3 of Part II of the C.C. gives the geographical divisions. The use of this schedule in securing parallel sequence of classes in all geographical arrays, wherever they may occur, is laid down by rule " 62 Geographical Device " of Part I of the C.C. This " consists in using the appropriate Geographical Number (that is, of continent, country, state, district, etc., as the case may be) for the further subdivision of a focus that is capable of geographical division, or when the individualisation of the sub-isolates may be made to depend conveniently on the place of origin, or prevalence, or habitation, or one that may be definitely associated with the respective sub-isolates in any manner or for any other reason. The cases where this device may be applied are generally indicated either in the Schedules of Classification in Part II, or in the Rules of Classification in this Part."

Examples

The geographical classes of Geography, History, Economics and Sociology fall in a sequence parallel to the one given in Part 2, chapter

3. The Geographical Device is used in several other places, such as the classification of dialects and jargons in Linguistics, certain religions in the main class Religion, and certain systems of philosophy in the main class Philosophy. Further, several common subdivisions such as laboratories, exhibitions, periodicals of all kinds, statistics, commissions, travels and history are also subdivided by the Geographical Device. The result is that in all these and other similar cases the geographical classes, in whatever array they may be found, follow in parallel sequences.

14443   Chronological Device

Schedule 5 in part II of the C.C. is entitled " Chronological Divisions." Rule 683 of its part I enunciates the Chronological Device, and shows how the arrangements of periods given in this schedule should be automatically adopted in all cases where classification proceeds on a chronological basis.

The chronological device is used in quite a large number of cases in the C.C.—several times almost in all subjects.

Examples

   (1) In the main division Mathematics,
      special forms of Diophantine equations,
      special arithmetic functions,
      special forms of algebraic equations,
      special determinants,
      special algebraic transformations,
      special types of infinite series,
      special integrals of real variable, and
      special functions of complex variable

are divided by the chronological device. In all these cases the chronological classes are arranged in parallel sequences.

   (2) In the main class Economics, special theories of distribution and special types of organisation are classified by the chronological device.

In fact, there is hardly any subject where this device is not employed.

14444   Facet Device

In the tables relating to most of the subjects in the C.C., two or more schedules based on different characteristics are given.

For example, in the table for Medicine, we have the Organ Schedule and the Problem Schedule. The organ schedule contains about 200 classes. The problem schedule contains an even larger number of classes. Some of them are: Morphology, Physiology, Disease and Growth. As a result of using the facet device, the problem divisions of all the approximately 200 classes of organs are automatically arranged in one and the same sequence, that is, the sequence in which the classes are given in the problem schedule.

Such an automatic conformity to the canon of consistent sequence is secured by the facet device in every subject. As stated in the Introduction to the Colon Classification, it consists of a number of standard schedules, which correspond to the standard pieces in a Meccano set, the connecting symbols playing the role of the nuts and bolts. By picking out one class at a time from some of the unit schedules according to assigned combinations, and arranging those classes in assigned permutations, the class numbers of all possible classes are constructed. The standard sequence of classes fixed in the unit schedules automatically persists in all arrays where these classes figure, no matter what the subject may be, and no matter what the sequence of the array may be.

14445   Subject Device

The Subject Device is enunciated in rule 684 of Part I of the C.C. " The Subject Device consists in using an appropriate Class Number for the formation or sharpening of a focus which is capable of such subdivision, or when the individualisation of the sharper foci may be made to depend conveniently on a Class Number that may be definitely associated with the respective sharper foci in any manner or for any reason. The cases where this device may be applied are generally indicated either in the Schedules of Classification in Part II, or in the Rules of Classification in Part I."

This rule adds greatly to the profuseness as well as to the minuteness of the classes. At the same time, parallel sequences are automatically secured wherever it is possible, in all similar arrays. This device also is employed frequently in almost all subjects.

Examples

Most of the buildings under the utility-characteristic in Architecture; most of the subjects under the figure-characteristic in Sculpture; most of the special views under the view-characteristic, and all the classes under the subject-characteristic of Metaphysics; the classes under the divisions rights, duties, administration, records, in History; the classes of *ad hoc* bodies for special functions in Political Science; most of the industries in Economics; and most of the implements, other material equipment and activities under the problem-characteristic in Sociology; are arranged by the subject device, and their sequences are thus automatically made parallel.

We find the subject device in an incipient stage in a few places in the D.C., though it is not applied as frequently as it could be. Under " Subject of study " in Education, we find the note " divided like the classification 010-999, e.g. 375.5 Place of science in the curriculum, 375.84 French literature in the curriculum, 375.88 Classics in the curriculum." Again, under " Relations of capital to labour. By industry," in Economics, we find the note " divided like 620-699. For occupations not included in 620-699, use 331.181 divided like main classification." This device is also applied twice in the class " Bibliography."

14446   Further Parallels from the C.C.

Example 1

In Psychology: Array formed on the basis of Entity characteristic	In Education: Array formed on the basis of Educand characteristic	In Sociology: Array formed on the basis of Group characteristic

Child
  Newborn
  Toddler
  Infant
Pre-adolescent
Adolescent
Post-adolescent
  Middle age
  Old age
	Pre-secondary
	
	  Pre-school
	  Elementary
	Secondary
	Adult
	Literate
	  Foreigner
	  Illiterate
		Groups arising from age and sex
		
		Children
		Youths
		Old persons
		Women
		Family
		Groups arising from residence

Vocational	University	Groups arising from occupations

Sex
  Male
  Female
	Sex
	  Male
	  Female
		Groups arising from birth or status

Abnormals
  Genius
  Subnormal
  Insane
  Sick and Infirm
  Criminal
  Deaf and dumb
  Blind
	Abnormals
	  (To be divided as in Psychology)
		Abnormals
		  (To be divided as in Psychology)

Race Social	Backward classes	Race as a social group Groups arising from association

Other
  (To be divided by the Subject Device)
	Other
	  (To be divided by the Subject Device)
		Other
		  (To be divided by the Subject Device)

Example 2

In each of the Natural Sciences and in Medicine: (Problem divisions)	Morphology	Physiology	Diseases
In Philology: (Problem divisions)	Structure, morphology	Function syntax	
In Politics: (Problem divisions)	Parts of Government	Functions of Government	
In Sociology: (Problem divisions)		Activities	Social Pathology

Example 3

In Mathematics	Dynamics	Hydro-dynamics	Aero-dynamics
In Physics	Solids	Liquids	Gases
In Civil Engineering	Land transport	Water transport	Air transport
In Mechanical Engineering	Principles of Mechanism	Hydraulic Engineering	Pneumatic Engineering
In Dynamic Geology	Glacial Geology	Action of water	Action of air
In Ecology (Physiographic regions)	Land	Water	Air
In Sports and Games	Athletics	Aquatic sports	Air sports
In Geography	Geomorphology	Oceanography	Meteorology
In History	Military history	Naval history	Aerial history
In Economics	Land transport	Water transport	Air transport
In International Law (Laws of War)	Invasion, etc.	Maritime warfare	Air warfare

Such examples can be multiplied to any extent.

14447 Phase Device

The Phase Device is another means by which sequences of the same classes are made to be the same in all the different arrays in which they occur.

1445 LIBRARY OF CONGRESS CLASSIFICATION

The L.C. is quite indifferent to the Canon of Consistent Sequence, as the following examples show.

14451 Geographical Sequence

Arrays of geographical isolates occur in hundreds of places in the schedules of the scheme. But in comparing them, one is tempted to say, " Inconsistency, thy name is geographical array! "

Examples

(1) In " Palaeontology," the countries of continental Europe are arranged strictly by the alphabet.

(2) But in several classes of " Natural History," " Botany " and " Zoology," some of the countries of continental Europe are grouped and the groups are alphabetised, with the result that Holland, Belgium amd Luxembourg are placed under N, Netherlands, Poland and Finland are placed with R under Russia, and so on.

(3) Here is another whimsical variation. Under " Fauna," Holland precedes Belgium, but under " Flora " Holland succeeds Belgium.

Again, the countries of Africa are arranged alphabetically under " Fauna," but are grouped under " Flora," with the result that Natal, Transvaal, East Africa, Nigeria and Uganda come with B under British Africa, Abyssinia comes before British Africa. But West Africa comes before Abyssinia, and so on.

(4) In " History of Printing," the continents are arranged in the order: Europe, Asia, Africa, America, Australia; and Great Britain comes after Germany among the subdivisions of Europe.

(5) But in " History of Copyright Laws " all the countries of the world are arranged in one alphabetical sequence which gives no quarter to names of continents.

(6) On the other hand, under " Bibliography in Botany " the countries of the world and the names of the continents, including oceanic areas like Arctic Regions, are merged in one alphabetical sequence.

(7) The geographical array prescribed for arranging " Library reports " lays down yet another sequence, giving the first place to the United States, and giving Great Britain precedence over Austria, in a sequence otherwise alphabetical by countries.

(8) An altogether different sequence is prescribed for the geographical isolates under the sub-class " Lighthouse Service " in the class " Naval Sciences." It is as follows: Europe, Great Britain, Norway, Denmark, Sweden, Russia, Germany, . . . Africa . . . Asia . . . Australia . . . South America.

The illustrations of the richness of inconsistency can be continued to any extent. It is not clear what purpose is served by arranging the geographical isolates in so many ways, ruthlessly flouting the Canon of Consistency, conformity to which would have considerably shortened the bulk of the schedule, would save classifiers a good deal of unnecessary strain in their daily work, and would cause less irritation to readers, in whom curiosity is not altogether dead.

144 5 2   Subject Sequence

The idea of Subject Device—explicitly exploited in the C.C., incipient in the D.C., and figuring, though meagrely and in an un-recognised form, in the categorical tables of the S.C.—is quite foreign to the Library of Congress Classification. One example will suffice. We find the following different sequences:

In the schedule of " Fine Arts "	In the schedule of " Bibliography by subjects "
Architecture	Architecture
Sculpture	Engraving
Drawing	Painting
Painting	Sculpture
Engraving	Decoration and ornament
Decoration and ornament	Drawing

144 5 3   Common Subdivisions

The pestering trivial discordance in the sequence of common sub-divisions is endless. None but the law of permutation can find delight in such eccentricities.

Examples

(1) In most subjects, no distinction is made between *Periodicals* and *Societies*. In some, they are distinguished but put consecutively. But in certain subjects, like " Science (General) " and " Decoration and Ornaments," they are separated by *Yearbooks*.

(2) In most subjects, *Exhibitions and museums* come after *Study and teaching* and *Laboratories*, very near the end of the common subdivisions. But in " Chemistry " and " Sculpture " they come very near the beginning—immediately after *Periodicals* in the former, and one place later, i.e. after *Congress*, in the latter—while in the subject " Engraving " it comes still later, after *Dictionaries* and *Directories*. A more meaningless variation is that of *Museums* preceding *Exhibitions* in some subjects, like " Fine Arts (General)," while the sequence is the reverse in other subjects, like " Sculpture," " Graphic Arts " and " Chemistry."

(3) In " Fine Arts (General)," *Directories* comes about the middle, and occurs between *Biography* and *History*. But in " Engraving " it comes much earlier, immediately after *Yearbooks* and *Dictionaries*, while *History* and *Biography* come several places later. On the other hand, a place near the end is found for *Directories*, after *History* and *Biography*, in " Science (General) " and " Geology."

(4) *Yearbooks* is usually given the second place. But in " Geology " it is taken a long way down and is put together with *Directories*.

(5) *History* and *Biography* are separated by *Directories* in " Fine Arts (General)." But in most other subjects they are put consecutively. Again, *History* comes before *Biography* in " Sculpture," " Engraving " and in most of the " Natural Sciences." But Biography comes before History in " Fine Arts (General)," " Graphic Arts " and " Painting."

(6) *Nomenclature* comes at the very end in " Anatomy," very early in " Botany," " Geology " and " Chemistry," but somewhere in the middle in " Science (General)."

(7) *Studies and Teaching* usually comes immediately after *Essays and Lectures* and about two-thirds of the way down in the array of common subdivisions. But it comes last, and is separated from *Essays and Lectures* by many divisions, in " Physics." In " Anatomy," " Botany " and " Zoology," on the other hand, *Studies and Teaching* retains its usual place two-thirds of the way down the array, but *Essays and Lectures* comes last.

(8) *Study and Teaching* comes after *History* in most subjects, but many classes before *History* in " Decoration and Ornaments."

(9) *General works* usually comes immediately before *Study and Teaching* in most of the subjects, and is about two-thirds of the way down the array. But in " Decoration and Ornaments " *General works* comes near the end of the array, and *Study and Teaching* occurs somewhere in the middle.

(10) *Essays and Lectures* usually comes near *General works*, about two-thirds of the way down the array. But in " Botany " it comes almost near the end of the array.

Surely no useful purpose can be served by such haphazard variations. A little co-ordination and forethought would have secured conformity with the Canon of Consistent Sequence, which would have resulted in compactness, convenience, and economy of space, time and energy.

14454   Further Example

Here is another example of purposeless variation of sequence:

In Physics	In Chemistry	In Therapeutics
Heat	Thermo-chemistry	Photo-therapy
Light	Electro-chemistry	X-ray therapy and Radio-therapy
X-rays and Electric radiations	Magneto-chemistry	Thermo-therapy
Electricity	Photo-chemistry	Electro-therapy
Magnetism		Magneto-therapy

1446   BIBLIOGRAPHIC CLASSIFICATION

The Bibliographic Classification of Bliss secures automatic conformity to the Canon of Consistent Sequence with the aid of its Auxiliary Schedules; this, to a limited extent, is equivalent to the use of the facet device in the C.C. But the B.C. has been slowly increasing the number of these auxiliary schedules—that is, increasing the scope for the facet device. In the first edition (1935), Bliss began in effect with fifteen schedules, but the fuller edition in four volumes, completed in 1953, states the position as follows, on page 7 of the first volume: " The number of systematic schedules has been increased to twenty-one, and to these twenty-four adaptations are supplementary, making the total forty-five. Of these, only four are of general applicability, the others being for special classes or subjects or groups of these, and distinguished as Special Auxiliary Schedules."

CHAPTER 15

CANONS FOR CHAIN

150 Two Canons

EACH CHAIN OF CLASSES in a scheme of classification should satisfy the following two canons:

(1) Canon of Decreasing Extension.
(2) Canon of Modulation.

151 Decreasing Extension

While moving down a chain from its first link to its last link, the intension of the classes should increase, and the extension of the classes should decrease. This is the **Canon of Decreasing Extension.**

The terms extension and intension require elucidation. Much controversy exists in logic about the proper use of the terms and the inverse relation between them implied in the Canon of Decreasing Extension. But as applied to a chain of classes in a scheme of classification as defined in chapter 12, these can be determined without complicating ourselves with this controversy. Applying only to classes subordinate one to another in a chain, the canon is an attempt to explain the nature of classification. In a scheme of classification, the classes in a chain are so related that each class is of wider extension and smaller intension than the next below it in *its* chain.

For practical purposes, we may say that Extension of a class has for its measure the number of entities or the range comprised in the class, while its intension has for its measure the number of characteristics used in deriving the class from the original universe. This measure is the same as the order of the class.

In a certain sense we may also say that Extension is a quantitative measure of a class, and Intension is a qualitative measure of it.

1511 ELUCIDATION

On page 13 of his *Introduction to library classification* (1935), Sayers elucidates the matter in this way. A main class covers a wide field, a great number of things. Its compass is its *extension. Intension,* on the other hand, signifies meaning: the broader the class, the fewer are the attributes that can be predicated of it; or the greater the extension, the smaller the intension. Philosophy has great extension; Ethics, which is a division of Philosophy, is of less extension but of very much greater intension. Sobriety, which is a division of Ethics, is of much less extension but of much greater intension; Abstinence has still further reduced extension and increased intension, and Total Abstinence is of very small extension and very great intension. Classification moves according to that method.

Examples

(1) Let us take the chain relating to chemical substances—Substances, Inorganic Substances, Elements, Halogens, Chlorine. The number of entities comprised in each class decreases, and the number of characteristics that have been used to derive it from the original universe Substances increases, as we go down the chain and reach Chlorine.

(2) Let us take the chain—World, Asia, India, Bengal. The range comprised in the class decreases, and the order of the class increases, as we progress from the class World to the class Bengal.

1512   WHEN APPLICABLE?

It may be emphasised here that the Canon of Decreasing Extension is applicable only to the classes in *one and the same* chain, i.e. to classes that have lineal kinship, and not to any set of classes. Obviously, it would be ridiculous to compare in this manner such different classes as *democracy* and *steam engine*; it is equally without meaning to compare classes which, though belonging to the same main class, occur in different chains of subordination; *bird* and *reptile*, for example, both belong to the class *animals*, but are not subordinate one to the other (that is, they do not occur in the same chain), and nobody can tell which has the greater intension; nor, if that were decided, could anyone infer from the decision which had the greater extension, or comprised the larger number of subordinate species.

152   Modulation

A chain of classes should comprise one class of each and every order that lies between the orders of the first link and the last link of the chain. This is the **Canon of Modulation.**

Examples

(1) To take the first example given in the preceding canon, " Substances " is the first link and " Chlorine " is the last link of the chain. " Substance " is a class of order zero and " Chlorine " of order four. According to the Canon of Modulation, the scheme of classification would be defective if the chain omitted to give either " Inorganic substances," or " Elements," or " Halogens." These are the classes of the intermediate orders—one, two and three—of the chain in question.

(2) Again, if we take the second example given under the preceding canon, " World " is the first link and " Bengal " is the last link of the chain. " World " is a class of order zero, and Bengal of order three. According to the Canon of Modulation, the scheme of classification

would be defective if the chain omitted to give either " Asia " or " India." These are the classes of the intermediate orders—one and two—of the chain in question.

(3) The Canon of Modulation needs further investigation. It implies a certain necessary set of links in a chain, and this unexpressed implication is responsible for a great deal of difficulty. Ultimately, modulation appears to depend on (*a*) the relevant characteristics allowed in a train of characteristics, and (*b*) the sequence of application of those characteristics. Thus the concept is severely relative. There is hardly anything absolute about it, and in spite of difficulties in unexplored regions at great depths, the canon may not be difficult to apply in ordinary superficial contexts.

CHAPTER 16

CANONS FOR FILIATORY SEQUENCE

160 Two Canons

FILIATORY SEQUENCE CALLS FOR the following two canons:
- (1) Canon for Subordinate Classes.
- (2) Canon for Co-ordinate Classes.

161 Subordinate Classes

All the subordinate classes of a class, in whatever chain they may occur, should immediately follow it, without being separated from it or among themselves by any other class. This is the **Canon for Subordinate Classes.**

This canon has been illustrated in the diagram facing chapter 11, and by the analogy of the Siddha family described in section 1261.

162 Co-ordinate Classes

Among the classes in an array, no class with less affinity should come between two classes with greater affinity. This is the **Canon for Co-ordinate Classes.**

CHAPTER 17

CANONS FOR TERMINOLOGY

170 Terminology

TERMINOLOGY, IT MAY BE recalled, is the system of Terms used to *denote* or name the classes in a scheme of classification.

1701 TWO PARTIES

Two parties are to be recognised in the discussion of Terminology. There is the classificationist, including the accredited revisers and editors of the scheme of classification on the one hand, and there is the classifier or the user of the scheme on the other. We shall have to search for the canons to be observed by each of these parties in regard to Terminology—the canons to be observed in the construction of the schedule, and those to be observed in interpreting the Terms in the schedule while applying them in the process of actual classification.

1702 VAGUENESS

We humans pride ourselves on our possession of articulate speech or language, denied to other creatures. Yet many of our social, economic, political and even domestic ills are traceable to the imperfection and vagaries of language. Classification schemes will have to share, with other human endeavours, some consequences of such imperfections and vagaries. The language of every conversation is notoriously vague. The language of even carefully prepared documents yields several interpretations, and hides or confuses the original intention to such an extent that society is forced to maintain the costly profession of advocates. What is worse, this results in the diversion to that profession, by the lure of disproportionate emoluments, of some of the best brains, which should be used in more substantial creative work.

The language of even technical treatises is not always very much better. Everybody is familiar with the difficulty of deciding whether certain micro-organisms are " plants " or " animals," whether a given society is or is not a " democracy," whether we do or do not have certain rights. Such words are vague, because their denotation shades off imperceptibly into the denotation of other words. The vagueness of ordinary words is one of the principal reasons why technical vocabularies must be constructed in special sciences.

77

Much of the best effort of human thought must go, therefore, to delimit the vagueness of words and eliminate ambiguity. This is the justification for standing committees on terminology, appointed on an international basis in different departments of knowledge. With all these measures, vagueness may be reduced, but it can never be completely eliminated; neither can ambiguity.

1703 CREATION OF NEW TERMS

To add to this difficulty, new words are coined and brought into use, sometimes to express new ideas, but sometimes to express even old ideas. The publication of the sumptuous supplementary volume of the *New English dictionary* is a proof of this phenomenon as far as a single language is concerned. This volume and the original volumes together demonstrate also the changes that have taken place in the meaning of terms with the progress of time, with nobody in particular shouldering the responsibility for such changes.

Then we may have the multiple meanings of certain terms. Etymologists may find justification for them, and may even enjoy the semasiological pleasure given by them. But they are a source of trouble to the inventor and the user of a scheme of classification, and this trouble has necessarily to be met by some carefully framed canons.

1704 CANONS

The following four canons relating to Terminology should be observed in the construction and use of a scheme of classification:

(1) Canon of Currency.
(2) Canon of Reticence.
(3) Canon of Enumeration.
(4) Canon of Context.

171 **Currency**

Each of the terms used to denote the classes in a scheme of classification must be the one currently accepted by those specialising in the universe to which the scheme is applicable. This is the **Canon of Currency.**

This canon has two implications. In the first place, the terms chosen at the time of the design of a scheme of classification should accord with the usage then currently accepted. In the second place, there should be some arrangement for changing over obsolete terms to current ones, as and when the need arises.

1711 LIBRARY OF CONGRESS CLASSIFICATION

In this matter, the best-provided scheme today is the L.C. Classification. The library-minded Government of the United States of America is at the back of the organisation, and it has provided a liberal establishment of specialists to be in constant charge of the revision of the classification. This staff of specialists has one of the biggest libraries in the world, adding books at a far greater rate than any other library, as the testing laboratory for the terms of the scheme. Thus financial, human and book resources are at their maximum to help the perpetual fulfilment of the Canon of Currency by the L.C.

1712   DECIMAL CLASSIFICATION
17121   Business Side

Astute organiser that he was, Melvil Dewey provided the necessary machinery for the fulfilment of this canon by his scheme, by entrusting the future editions of the D.C. to the Lake Placid Education Foundation chartered by the University of the State of New York, January 26th, 1922. He turned over to this Foundation the considerable property owned by the Lake Placid Co., thus assuring permanent financial support. This was further increased by gifts and bequests from interested friends. One important condition that was imposed on the publication of the future editions of the D.C. was that the entire receipts, above the necessary expenditure, should be used for ever solely for improving the classification. A committee consisting of the most interested Foundation Trustees, in consultation with committees of the American Library Association and the International Federation for Documentation (its present name), acts to ensure the observance of this condition. So much for the first steps taken on the business side.

17122   Academic Side

On the academic side, the editor appointed had been in close association with Dewey and the D.C. from the seventh edition onwards. During this period, the classification had grown from 792 pages to 1,645, which shows the good preservation of continuity of policy.

17123   Nunc Dimittis

But the irrepressible ambition and uncanny foresight of Dewey did not allow him to be satisfied with these provisions. By persistent efforts, spread over many years, he ultimately succeeded in turning all the resources of the Congress Library to the advantage of the D.C. from the year 1930. How much he had set his heart on the consummation of this ambition of his can be inferred from his remark, " When I see the Decimal Classification Numbers on the Library of Congress Cards, I shall be ready for the *nunc dimittis*."

17124   Ambition Fulfilled

1930 saw the establishment of the Office for D.C. Numbers on L.C. cards; 1933 saw the formation of a D.C. Section as part of the staff of the Library of Congress. The editorial office of the D.C. was also located there. The intimate way in which the resources of the Library of Congress were exploited for the fulfilment of the Canon of Currency by the D.C. was described in the following words by J. C. Pressy, Assistant in Charge, D.C. Section, Library of Congress, in *Catalogers' and classifiers' yearbook* (American Library Association, Catalog Section), Vol. 6, 1937, pages 54-56: " Of necessity, the Decimal Classification Section must work in close cooperation with the editors of D.C. *They* are constantly at work rounding out and expanding D.C., and re-interpreting the older parts in modern terms; *we* are constantly at work applying the D.C. to the stream of printed material, new and old, which is entering the Library of Congress. They help us when we are puzzled by the interpretation of numbers and topics in the tables, and by new subjects; we help them—and hope to do so still more in the near future—by serving as a kind of testing laboratory for their work."

17125   Testing Laboratory

" As a ' testing laboratory ' our shelf list is available to the editors of D.C., whenever they wish to examine it. And they, in turn, send copies of tentative expansions for us to consult and to criticise. These tentative expansions cannot be used until they are surely permanent. But they do offer suggestions to us, for new sub-topics included under a heading that has already appeared in the printed tables are not likely to be shifted and put under another, even though their order, and therefore the numbers assigned to them, may be altered. These schedules, though tentative, are useful to us in that they indicate the scope of many numbers now printed in Edition 13. And as we study them and compare them with our shelf list, we hope to be able to make practical suggestions to the editors as to the application of these schedules to classification of books."

1713   HELP FROM CATALOGUE

As a secondary means of meeting the second implication of the Canon of Currency the class index cards in the catalogue of a library should be constantly revised. Cards with an old obsolete term for heading should be marked obsolete, and, if practicable, should be furnished with an additional note in distinctive style showing the period of its currency. Also, new cards should be written in terms of the current equivalent headings. This impact of the theory of classification on the theory of cataloguing has been set forth in the following terms in my *Classified catalogue code,* ed. 3, 1951, Rule 3116 commentary: " One of the basic Canons of Classification is that the term used to denote a Class in the Schedule of Classification should have a fixity of meaning. In deference to this canon, individuals that have to do with the administration of libraries may use the same term with the same meaning at all times. But there are forces, beyond the control of individuals, which change the meaning of terms in course of time. The vicissitudes in the meaning of terms like Philosophy, Philology, Anthropology, Sociology and so on, are cases in point. Nobody in the world, much less the classifier and the cataloguer, can arrest this semasiological change and evolution of the words in human use. Apart from the changes that comes through ages—a library catalogue, being a permanent entity, has no doubt to take note of these—the recent publication of the supplementary volume of the Big Oxford Dictionary demonstrates the extraordinary rate at which new terms are born and old terms change their colour and meaning even *in* a single generation.

1714 Internal Repair

" What cannot be prevented must be met with suitable adjustments. It is here that the need for repair of the catalogue comes—internal repair as distinct from the repair of the physical card. As the terms used as Headings of Class Index Entries become obsolete, their cards should be replaced by ones having their more up-to-date equivalents as Headings. This process requires constant vigilance and industry. Otherwise, instead of the catalogue helping the people, it may prove to be harmful and misleading. Again, the need for such replacement of isolated entries from time to time makes it imperative that the physical form of the catalogue should be such that any given entry can be removed, corrected or replaced without disturbing the other entries. This would rule out the ledger form of the catalogue and make the Card Catalogue the form *par excellence*."

172 Reticence

The terms used to denote the classes in a scheme of classification should not be critical. This is the **Canon of Reticence.**

Common sense will usually lead one to the observance of this canon. But the inclusion of this commonsense rule among the canons has been necessitated by the use of certain terms in the Decimal Classification.

1721 Humbugs

The D.C. used the term " Humbugs " to denote a class in Metapsychology. This is a privilege or rather a freak of genius. It can be tolerated only in Dewey even as the Johnsonian definition of oat as " A grain which in England is generally given to horses but in Scotland supports the people " was tolerated in his famous lexicon.

But the classifier must learn to subordinate his own opinion about classes. He should use only such terms as are purely descriptive, and not ratiocinative.

1722 Minor Authors

Another term frequently occurring in the D.C. much against the Canon of Reticence is " Minor." " Minor Authors " is found scattered over all the pages of the Literature schedule. How is it the province of a classifier to adjudge men of letters as " Major " and " Minor "? Even among literary critics, opinion is divided. What is worse, the valuation changes. According to the famous gentleman whose name is used by the Library of the University of Oxford, Shakespeare was worse than a minor author. His plays were simply thrown out of that library. But a century or two later, the " worse than ' Minor ' author " had shot up in public estimation as the " Majormost " author and the successors of Bodley had to pay out fabulous sums of money to secure for that library representative copies of the Quartos thrown out by him. The purpose of the scheme of classification could very well have been served by replacing the critical word " Minor " by the colourless descriptive word " Other."

173   Enumeration

The denotation of each term in a scheme of classification should be decided in the light of the classes enumerated in the various chains (lower links) having the class denoted by the term as their common first link. This is the **Canon of Enumeration.**

There is no agreement or uniformity in the denotation of terms as used by different persons and by different schemes. Nor is it possible to force any such uniformity by the fiat or the order of any government or academy. Hence, the only course open to the users of a scheme of classification is to find out the denotation of a term by a reference to the classes and the chains of sub-classes shown to be comprehended by it in the scheme.

1731   ARITHMETIC

The enumeration of the sub-classes of the class denoted by the term " Arithmetic " shows that it comprehends only what is known as " Lower Arithmetic " in the D.C. and L.C. But " Higher Arithmetic," otherwise known as " Theory of Numbers," is also comprehended by the term " Arithmetic " in the C.C. " Theory of Numbers " is not comprehended either in " Arithmetic " or in " Algebra " in the S.C., in fact it does not appear to occur anywhere in that scheme.

1732   GEOMETRY

In the D.C., according to the enumeration of the sub-classes of the class denoted by " Geometry," this term includes " Pure Geometry," " Infinitesimal Geometry," " Systems of Geometry " and " Analytical Situs." But it does not include " Descriptive Geometry " or " Analytical Geometry." But in the C.C. the term " Geometry " is shown by enumeration to include all these except " Analytical Situs," which is shown under Analysis as " Foundations." The enumeration in the S.C. and L.C. agrees with that of the C.C.

1733   RADIATION

The class in the D.C. denoted by the term " Light " and the alternative term " Radiation " presents a hopeless deviation from accepted usage. It violates the Canon of Currency so much that, but for the Canon of Enumeration, a classifier would surely experience many pitfalls. We have to read the enumeration of sub-classes with the index to escape these pitfalls. " Ultra-violet Ray " is a colourless invisible ray, and it is comprehended under the term " Radiation " or " Light." But the place shown for it by the index is denoted by the term " Colour " in the Schedule! This is indeed an irony in the eyes of those having even a smattering of knowledge of modern developments in physics. But another radiation, " X-rays," is shown by the index to be comprehended not by the term " Radiation " but by the term " Electricity," in the sub-class " Induction spark in rarefied gases." This is a grievous violation of the Canon of Currency. " Infrared Rays " and " Cosmic Rays " do not find a place either in the enumeration under the term " Radiation " or in the index.

On the contrary, the enumerations of the sub-classes of the class denoted by the term " Light " in the C.C. and L.C. show that all the radiations mentioned above are comprehended by the term " Light." The S.C. does not recognise so many rays. There is no enumeration of different kinds of radiation under the class denoted by the term " Light." However, from the index entry one has to infer that the sub-class " Light Rays " of " Light " includes also " X-rays." But no mention of any other radiation is made, either in the enumeration or in the index.

1734 PHILOSOPHY

In all the schemes, except the C.C., the enumeration of the sub-classes of the class denoted by the term " Philosophy " includes Psychology. In the C.C., on the contrary, Psychology is left out of the enumeration under the class Philosophy, and is given a place co-ordinate with it.

1735 POLITICAL SCIENCE

The enumeration of the sub-classes of the class denoted by the term " Political Science " in the C.C. excludes Constitutional History, and this is also confirmed by a special rule, V32. But in the other schemes, the enumeration under the class Politics explicitly mentions Constitutional History.

174 Context

The denotation of each term in a scheme of classification should be decided in the light of the different classes of lower order (upper links) belonging to the same primary chain as the class denoted by the term. This is the **Canon of Context.**

This canon is necessitated by the fact that one and the same term denotes several different entities, in popular as well as in technical usage. It may be stated that this canon is usually overlooked by beginners, which leads to many absurd placings. The tutorial hours in my School of Library Science are usually rendered most enjoyable to the teacher as well as the taught on account of the fund of humour so amply provided by the neglect of this canon by the beginners. The importance of the canon has to be rubbed in for many hours, in discussing class numbers in the tutorial hours.

Prolegomena to Library Classification

1741 ACCIDENT

The term " Accident " naturally occurs in Mining Engineering, in Insurance, in the sub-class Labour in Economics, and in Sociology. If we have a book which has the word " Accidents " as a prominent word in its title, we should not put it into any one of these classes at random. We must see that the context in which the term is used in the book agrees with the context in which it is used in the schedule when fixing the class number of the book.

1742 FOUNDATION

The term " Foundation " occurs under the class " Analysis " (Mathematical), as well as under the class " Buildings." But the denotation of the term is obviously different in the two cases. We must be guided by the Canon of Context when placing a book in whose title the substantive word is " Foundations."

1743 MORPHOLOGY

The term " Morphology " occurs in General Biology, Botany, Zoology, Medicine, Crystallography and Philology. One can easily imagine the funny situation that will arise in a tutorial class when a " Textbook of Morphology " is classified by different freshmen differently.

1744 STONE

A treatise on " Stone " may treat of its geology or of its use as a building material. It may even be a book on the stone in the bladder. It is the province of the Canon of Context to establish correct correlation between the books under consideration and the different classes denoted by the term " stone " in the scheme of classification.

CHAPTER 18

CANONS FOR NOTATION

180 Notation

NOTATION IS THE SYSTEM of ordinal numbers used to represent the classes in a scheme of classification. The term " numbers " brings to one's mind the ten Arabic numerals and use of them as in integers. But it requires only a slight effort to realise that neither of these restrictions is essential. To deal with this question, it will be convenient to introduce certain terms.

181 Digit and Base

A Digit is a single, isolated, primary symbol occurring in a notation. The total number of digits used by a notation is its Base.

The base of a notation using only the Arabic numerals is 10; the base of one using Roman capitals is 26; the base of one using both of them is 36; and so on.

182 Structure

The term " Structure of Notation " denotes the mode of arranging the digits of a class number.

In Linear Notation, the digits of a class number are arranged in a straight line.

In Horizontal Notation the digits of a class number are arranged in a horizontal straight line.

In Right-Handed Notation the digits of a class number are arranged from left to right in a horizontal line.

Example: 75437

In Left-Handed Notation the digits are arranged from right to left in a horizontal line.

Example: 73457

In Vertical Notation the digits are arranged in a vertical straight line.

In Downward Notation the digits are arranged from the top downwards in a vertical line.

Example: 7
    5
    4
    3
    7

In Upward Notation the digits are arranged from the bottom upwards in a vertical line.

Example: 7
3
4
5
7

In Curved Notation the digits are arranged along a curve, and the notation takes the name of the curve used for arranging them, e.g. Circular Notation, Parabolic Notation.

In Plane Notation the digits are arranged in two dimensions.

Example: 7345
6231
9586

Suffix Notation is right-handed horizontal notation with one or more digits having a suffix digit added.

Example: $3_2 5 7 2_6$

Superior Notation is right-handed horizontal notation with one or more digits having a superior digit added.

Example: $5 7^2 8 2^9$

The notation usually preferred in classification is Right-Handed Linear Notation without suffixes or superiors. When a class number has to be written on the back of a thin book Upward Notation is used. The other kinds of notation have not yet been exploited in classification.

183 Place Value

In right-handed notation two further subdivisions can be recognised by the effect produced by the addition of another digit at the right-hand end of a number.

1831 INTEGER NOTATION

In Integer Notation the place value of a digit of a number is changed by adding an extra digit at the end of the number.

Begin with the number 346. Let us add 5 at the right-hand end: we get 3465. Reading the numbers as integers, in the former the place value of 3 is 300; that of 4 is 40; and that of 6 is 6. In the latter the place value of 3 is 3000; that of 4 is 400; that of 6 is 60; and that of the newcomer 5 is only 5. In other words, the addition of a digit at the right-hand end changes the place values of the digits existing already.

1832 DECIMAL FRACTION NOTATION

In Decimal Fraction Notation the place value of a digit of a number is not changed by adding an extra digit at the right-hand end of the number.

In the example given under section 1831, let us imagine a decimal point to be inserted to the left of the digit 3. Then, in both the numbers, the place value of 3 is 3/10; that of 4 is 4/100; and that of 6 is 6/1000; that of the newcomer in the second number is 5/10,000. In other words, the addition of a digit at the right-hand end does not change the place values of the digits existing already.

184   Species of Digits

The digits belonging to any one conventional group are of one Species.

Here are some examples of different species:

(1) Arabic numerals.
(2) Capital letters of the Roman alphabet.
(3) Small letters of the Roman alphabet.
(4) Letters of the Greek alphabet.
(5) Letters of the Sanskrit alphabet.
(6) Punctuation marks.
(7) Mathematical symbols.

Pure Notation uses one and only one species of digit.

Examples: 365
        HPF

Mixed Notation uses two or more species of digit.

Examples: N24
        XM,8,D:*w*

185   Absolute Value

Regarding the absolute ordinal values of the digits, they are conventionally fixed in the species of Arabic numerals, as of increasing sequence while progressing from 0 towards 9. The scale may be similarly fixed for other species, and so also may any convenient scale be fixed for the relative values of digits of different species. For example, the Roman capitals are taken to be of higher ordinal value than the Arabic numerals in both the Colon and Bibliographic Classifications.

186   Notations of Schemes

1861   Decimal Classification

In the simplest form of the D.C., only two species of digit are used—Arabic numerals and a dot. Thus it is impure, and its base is 11. It is linear, right-handed and decimal fractional. The need for fixing the absolute value of the dot does not arise, since it occurs in the fourth place and the fourth place only, and no other digit ever occurs in the fourth place. It is used only to relieve the eye of monotony, and has no meaning or ordinal value. If it is ignored, the notation of the D.C. is pure.

1862 Colon Classification

In the C.C., the following five species of digit are used:

(1) the 10 Arabic numerals;
(2) the 26 Roman capitals;
(3) the 24 Roman smalls (excluding *i* and *o*);
(4) some letters of the Greek alphabet; and
(5) the punctuation marks, arrows and brackets.

Thus its notation is mixed—more mixed than that of any other commonly known scheme. Its base is elastic; it can be varied. It is linear, right-handed and decimal fractional. The absolute values are fixed by rules.

There is a queer rule according to which a number followed by a small letter occupies a lower place in the scale than the number itself. By this rule, the so-called "anteriorising" divisions are secured in "anterior" places.

1863 Subject Classification

In the S.C., the following three species of digit are used:

(1) the 10 Arabic numerals;
(2) the 26 Roman capitals; and
(3) a dot.

Thus its notation is mixed, though less mixed than the C.C., and its base is 37. It is linear, right-handed, and may be treated as decimal fractional.

1864 Congress Classification

In the L.C., the following three species of digit are used:

(1) the 10 Arabic numerals;
(2) the 26 Roman capitals; and
(3) a dot.

Thus its notation is mixed, to the same extent as the S.C. Its base is 37. It is linear and right-handed, but *integral* and not decimal fractional. The question of fixing the absolute values of the digits of the different species relative to one another does not arise, because in this scheme the capital letters and dots can come in only at particular places. For example, the first digit must always be a capital letter. The second digit may be a capital letter. But without explicitly stating a rule, in such classes the schedule is arranged as if the capital letter had greater value than an Arabic numeral. In certain subjects, the capital letter again appears when alphabetic arrangement is prescribed, which is after the third digit in some subjects, after the fourth in other subjects, and so on. Such a rigid prescription of the place where a capital letter can follow an Arabic numeral obviates the necessity for considering the relative absolute values of Arabic numerals and Roman capitals. The dot usually precedes a capital letter, and hence there is no need to fix its absolute value either.

1865   EXPANSIVE CLASSIFICATION

In the E.C., the following three species of digit are used:

(1) the 26 Roman capitals;
(2) the 10 Arabic numerals; and
(3) a dot.

Thus its notation is mixed, although the original intention of the author of the scheme was to make it a pure notation consisting of Roman capitals only. It has a base of 37, and is linear, right-handed and decimal fractional.

1866   UNIVERSAL DECIMAL CLASSIFICATION

In the U.D.C., the following five species of digit are used:

(1) the 10 Arabic numerals;
(2) the 26 Roman capitals;
(3) some punctuation marks;
(4) some mathematical symbols; and
(5) the 26 Roman smalls (when alphabetical device is used).

Thus its notation is mixed, linear, right-handed and decimal fractional.

1867   BIBLIOGRAPHIC CLASSIFICATION

In the B.C., the following five species of digit are used.

(1) the 9 Arabic numerals, excluding 0;
(2) the 26 Roman capitals;
(3) the 26 Roman smalls;
(4) some punctuation marks; and
(5) some other improvised digits, such as & and *.

Thus its notation is mixed, linear, right-handed and decimal fractional.

187   Length

The length of a class number is the number of its digits.

1871   LONG VERSUS SHORT NOTATION

The question of long versus short notation is illusory, unless it is stated with special care. Notation is a system of numbers used to represent the classes in a scheme of classification. The term " Length of Notation " has no meaning unless all the numbers of the system are of equal length, and in no scheme in use are all the class numbers of equal length. On the contrary, variation of length of class numbers is common.

Under these circumstances, there is only one method of comparing the length or shortness of notations. That is the statistical method, which tries to give some definite shape to such elusive material by comparison of averages. But the statistical method, in its anxiety to look round all the sides of questions, invented a number of averages. All these points, and the application of these points to the problem of long versus short notation, have been illustrated by K. M. Sivaraman, my colleague and classifier in the Madras University Library. The discussion was published in the *Modern librarian* and in the *South Indian teacher*, and it is extracted here with slight modifications.

1872 The C.C. and D.C.—a Statistical Study

Occasionally a critic of the C.C. expresses the opinion that the notation of the scheme is long when compared with the notation of the D.C. The terms " long " and " short " are amenable to quantitative examination. Hence, in comparing the lengths of the notations, fallacies possibly implied in dependence on vague feelings and general impressions can be avoided. With a view to testing the correctness of such general remarks, not founded on any quantitative examination, a statistical analysis was undertaken, and the result is set down below. This analysis shows that the C.C. notation is not longer than that of the D.C., but, on the contrary, is definitely shorter. The meaning of the terms " longer " and " shorter " will be defined in the later sections.

1873 Material

The sample taken for this analysis consists of the class numbers of books taken out on loan in February, 1934, from the Madras University Library, in subjects other than the class " Literature." It was intended to deal with the class " Literature " separately. Further, periodical publications were excluded from the study.

1874 Method

The loan slips of the books issued in February, 1934, were used for study. They already contained C.C. numbers at the top. The number of digits in the class number was counted, and this was noted prominently at the top left-hand corner. The corresponding D.C. numbers were written at the bottom, and the numbers of digits in these class numbers were counted and noted at the right-hand bottom corner. The slips were sorted in the usual way by the number of digits in the two schemes, and the following correlation table was obtained.

The frequency distributions for the two schemes were plotted, representing the number of digits in the class number along the x-axis,

No. of digits (Decimal Number)	Colon Number												Total
	1	2	3	4	5	6	7	8	9	10	11	12	
3	108	66	27	59	16	2	9	3	1				291
4													
5	2	60	122	54	60	44	74	11	16	9		1	453
6	3	5	34	49	43	39	49	30	14		1	1	268
7			9	16	33	45	31	25	11	2	1	1	174
8		2	2	10	10	10	11	14	5	3			67
9		1	1	1	4	2	5	9					23
10			1		4	2	9	1				1	18
11					2	3							5
12											1		1
Total	113	134	195	190	166	148	181	104	48	15	2	4	1300

and the number of books having the given number of digits in their class numbers along the *y*-axis. The frequency curves thus plotted, shown on page 92, visualise the distribution of books in the samples taken in accordance with the two systems of classification. The taller and sharper curve corresponds to the D.C., the shorter and flatter curve corresponds to the C.C.

1875 CONSTANTS OF DISTRIBUTION

The following are the chief constants of distribution of the two schemes of classification:

	C.C.	D.C.
(1) Mode (most frequently occurring number of digits)	3	5
(2) Median (number of digits which is not exceeded by half of the class numbers)	4	5
(3) Mean (the average number of digits in the class numbers)	4.77	5.75
(4) Standard deviation (a measure of the spread of the range of the length of notation)	2.35	1.67
(5) Correlation coefficient	+ 0.56	

The *mode* in the D.C. is 5, but only 3 in the C.C. In other words, the peak in the former corresponds to a " longer " class number than the peak in the latter, that is, the length of the class number that occurs most frequently in the C.C. is less than the corresponding one in the D.C. by two digits. In this sense, the notation of the C.C. is distinctly " shorter " than that of the D.C.

Then let us take the *median* as the basis of comparing the lengths of notation in the two schemes. In the C.C. the median is 4; that means that 50 per cent. of the books in the sample have in their class numbers four or less digits. On the other hand, the median in the D.C. is 5. In this sense also, the C.C. has a " shorter " notation.

Perhaps a more popular measure of the length of the notation is the *mean*, i.e. the arithmetic mean of the number of digits in the class numbers of all the books in the sample. Here again, the average in the D.C. is one digit more than the average in the C.C. In this sense also, the C.C. has a " shorter " notation.

18751 Standard Deviation

Perhaps the features disclosed by the *standard deviation* of the two schemes are much more vital. They bring to the surface a factor which lies much deeper. The " Colon Curve " with its standard deviation of 2.35 is much more spread out than the " Decimal Curve " with its standard deviation of 1.67. Is this difference significant at all, and if so, what is its significance? To answer this question, we should remind ourselves that the class number in either scheme may be taken to be a translation into ordinal numbers of the names of the subject of a book. Further, in either scheme, the length of the class number is obliged ultimately to vary directly as the " intension " of the subject-matter of the book, and inversely as its " extension."

18752   Flatness

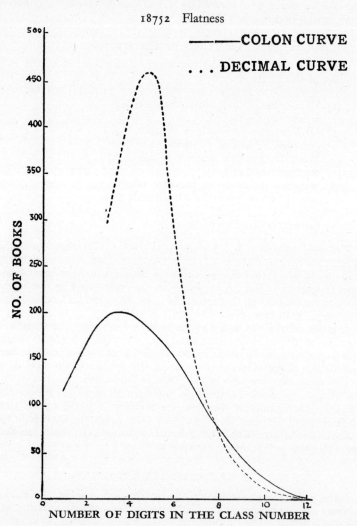

Now, with our knowledge of books, we may state that the distribution of the " intension " of the subject-matter of the books in a random sample is more likely to be spread out and graduated in a manner that would correspond to the   " Colon Curve." In other words, the C.C. notation imitates more closely the variation of the " intension " of knowledge which is to be found in the sample of books. The comparative flatness of the " Colon Curve " visualises it. In this sense, the C.C. is a more natural scheme than the D.C.

On the other hand, it is clear that in the D.C. the class numbers lean more towards artificiality. They get unnaturally crowded within a narrow range in the neighbourhood of five digits. This is prominently visualised by the steep and narrow shape of the " Decimal Curve."

18753   Correlation Coefficient

The correlation coefficient is 0.56. Perhaps this low figure may also be taken as a measure of some fundamental difference between the two schemes. If they are not fundamentally different, remembering that they are both intended to serve a similar purpose and that they both use the digits as in decimal fractions, one would expect a much higher value for the correlation coefficient; something as high as 0.8 or 0.9. In what direction has one to look for this fundamental difference? One aspect of it is already indicated, viz. that the D.C. leans more towards artificiality; the C.C. leans more towards a faithful expression of the nature of books.

18754   Conclusion

It is evident from this quantitative examination that only those people with a limited experience, who have not had either the inclination or the opportunity to classify a large number and variety of books, would consider the C.C. notation as lengthy when compared with the D.C. notation. It has been shown that the number of digits in the class numbers of books used by half the number of readers is four or less than four in the C.C., whereas it goes up to five in the D.C.

But, after all, what is the value that should be attached to the length of the notation? Here is the opinion expressed by Berwick Sayers in a paper on *Systems of classification, with special reference to those used in special libraries,* included in page 68 of the Report and Proceedings of the Third Conference of the Association of Special Libraries and Information Bureaux:

" . . . The length of a notation should always be judged in relation to its effectiveness. To object to a sign that consists of five or six symbols—letters or figures—is unworthy of present-day librarianship. Minute classification must always have a fairly long notation."

The function of the notation in classification is to facilitate the arrangement of books on shelves, and their entries in a catalogue or other documentation list, in a systematic and helpful manner. A librarian who chooses or advocates the adoption of a classification scheme solely because of a simpler or shorter notation shows a lamentable disregard for what is essential in classification.

Let it not be understood, therefore, that the preparation of this paper implies a plea for a short notation because the C.C. has a " shorter " notation than the D.C., in spite of the former being more minute than the latter. The primary object of the paper is merely to indicate a more reliable and responsible way of comparing the lengths of notation, if such a comparison is deemed to be necessary at all.

188 Canons

The following three canons relating to Notation should be observed in a scheme of classification:

(1) Canon of Relativity.
(2) Canon of Expressiveness.
(3) Canon of Mixed Notation.

1881 RELATIVITY

The length of a class number in a scheme of classification should be proportional to the order or the intension of the class it represents. This is the **Canon of Relativity.**

We may perhaps use the word Uniformity to express the opposite of Relativity as applied to lengths of class numbers. It would have been more appropriate to have called this canon the Canon of Elasticity. We speak of, for example, elastic ribbon. But some have popularised the use of this word in the sense of hospitality, and therefore I refrain from using it with a new significance. Hence the term Canon of Relativity.

Examples

(1) Consider the following table, where Physics is taken as the universe.

Treatise on	Class Number			
	D.C.	C.C.	S.C.	L.C.
Science	500	A	B000	Q158
Physics	530	C	B001	QC21
Light	535	C5	C100	QC355
Dispersion	535.4	C5:3	C110	QC431
Spectrum technique	535.84	C5:31	C110	QC465
Ultra-violet spectrum	?	C52:31	?	QC459
Zeeman effect	?	C5:38M9	?	QC675

The following table displays the relation of the length of the class number to the order (intension) of the class represented by it in the different schemes.

Order	Number of Digits			
	D.C.	C.C.	S.C.	L.C.
0	3	1	4	4
1	3	1	4	4
2	3	2	4	5
3	5	4	4	5
4	6	5	4	5
5	?	6	?	5
5	?	7	?	5

Here are some observations on this table. The Canon of Relativity is observed loyally by the C.C. It is observed by the D.C. from the third order classes only. It is meagrely satisfied by the L.C., and not at all by the S.C.

(2) Here is another example.

Treatise on	Class Number			
	D.C.	C.C.	S.C.	L.C.
Geography	551	U	O200	G115
Physical geography	551.4	U2	D000	GB53
Oceanography	551.46	U25	D101	GC11
Dynamics of the ocean		U256		GC201
Current	551.47	U2562	D120	GC231
Current in the Atlantic	551.471	U2562:95	D102.431	GC271
Current in the Mediterran-ean	551.472	U2562:951	Q041.431	GC277

	Number of Digits			
Order	D.C.	C.C.	S.C.	L.C.
First	3	1	4	4
Second	5	2	4	4
Third	6	3	4	4
Fourth	—	4	—	5
Fifth	6	5	4	5
Sixth	7	8	8	5
Seventh	7	9	8	5

The above table displays the length of the class number in relation to the order (intension) of the class represented by it in the different scheme. The C.C. shows the greatest degree of loyalty to the Canon of Relativity, the D.C. comes next in order, the S.C. and L.C. respect the canon least.

1882 EXPRESSIVENESS

A class number should be expressive of the relevant characteristics of the class represented by it. This is the **Canon of Expressiveness.**

Section 123 defines the order of a class as the number of successive characteristics used to derive it from the original universe. Let us read the Canon of Relativity with this definition. Every characteristic used in deriving the class from the original universe will be represented by a digit in the class number. Thus all the characteristics of the class that are considered relevant to the purpose of the classification will be represented by the successive digits in the class number. There may, however, be occasional exceptions to this. One will be when the number of classes in an array is definitely known to be considerably smaller than the number of places normally available in the array. Then classes of two successive orders may have the same number of digits. In such a case, the resulting array is called a Telescoped Array, which will be discussed in section 3667. The use of a long base, such as Roman capitals, will often lead to a telescoped array. In such a case, the Canon of Expressiveness will not be fulfilled. This is often the case in the Bibliographic Classification.

1883 MIXEDNESS

The notation of a scheme of classification should be mixed. This is the **Canon of Mixed Notation.**

A pure notation will be practicable only if the universe classified is a finite one, and if all its entities are known before the notation is designed. Such a case is trivial. Yet, on page 112 of his *Manual of classification* (1926), Sayers enunciated as his twelfth canon that " The notation should be pure; that is to say, it should be composed entirely of one kind of symbol." But on page 53 of his *Introduction to library classification* (1935), Sayers himself appears to endorse the statement of E. C. Richardson that an ideal notation is one " using mixed symbols but with a predominatingly decimal base," and also that " every practical system sooner or later does make use of both letters and figures." According to Bliss, on pages 54 to 56 on his *Organisation of knowledge in libraries* (1934), there is psychology as well as common sense behind this statement.

In any case, if the entities of a universe are likely to be known only in successive instalments in the future, and particularly if the universe is infinite, pure notation is impossible. Mixed notation is essential. The advantages of a mixed notation in knowledge classification, and the gravitation towards it of practically every scheme of library classification, have been brought out in the *Fifth Report* furnished by myself in 1955 to F.I.D./C.A., the Committee on General Theory of Classification of the International Federation for Documentation. The need for mixed notation will be demonstrated in detail in part 3 of this book, which is on Analytico-Synthetic Classification.

A mixed notation of letters and arithmetical figures, with suitable punctuation marks inserted at convenient points, is more legible and convenient than a long string of either letters or figures. The punctuation marks give some relief to the eye, and also cut up a class number into quanta of a sufficiently small size to be carried in the mind with comfort during the short interval that they may have to be kept in mind. It is conjectured that a block of three digits is the optimum length for one comfortable sweep of the eye and pick-up by the mind. It is for this reason that the U.D.C. introduces its dummy " decimal point " after every three digits. The C.C. makes its punctuation marks functional in the idea plane as well. All the common punctuation marks are included in its notational system, and are given definite meanings. They are called Connecting Symbols. Connecting symbols are also to be found in the B.C. and in the U.D.C., which uses certain mathematical symbols and punctuation marks.

PART 2

THEORY OF KNOWLEDGE CLASSIFICATION
First Approximation
ENUMERATIVE CLASSIFICATION

CHAPTER 21

UNIVERSE OF KNOWLEDGE

211 Library

IN THE LIBRARY, the universe is that of books embodying expressed and recorded thought. The purpose of a library is indicated by the laws of library science, which are: (1) Books are for use; (2) Every reader his book; (3) Every book its reader; (4) Save the time of the reader; and (5) A library is a growing organism. The implications of these laws in the field of classification will be found elucidated in my *Five laws of library science* (1931). The upshot of that elucidation is that (1) the most popular approach to books by readers is subject approach; hence (2) the subject-matter, or the knowledge embodied in them, should form the primary basis for the classification of books; and (3) the more minute the classification the more helpful it is in the fulfilment of the laws of library science. Hence, it will be convenient to consider the Theory of Knowledge Classification before we take up the theory of Book Classification.

The Theory of Knowledge Classification is concerned with the elucidation and solution of the special problems arising when the original universe classified is the Universe of Knowledge.

212 Future Knowledge

Knowledge has been defined as the sum of information conserved by civilisation. We speak of the *boundaries* of knowledge and of the *extension* and *deepening* of knowledge by research. The boundaries of knowledge change with time. Thus, at any moment we may speak of future knowledge. This is now only potential: it is not knowable at the moment.

Examples

(1) From the standpoint of 1876, the year of publication of the first edition of the D.C., the following related to future (inaccessible or potential) knowledge:

Highly composite numbers	Anthroposophy
X-rays	Existenz philosophie
Cosmic rays	Psycho-analysis
Raman effect	Gestalt psychology
Wave mechanics	We-psychology
Pile foundation	Dalton plan

Radio	Project method
Television	Visual instruction
Radium	Stratosphere
Heavy water	Fascism
Diphtherial bacteria	Passive resistance
Malarial protozoa	Non-co-operation
Air ports	Mandatory powers
Cinema production	Social credit
Surrealism	Scout movement
Hom-idyomo	Quasi contract

(2) From the standpoint of 1933, the year of publication of the first edition of the C.C., the following related to future (inaccessible or potential) knowledge:

Fundamental particles	Field psychology
Spin of an electron	United Nations
Jet plane	Pakistan
Radar	Full employment
Penicillin	International monetary fund

(3) Similarly, from the standpoint of the present time, there no doubt exist in the potential future many fields of knowledge now unknown.

213 Infinite Universe

The Universe of Knowledge will be taken to include *all knowledge*, past, present and future: i.e. *known* as well as *unknown* knowledge. It is an Infinite Universe.

Thus, in the Universe of Knowledge:

(1) The number of entities known at any moment may be finite.
(2) The number of entities not known at any moment is infinite.
(3) Some of the entities unknown at any moment will be known from time to time in the future.

2131 Some Issues

The following are some issues arising about the Universe of Knowledge:

(1) Can we speak of entities at all in the Universe of Knowledge?
(2) Will it not be more appropriate to look upon the Universe of Knowledge as an Amplified Universe, in which the entities are all lost sight of amidst the classes (pseudo-entities)?
(3) In simpler terms, will it not be more appropriate to look upon the Universe of Knowledge as a Universe of Classes rather than a Universe of Entities proper?

2132 Implications of Infinity

The implications of a universe being infinite will become clearer by an examination of a Chain of Classes in the Universe of Knowledge;

for we have agreed to say that each entity is linked up to the Original Universe by a Chain of Classes. Consider the following chain:

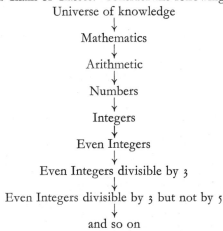

Universe of knowledge
↓
Mathematics
↓
Arithmetic
↓
Numbers
↓
Integers
↓
Even Integers
↓
Even Integers divisible by 3
↓
Even Integers divisible by 3 but not by 5
↓
and so on

This chain can be continued *ad infinitum* by the use of further and further characteristics, of which there can be no end. Until we reach the last link of the chain, we cannot discover an Entity proper. The other links in the chain are all classes. Mathematics is a class, Arithmetic is a class, Numbers is a class, Integers is a class, and so on. The chain can be continued *ad infinitum*; that is, however far we go down the chain, we can increase the intension and decrease the extension one step further. We can thereby reach a link of the next greater order.

2133 CLASSES ONLY

Consequently, the Last Link of a chain can *never* be reached in actual practice in a scheme of classification of the Universe of Knowledge. That is, all the reachable links are only classes (pseudo-entities). Entities proper can never be reached.

Hence, for all practical purposes, we shall have occasion to deal only with the classes of the Universe of Knowledge; we shall seldom have to deal with its entities proper. Nor does this present any difficulty, for the entities themselves do not figure in a scheme of classification. This was shown in section 1273.

The above statement implies another, which is that every chain explicitly described in a scheme of classification of the Universe of Knowledge is an incomplete chain. We can now bring together some relevant peculiarities of a scheme of knowledge classification.

214 Scheme of Knowledge Classification

A scheme of classification for the Universe of Knowledge must provide for:

(1) An indefinitely large number of classes, tending to infinity we may say.

(2) The creation of any number of new classes as and when the need arises.

(3) The accommodation of the new classes in the scheme without violence to the Canons of Filiatory Sequence and Helpful Sequence, and without the need to change the already existing class numbers.

The most difficult and at the same time the most vital of these requirements is the last. Should this not be fulfilled, a scheme of classification will cease to be a scheme, and will slip into chaos. Its fulfilment involves two different factors: (1) finding a helpful place for a new class amidst the existing ones, and (2) finding for the new class a class number which will secure the helpful place found for it.

215 Place for New Class

The helpful place for a new class should be found without violating the Canons for Characteristics, Arrays, Chains and Filiatory Sequence laid down in part 1. This work has many inherent difficulties; but we shall not consider them in this part: they will be studied later. Here, we shall assume that the proper place has been found for the new class.

216 Class Number for New Class

This part will be devoted entirely to the problems arising in finding for the new class the class number capable of implementing the decision about its helpful place. This work concerns the notation of the scheme. The infinite nature of the Universe of Knowledge puts a great burden on the notation in the execution of this work. The success of a scheme therefore depends on the efficiency of its notation.

2161 THE IMPORTANCE OF NOTATION

This is the implication of the following statement of Sayers on page 51 of his *Introduction to classification* (1935): " A good notation cannot make a bad classification good, but a bad notation may destroy a large part of the usefulness of a good one. This last fact has been the reason why some librarians have apparently chosen their classifications only by their notations." It accounts again for the apparently undue prominence given to notation in the very names of the chief modern schemes of classification. Witness, for example, the two American schemes, the Decimal Classification and the Expansive Classification, which give the substantive part of their names to the words " Decimal " and " Expansive." These describe the nature of the notation. So also the Subject Classification was first named " Adjustable." The Indian classification is called Colon Classification. In these cases also, the substantive words in the names " Adjustable " and " Colon " relate to notation.

2162 WHY NOTATION IS GLORIFIED

Let is be repeated here that if notation is unduly glorified in these names, it is not because " librarians have chosen their schemes exclusively by their preference for this or that form of notation, and have quite ignored the fact that the primary virtues of classification are scientific order, consistence of division, mutual exclusiveness of terms and generalness of application." Loyalty to these primary virtues would become impossible in a scheme of knowledge classification but for a highly efficient notation. It is no wonder that, " if you consulted the files of the professional library magazines, you might be forgiven for concluding that the only thing that mattered in a scheme of classification was its notation; because nearly every discussion of classification has been a wrangle about the merits of the notations of rival classification schemes." These are observations found on page 60 of Sayers' *Manual of classification*, ed. 3, 1947.

In fact, conformity to the canons of the general theory of classification is largely dependent on notation, if the universe is infinite and not wholly known. We shall therefore begin with the study of notation. We shall search for any new canons of classification necessary for the application of the general theory to the Universe of Knowledge.

217 Development of New Canons

As some of the now unknown classes of knowledge come to be known, need will arise from time to time for accommodating an infinity of co-ordinate classes in any array. This will have to be done to conform with the Canon of Exhaustiveness. Need will also arise for accommodating an infinity of successively subordinated classes at the end of any chain. This will have to be done to conform to the Canon of Decreasing Extension. The Canon of Consistent Sequence also will put its own pressure on notation. The Canon for Subordinate Classes and the Canon for Co-ordinate Classes will also demand conformity with them. Thus the Canons for Array, Chain and Filiatory Sequence stated in part 1 lead to the development of some new canons for the notation of a scheme of classification for an infinite universe, such as the Universe of Knowledge.

218 New Canons

Six additional canons must be observed in the construction of the notation of a scheme of classification for the Universe of Knowledge.

This is because the universe consists of an infinity of entities some of which are now unknown and may become known in the future. The additional canons are:

(1) The Canon of Hospitality in Array.
(2) The Canon of Hospitality in Chain.
(3) The General Canon of Mnemonics.
(4) The Canon of Verbal Mnemonics.
(5) The Canon of Scheduled Mnemonics.
(6) The Canon of Seminal Mnemonics.

All these six canons concern the notation of the scheme.

CHAPTER 22

HOSPITALITY IN ARRAY

221 The Canon

THE CONSTRUCTION OF A class number should admit of an infinite number of new co-ordinate class numbers being added to an array without disturbing the existing class numbers in any way. This is the **Canon of Hospitality in Array.**

This canon is needed to implement the Canon of Exhaustiveness enunciated in section 141 while discussing the general theory. It is made necessary by the Universe of Knowledge being infinite. Any of its arrays may have to accommodate, in course of time, an indefinitely large number of classes of its immediate universe, based on one and the same characteristic. The efficiency and enduring capacity of a scheme of classification will depend mostly on the devices employed to secure compliance with this Canon of Hospitality in Array. A scheme not providing for infinite hospitality in array is bound to break down sooner or later.

222 Decimal Classification

In the D.C., the fulfilment of this canon is sought by the following principle, stated on page 16 of the *Decimal classification*, ed. 13, 1933: " When more than nine divisions are needed, the difficulty is commonly obviated by grouping on single numbers the subjects most closely allied or by assigning 1-8 specifically to the most important subjects and grouping minor subjects on 9 as ' other '."

The " grouping of other subjects on 9 " implies " no classification for more than eight subjects." This failure in classification is due to inefficiency of notation. The Canon of Hospitality in Array insists upon a more efficient notation. Moreover, this " Other " device is not freely used. On the contrary, all the nine places are found filled up n many arrays.

2221 ARRAY OF THE FIRST ORDER

The main classes form the array of the first order. All the ten digits have been used up. Any new main class taking shape in future will have perforce to be treated as a sub-class of an existing main class. Forced billeting of a main class has already been resorted to in the case of Sociology. This became an independent discipline only after the first edition of the D.C. appeared. The improvisation of the main classes 300, 500 and 600 to accommodate several independent disciplines is also due to inefficiency of notation. The Procrustean Bed of ten digits is too cruel to the expanding Universe of Knowledge.

2222 ARRAY OF THE SECOND ORDER

Out of the ten arrays of the second order, only the three shown below have followed the " Other " device.

290 Non-Christian religions
490 Other languages
890 Literature in other languages

The other seven arrays break the Canon of Hospitality in Array.

2223 ARRAY OF THE THIRD ORDER

Out of the eighty-one arrays of the third order, only the eighteen shown below have followed the principle.

149 Other philosophical systems
179 Other ethical topics
199 Other modern philosophers
259 Other ministrations
289 Other Christian sects
299 Other Non-Christian religions
369 Other associations
439 Other Teutonic languages
499 Malay-Polynesian and other languages
629 Other branches of engineering
668 Other organic chemical industries
689 Other trades
719 Other topics in landscape gardening
879 Other Italic literatures
889 Other Hellenic literatures
899 Malay-Polynesian and other literatures
939 Ancient History of other countries
949 Other countries of Europe.

The other sixty-three arrays break the Canon of Hospitality in Array.

223 Colon Classification

In the C.C. mixed notation increases the Hospitality in Array. This is simply the result of the digits of several species being available for use in an array. This will be studied in detail in section 3612. Apart from this, it may be stated here that the C.C. uses the following six devices to increase the efficiency of its notation in the implementation of the Canon of Hospitality in Array: Interpolation Device, Octave Device, Chronological Device, Alphabetical Device, Common Isolate Device and Subject Device.

2231 INTERPOLATION DEVICE

The Interpolation Device consists in (1) interpolating between two consecutive digits of one species a digit of another species; and (2) defining its ordinal value accordingly.

22311   Array of First Order

The first eight Arabic numerals and the twenty-six Roman capitals in the C.C. form an ascending sequence. They are used to represent the traditional main classes. These classes form the Array of First Order. With this restricted base, in the first edition of the C.C. (1933), the array of order 1 had capacity to accommodate only thirty-four main classes. The remaining main classes had to be demoted to an array of order 2, and this also led to their being taken away from their filiatory position. For example, Animal Husbandry had to be billeted between Rope-Making and Musical-Instrument-Making. The D.C. tradition of billeting trans-intellectual intuitive Spiritual Experience and Mysticism amidst the severely intellectual subdivisions of Philosophy had to be followed. Sub-Generalia materials covering Humanities alone, or Social Sciences alone, or both of these, had to be numbered as if they were full-fledged Generalia covering all subjects—Natural Sciences, Humanities and Social Sciences. All these makeshifts violated the Canons of Helpful Sequence and of Filiatory Sequence. This violation marred the quality of hospitality. Hospitality virtually failed in the array of order 1.

This fault was removed in the fourth edition of C.C. (1952). It was the experience faced in the compilation of the *Union catalogue of learned periodicals in South Asia* (1953) and of the *Retrospective directory of Asian periodicals* (completed in 1955)—each as a project sponsored by Unesco —that gave courage to the C.C. to use the Interpolation Device to remove the fault. It interpolated letters of the Greek alphabet amidst those of Roman. By this, it accommodated all the classes mentioned above in helpful, filiatory places. It also learnt a way to accommodate new main classes taking shape in future. Here are the interpolations made:

Greek Letter	representing Class	between Class	and Class
β (beta)	Mathematical Sciences	A Natural Sciences	B Mathematics
Γ (gamma)	Physical Sciences	B Mathematics	C Physics
η (eta)	Mining	H Geology	I Botany
λ (lambda)	Animal Husbandry	K Zoology	L Medicine
μ (mu)	Humanities and Social Sciences	M Useful Arts	Δ Spiritual Experience
Δ (delta)	Spiritual Experience and Mysticism	μ Humanities and Social Sciences	ν Humanities
ν (nu)	Humanities	Δ Spiritual Experience	N Fine Arts
Ω (omega)	Language and Literature	N Fine Arts	O Literature
Σ (sigma)	Social Sciences	S Psychology	T Education

Except on grounds of more compelling considerations, a Greek letter is put close to its phonetic equivalent in the Roman alphabet. Rather, the Greek letter for interpolation is chosen on this phonetic ground, the position for the new subject having been determined in the idea plane without any influence by the notational plane. The reason for choosing △ to represent Spiritual Experience and Mysticism, in spite of its phonetic misfit, has been explained in brief in the *Colon classification,* part 1, chapter △. A fuller account is given in my *Spiritual experience and mysticism: A problem in classification,* forming pages 121 to 146 of the *Memoirs* of the Madras Library Association for 1940.

22312 Cardinal *versus* Ordinal Number

The courage of the C.C. to interpolate came from a conscious realisation of the implications of a number being an ordinal number and not a cardinal number. Ordinal numbers are used only for arranging, not for counting. Cardinal numbers are used for counting, not for arranging. But tradition has accustomed us to use the same digit for cardinal and ordinal purposes. Further, mathematics has studied cardinal numbers intensively. But ordinal numbers have been studied only meagerly. As a result, the distinctive properties of ordinal numbers have not made themselves felt and applied in popular usage. In particular, the addition of an extra digit in the scale of cardinal numbers involves violent implications. Practically all the results are now stated in the decimal scale. They will all get changed, and will require a new formulation in the new scale set up by the addition of the new digit. Therefore, new digits are not introduced in the field of cardinal numbers. This produces inhibition in the field of ordinal numbers also. However, the introduction of a new digit in the scale of ordinal numbers need not be matched by a corresponding new introduction in the cardinal scale. Again, no involved or far-reaching implications are generated in the manipulation of ordinal numbers by the admission of a newcomer. It took nearly thirty years for the C.C. to exploit this freedom in regard to ordinal numbers. The exploitation of this freedom to introduce new ordinal numbers without the obligation to introduce a corresponding cardinal number has endowed the array of order 1 in the notational plane with infinite hospitality.

2232   OCTAVE DEVICE

The Octave Device consists in taking

(1) the digits 1 to 8 only to be Significant Digits—i.e. representatives of divisions of a universe;

(2) the digit 9 to be Non-significant—i.e. only an Octavising Digit;

(3) the numbers 91, 92, . . . 98 to be co-ordinate with the numbers 1, 2, . . . 8;

(4) the numbers 91, 92, . . . 98 to succeed the number 8 immediately;

(5) the numbers 991, 992, . . . 998 to be co-ordinate with the numbers 1, 2, . . . 8;

(6) the numbers 991, 992, . . . 998 to succeed the number 98 immediately;

(7) and so on *ad infinitum* for numbers with any number of 9's followed by a significant digit.

The first eight numbers form the first octave, the second eight numbers form the second octave, and so on. The number of possible octaves is infinite, and so the Octave Device secures infinite hospitality in array. In practice, however, we have not had occasion to use more than three or four octaves.

In the C.C., the octave device is used extensively. Indeed, it is used in all but a few arrays. Here is an example:

Y58   Slum
Y591   Groups arising from titles of distinction
Y592   Groups arising from caste

At the time of the first edition of the C.C., the octave device was not consciously applied. Therefore in a few cases the development of the second octave has been blocked by the use of 9 to represent a division in the array, as if it were a significant digit. " 9 Labour " in Economics is an example. Such cases are giving trouble. Some makeshift is being made to get over the trouble. But all such obstructions to the free use of octave device should be removed from future editions.

22321   Extension of Use of Term " Octave "

The term Octave is extended in its use to cover also the set of numbers A, B, . . . Z. Thus the whole spectrum of octaves is as follows:

Number of the Octave	Numbers in the Octave
1	1, 2, . . . 8
2	91, 92, . . . 98
3	991, 992, . . . 998
* * *	* * * * * * * * *
* * *	* * * * * * * * *
Third Last	99A, 99B, . . . 99Z
Second Last (penultimate)	9A, 9B, . . . 9Z
Last	A, B, . . . Z

It can be seen that there are an infinity of octaves with an Arabic numeral as the first significant digit. It can be further seen that there is a similar infinity of octaves with a Roman capital as the first significant digit. The first set of infinity of octaves is called the First Octaves. Similarly, the second set of infinity of octaves is called the Last Octaves. This nomenclature will be found to be convenient for reference, when there are two species of digits in an array.

22322   Other Octavising Digits

The last digit in any species of digits used to represent divisions can be made an Octavising Digit. For example, ꝫ can be made an octavising digit for Roman smalls. Similarly, Z can be made an octavising digit for Roman capitals. This will make each such species of digits infinitely hospitable.

2233 CHRONOLOGICAL DEVICE

Another sharp device used by the C.C. to secure conformity with the Canon of Hospitality in Array is the Chronological Device. This device has been explained in section 14443.

Examples

(1) The authors in any form of literature are individualised by the chronological device. Hence any number of them can be accommodated in an array. We have in English Drama, for example:

O-,2J64 Shakespeare (born in 1564)
O-,2L51 Sheridan (born in 1751)
O-,2M56 Bernard Shaw (born in 1856)
O-,2Noo Richard Hughes (born in 1900)

(2) The grammar of artificial languages is individualised by the chronological device and any number of these languages can be accommodated in the array of the first order in P, Linguistics. For example:

PM   Esperanto (invented 1887)
PN   Hom-idyomo (invented 1923)

(3) Different systems of physics are individualised by the chronological device. For example:

CK   Gravitation theory (first enunciated in 1686)
CM65   Electro-magnetic theory (first enunciated in 1865)
CNo   Quantum theory (first enunciated in 1901)

A chronological isolate number may have one, two, three or even a larger number of digits. Whatever be the number of digits, they are all taken to be co-ordinate and to form a single array. This is a convention in the C.C.

2234 ALPHABETICAL DEVICE

As a last resort, the Alphabetical Device is used to secure conformity with the Canon of Hospitality in Array. This is used only when alphabetical sequence is no less helpful than any other. For example, in *Depth classification* (9), appearing in *Annals of library science*, vol. 2, 1955, page 20, Krishna Rao says: " The number of cultivars in any species is very large. . . . No one particular sequence of the cultivars in any species is more helpful than any other. In the circumstances, alphabetical device is indicated for representing cultivars." J3811 is the species *sativa* of the genus *oryze*. Its popular name is Rice. Its cultivars are enumerated by alphabetical device, as follows:

J3811K Kuruvai
J3811S Sirumani
J3811V Vadansamba

2235 COMMON ISOLATE DEVICE

In the C.C. some common subdivisions are represented by the small letters of the Roman alphabet. The small letters are of lower ordinal value than 1, therefore the use of these digits to denote common subdivisions results in increasing the hospitality of the array to the left of division 1. This happens in some arrays only.

Examples

    2:*k* Library publicity
    2:*p* Library organisation
    2:*w* Library administration
    2:1 Book selection
    2:6 Issue work
    2:7 Reference service

2236 SUBJECT DEVICE

In the C.C., Subject Device is used to increase the hospitality in several arrays. This device has been explained in section 14445.

Examples

    D6,9(M14) Printing machinery
    R39(Y)   Humanistic metaphysics
    W:58(Q)   Freedom of religion
    W:58(X5)   Freedom of trade
    W:58(Y8)   Freedom of association

224 Subject Classification

In the S.C., the Canon of Hospitality in Array is sought to be served by leaving a finite number of gaps between any two consecutive class numbers. There are about 10,000 such gaps in the whole scheme of classification. Obviously, this puts a very definite limit on the extent to which the canon can be satisfied by the scheme. In the realisation that this limitation would be too hampering, the scheme makes an additional provision in the following words: " If any new or other subject is found unrepresented in the tables, . . . at a general covering head . . . the place for it can be made at any point by treating the existing numbers as decimals and adding the units from 0 to 9 as found necessary," as stated on page 14 of the *Subject classification* of Brown, ed. 3, 1939. These are then called intercalated numbers.

However, no rule of procedure has been laid down by which the intercalation of numbers made independently by different users of the scheme may agree.

225 Library of Congress Classification

In the L.C., also, an attempt to satisfy the Canon of Hospitality in Array has been made by leaving gaps in between consecutive class numbers. The number of vacant numbers left in the L.C. is many times greater than that in the S.C. In spite of this, however, there is only limited provision for accommodating new classes. This is realised by the makers of the scheme, hence there is the makeshift arrangement of using the decimal point to provide additional class numbers. " A decimal, therefore, does not necessarily imply sub-arrangement, for it may have been employed as in DC369 merely because no whole number happened to be available at that particular place." This prescription is found on page 6 of *Classification, class D, universal and old world history* (1916) of the Library of Congress.

226   Universal Decimal Classification

At the 1948 meeting of F.I.D. at The Hague, I pressed for the Octave Device to be adopted by the U.D.C., and this has eventually been accepted. Its adoption is recorded in section 224 of F.I.D. publication 268 entitled *Guiding principles and procedure for the development and revision of documentary classification with special reference to U.D.C.* (1953). In other respects, the hospitality in array of the U.D.C. is virtually of the same order as of the D.C. which forms its core.

227   Closed and Open Array

An array of class numbers not admitting of extrapolation at the right-hand end is called a Closed Array. An array of class numbers admitting of extrapolation at the right-hand end is an Open Array.

Examples

(1) As shown in sections 2222 and 2223, in the D.C. three arrays of the second order and eighteen arrays of the third order are kept as open arrays by the " Other " principle. The remaining seven arrays of the second order and sixty-three arrays of the third order are closed arrays.

(2) In the C.C., practically all the arrays are kept as open arrays. The few remaining closed arrays should be made into open ones in future editions.

(3) The integral notations of the L.C. and S.C. do not admit of keeping their arrays open.

CHAPTER 23

HOSPITALITY IN CHAIN

231 The Canon

THE CONSTRUCTION OF a class number should admit of an infinity of new class numbers being added at the end of its chain without disturbing any of the existing class numbers in any way. This is the **Canon of Hospitality in Chain**.

This canon is needed to implement the Canons of Decreasing Extension and of Modulation enunciated in sections 151 and 152 while discussing the general theory. It is made necessary by the universe of knowledge being infinite. Any of its chains may have to accommodate, in course of time, an indefinitely large number of classes derived by a succession of independent additional characteristics. The efficiency and enduring capacity of a scheme of classification will therefore depend mostly on the devices employed to secure compliance with this Canon of Hospitality in Chain. A scheme not providing infinite hospitality in chain is bound to break down sooner or later.

232 Devices

Various devices may be used for securing hospitality in chain. Here are some of them.

(1) Gap Device.
(2) Decimal Fraction Device.
(3) Facet Device.
(4) Phase Device.
(5) Auto-bias Device.

233 Gap Device

The Gap Device consists of leaving a finite gap between the class numbers of two classes appearing to be consecutive at the time of their construction.

This device is employed by any system of classification using an integer notation. Obviously the gap left can accommodate only a limited number of class numbers. As stated in 225, the gap has to serve the needs of hospitality in array also. Thus the number of class numbers available for hospitality in chain is further reduced. Thus the gap device can give only limited hospitality in chain. Infinite hospitality is not possible, nor is it possible to improve matters by anticipating regions likely to receive a large number of new classes and leaving proportionately large gaps in them.

Since the gap device is not suited for the classification of any infinite universe, schemes of classification for the universe of knowledge should avoid it. However, it was adopted about half a century ago by the L.C. and S.C.

New classes often crop up, as if spitefully, in gaps already choked up. This is a recurring phenomenon with integer notation. Therefore, schemes with integer notation are driven to the adoption of makeshifts to receive new classes.

2331 LIBRARY OF CONGRESS CLASSIFICATION

In the L.C., further amplification of given integral numbers by the alphabetical device is frequently resorted to in order to secure greater hospitality in chain as well as in array. The alphabetical digit is preceded by a dot, as in a decimal fraction. Thus the alphabetical digit has to be valued as a decimal fraction part of the class number. However, the set of arabic numerals following it should be read as integers. This appears to be the intention, though not so stated.

Examples

(1) In DK History of Russia, we have
    (11) Ethnology. Races
DK33   General works
DK34   Special, A-Z, e.g. .K14 Kalmucks
DK35   Cossacks
    (12) Biography of Historians
DK38.5   Collective
DK38.7   Individual, A-Z. e.g. .K8 Kunik
    (13) Diplomatic History
DK68.A2 to 1800 Chronicles
DK68.A3-Z 1801-
    (14) Local History
DK511   Provinces, governments, etc.
   .B2   Baku
   .C35   Biography, A-Z
   .L2-25   Lithuania
   .W2   Warsaw.
    (15) Buildings of Petrograd
DK573   General works
DK574   Special, A-Z
(2) In GN Anthropology, we have
   (21) GN37   Special museums, A-Z
   (22) Psychological Anthropology
GN295   Other special, A-Z, e.g., .T9 Twins
    (23) GN419   Ornaments
      .A1-A5   General
      .A6-Z5   Special

.1   Head dresses
.3   Tattooing
(24) Industries
GN434   Others, A-Z, e.g. .F3 Featherwork
.S6 Skin dressing
(25) GN447   Articles for special purposes, A-Z
e.g.   .D77 Drilling instruments
.K7   Knives
.T9   Traps
(26) Prehistoric Archaeology
GN799   Other special topics, A-Z
e.g.   .F5   Fishing
.N3   Navigation
.S4   Sculpture
.W3   Weapons
(3) In HV Social Pathology, Philanthropy, etc., we have
(31) Cripples
HV3018   Occupations for cripples ·
HV3019   By trade, A-Z
(32) Special classes, by occupation
HV3174   Other, A-Z by profession
.A5   Actors
.P7   Professional men
(33) Alcoholism in the United States
HV5289   Collections
.A1-5   Documents
.A1-49   Serial
.A5   Special, by date
.A7-Z   Non-official
(34) Drug habits
HV5822   Other, A-Z
(35) Penology.   United States
HV9474   Federal prisons, A-Z

2332 Subject Classification

In the S.C., the categorical table and the provision for the further
division of any class geographically or linguistically goes some way in
satisfying the Canon of Hospitality in Chain. Reference has also been
already made to the suggestion of the intercalation of five digit
numbers in connection with providing hospitality in array. Hospitality
in chain is also expected to have a share in this intercalation. But, as
already remarked, apart from the mention of this possibility, the
details of this device have not been gone into and no attempt has been
made to secure uniformity of treatment.

234 Decimal Fraction Device

The Decimal Fraction Device consists of treating each class number
as a pure decimal fraction.

In using this device, every class number without exception is treated as a pure decimal fraction. No class number whatever is treated as an integer or as a mixture of integer and fraction. There is, therefore, no need at all to use the decimal point. Indeed, it is taken as understood before every class number. This satisfies the law of parsimony.

A new class is created in a chain by subdividing the class forming its last link on the basis of a new additional characteristic. By the Canons of Relativity and Expressiveness this should result in the addition of a digit to the class number of the class subdivided. The subdivision may have to be continued *ad infinitum*. In other words, the chain may be lengthened *ad infinitum*. The decimal fraction device will give a distinct helpful class number to each new class, because it provides for the addition of digits *ad infinitum* without disturbing the ordinal value of any existing class number. Thus the decimal fraction device provides infinite hospitality in chain.

The decimal fraction device was brought into popular use by the D.C. It has been adopted by the U.D.C., C.C. and B.C. Probably it will be adopted by any worth-while new scheme of knowledge classification. It is likely, indeed, to be adopted by any scheme for the classification of any infinite universe. Decimal fraction notation is a contribution by the D.C. of permanent value.

But the Canon of Hospitality in Chain is voracious without limit. That the decimal fraction device is inadequate to satisfy its voracity will be seen in the next three sections on D.C.

2341 DECIMAL CLASSIFICATION

(1) Consider the following chain in the D.C.

Universe of Knowledge
↓

3	=	Social sciences
33	=	Economics
331	=	Labour
331.8	=	Labouring classes
331.81	=	Duration of work

For our purpose, we shall call the last of the above links the " starting point." The above chain can be lengthened beyond the starting point on the basis of the following two independent trains of related characteristics:

(1) Nature of duration.
(2) Geographical area.

The D.C. provides for the lengthening of the chain beyond the starting point on the basis of either of the above-mentioned trains of characteristics.

The array based on the first train of characteristics is scheduled as follows:

331.811	Length of day
331.812	Night work
331.813	Sunday work
331.814	Overtime
331.816	Leave
331.817	Holidays

The following is the prescription for lengthening the chain beyond the starting point on the basis of the second characteristic:

331.819   In special countries, divide like 930-999

Let us now classify the subject " Overtime in India." It has to be put into *either*

	331.814	= Overtime
or	331.81954	= Duration of work in India

Each library has to make its own convention as to which one of the above classes must be chosen. Whatever the convention, the subject only gets a class of greater extension than itself. It ought to be placed in a class of greater intension than either of the above classes.

The D.C. has recognised the possibility of using the above two trains of characteristics, but its notation prevents the use of both in succession. This shows the limitation of the decimal fraction device. It can provide hospitality in chain for a singlefold infinity of links; but subjects call for a twofold infinity of links in the chain beyond the starting point, for the chain can be lengthened *ad infinitum* on the basis of the trains of both the time and geographical characteristics.

(2) Let us take 59 Zoology as the starting point. This can start two chains on the basis of the following two independent trains of related characteristics:

(1) Problem, viz. morphology, physiology, ecology, etc.
(2) Natural group, viz. group, class, order, family, etc.

The D.C. provides for a chain to be developed on the basis of either of these trains of characteristics. Here is a portion of the train based on the *problem* chain:

59	=	Zoology
		↓
591	=	General
		↓
591.5	=	Ecology
		↓
591.57	=	Means of protection and attraction
		↓
591.573	=	Protection
		↓
591.5737	=	Mimicry

Here is a portion of the chain based on the *natural group* train:

59	=	Zoology
		↓
595	=	Articulate
		↓
595.7	=	Insecta
		↓
595.78	=	Lepidoptera
		↓
595.787	=	Bombyces

Let us classify the subject " Mimicry in lepidoptera." It has to be put in *either*

	595.78	= Lepidoptera
or	591.5737	= Mimicry

(3) Let us take o2 Library Economy for the starting point. This can start two chains on the basis of the following two independent trains of related characteristics:

(1) Problem.
(2) Library.

The D.C. provides for a chain to be developed on the basis of either of these trains of characteristics. Here is a portion of the chain based on the problem train:

o2	=	Library Economy
		↓
o25	=	Administration
		↓
o25.2	=	Accession
		↓
o25.21	=	Book selection
		↓
o25.215	=	How?

Here is a portion of the chain based on the library train:

o2	=	Library Economy
		↓
o27	=	General library
		↓
o27.8	=	School, etc.
		↓
o27.82	=	School
		↓
o27.822	=	Elementary
		↓
o27.8222	=	Kindergarten

Let us classify the subject " Book selection in the elementary school library." It has to be put in *either*

025.21 = Book selection

or   027.8222 = Elementary school library

All three examples show the limitation of the decimal fraction device. It can provide hospitality in chain for a singlefold infinity of links; but a subject may call for hospitality in chain for a manifold infinity of links beyond a class number of any order whatsoever taken as the starting point. These examples point to the need for an additional device to provide for a manifold infinity of hospitality in chain to be developed from any starting point in any primary chain.

235 Facet Device

Facet Device consists of adding, after a class number of any number of links, a digit of ordinal value less than that of the least of all the substantive digits and adding thereafter a set of digits constructed on the basis of a train of characteristics related to one another but unrelated to those previously used.

The digit first added is called a Connecting Symbol.

The set of digits added thereafter is called a Facet.

This device secures a Manifold Infinite Hospitality in Chain, for it can be applied repeatedly. It is used by the U.D.C. and C.C. We shall show how they solve, with facet device, the problem shown in section 2341 to be insoluble in the D.C.

Subject	U.D.C. No.	C.C. No.
(1) Overtime in India	331.814(54)	X:95512.44
(2) Mimicry in lepidoptera	595.78-157	K867:5647
(3) Book selection in elementary school library	027.822.2:025.21	231:i

In example 3, the numbers of the facets are taken from the D.C. instead of the U.D.C., as the former is more detailed.

The points of facet-attachment in the U.D.C. and C.C. are as shown below:

In Words	In U.D.C. No.	In C.C. No.
(1) Overtime	331.814	X:95512
(2) Lepidoptera	595.78	K867
(3) Elementary school library	027.822.2	231

The following are the set of digits attached as facet:

In Words	In U.D.C. No.	In C.C. No.
(1) India	54	44
(2) Mimicry	157	5647
(3) Book selection	025.21	I

The following table gives the names of the facets and the connecting symbols used to attach them, in the U.D.C. and C.C. respectively:

Name of Facet	Connecting Symbol in U.D.C.	Connecting Symbol in C.C.
(1) Country (space) (2) Problem (energy) (3) Problem (energy)	( ) - :	: : :

Each connecting symbol is given a distinct ordinal value. Each is less than the least of the substantive digits. There are also other connecting symbols for attaching other kinds of facets. These will be given in section 3621.

2351 MOBILITY OF FACET

A facet may be attached at any point of intension. The following examples illustrate the mobility of facet:

Subject	U.D.C. No.	C.C. No.
Work hours in India	331.81(54)	X:95512.44
Mimicry in insects	595.7-157	K86:5647
Book selection in academic library	?	23:1

2352 SPACE FACET

Both the U.D.C. and the C.C. give a general specification to attach, whenever warranted by the subject, a space facet to any class number, i.e. at any point of intension. A separate geographical schedule is given by each of them. It is independent of the subject to which it can be attached. In other words, it is a schedule common to all subjects.

2353 ENERGY FACET

The U.D.C. and C.C. do not go together the whole way in the energy or problem facet. Examples 2 and 3 in section 235 show this.

A schedule of the problem facet is called a schedule of analytical divisions in the U.D.C. It is prescribed only in a few cases, as the result of the U.D.C. having adopted as its core the D.C., which does not have the facet device. The U.D.C. is able to adopt the facet device only in the periphery enveloping the D.C. core. As a result, the facet device is not fully developed by the U.D.C.—its potentialities are not fully exploited.

2354 COLON CLASSIFICATION

The C.C. prescribes a problem facet for each class needing it. Some problem facets are common to all classes, some are common to several classes, and some are special to the respective classes for which they are scheduled. These will be discussed and illustrated in section 363 and in chapter 45. In fact, the C.C. makes unrestricted use of the facet device. Whenever the quality of the train of characteristics forming the basis of classification changes totally, the C.C. uses the facet device.

Practice with class numbers having adequate hospitality in chain secured in this way, eventually led to an objective study of the facet device. In fact, the term " facet " had not been improvised in the first edition of the C.C., for the concept itself was not consciously applied.

It was not consciously seized even in the first edition of the *Prolegomena* (1937), and had not taken shape even in the second edition of the *Colon classification* (1939). The term " facet " and the concept denoted by it became objective only in my *Library classification: fundamentals and procedure* (1944).

Since 1948, the concept of " facet " has been systematically pursued. This has led to many helpful ideas in the theory and practice of Knowledge Classification. These may be grouped under the three heads, Analytico-Synthetic Classification, Depth Classification and Abstract Classification. These will be studied in parts 3, 4 and 8 respectively. Facet Notation and Facet Analysis form a valuable contribution of the C.C. Perhaps no worthwhile scheme of classification of the future will fail to use it.

Pages 262 to 268 of volume 57 (1955) of the *Library Association Record* give the latest formulation of the potentiality of the facet concept. These pages reproduce a memorandum of the Classification Research Group of Great Britain, given to the Library Association's Library Research Committee in May, 1955. The memorandum is entitled *The need for a faceted classification as the basis of all methods of information retrieval*. At the time of The International Congress at Brussels in 1955, the following resolution, sponsored by D. J. Foskett, was adopted by the General Assembly of F.I.D.: " The F.I.D. recommends that a deeper and more extensive study should be made of the general theory of classification, including facet analysis, and also of their application in the documentation of specific subjects."

236 The Phase Device

The Phase Device consists of attaching one class number to another by means of a connecting symbol of ordinal value less than that of any connecting symbol for a facet.

This phase device secures an additional singlefold infinity for hospitality in chain. It is generally used to represent a subject resulting from or appearing in the form of the exposition of a relation between two subjects. The resulting subject is a Phased Subject, the two latter subjects are its phases.

Examples

Phased Subject	U.D.C. No.	C.C. No.
(1) Mathematics for economists	51:33	Bo*b*X
(2) Economics for mathematicians	33:51	Xo*b*B
(3) Comparison of economics and mathematics	33:51	Bo*c*X
(4) Economics as influenced by mathematics	33:51	Xo*g*B
(5) Mathematics as influenced by economics	51:33	Bo*g*X

The order of the intension of each of the above-mentioned subjects is certainly greater than that of the subject forming the first phase. The class numbers in the second and third columns keep in step with the increase in order. Thus the Canon of Hospitality is satisfied. Each of the phased subjects gets a class number distinct from that of either of its phases. Moreover, the new class number satisfies the Canons of Expressiveness and of Relativity.

2361 THE COLON CLASSIFICATION

The C.C. numbers in the third column of the examples in section 236 are all different. This is due to two causes. Firstly, the digits b, c, g represent the respective phase relations; each of these digits uniquely represents one and only one phase relation. Secondly, the arrangement of the phases follows the nature of the new subject created. For instance, in the first example, the subject of the exposition is mathematics; it is therefore made the first phase. The same is true of the fifth example. On the other hand, in the second example the subject of the exposition is economics; this is therefore made the first phase. It is the same with the fourth example also. But in the third example such a distinction between the two phases is not possible. In such a case the subject which comes first in the schedule of main classes is treated as the first phase, by convention.

2362 U.D.C.

The U.D.C. class numbers in the second column of the table of examples in section 236 are not all different. This is due to the same bare connecting symbol being used in all cases, without any digit to represent and individualise the different kinds of phase relation. Thus classification fails in the set of examples 2, 3 and 4. So also it fails in the set of examples 1 and 5. A specification in the U.D.C. will obliterate even the difference between examples 4 and 5. The specification is given in table (6), section B of volume 1, part 1, of the English edition of the U.D.C. of 1943. It reads: " The compound is reversible, since reversal does not materially affect the significance (*sic*) . . . the usual practice is to file under the lower number of the pair." Thus all the five numbers will be 33:51. The U.D.C. could, with advantage, give up this reversal idea.

237 **Auto-bias Device**

The Auto-bias Device consists of attaching to one number within a facet another number within the same facet with a distinctive connecting symbol chosen for this purpose.

This device helps to enrich the Canon of Hospitality in Chain within a facet. Hospitality in chain is already endowed with singlefold infinity of links within a facet by the decimal notation device. The auto-bias device endows a second singlefold infinity of links within a facet. Thus a facet is able to give twofoldedly infinite hospitality in chain within itself.

Subject	U.D.C. No.	C.C. No.
(1) Botany	58	I
(2) Tissue	581.8	I,12
(3) Secretory tissue	581.822	I,126
(4) Leaf	581.45	I,5
(5) Tissue of leaf	581.845	I,12-5
(6) Secretory tissue of leaf	581.822:581.845	I,126-5

2371   U.D.C.

The U.D.C. has not yet adopted the auto-bias device. It has utilised its D.C. core to manage example 5 without the use of any special device. The tactics of the D.C. in such a situation are well known; it provides in the same array for division on the basis of more than one characteristic. But in example 6, the U.D.C. has made the phase device also bear the burden of the auto-bias device. Already it has to bear that of the facet device, as was shown in example 3 of section 235. Thus a class number formed by the joining of two class numbers by means of a colon may have to represent several classes. This means a failure of classification.

2372   COLON CLASSIFICATION

The C.C. uses a hyphen (-) as the connecting symbol for the auto-bias device. It has the greatest ordinal value of any of the connecting symbols. Thus the subjects given as examples in section 237 will get arranged in the following sequence:

	C.C. No.	Subject
(1)	I	Botany
(2)	I,12	Tissue
(3)	I,12-5	Tissue of the leaf
(4)	I,126	Secretory tissue
(5)	I,126-5	Secretory tissue of the leaf
(6)	I,5	Leaf

The C.C. adopts a convention in the application of the auto-bias device. The number occurring earlier in the schedule of the facet is always made the first member of the auto-biased number. There is a provision for waiving this convention where the reversal of the combination will represent the subject better. This is a weak point which must be rectified in later editions.

Perhaps the auto-bias device is a useful contribution to classificatory science by the C.C. It could be adopted with advantage by other schemes of classification. Equally useful contributions by the C.C. are the facet and phase devices used as distinctive devices for distinctive purposes.

238 Minute Classification

Even as late in the day as this there is probably somebody damning the whole subject of classification with the epithet " of purely academic interest." He may be saying " it is all very well to demonstrate such possibilities as hospitality in chain, but of what practical use can it be? Whoever wants such minute classification as these devices bring out?" The best answer to such a question is given in the best possible way in the words of the pioneer of the profession, in Dewey's *Decimal classification*, ed. 13, 1933, pages 17-18.

" *Minute classing*. On the first publication in 1876, a common criticism was that 1,000 heds cud never be successfully uzed, however desirabl so close classification myt be. As soon, however, as actual experience proved it as eazy to use 1,000 heds in the new sistem as 100 in the old, the obviously great practical value of close clasing led one uzer after another to urj strongly publication of more subdivisions. Minute as ar many now given there ar none that sum hav not askt for and almost none that others hav not declared needless. Subdivisions ar made in such way that one may uze all, or any part and ignore the rest without difficulty or confuzion, thus allowing each to uze minute subdivisions where he wishes or needs them, without being forst into refinements in subjects where he has few books or litle interest. Since the degree to which any skeme shall be applyd is optional with each clasifyer and close analisis is useful to everyone in defining content or in clarifying differences between related subjects, even elaborate skemes ar printed in ful if no essential objection has been bro't against them by the best qualifyd critics. . . . On many topics minute subsections ar printed . . . for use in indexing periodicals and society transactions, and in keeping notes.

" The advantaj of close clasing is unquestioned, if the uzer knows just what it is. With this plan it is not only practicabl, but comparatively eazy. If there ar only 10 books on a given topic, it is useful to hav them in groups amung themselves, for otherwize they wud hav only accidental order, which is of servis to no one. A reader wishing a specific book shud go not to the shelvs, but to the catalog, where he can find its place quickest. If he wishes a specific subject, he is sent instantly to its exact place by the Subject Index. If he wishes to study the library's resources at the shelvs, he will be *greatly helpt by minute clasing*. A teacher showing his pupil the material on any subject wud, if there wer only 20 books, surely put together those covering the same points, even if there wer only 2. Much more shud librarians group closely their colections, that readers may gain sumthing of the advantajes of an experienst gyd."

2381 Then and Now

Seventy years ago, Dewey had to put forward a special plea like the foregoing to justify even a three-digited class number. The fact of this special pleading for the defence of such a slight minuteness of classification has left a bad tradition behind. There are still enough left of the old guard to resist, stage by stage, (1) any classification whatever, (2) any classification other than broad classification, (3) any classification seeking to obtain a class number coextensive with the subject classified, (4) any classification seeking to obtain an expressive class number, and (5) any classification giving short simple class numbers to commonly sought popular subjects, if it also manages to provide class numbers—necessarily long and complex—for subjects of great intension, usually embodied only in articles in periodicals.

But the fulfilment of the laws of library science in the service of the intellectual vanguard of humanity requires classification to march forward unperturbed by the attitude of the old guard.

CHAPTER 24

MNEMONICS

THE CANON OF CONSISTENT SEQUENCE, prescribed for the classes in an array, has as its counterpart certain canons to be satisfied by the notation. These canons gain in importance in the classification of an infinite universe. It is particularly so in the ever-expanding infinite Universe of Knowledge.

241   General Canon of Mnemonics
The digit or digits used to represent a specified concept in a class number should be the same in all class numbers having that concept represented in them, provided that insistence on such consistent representation does not violate more important requirements. This is the **General Canon of Mnemonics.**

On page 96 of his *Manual of classification,* ed. 3, 1947, Berwick Sayers remarks: " There is a very general quality in modern classification notations which is ingenious, and, within limits, of great value to the classifier. This is its mnemonic quality; its power of assisting the memory and of reducing the work of reference to tables and indexes to the minimum. By mnemonic notation we mean a notation which has always the same significance wherever it appears in the classification." This passage contains at once a neat definition of mnemonics and a pithy description of its benefits.

On pages 58-59 of his *Organisation of knowledge in libraries,* ed. 2, 1939, Bliss comments on the value of mnemonics in the following words: " Notation, as a kind of symbolic language, depends extensively on memory of meanings. In learning to read and write a new language we gradually learn the words and their meanings and remember more and more of them. In like manner librarians and users of libraries gradually learn the order of the classes and remember the class-marks, though they continue to make use of the catalogs, shelf-lists and index to schedules. The more systematic the system is the more readily they will learn and the more efficiently they will remember. This is the natural and rational ground for a system of *mnemonics,* or symbols that may be readily and systematically remembered."

242   Definition
Mnemonics originates from a Greek word meaning " to remember." Its dictionary meaning is " the art of assisting memory; a mode of

recalling to mind any fact or number, or a series of disconnected terms or figures." Arumugam and Sakuntala, the contemporary arithmetical prodigies, use some extraordinary mnemonics in the amazing feats of multiplication and other calculations. Magicians reproducing accurately a number of disconnected statements made to them some time earlier, exactly in the sequence in which they were made, use their own mnemonic to fix the statements in their memory in the sequence in which they hear them. Each of us improvise some sort of mnemonics for the moment. When we go to the market, we remember apples by A, grapes by G and raspberry by R. Some tie a knot in the handkerchief to recall something to memory. These mnemonics are mostly private and individual, and are often temporary. In the *Ramayana,* Valmiki describes the cruel effect of mnemonics in certain circumstances. Maricha had once received a severe thrashing from Rama the hero, when he was a marauder terrorising the sages in the forest. Years later, he confesses to Ravana the anti-hero, " The phoneme R, written or spoken, brings Rama and his thrashing to mind. The memory of it makes me quiver."

243 Kinds of Mnemonics

In the building of a class number for public use, and not merely for private use, such fortuitous, temporary or private improvisation of mnemonics cannot be of help. A different definition of the term " mnemonics " is implied in the enunciation of the General Canon of Mnemonics. It denotes a mode of securing consistent sequence among the categories figuring in classifying work. It is indeed a mode of choosing digits or numbers of several digits to represent categories in such a way that their sequence is consistent in whatever subjects they occur. The following three kinds of mnemonics are possible in notation:

(1) Verbal mnemonics.
(2) Scheduled mnemonics.
(3) Seminal mnemonics.

These are explained in the three succeeding chapters.

CHAPTER 25

VERBAL MNEMONICS

VERBAL MNEMONICS ARE QUITE common in life. Their application to the construction of a number in classification is the Alphabetical Device. This consists in representing a category by the first letter or the first few letters in its name.

A for apple, B for boat and C for cat are trivial examples. If the names of two or more categories, coming in the same array, begin with the same letter, then one of them is represented by that letter, and the others are represented by the first two letters in their respective names. If the names of two or more categories begin with the same two letters, then one of them is represented by these two letters, and the others are represented by the first three letters in their respective names. And so on.

251 When to Use

Alphabets have ordinal values in respect of their mutual sequence. They can also be used as decimal fractions. Thus they are quite suited for use as digits in the construction of class numbers. In fact the construction of class numbers or any parts of them by the alphabetical use is quite easy. It does not need the prior construction of a schedule or its use while classifying. On the other hand, the construction of a class number based on characteristics intrinsic to the entities of a universe requires more work. It requires a schedule to be set up by a classificationist. It requires a knowledge of the classificatory language set up by the schedule.

Alphabetical arrangement does not give a helpful sequence in most cases. However, when arrangement on the basis of a characteristic is not more helpful than alphabetical arrangement, in any subject or in any array derived from it, the alphabetical device may be preferred with advantage. The arrangement of makes of bicycles or motor cars, of different variant forms of an instrument having distinctive names, and of the different strains of an agricultural crop or cultivars, are instances justifying the preference of verbal mnemonics to the use of specially constructed ordinal numbers.

252 Canon of Verbal Mnemonics

Verbal mnemonics should be rejected, without any hesitation, if a sequence more helpful to readers or more filiatory than alphabetical sequence exists. Verbal mnemonics by alphabetical device should be preferred if the alphabetical sequence is as helpful as any other sequence. The word forming the basis of verbal mnemonics should be that of international nomenclature whenever it has been set up. This is the **Canon of Verbal Mnemonics.**

The classificatory language of ordinal numbers is intended to be an international language. This is essential to facilitate international communication through classification. The use of a vernacular name in the alphabetical device will militate against this. The only means of avoiding this fault is to use international nomenclature for alphabetical device. It is true that international nomenclature does not exist in several fields, but this is compensated for by the number of occasions calling for alphabetical device being small. Further, in several cases calling for the use of alphabetical device, such as makes of machinery, laws of a subject derived by induction or deduction such as Hooke's Law, or manufacturing processes, the words concerned are often virtually proper nouns. They are therefore suitable for use in verbal mnemonics.

253 Prescription

Division by alphabetical device is usually prescribed by most of the schemes in the light of the Canon of Verbal Mnemonics. The L.C. scheme prescribes it more often than others in preference to numbers based on a characteristic giving a more helpful and filiatory sequence. The use of English words as the basis of alphabetisation, coupled with far too many resorts to alphabetisation, increases the unsuitability of the L.C. for international use. The U.D.C. is more sparing in the prescribing of alphabetical device, and the C.C. is even more sparing. Some differences between the U.D.C. and C.C. may be mentioned. Poets are arranged by the U.D.C. alphabetically, whereas the C.C. arranges them on the basis of their year of birth as characteristic. So it is with authors in drama, fiction and other forms of literature. Again, periodicals are arranged by the U.D.C. alphabetically, but the C.C. first groups them by the country of origin, and in each country-group arranges them by the chronological device, using their year of beginning as the epoch. The D.C. does not prescribe alphabetical device at all.

254 Amateur Classification

Many an amateur designs a classification based on verbal mnemonics from beginning to end. He gets disillusioned when it is too late. This temptation to play with the so-called mnemonic classification—mnemonic in the sense of verbal mnemonics—is caused by the very limited nature of the universe with which the amateur is concerned at the beginning. Usually, it is small in extent; it does not grow with sufficient rapidity to give him a shock early enough; perhaps it does not call for a particularly helpful sequence. Many eminent scientists have been tempted into such amateurish attempts at designing a classification. They did not realise at the beginning the chaos—the very opposite of classification—towards which it was leading. The first influential pronouncement on the futility of amateurish design of classification came from the scientists themselves in 1950. It came through the Standing Committee on Subject Classification in Science set up by the Royal Society of London, in pursuance of a resolution of the Scientific Information Conference convened by it in 1948. At the end of 1950, this committee reported that " the problem of classification is far more complex than was imagined at the outset." Its secretary, Professor J. D. Bernal, has given the right lead in the matter by commending to the library profession a serious and systematic pursuit of the discipline of classification along the lines of scientific method. The library profession should have the sensibility and courage to pursue the subject uninhibited by the howlers among old guards and newcomers without experience of the exacting needs of the social implications of precise documentation work expected of libraries today.

255 Unnecessary Numeralising

At the other extreme, we find blind enthusiasts for numeralisation. Even where it is decided that alphabetical device gives as good a help as any other, they retain only the first letter in the name concerned. They translate the succeeding letters into Arabic numerals. It is difficult to see the purpose served by such translation of letters into numerals. For the letters have as much ordinal quality as numerals. Early in the century many able librarians wasted their powers in designing schedules for such letter-numeral translation. The vogue set by them is not yet dead; it appears even in professional examinations, and the L.C. perpetuates it in its schedules. Here are some examples from page 240 of the volume on Class T Technology: A6 apple; M2 Maize; W5 Wheat.

CHAPTER 26

SCHEDULED MNEMONICS

261 The Canon

A SCHEME OF CLASSIFICATION should include a preliminary set of schedules of divisions based on characteristics likely to recur in an array of some order or other of all or many classes, or refer any recurrent array of divisions to the one schedule of them giving in connection with an appropriate class. This is the **Canon of Scheduled Mnemonics.**

Obviously, this canon will automatically secure conformity to the Canon of Consistent Sequence. It will also satisfy the law of parsimony in regard to the bulk of the schedules of the classification. The work of the classificationist also will conform to the law of parsimony.

262 Decimal Classification

In the D.C., scheduled mnemonics are automatically secured by some of the devices used in constructing class numbers.

The geographical schedule is covered by the numbers 940-999 in 9 History. It is prescribed for mnemonic subdivision in many of the cases admitting of geographical arrangement. For example, under 371.839 Students organisations, by country, we find the following note: " Divided like 940-999."

The entire schedule is prescribed for mnemonic subdivision by subject device wherever such a prescription is warranted. For example, under 375.01-375.9 Subjects of study, we find the following note: " Divided like the classification 010-999."

The main classes only are prescribed for mnemonic subdivision in certain cases. Thus under 371.84 Student life and customs by subjects, we find the note: " Divided like the main classification, e.g. 371.845 Scientific, 371.848 Literary." Some part of the scheme only is sometimes prescribed for mnemonic subdivision. In several classes in 330 Economics, division as in 620-699 is prescribed. An appendix gives a schedule of languages for use in mnemonic subdivision wherever necessary.

2621 MNEMONICS MISSED

Opportunities for mnemonics are also missed by the D.C. in several places. In the following examples the class numbers of the C.C. are also given in parallel columns to show the possibility for mnemonics.

The mnemonic digits of the C.C. are shown in black type. The corresponding digits of the D.C. are also shown in black type.

Examples

(1) Literary authors

In the schedule of 800 Literature, an author is not represented by the same digit in each of the form divisions of the class.

Class	D.C. No.	C.C. No.
Oliver Goldsmith as poet	821.64	O:1**L28**
Oliver Goldsmith as essayist	824.66	O:6**L28**

(2) Cereals

Compare the digits representing " cereals " in the following class numbers.

Class	D.C. No.	C.C. No.
Farming of *cereals*	633.1	**J38**
Adulteration of *cereals*	614.312	L:523:**J38**
Diet of *cereals*	612.39273	L:533:**J38**
Trade in *cereals*	338.1	X9**J38**

(3) Marine

Compare the digits representing " marine " in the following class numbers.

Class	D.C. No.	C.C. No.
Marine biology	574.92	G:**5255**
Marine zoology	591.92	K:**5255**
Marine botany	581.92	I:**5255**
Marine corps	359	MV**45**
Marine engines	621.12	D64:5255
Marine insurance	368.2	X89**5**
Marine law	347.7	Z9**25**
Marine libraries	027.644	2:**55**
Mariner's occupation	613.64	MD5**255**

(4) Transport

Compare the digits representing " transport " in the following class numbers.

Class	D.C. No.	C.C. No.
Air *transport* service	629.1382	X**43**
Architecture of *transport* buildings	725.3	N1:9D**4**
Transport facilities for industrial plant	658.214	X9:20X:**4**
Transport in mines	622.6	D3:**4**
Transport of goods	658.7885	X9:**4**
Transport business	658	X**4**

2622 RESULT OF NEGLECT OF MNEMONICS

How such missing of opportunities for mnemonics causes unnecessary situations in the application of the D.C. is illustrated by the following statement in the *Cataloguers' and classifiers' yearbook* Vol. 6, 1939, page 59, by the Head of the D.C. Section of the Library of Congress: " One policy of ours should be mentioned here, because it must be puzzling at times. Take 338.1 Production of agricultural products considered from an economic standpoint. Books on that general subject, not limited geographically, we class in 338.1. If limited to the U.S. we class in 338.10973. Now wheat is an agricultural product; so books on wheat are classed in 338.1 since no subdivision by products has yet been made. When we have a book on wheat in the U.S. we still class it in 338.1, not 338.10973. Why? Because some day we expect to have a definite number under 338.1 for wheat, and when that time comes we want to be able to add figures to 338.1 on cards without first removing 0973. You may want to do the same thing, in anticipation of future expansions. Or you may prefer, either permanently or temporarily, to put all wheat in the U.S. with general agricultural products in the U.S."

How unnecessary and ridiculous this situation is will be realised if we remember that in 630 Agriculture, 633.1 is Cereals and 633.11 is Wheat. In the number 338.1, 338 stands for Production and .1 stands for Agricultural products. If the Canon of Scheduled Mnemonics is sufficiently enforceable in the scheme, obviously 338.1311 should be taken as the class number for the Production of Wheat not only by the official editor of the D.C., but by any and every classifier using the scheme. That being so, Production of Wheat in the U.S. could immediately receive its permanent number as 338.13110973, without waiting for the time to come when figures can be added to 338.1 in order to represent Production of Wheat. Surely classifiers using the D.C. should not be made to depend on the official editors for such trivial extensions? The thought of the official editors, too, should be released from such trivia and be concentrated upon more far-reaching and fundamental improvements of the scheme. Autonomy should be given to the classifier.

This ridiculous situation cited by the Head of the D.C. section is typical of thousands of similar avoidable situations. They are not avoided in the D.C. because it has not set up the necessary apparatus for exploiting the Canon of Scheduled Mnemonics to the maximum possible extent.

The unerring way in which the one and the same class number can be derived by every trained classifier with the aid of prescribed apparatus and without aid from the official editor will be illustrated further at the end of the next subsection on the C.C.

263   Colon Classification

In the C.C., scheduled mnemonics are secured in five ways: by the facet device, the common isolate device, the geographical device, the chronological device, the subject device and the phase device. The mnemonic digits are shown in black type in the examples given.

2631   Facet Device

Class	C.C. No.
Gall bladder	**L292**
Anatomy of the *gall bladder*	**L292**:2
Physiology of the *gall bladder*	**L292**:3
Imflammation of the *gall bladder*	**L292**:4**15**
Embryology of the *gall bladder*	**L292**:73
Inflammation	**L**:**415**
Inflammation of the eyes	L183:**415**
Inflammation of the joints	L191:**415**
Inflammation of the tonsils	L219:**415**
Inflammation of the stomach	L24:**415**
Inflammation of the pericardium	L31:**415**
Inflammation of the bronchi	L44:**415**
Inflammation of the kidneys	L51:**415**
Inflammation of the meninges	L711:**415**
Rural community	**Y31**
Pastimes of the *rural community*	**Y31**:3MY
Opium habits of the *rural community*	**Y31**:413
Underpopulation in *rural areas*	**Y31**:51
Residences of the *rural community*	**Y31**:81
Ornaments of the *rural community*	**Y31**:86
Apparel of the *rural community*	**Y31**:88
Ornaments	Y:**86**
Ornaments of children	Y11:**86**
Ornaments of youth	Y12:**86**
Ornaments of women	Y15:**86**
Ornaments of musicians	Y41(N8):**86**
Ornaments of aristocracy	Y52:**86**
Ornaments of aristocratic children	Y52-11:**86**
Ornaments of aristocratic women	Y52-15:**86**
Ornaments of primitive people	Y72:**86**
Ornaments of Muslims	Y9(Q7):**86**
Ornaments of Muslim women	Y9(Q7-15):**86**

2632   Common Isolate Device

Class	C.C. No.
Bibliography of library science	**2a**
Bibliography of science	**Aa**
Bibliography of mathematics	**Ba**
Bibliography of geometry	**B6a**
Bibliography of Shakespeare	**O-,2J64a**
Bibliography of foreign language teaching in elementary schools in India	T15:3,(P5).44**a**
Bibliography of overtime in the textile industry in India in the twentieth century	X9(M7):9:511.44.**Na**

2633   GEOGRAPHICAL DEVICE

Class	C.C. No.
Flora of *India*	I:12.44
Fauna of *India*	K:12.44
Indian sculpture	ND44
Psychology of *Indians*	S744
Geography of *India*	U.44
History of *India*	V44
Double taxation in *India*	X7:32.44
Evolution of the ornaments of women in *India*	Y15:86:6.44
Indian criminal law	Z44:5

2634   CHRONOLOGICAL DEVICE

Class	C.C. No.
G. K. *Chesterton* as a poet	O-,1M74
G. K. *Chesterton* as a dramatist	O-,2M74
G. K. *Chesterton* as a novelist	O-,3M74
G. K. *Chesterton* as a prose writer	O-,6M74
Collection of G. K. *Chesterton's* critical essays	O-,9xM74

2635   SUBJECT DEVICE

Class	C.C. No.
X-rays	C53
X-ray diagnosis	L:4:40253
X-ray therapy	L:4:6253
Making *X-ray* apparatus	MC53
Economics of the *X-ray* apparatus industry	X9(MC53)

2636   PHASE DEVICE

Class	C.C. No.
Psychology	S
Mathematics for *psychologists*	BobS
Statistics for *psychologists*	B28obS
Endocrinology and *psychology*	L6ogS
Psychology in Shakespeare's plays	O-,2J64:gS
Psychology of travel-mindedness	U8ogS
Economic wants and *psychology*	X:1ogS

264 Subject Classification

In the S.C., scheduled mnemonics are provided for the geographical divisions and the language divisions. In addition, the Categorical Table provides a rich source of scheduled mnemonics.

265 Library of Congress Classification

The L.C. scheme pays no heed whatever to mnemonics. It has no scheduled mnemonics. For lack of them it is encumbered with hundreds of pages of repetitive details. The repetition of geographical divisions almost on every other page with entirely different numbers to represent them is most irritating. So also with other repetitions.

Let us take the schedule for Political Science. It runs through 374 pages. Of these, above 100 pages are due to the repetition of geographical areas some forty or fifty times, each time with different significant digits, besides the prescription of the alphabetical device for geographical division in more than a hundred places. Again, the Problem divisions such as Crown, Legislature, Executive, Judiciary and so on, and their subdivisions, are repeated under practically every country, with different significant digits. A mnemonic schedule for these would have eliminated more than 100 pages. With the full economy procurable by scheduled mnemonics the number of pages in the volume could have been reduced to far less than fifty.

266 Bibliographic Classification

The B.C. secures conformity to the Canon of Scheduled Mnemonics rather sparingly, and does not use it consistently. The following table is illustrative.

B.C. No.	Class	C.C. No.
FAB	Morphology of plant	I:2
FOH	Morphology of stem	I,5:2
FT,A	Morphology of monocotylac	I7:2
FTH,A	Morphology of palmae	I75:2
FVD	Morphology of micro-organism	G91:2

The abandonment of the facet device in the first, second and third subjects has thwarted conformity to the Canon of Scheduled Mnemonics. The advantage of shortening the class number by one digit accrues from this abandonment of the facet device. Is this economy in notation a sufficient offset to the economy in thinking secured by the facet device?

CHAPTER 27

SEMINAL MNEMONICS

271 The Canon

A SCHEME OF CLASSIFICATION should use one and the same digit to denote seminally equivalent concepts in whatever array of whatever class they may appear. This is the **Canon of Seminal Mnemonics.**

In scheduled mnemonics, the same concept is represented by the same term and the same number, in all its places of occurrence. It is possible to have the same concept represented by the same *number* in all places of occurrence, but with different *terms* denoting it in the different places. The identity of the concept is cognisable at great depths, beyond the reach of natural language. As and when the concept came up to the surface in particular contexts, a word in the natural language has been coined to denote it in that context. At the unmanifest depth of identity, there has been no need to denote that primordial concept by a term in the natural language. In classificatory language it is possible to denote it by a definite digit. But in the different schedules where that concept is denoted by that digit, the equivalent term current in the natural language has to be different in each schedule. Therefore it cannot be called a scheduled mnemonic. I denoted these deep mnemonics by the negative term " Unscheduled Mnemonics " in the first edition. But my friends B. I. Palmer and A. J. Wells have hit upon the more happy and more truly descriptive term " Seminal Mnemonics " to denote it. I gladly change over in this edition from " Unscheduled " to " Seminal."

Examples

(1) " Function " in Political science, " Physiology " in Biological sciences and " Social activities " in Sociology are equivalent at the unexpressed seminal level. They are all denoted by the digit 3.

(2) " Constitution " in Political science, " Morphology " in Biological sciences, " Physical anthropology " in Sociology and " Morphology " in Linguistics are equivalent at the unexpressed seminal level. They are all denoted by the digit 2.

(3) " Disease " in Biological sciences, " Social pathology " in Social sciences, " Tort " in Law are equivalent at the unexpressed seminal level. They are all denoted by the digit 4.

272 Forgotten Tradition

In the mystic tradition of Chaldea and India, many such equivalences are believed to have been recognised. I have not yet been able to get hold of that tradition. It gives seminal mnemonic significance to letters as well as numerals. A correct knowledge of it ought to make the use of digits conform with seminal mnemonics. The forgotten tradition needs to be recaptured. Class numbers formed with such seminal mnemonic digits will satisfy the Canons of Filiatory Sequence and of Helpful Sequence in an ideal way. The Canon of Consistent Sequence would also be satisfied even at a subtle level.

The pathetic phenomenon of freezing a digit representing a bibliographically poverty-stricken class, keeping it in quarantine for a prescribed number of years, and releasing it thereafter to represent some other concept needing a digit will not become helplessly necessary as it is with the use of digits in the U.D.C.

The seminal concepts and the digits have a "many-one" relationship. Many related seminal concepts may be denoted by the same digit. As an example, Aesthetics, Painting, Women, Love and Radiation are all represented by the digit 5.

The subject is discussed in greater detail in sections 266 to 27 of my *Philosophy of library classification* (1951). Several uses of seminal mnemonics will be found in the C.C., but they are all tentative. I have not yet achieved a full insight into seminal equivalences.

Moreover, as the deep region of seminal equivalences transcends expression in words alone, communication through the written or printed word is difficult. Seminal equivalences are ineffable, but they get permeated by personal association and communication in a "school."

CHAPTER 28

STRUCTURE AND DEVELOPMENT

281 Enumeration

IN AN ENUMERATIVE CLASSIFICATION of the universe of knowledge the classes are enumerated in a single schedule, with or without a few auxiliary ones, to cover all known subjects more or less exhaustively.

The L.C. scheme is severely enumerative. So is the S.C., but its categorical divisions form a long auxiliary schedule. The D.C. is largely enumerative, but its common subdivisions form an auxiliary schedule.

The U.D.C. is mainly enumerative, it has five auxiliary schedules. These concern (1) Language, (2) Form, (3) Place, (4) Time and (5) Point of View. There are also short schedules of special analytic divisions scattered at many points of the main schedule. But the length of the main schedule is considerably larger than the total length of all the auxiliary schedules taken together.

The B.C. is virtually enumerative. But it deviates from pure enumeration more or less like the U.D.C. Its auxiliary schedules for general use are four. These are devoted to (1) Approach materials, (2) Place, (3) Language and (4) Time. In addition it has forty-one auxiliary schedules for use in particular main classes. These correspond to the special analytical divisions in U.D.C. The length of the main schedules is much greater than the total length of all the auxiliary schedules taken together. Moreover, the main schedule is interspersed with classes formed with the aid of the first auxiliary schedules. This increases its enumerative quality.

The C.C. is far from enumerative. It has four auxiliary schedules for general use. These are devoted to (1) Approach materials, (2) Place, (3) Language and (4) Time. There are also auxiliary schedules of other common isolates. It has a schedule of main classes, one page long. For each main class, a set of schedules of isolates is given. A class number is synthesised by assembling numbers taken from the schedules of the set and the auxiliary schedules.

However, there are versions of C.C. reduced to enumerative status. These are given in

(1) *School and college libraries* (1944) by S. R. Ranganathan.
(2) *Organisation of libraries* (1945) by S. R. Ranganathan.
(3) *Library manual* (1950) by S. R. Ranganathan and K. M. Sivaraman.

(4) *Granthalaya prakriya* (1951) by S. R. Ranganathan and M. L. Nagar.

(5) In the pages of printed library catalogues, such as the volumes of the catalogue of the Madras University Library and of the Library of the Ministry of Labour of the Government of India.

The enumerative schedules giving ready-made class numbers by the above publications were designed to help persons in charge of small libraries but without opportunity to learn the technique of classification.

282 Dependence of Classifier

An enumerative classification gives little autonomy to the classifier. On the appearance of any new subject, he has to look to the classificationist for its class number. On the other hand, the universe of knowledge is dynamic. It repeatedly throws forth new subjects here, there and everywhere. This makes the utter dependence of the classifier on the classificationist offend against the Laws of Library Science. For books embodying new subjects may have to be kept away from public use till the arrival of the class number from the classificationist, or they may have to be given class numbers of greater extension than the embodied thought would warrant.

283 Autonomy of Classifier

A scheme satisfying the Canons of Scheduled and Seminal Mnemonics and using the octave device, decimal fraction device, facet device and phase device, gives some autonomy to the classifier. At the same time there is a high probability of the same class number being hit upon by every classifier, to denote a new subject. Of course, the classifier must be well disciplined in the grammar of the classificatory language chosen. He should also have been attuned to the feel of seminal equivalences. The autonomy of the classifier has been put in other words, such as " A scheme of classification should be self-perpetuating," and " Each new subject should bring its own class number in its pocket." In *Some new placings in the Colon Classification,* published in page 28 of the *Proceedings* of the Second All-India Conference, 1935, I gave cases of new subjects in all of which the few librarians with training in the School of Library Science of the Madras University Library, and working with me, independently arrived at the same class numbers. A few cases are extracted here from that paper. These have been subjected to improvements made later.

284 Hilbert Space

The first placing for consideration refers to Function-spaces, or spaces of many dimensions. In the words of M. H. Stone, " The systematic study of the possible internal relationships with which a general class or space may be endowed, and of the various types of space characterised by such internal properties, was begun by Frechet and Handsdorff; to the efforts of these mathematicians and their numerous followers we now owe an independent and fertile mathematical discipline." Such function-spaces belong to the foundation of analysis. Hence they should form a class under B31. As the digit 3, when applied to the canonical divisions of Mathematics, specialises in Analysis, Function and Transcendental operations, we have fixed the number for function-space as B313 by adding the mnemonic digit 3 to B31. This placing was necessitated by the arrival in the library of Stone (Marshal Harvey), *Linear transformations in Hilbert space and their applications to analysis,* 1932. Now the Hilbert space is but one of a great variety of function-spaces. The basic article on Hilbert space was published in 1908. Hence, by the application of the chronological device, we get the number B313N for Hilbert space.

285   Periodogram Analysis

The second placing in Mathematics refers to Periodogram Analysis and it is a branch of B28 Statistics. The problem is to find a place for it among the subdivisions of B28. The outstanding elements in periodogram analysis are the crests and troughs, i.e. the maxima and minima. A reference to the problem divisions of the Function Theory will show that the digit 7 is mnemonic for maxima-minima principles. Hence the number B287 has been assigned to Periodogram Analysis.

286   Crystals

The first new placing in Physics relates to Crystals. Following the Dewey tradition we had given places for Crystals in Geology and Chemistry. But in recent years, particularly under the leadership of Bragg, much work has been done on the pure physics of crystals. It is the classification of the works published by this school of workers that has led to the new placing in question.

Crystals refers to a *state* of matter; it is one of the possible states of matter. Hence, Crystals should be a subdivision of 1 Solids of the canonical division C2 Properties of matter in C Physics. Again, that which distinguishes the crystal state from the glass state is that the former has differential directional properties. The digit that specialises in direction is 6 (cf. B46 Vector analysis, B6 Geometry, and the number 6 Polarisation under C5, Light). These mnemonic considerations led us to assign the number C216 to Crystals.

287   Ultra-sound

According to the printed schedule of the C.C., C5 Light is to be divided on the basis of two characteristics, viz. Wavelength characteristic and Problem characteristic. But C3 Sound is divided only on the basis of the problem characteristic. Is it not anomalous that such different treatment should be given to two topics both of which are vitally based on wave motion? But within one year of the publication of the first edition of the C.C. this anomaly was violently brought to my notice by the publication of Teil 1 of Band 17 of the *Handbuch der experimental physik* under the title *Schwingungs und Wellenlehre ultraschallwellen.* A complete section of this book is devoted to ultra-sound. We also learnt that Sir C. V. Raman's laboratory in Bangalore had just begun to work on ultra-sound. This led us to set the anomaly right. We opened under C3 Sound a new schedule based on wavelength as characteristic. The number C35 was assigned to ultra-sound.

288   **Bhakti** (devotion)

Narada's *Bhakti-sutras* and the allied works presented a problem. It was finally decided to place them in the problem division 4 Religious practice, 41 Personal, 419 Other topics. The mnemonic digit for Bhakti had to be decided. There is an element of mysticism in Bhakti; 6 is the mnemonic digit for mysticism. Therefore, 4196 was fixed for Bhakti.

PART 3

THEORY OF KNOWLEDGE CLASSIFICATION
Second Approximation
ANALYTICO-SYNTHETIC CLASSIFICATION

CHAPTER 31

MULTI-DIMENSIONAL UNIVERSE

311 Challenge to Notation

IN CHAPTER 21, THE starting point was the assumption of the attribute of infinity in the universe of knowledge. In chapter 22, the implication of potentially infinite expansion of the universe, in any array, was considered. The octave device was described as a means of endowing the notational system with Infinite Hospitality in Array. In chapter 23, the implication of potentially infinite expansion of the universe, in any chain, was considered. The decimal fraction device was described as a means of endowing the notational system with Infinite Hospitality in Chain. Reference was also made to the universe of knowledge being characterised by manifold infinity in chain. This character of the universe threw a challenge to the notational system. It transcended the capacity of the bare decimal fraction device. This could provide only a Onefold Infinite Hospitality in Chain. To meet the challenge, Manifold Infinite Hospitality in Chain had to be provided in the notational system. In this respect, the facet device was described as a helpful supplement to the decimal fractional notation. So was the phase device. The four devices jointly enabled the notational system to meet the challenge of the universe of knowledge.

312 Genesis of the Challenge

To get a closer view of the challenge of the universe of knowledge to the notational system, an examination of the genesis of the challenge is necessary. The challenge is an inevitable consequence of the incommensurability of the number of dimensions of the universe of knowledge and that of the universe of class numbers. The universe of knowledge is of many dimensions. The universe of class numbers is only of one dimension. This is imposed on it by the very purpose of the notational system. Its purpose is to serve as a tool for mechanising arrangement of entities along a line, i.e. in one dimension. There are reasons for arrangement along a line, be it documents or entries of them.

313 Sensory Capacity

In a library, books have to be arranged in a line. We have to do so to facilitate the picking out of any book needed at any time. We have to do so also to facilitate the restoring of any book to its original place.

145

Linear arrangement of materials provides greater facility than arrangement in a plane or in space of three dimensions. Our sensory capacity has just reached the stage of sensing space of three dimensions and no more. The sensory capacity of some animals has reached the stage of sensing space of two dimensions only. The sensory capacity of lower organisms has reached the stage of sensing space of one dimension only. Perhaps some primitive organisms have not developed capacity to sense space at all. In the development of man, all these stages occur. A well-known case study on the subject is the " Hanna Case." Up to a few weeks, perhaps, a child has no sense of space. Then it acquires capacity to sense space of one dimension. After some more months it acquires capacity to sense space of two dimensions. The capacity to sense space of three dimensions develops still later. Thus, sensory capacity to deal with space of one dimension has been exercised longer in the evolution of the human species and in the development of the individual man. The preference for arrangement of materials in one dimension is perhaps due to this factor.

3131   COROLLARY

In library classification, arrangement of the universe of books has to be made on the basis of the subjects embodied in them. This was seen in section 211. Consequently arrangement of the universe of knowledge became the first step in library classification. As stated in section 2133, the universe of knowledge has only pseudo-entities, i.e. classes. Thus arrangement of classes has to be along a line.

314   Intellectual Habit

In addition to reasons of sensory capacity, intellectual habit also calls for arrangement of classes in a linear series. The intellect prefers to enumerate the classes of an array one at a time in succession. This creates a time-sequence, which is one-dimensional. Again, the intellect prefers to apply the relevant characteristics of classification one at a time in succession. This also creates a time-sequence, which too is one-dimensional. A great contribution of Descartes to facilitate the study of space of two or more dimensions was his reduction of such a space to two or more spaces of one dimension. The phenomenal advance in the study of spaces of two or more dimensions made possible by the Cartesian co-ordinate system is well known. This indicates our intellectual preference for arrangement in one dimension.

315   Dimension

" Dimension " is an undefined term as applied to the universe of knowledge. We are yet to get a sufficiently objective method of distinguishing one dimension from another. At present, we can only illustrate. It may be illustrated as follows. Consider the subject Zoology.

3151 DIMENSION OF NATURAL GROUP

We have the following successive subdivisions of Zoology: Invertebrate; Arthropoda; Insecta; Lepidoptera; Heteroptera; and so on. These are animal kingdoms of increasing intension got by the use of successive additional characteristics. Each characteristic has landed us only on animal kingdoms. We say that all these classes belong to one dimension of zoology. We call this the dimension of "Natural Group." The chain described above lies in this dimension.

3152 DIMENSION OF PROBLEM

Let us next consider the following successive divisions of Zoology: Ecology (=relation to environment); Interrelation (with other animals); Protective aids; and so on. These are all problems capable of being studied in relation to any animal kingdom. The problems are mentioned in the sequence of increasing intension, got by the use of successive additional characteristics. Each characteristic has landed us only on problems. We say that all these classes belong to one dimension of zoology. This dimension is obviously different from the dimension of "Natural groups." We call the new dimension the dimension of "Problem." The chain described above lies in this dimension.

3153 DIMENSION OF SPACE

Let us next consider the following successive divisions of Zoology: Physiographical habitat; Land; Mountain; Alpine mountain; and so on. The ecology of the animal kingdom varies with these physiographical divisions. These divisions have been mentioned in the sequence of increasing intension, got by the use of successive additional characteristics. Each characteristic has landed us only on physiographical regions. We say that all these classes belong to one dimension of zoology. This dimension is obviously different from the two dimensions already mentioned. We call the new dimension the dimension of "Space." The chain described above lies in this dimension.

316 Variety of Subjects

A subject may lie wholly in any one dimension of Zoology. It may also lie in any two dimensions. Or it may lie in all three dimensions. The next three sections give examples of these three varieties of subjects.

3161 SUBJECTS OF ONE DIMENSION

11 Zoology of Arthropoda
12 Zoology of Insecta
13 Zoology of Lepidoptera

21 Ecology of animals
22 Social life among animals
23 Protective features of animals

31 Land animals
32 Animals of mountain
33 Animals of Alpine mountain
There are 9 such subjects.

3162 Subjects of Two Dimensions

111 Ecology of Arthropoda
112 Interrelation of Arthropoda
113 Protective features of Arthropoda
121 Arthropoda of land
122 Arthropoda of mountain
123 Arthropoda of Alpine mountain

211 Ecology of Insecta
212 Interrelation of Insecta
213 Protective features of Insecta

221 Insecta of land
222 Insecta of mountain
223 Insecta of Alpine mountain

311 Ecology of Lepidoptera
312 Interrelation of Lepidoptera
313 Protective features of Lepidoptera

321 Lepidoptera of land
322 Lepidoptera of mountain
323 Lepidoptera of Alpine mountain

411 Ecology of land animals
412 Ecology of animals of mountain
413 Ecology of animals of Alpine mountain

421 Interrelation of land animals
422 Interrelation of animals of mountain
423 Interrelation of animals of Alpine mountain

431 Protective features of land animals
432 Protective features of animals of mountain
433 Protective features of animals of Alpine mountain
There are 27 subjects of two dimensions.

3163 Subjects of Three Dimensions

111 Ecology of Arthropoda of land
112 Ecology of Arthropoda of mountain
113 Ecology of Arthropoda of Alpine mountain

121 Interrelation of Arthropoda of land
122 Interrelation of Arthropoda of mountain
123 Interrelation of Arthropoda of Alpine mountain

131 Protective features of Arthropoda of land
132 Protective features of Arthropoda of mountain
133 Protective features of Arthropoda of Alpine mountain

There are similarly nine such subjects relating to each of Insecta and Lepidoptera. Thus the total number of subjects of three dimensions is twenty-seven.

3164 Number of Subjects

By adding up all the possible constructions of dimensions in the subject-field considered, we get sixty-three subjects.

317 Measure of Challenge

In general let us suppose that there are
p links in a chain of the first dimension;
q links in a chain of the second dimension;
r links in a chain of the third dimension;
etc., etc., etc., and
z links in a chain of the nth dimension.

The number of subjects of one dimension is Σp. This is the sum of all numbers of links in each dimension.

The number of subjects of two dimensions is Σpq. This is the sum of all the binary products of the number of links in different dimensions, taking the number from two different dimensions in all cases.

The number of subjects of three dimensions is Σpqr. This is the sum of all the ternary products. And so on.

Thus the total number of subjects is

$$\Sigma p + \Sigma pq + \Sigma pqr + \ldots + \Sigma pqr \ldots z.$$

This is a measure of the challenge of the multi-dimensional universe of knowledge to the one dimensional universe of class numbers.

Let us simplify the matter, without loss of generality, by taking

$$p = q = r = \ldots = z.$$

Then the total number of subjects is

$$np + {}_nC_2 p^2 + {}_nC_3 p^3 + \ldots + {}_nC_n p^n = (1 + p)^n - 1.$$

Putting $p = 3$ and $n = 3$, for the case considered in section 316, we get 63 as the number of subjects. This was the figure got in section 3164.

318 Pressure on Notational System

The notational system should provide class numbers for all the subjects lying in one or more dimensions. The class numbers should be capable of throwing the subjects in the preferred, helpful, filiatory sequence. But we do not now know all the links likely to appear in each chain. Further, in each dimension the number of chains is many. For from each link in each chain any number of new chains may branch off. This number also is not fully known. Thus, the challenge of the multi-dimensional universe of knowledge is immense. The notational system has to bear a tremendous pressure. To do so, it must be endowed with capacity to grow from everywhere. It should be like a tree with an infinity of apical buds scattered over all its twigs, branches and stem. It should be like a banyan tree and not like a palmyra tree. There should be no rigidity anywhere in its structure. Suitable devices should be provided to remove every possible rigidity at every point in the structure of a class number.

CHAPTER 32

REDUCTION OF RIGIDITY

THE HISTORY OF NOTATION is a vital part in the history of classification. The history of reduction of rigidity is a vital chapter in the history of notation. It will be helpful to trace this history. This will clear the ground to be covered.

321 Fullness of Rigidity

The primitive notational system uses the integers alone as ordinal numbers. It numbers the subjects in the sequence of their appearance.

3211 VIOLATION OF CANONS

This integral notation is too rigid to satisfy either

(1) The Canon of Helpful Sequence; or
(2) The Canon of Modulation; or
(3) The Canons of Filiatory Sequence.

The co-ordinate subjects do not appear together at their first appearance. Therefore they cannot be put in juxtaposition, nor can they be put in helpful sequence. The subjects subordinate to a host-subject do not appear for the first time in the sequence of their modulation. Therefore they cannot be arranged in a modulated sequence, and do not appear immediately after their host-subject. Subjects co-ordinate with their host-subject may appear earlier than the subordinate subjects. The co-ordinate subjects themselves may not appear in the sequence of their degree of affinity. Therefore the arrangement of subjects cannot be filiatory.

322 Limited Reduction

The gap-notational system comes second in order of primitiveness. This system also uses only integers as ordinal numbers. In this system, all known subjects are arranged in a filiatory, helpful sequence. They are not, however, assigned consecutive integers. A gap of integers is left between the integers denoting any two consecutive subjects in the arrangement. This has been called Gap Device in section 233. The gap is not filled consecutively from end to end. Even in filling a gap, gaps are left. The L.C. used this device to effect limited reduction in rigidity.

3221 VIOLATION OF CANONS

In the first place, classes co-ordinate with and subordinate to the class represented by the number at the left end of the gap will have to be put into the gap. They may not appear for the first time in a helpful sequence. Therefore the Canon of Filiatory Sequence for Subordinate Classes will be violated. Again, more subjects may appear in a gap than there are numbers in it. This will bring the position back to the one described in sections 321 and 3211.

323 Rigidity in Chain

3231 FIRST REDUCTION

The decimal fraction device, described in Section 234, reduces rigidity in all chains belonging to one dimension. This device was popularised by the D.C., and is now used by most schemes, the only exception being the L.C. On account of the great influence of the Library of Congress, this is unfortunate.

3232 SECOND REDUCTION

The auto-bias device, described in section 237, further eliminates rigidity in chain. The C.C. made this second reduction of rigidity in chain by postulating an additional digit, the hyphen, to connect two numbers belonging to the same domain. Fixing its ordinal value as greater than the ordinal value of any connecting symbol and smaller than that of any substantive digit is the essence of the success of this device.

3233 RESIDUAL RIGIDITY

But there is difficulty in applying it at once consistently and helpfully. To mechanise its use, the members of an auto-biased number are, by prescription, made to follow their own ordinal sequence. But the result does not always give a helpful sequence. This *ex cathedra* fixing of the sequence of the two members of an auto-biased number amounts to playing into the hands of the notation, whatever be the demand of the Canon of Helpfulness. This leaves a residual rigidity in chain, the removal of which is still a standing challenge.

3234 EXAMPLE

Consider " Arteries of the hands." Both " Arteries " and " Hands " are assumed to fall in one and the same dimension—the dimension of organs. Their numbers are given below.

C.C. No.	Subject	D.C. No.
L167:2	Anatomy of hands	611.96
L37:2	Anatomy of arteries	611.13
L167-37:2 or L37-167:2	Anatomy of the arteries of hands	611.1344

The D.C. number 611.1344 is equivalent to the C.C. number L37-167. This method of assembling together the two numbers 37 and 167 of co-ordinate status will form a sequence helpful to the persons specialising in the "Anatomy of the circulatory system." But surgeons would prefer to assemble the numbers in the reverse order. The other C.C. number L167-37 assembles the numbers in this way.

But it is fatal to give two numbers to one and the same subject, for absence of synonyms is an essential attribute of a classificatory language, as stated in section 12832. One of the numbers has to be forcibly preferred and the other discarded. The prescription of the C.C. prefers L167-37, which, as stated above, is no doubt helpful to surgeons. But it is not helpful to specialists in the circulatory system. This appears to be an insoluble problem. Is this residual rigidity in chain irremovable?

324 Rigidity in Array
3241 REDUCTION

The decimal fraction device is necessary to eliminate rigidity in chain. This device automatically restricts the number of places available for co-ordinate classes,

> to 9 if Arabic numerals are used;
> to 26 if Roman capitals are used;
> to 50 if Roman capitals and smalls, excluding certain letters like i, l and o, are used;
> to 59 if numerals and Roman letters are used;

and so on. This is too severe a rigidity. For in many arrays several co-ordinate classes can crop up in course of time. The octave device, described in section 2232, reduces this rigidity to a considerable extent. This is a contribution of the C.C.

3242 RIGIDITY IN ZONES

In the application of the octave device, the C.C. experiences a certain amount of residual rigidity. It is not able to arrange all the co-ordinate classes of an array in a strictly helpful sequence. Actually, it breaks up an array into four zones, and further breaks up the second and the third zones into several octaves, as will be described in detail in section 363 and its subdivisions. This forcibly distributes the isolates into several zones and octaves, which may violate the Canon of Helpful Sequence in some subjects, due to the rigidity of the notation. This is particularly serious in the first few octaves of the second zone. Is this residual rigidity due to zones and octaves irremovable?

325 Rigidity in Dimension
3251 FIRST REDUCTION

A more serious rigidity is the one due to the incapacity of a notation to satisfy the Canons of Filiatory Sequence. The first reduction of this rigidity is made by the decimal fraction device. But as shown in sections 233 and 323, this device is effective only if the chain lies wholly within one dimension. It blocks the way to the arrangement of classes of chains lying in two or more dimensions, in conformity with the Canons of Filiatory Sequence.

3252 SECOND REDUCTION

The examples considered in section 2341 show the way of incidence of rigidity in regard to dimension. Section 235 and its subdivisions showed the reduction of this rigidity by facet device in the C.C. This is the second reduction of rigidity in relation to dimension.

3253 U.D.C.

The U.D.C. was the first scheme to make this second reduction of rigidity in dimension. Its facet device consisted of the use of three digits to mark off three dimensions.

Dimension	Digit
Time	" . . . "
Space	(. . .)
Special Analytical	-

Fixing the ordinal value of these new digits below 1 was the essence of the success of this device.

3254 INCIPIENT STAGE

However, the U.D.C. did not go the whole way in the matter, for it did not take freedom to separate out the dimensions fully. Its adoption of a D.C. core implied the acceptance of the rigidity in dimension already in the D.C. core.

The examples given in the table in section 235 illustrate this weakness.

Example	Subject	U.D.C. No.
(1)	Overtime in India	331.814(54)
(2)	Mimicry in Lepidoptera	595.78-157
(3)	Book-selection in elementary school library	027.822.2:025.21

In the first example, the starting subject is " 33 Economics." The link " 1814 Overtime " belongs to the dimension of problem. The link " 54 India " belongs to the dimension of space. The chain of the subject " Overtime in India " lies in both of these dimensions. The class number 331.814(54) itself assembles the numbers of the links of the two dimensions by the connecting symbol (. . .). The facet device is in full use. So it is in the second example also.

It is, however, different in the third example. Here the starting point is " 02 Library economy." The link " 78222 Elementary school library " belongs to the dimension of library. The link " 521 Book-selection " belongs to the dimension of problem. The chain of the subject " Book-selection in elementary school library " lies in both of these dimensions. But the U.D.C. has not prescribed for the connection of the two links in the two respective dimensions. Therefore, the whole chain of a subject belonging to the dimension of Problem and beginning with the main class number has to be attached to the whole chain of a subject belonging to the dimension of Library and again beginning with the main class number. This gives the long number 027.822.2:025.21. In this, the facet device has been abandoned. It could have been retained, and the shorter number 027.822.2-521 would have resulted.

Such abandonment of the facet device occurs more often than its adoption. Probably this justifies the following inference. The " rigidity in dimension " of the D.C. core has mesmerised the U.D.C. This mesmerism has prevented the U.D.C. from exploiting fully its facet device to remove rigidity in dimension. The sensitiveness to " rigidity in dimension " appears to have been thus arrested in the U.D.C. even at the incipient stage.

3255 COLON CLASSIFICATION

The C.C. escaped the mesmerism and recognised the different dimensions with greater thoroughness than U.D.C. It consciously worked out the chains in each dimension independently, and fitted the links in each dimension with its own numbers. For a subject lying in two or more dimensions, it could spot out the part of it lying in the respective dimensions. It could then find the number for each such part, and finally assemble with connecting symbols the numbers of the various parts. The connecting symbol used was the colon. The second reduction of rigidity in dimension started by the U.D.C. was completed by the C.C.

326 Rigidity of Facet-Formula

3261 NIGHTMARE

In its earlier years—1924 to 1949—the C.C. seems to have been obsessed with the idea of dimensions. The force of its first contact with dimensions seems to have caused a nightmare. Its plight was reduced to that of Maricha, who began to see a Rama in every tree about him, such was the force of his first contact with Rama. So also the C.C. began to see dimensions in every subject—all dimensions in every subject—and it provided a dimension-formula for every main or canonical class. It called this a facet-formula, for the C.C. uses the word " facet " as the equivalent of the word " dimension." It compelled the class number of every subject to show forth all the facets prescribed by the formula, in spite of the absence of any particular facet in a subject.

3262 EFFECT OF FACET-FORMULA

The rigidity-effect of such a formula can be illustrated by an example. For " X Economics " the facet-formula prescribed was

X [B] : [P] : [S] : [T]
[B]=Business facet=Dimension of business;
[P]=Problem facet=Dimension of problem;
[S]=Space facet=Dimension of space; and
[T]=Time facet=Dimension of time.

The subject " Overtime for labour in the railways of India in 1950s " has the parts of its chain spread over four dimensions, as shown below:

" 415 Railway " in dimension [B];
" 9511 Overtime for labour " in dimension [P];
" 44 India " in dimension [S]; and
" N5 1950s " in dimension [T].

Then, the C.C. number according to the third edition, 1950, for this subject is

X415:9511:44:N5

The subject " Railways in India in 1950s " had to be given the number

X415::44:N5

No part of the chain of this subject belongs to the dimension of problem, yet the class number had to create a facet for it within itself and keep it vacant. This brought two colons together. This obsession about dimensions could bring any number of colons together, making the number clumsy.

3263 CAUSE OF CLUMSINESS

The cause of this clumsiness was the rigidity of the facet-formula. It amounted to thrusting every subject into a Procrustean mantle of a fixed number of sleeves.

3264 REDUCTION OF RIGIDITY

In 1949 a search was made for methods of reducing this rigidity. The first findings were given in my paper *Optional facets in library classification* (1) published in the *Annals* part of *Abgila*, Vol. 1, 1950, pages 25-36. These findings were expounded in a crisper form at the Fifteenth Annual Conference of the Graduate Library School of the University of Chicago held from July 24th to 29th, 1950. This exposition forms section 2 of Ranganathan's *Colon classification and its approach to documentation,* forming part of the proceedings of that conference, edited by Shera (Jesse H.) and Egan (Margaret E.) under the title *Bibliographic organisation: Papers presented before the fifteenth annual conference of the Graduate Library School July 24-29, 1950* (University of Chicago Studies in Library Science), 1951, pages 96-103. The findings were again discussed in the Delhi Seminar in Library Science on October 21st, 1950. The minutes of the discussion were published in the *Bulletin* part of the *Abgila,* Vol. 2, 1951, pages B25-B26. The device used to reduce the rigidity was to use different digits as the connecting symbols for the different dimensions or facets.

327 Hornets' Nest

This method of reduction of the rigidity of the facet-formula disturbed a hornets' nest. Every main or canonical class had its own facet-formula. In other words, every one of them had its own dimensions. Let us take, for simplicity, the average number of dimensions for each of them as three, and the number of main and canonical classes as one hundred. This implies the provision of different connecting symbols for each of three hundred dimensions. It was like having three hundred hornets hovering round and each one stinging us for its own linkage—for a distinctive connecting symbol.

328 Fight for Precedence

Another result of removing the rigidity of the facet-formula is a dog-fight among the dimensions themselves for precedence. Which facet of the subject should be given the first place in its class number? Which facet should be given the second place in the class number? And so on. The Canon of Filiatory Sequence passes the problem on to the Canon of Helpful Sequence. This in its turn passes the problem on to the Laws of Library Science. They pass it on to Observed Data on readers' approach. The observed data are promiscuous, and refer the matter to Mathematical Statistics. This in its turn passes it on to the Law of Probability, which passes the problem on to the Law of Large Numbers. This law asks the libraries of the world to collect millions and millions of observed data. This collection should be made for every subject of more than one dimension. This is the empirical method of fixing precedence.

3281 FAILURE OF EMPIRICAL METHOD

Such a severely empirical method of deciding precedence among dimensions is impracticable though not impossible. The cost in time, man-power and money needed will not be worth the result obtained. One has to accept the virtual failure of the purely empirical method in this matter.

CHAPTER 33

THREE PLANES OF WORK

THE NOTATIONAL SYSTEM CAN be enabled to reduce its rigidity. With the notational devices described so far, it can stand a good deal of the pressure of the universe of knowledge in spite of its many dimensions. This very efficiency of the notational system has laid bare a conflict among the dimensions themselves. This has been mentioned in section 328. In section 3281 the impracticability of a purely empirical method of resolving the conflict was pointed out. We have therefore to make a theoretical attempt to resolve the conflict. This requires a clear and ruthless analysis of the factors involved in the work of knowledge-classification. It is helpful to break down this work into work in three different planes. These planes are: (1) Idea Plane, (2) Notational Plane and (3) Verbal Plane. The construction of a scheme of classification involves work in each of these planes. It is helpful first to consider work in each of these planes independently. Then we may examine how work in one plane influences work in any other.

331 Idea Plane

To classify a subject, we should find out, in the idea plane, answers to many questions about it. To set up a scheme of classification, a similar set of questions should be answered. An illustrative set of questions is given below.

3311 MAIN CLASS

First question: What is the main class to which the subject belongs? Here " main class " means one of the classes marked as " main class " in the preferred scheme of classification. The main classes are the classes of the first order of the universe of knowledge. They form the first order array. What are the subjects to be given the status of main class? In other words, what are the subjects to be enumerated in the first order array? In the past, the number of subjects to be enumerated in the first order array was determined by rigidity of notation. But rigidity in this respect has been removed by the Interpolation device described in section 2231.

The notational plane no longer imposes any limit on the idea plane. Thus work in regard to enumeration of main classes can be done in the idea plane on the merits of the relation between subjects. Selection of subjects to the status of main class depends entirely on the degree of their mutual independence. Their sequence depends entirely on their filiatory relations on the basis of co-ordinate status.

3312 CHARACTERISTICS

Second question: What characteristics of the main class are represented in the subject considered? Here all the characteristics are to satisfy all the canons prescribed in chapter 13, Canons for Characteristics. What are the characteristics likely to go with the main class of the subject? These questions have to be examined entirely in the idea plane. In what sequence should the characteristics be used? The answer to this question also is to be found entirely in the idea plane. The helpful sequence of characteristics is more difficult to decide than the helpful sequence of divisions in an array. To choose a more or less helpful sequence in an array, some principles were enumerated in sections 1431 to 1438, but no principle has been so far enunciated to choose a more or less helpful sequence among characteristics. Till now each classificationist has been depending entirely on his own unexpressed transconscious guidance. This has been denying any autonomy whatever to the classifier. The discovery of objective principles for sequence of characteristics is one of the important problems needing pursuit in the idea plane.

3313 DIMENSION OR FACET

Third question: Into what homogeneous groups do the characteristics fall? What are the characteristics going into each such group? This is determined by their mutual congruity, which has to be determined in the idea plane. Each group of homogeneous characteristics corresponds to a different dimension or facet. This question also has not been consciously answered in most schemes of classification. The theory of classification too has not till recently pursued the question. The series of articles on *Optional facets* appearing in the *Annals* part of the first three volumes of the *Abgila* during the years 1949 to 1953, and its continuation as *Depth classification* in the *Annals of library science,* represent a beginning of the pursuit of the question in the idea plane. The answers got are still vague, and have not been sufficiently externalised. They are only tentative, and yet the fourth edition of the *Colon classification* (1952) incorporated these tentative ideas. They have been occupying the attention of the Library Research Circle in Delhi during the last five years. The Classification Research Group in London also has taken up the pursuit of the question along this line. This line of pursuit seems to be promising, and some account of it will be given in chapter 35, Five Fundamental Categories.

3314 SEQUENCE OF DIMENSIONS OR FACETS IN U.D.C.

The U.D.C. was the first to recognise and implement the facet idea. In regard to the peripheral facets of " Place " and " Time," U.D.C. has fixed a definite sequence. Paragraph 4 of section C under table (f) of VI part 1 of the complete English edition (1943) of *U.D.C.* reads " Its [= the subdivision of Time] place in the sequence of compound numbers is between the subdivision of Place and the subdivision of Form." Thus (" Place, Time ") is the prescribed sequence among these two facets or dimensions.

3315   U.D.C.'s FAILURE

But the U.D.C. had restricted its range of pursuit of this idea. This restricted its experience in working with facets or dimensions, and it thereby lost a splendid opportunity to make important advances in the idea plane. The initial restriction in the range of pursuit was due to its acceptance of the D.C. as its core. Thus in the vital part of a class number, dimension or facet was not recognised. The following example given in paragraph (*c*) of section B under table (e) of the *U.D.C.* illustrates its self-imposed surrender of opportunity. It reads as follows: " In bibliographies intended for publication, the tables (of place) may be employed only where indicated in the main tables (=D.C. core). Thus, in 58 Botany, the subdivision of place is added only to the section 581.9 and not to its subdivisions.

" *E.g.* 582.243:581.9(45) Myxogasteres in Italy
    not 582.243 (45)
" The former entry is reversed as
    581.9 (45):582.243 Italian flora. Myxogasteres.

" By adopting this method the entire Italian flora is collected under one heading."

This amounts to failure in the idea plane to indicate preference between the two sequences:

[Myxogasteres: Italy]; and
[Italy: Myxogasteres].

This may be generalised as follows:
Preference is not fixed in the idea plane between the two sequences:

[Natural group: Place]; and
[Place: Natural group].

This indecision is glorified as the " Principle of Reversibility." In reality it is an abdication on the part of the idea plane of its right to settle the " dog-fight " between dimensions. This question will be pursued further in section 3317.

3316   SEQUENCE OF DIMENSIONS OR FACETS IN C.C.

In its earlier editions, the C.C. took responsibility to settle the sequence of facets of each basic class definitely by a different facet-formula. This led to the setting up of many facet-formulae, which have since been reduced to a single master-facet formula. This will be described in chapter 35, Five Fundamental Categories.

3317 SYMBIOSIS IN C.C.

In the last paragraph of the extract quoted from the U.D.C. in section 3315, a certain advantage of giving two class numbers to one subject is pointed out. The first number will satisfy one subject approach. The second number will satisfy the opposite subject approach. The advantage of each approach should no doubt be given to the world of readers. But it is improper to give this advantage by sacrificing a fundamental attribute of the artificial language of class numbers, viz. absence of synonyms as prescribed in section 2833. The C.C. gives the advantage of double approach to readers by an alliance with the catalogue. Classification arranges the materials according to one approach. This approach corresponds to the facet-formula [Natural group. Place]. The classified part of the catalogue also arranges entries according to this preferred approach. The alphabetical index part of the catalogue takes care of the second approach. To make this alliance between classification and cataloguing produce the intended result without any fault, the Chain Procedure has been set up in Ranganathan's *Classified catalogue code*, ed. 3, 1951, section 31 and its subdivisions. This procedure has been found to lead to reciprocal enrichment of efficiency in classification and catalogue. Therefore the alliance between the two disciplines has been called " symbiosis." Each discipline should not attempt to do everything. By leaving to the other whatever can be better done by it, each discipline can improve its own efficiency better. Monopoly is as dangerous among disciplines as among industrialists. A holistic symbiosis should be preferred.

3318 SEQUENCE OF PHASES

The idea plane should also take responsibility of settling the sequence of phases.

33181 U.D.C.

The U.D.C. fails in this respect also. In the sub-section " Combination of Main Classes " in the section " Outline structure of classification " of *U.D.C.*, the following statements occur:

" 622:51 Mathematics adapted to mining technology
" A colon combination is reversible. Thus:
" 51:622 Mathematics adapted to mining technology."

In regard to the sequence of phases, loyalty to the Principle of Reversibility in the notational plane exposes it to a mistake in the idea plane. " Mathematics adapted to mining technology " means an exposition of those methods of mathematics that will be of use to specialists in mining technology in using mathematics as a tool in the study of their own subject. Reciprocally, a mathematician called upon to apply his subject to mining technology should be provided with facilities to know the problems in mining technology that will be amenable to mathematical treatment. For this facility, it should be possible to expound " mining technology from the angle of mathematicians." The number for this subject also has to be got by forming a " colon compound " of the same two " main classes." The U.D.C. makes this impossible by interpreting both forms of the " colon compound " to mean the former of the two subjects only.

33182   Colon Classification

The C.C. leaves it to the idea plane to decide which is the subject expounded, and which the subject affecting the exposition and thus playing the role of an auxiliary, i.e. a secondary role. This delicate decision should be made only in the idea plane. To satisfy reader's approach, this decision is essential. The notational plane has merely to carry out the decision of the idea plane.

332   **Notational Plane**

In the general design of a scheme of classification, work in the idea plane is paramount. Work in the notational plane is to implement the results reached in the idea plane. The design of notation is by no means simple. In chapter 31, we saw the ever-increasing pressure of the Universe of Knowledge on the notational system. In chapter 32, we saw the need for reduction of rigidity of all kinds. There is no end to the volume of work to be done in the notational plane.

3321   JURISDICTION

Work in the notational plane has often to be turned on deciding the admissibility of a problem within its jurisdiction. We have already referred in detail to the impropriety of U.D.C. introducing the Principle of Reversibility of the members of a compound number. Work in the notational plane indicates symbiosis with the catalogue as the only proper course.

3322   SPECIES OF DIGITS

The choice of the species of digits needed lies entirely within the notational plane. The efficiency of a scheme of classification depends on a judicious choice of the species of digits. Next to choice comes the use of the different species. To mention one outstanding example, it is now widely recognised to be an advantage to have a species of symbols for sole use as connecting symbols. Another happy use has been investing one species with anteriorising power. This was hit upon for the first time by the C.C. Rule 0251 of part 1 of the *Colon classification* has done it. It reads: " Any number followed by a small letter or an arrow shall have precedence over the original number." A third happy hit of the C.C. is the setting apart of the last digit in a species solely for octavising work.

3323   ORGANISATION OF NOTATION

Next to the choice of the species and the specialisation of their use comes the organisation of the notational system as a whole. This is the crux of the work in the notational plane. The general principles governing its organisation are the Canons of Expressiveness, Hospitality in Array, Hospitality in Chain, Scheduled Mnemonics and Seminal Mnemonics. These canons have been explained in chapters 18, 25, 26, 27 and 28. The organisation of notation will be examined in detail in chapter 36. It shows the value of the Canon of Mixed Notation stated in section 1883.

333 Verbal Plane

Generally speaking, work in the verbal plane has been neglected. In the first place, it has to be done separately for each natural language. Languages differ considerably in their etymology and semasiology. But a more effective reason has been the casual choice of the terms representing classes uncontrolled by the obligation of the classification schedules to give crisp, current terms for use in subject headings and class index headings in catalogues.

3331 Conformity to Canon of Context

Reliance on Canon of Context will reduce the flabbiness of many terms.

Example

U.D.C. No.	Name of the Subject	
	In the Schedule	Slimmed by Canon of Context
025.34	Various kinds of catalogues divided according to the basis of classification	Kinds of catalogue
025.341.1	Accession order	Accession
025.341.2	Topographical order	Topographical
025.342	Catalogue by authors	Author
025.343	Catalogue by subjects	Subject
025.343.1	Alphabetical catalogue by the name of the subject-matter	Alphabetical
025.343.2	Systematic catalogues	Systematic
025.343.3	Alphabetico-systematic	Alphabetico-systematic
025.344	Catalogue by title	Title

The terms in the third column are as effective as those in the second if the Canon of Context is applied. At the same time they are considerably slimmer.

3332 Conformity to Canon of Enumeration

Reliance on the Canon of Enumeration will render annotation unnecessary under many terms in the schedule. For example, we have in U.D.C.

" 025.3 Catalogue technique. Cataloguing.
Only questions and rules as to the editing and arrangement and organisation are put here."

The subdivisions under the above class describe the scope of the class more thoroughly than this annotation.

3333 HELP FROM CATALOGUING

The chain procedure described in section 31 of Ranganathan's *Classified catalogue code* links up the catalogue and the classification schedule. By this technique, the class number makes the choice and rendering of subject headings precise. Indeed it mechanises the two items of work. Reciprocally, the process of deriving subject headings discloses the faults in the natural-language part of the schedule. Words introduced in the schedule in negligence of the Canons of Context and Enumeration are high-lighted. This wholesome influence of the catalogue has disclosed faults in the terminology of the C.C., though it conforms to the two canons far more than the U.D.C.

3334 JARGON

The chain procedure often lays bare the inadequacy of natural language to supply terse terms either to subject-headings or to classification schedules. This inadequacy is common enough to lead to the development of a special jargon for the purpose. In the fourth edition (1952), the C.C. has coined such jargonish terminology to provoke thought on the question. Here are some examples, with the class numbers changed as they would be in the forthcoming editions.

C.C. No.	Term	
	In Natural Language	In Jargon
3	All questions concerning writings and books	Book-science
4	Journalism	Journalism
(a)	Art and science of compiling bibliography	Bibliographology
(k)	Art and science of compiling encyclopaedia	Encyclopaediology
(m)	All questions concerning writing and editing contributions to periodicals	Periodicalism
(w)	Art and science of writing biography	Biographology
(z7d)	Art and science of organising and administering institution	Institutionology
(z7e)	Art and science of organising and administering museum	Museology

Of these nine terms, " Journalism " and " Museology " have been already accepted by natural language.

3335 PROPOSAL ABOUT SCHEDULES

Here is a proposal to be considered by promoters of classification and cataloguing in an integrated manner. Classification schedules should be presented in three columns:

(1) Term in ordinal language;
(2) Term in jargon;
(3) Term in natural language.

CHAPTER 34

CLASSIFICATORY TERMINOLOGY

THE COMPLEXITY CHARACTERISING THE unpredictable development of the ever-expanding universe of knowledge calls for continuous and complicated work in the idea plane and in the notational plane. Communication has to cover these two planes, sometimes jointly and sometimes severally.

341 Need

This requires a precise terminology. Even apart from communication to others, precise terminology is required also to play productively with one's own thought. The terminology introduced in parts 1 and 2 is helpful as far as it goes. It is necessary, but it proves insufficient for communication—with brevity, ease and unequivocalness—of all the new concepts arising in the development of knowledge-classification. A vast specialised terminology has already come into vogue. More will be coming in future in spite of phlegmatic and rhetorical protests from old-guard and take-it-easy librarians. These come from those with little experience of the exacting demands of intensive reference service. These also come from those holding classification to be little more than shelf-marking. Thought on the discipline of classification must march on in spite of them. New terminology will continue to precipitate in its wake.

342 Inevitableness

Much of the work on any discipline has first to be done at the level of intuition. The results have then to be brought to the level of intellection. This is necessary for communication to others. As Goethe puts it, new experience at intuitional level needs a new divine language to communicate it to others. It also often happens that an intellectual analysis and examination of the results of intuition should be done to exploit them fully and to discover possible faults in them. It is also well known that intuition is fleeting. It often exhausts itself after giving us a start, often in a flash. The work has thereafter to be completed laboriously with the aid of intellect. Work through intellect can only be through analysis and synthesis. Terminology is essential to carry out any intellectual work. Natural words are often foggy, and lead us astray by imperceptible refractory suggestions. It is for this reason that special technical terminology has to be invented and used by each profession. Unlike common words, these terms of art are under the control of the profession and are protected from the onslaught of popular usage and the consequent incidence of a series of small deviations, undertones and overtones, leading ultimately to fogginess.

343 Resistance

Resistance to new terminology is in effect resistance to new ideas. For as the poet Kalidasa—the author of the famous drama *Sakuntala*—so elegantly puts it, idea and term are as inseparably fused to each other as Parvati and Parameswara—representation in Indian thought of the Father and Mother aspects of God fused in one body. As ideas grow, terms cannot help growing. As new ideas are created, we cannot help creating new terms. Resistance to new terminology and new ideas is born out of the absence of the new experience of the documentation service generating them. The resistance then gets nourished by indolence and inertia. Combines of the indolent are formed to multiply the resistance. Those that have the new experience and feel the need for fresh investigation with a fresh terminology should not allow themselves to be frightened out of their pursuit by the vociferous protests of the combines of the indolent and the inexperienced.

344 Tentativeness

It has also to be remembered that the new technical terminology being forged will have to be tentative and liable to adjustment from time to time and even to violent changes in certain situations. It is only after going a long way that it will be possible to stabilise them. It takes many attempts to hit at productive terminology. At this stage of trial and error, attempts at expression have to be tried on several platforms and published in several media. Those who feel pulled by the subject will not feel distracted by these attempts.

345 Additional Terms

Several terms have been already introduced in parts 1 and 2. More will appear in the later chapters. We give here a few terms necessary to get started on chapter 35.

The following equivalence must be remembered:

" Class " (Idea Plane) *is equivalent to*
" Class Number " (Notational Plane) *and to*
" Subject " (Verbal Plane).

Thus from each term defined in the idea plane two corresponding terms get automatically defined in the notational and verbal planes respectively.

(1) Main class: Any class enumerated in the first order array of a scheme of classification of the universe of knowledge. This definition is valid only for the scheme concerned.

(2) Amplified main class: (1) A class expounded according to a special system of thought, other than the currently favoured system,

and (2) A class with one or more of its characteristics lying within abnormal limits.

(3) Canonical class: Any traditional sub-class of a main class, not derived on the basis of definite characteristic(s). This definition is valid only for the scheme concerned.

(4) Basic class: Any main or canonical or amplified main class.

(5) Isolate idea: An idea belonging to a facet. It is not by itself a class. In association with a basic class, it creates a class of smaller extension than the basic class. Isolate is the generic name for Isolate Idea, Isolate Number and Isolate Term.

(6) Compound class: A basic class with one or more facets.

(7) Order of a compound class: The number of facets in it.

(8) Complex class: A class formed by the combination of two or more classes. Each constituent class is a phase.

(9) Order of a complex class: The number of phases in it.

(10) Focus: A class or an isolate. It can be used in all the three planes. Also Focus in Array, Focus in Facet, Focus in Phase.

(11) Sharpening a focus: Decreasing its extension on the basis of a characteristic.

(12) Lamination: Sharpening a class by attaching an isolate or a facet to it.

(13) Assemblage: Sharpening a class by attaching another class to it.

(14) Denudation: Sharpening an isolate by subdivision on the basis of an additional characteristic.

(15) Dissection: Assortment of an isolate into sub-isolates on the basis of a single characteristic.

(16) Common isolate: Isolate idea represented by the same isolate term and the same isolate number in more or less every class having it.

(17) Mnemonic isolate: Isolate idea represented by the same isolate number but not the same isolate term in every class having it.

(18) Special isolate: Isolate idea special to a basic class and not common to more or less every basic class.

Several other terms will be introduced in later chapters.

346 Glossary

B. C. Vickery has collected most of the current terms in his *Glossary of current terminology*. His collection includes 320 terms, and has been published in pages 27-46 of *Depth classification* (1953), edited by Ranganathan.

At the time of the International Congress at Brussels in 1955, the General Assembly of the F.I.D. accepted a resolution sponsored by G. Cordonnier, asking F.I.D. to promote the publication of the rapidly growing glossary of classificatory terms and bring it up to date from time to time.

CHAPTER 35

IDEA PLANE AND FIVE FUNDAMENTAL CATEGORIES

WE SHALL PURSUE THE following two problems in the idea plane:

(1) Establishment of a basis to divide characteristics into homogeneous groups. Each group should fall within one dimension. In other words, it should form one train of characteristics.

(2) Establishment of a basis to arrange dimensions or facets of a subject in a helpful sequence, consistent in the abstract, for all subjects.

The first problem was brought out in section 315. The second was brought out in section 3281. The need for establishing these bases by theoretical methods was also emphasised in the latter section. This and the succeeding chapters develop one such theoretical method.

350 Postulates

3501 POSTULATE 1

To begin with, the following five fundamental categories are postulated:

(1) Time; (2) Space; (3) Energy; (4) Matter; (5) Personality.

The use of these terms in the context of classificatory discipline has nothing to do with their use in metaphysics or physics. Their use here merely enables our employing them together in statements about dimensions (or facets)—their separation and their sequence.

3502 POSTULATE 2

Another postulate is as follows: every characteristic can be assigned to one and only one of these fundamental categories. This is easy in the case of many characteristics. In some, it is difficult, but not too difficult. It is possible to accustom oneself, by practice, to distinguishing them. There are some far too elusive characteristics. These need further study. All these will be illustrated in the later sections of this chapter.

3503 POSTULATE 3

We shall also postulate the following concepts:

(1) Whole; (2) Part; (3) Portion; (4) Organ; (5) Constituent.

Some explanation is given below of their connotation.

Whole is a typical individual of the universe of individuals classified.

In relation to universe of cycles, each cycle is a Whole.

Part is also used in relation to a typical individual of the universe of individuals classified. But it is not the whole of it. It is either a portion, or an organ or a constituent of the whole.

Portion is a part differing from the whole only in regard to the attribute of quantity. In relation to the universe of the milk contained in a cistern, the milk drawn from it into a cup is a Portion.

Organ is a functional Part. The different organs of a whole have usually different functions. They have also usually different structures. One organ differs from another in regard to the attributes of structure and function. An organ is distinguishable, and in some cases separable, from the whole. But its function ceases rapidly after separation from the whole or when considered by itself—i.e. independently of the whole.

In relation to the typical individual of the universe of cycles—that is, in relation to a typical cycle—the wheel is an Organ. For it is a functional part, with its own distinctive structure and function. The use of this term was suggested by B. C. Vickery, in his *Systematic subject indexing*, published in the *Journal of Documentation* of Aslib, Vol. 9, 1953, pages 48-57.

Constituent is a Part, with its own individuality and capable of occurring in the Whole of many different universes.

In relation to the rim of a typical cycle, iron and cobalt are constituents. In relation to milk, lacto-protein and water are constituents. In these examples one constituent differs from another only in its chemical make-up. A constituent is a substance. It is a manifestation of matter. This applies only to concrete entities. I have not yet succeeded in defining this term in regard to abstract entities. But recent experiments in depth-classification lead to the following suggestion. An attribute capable of characterising the wholes of many different universes may also be called a constituent. For example, (1) any physical or chemical or bio-property; (2) any use or commodity value; and (3) any spiritual, ethical or social value.

3504   POSTULATE 4

When a universe is classified on the basis of a characteristic, it may yield classes containing Wholes only, Portions only, Organs only, or Constituents only. This is the fourth postulate.

3505   FIRST TRAIN OF CHARACTERISTICS

A set of characteristics yielding successively only isolates containing whole entities or a portion of the universe considered forms the First Train of Characteristics.

The isolates yielded by the first characteristic of the train, chosen as basis, form the first order array. The isolates formed from an isolate of the first order by the second characteristic of the train, chosen as basis, form the second order array, and so on.

3506   FACET

The totality of the isolates formed on the basis of a single train of characteristics is a Facet, in the idea and the verbal planes.

The isolate number belonging to a facet is a Facet of the Class Number, in the notational plane.

35061   First Level Facet

The totality of the isolates formed on the basis of the first train of characteristics is a First Level Facet, in the idea and the verbal planes.

Each isolate number belonging to the first level facet occurs as the First Level Facet of a Class Number, in the notational plane.

3507   SECOND TRAIN OF CHARACTERISTICS

A characteristic yielding only isolates containing organs of a typical entity starts the Second Train of Characteristics.

35071   Second Level Facet

The totality of the isolates formed on the basis of the second train of characteristics is a Second Level Facet, in the idea and the verbal planes.

The isolate number belonging to the second level facet occurs as the Second Level Facet of a Class Number, in the notational plane.

3508   HIGHER LEVELS

And so on with the third, fourth, etc., levels.

These concepts will be illustrated in the later sections of this chapter.

351   **Time**

The Fundamental category " Time " occurs in every subject forming a local description or local history of any subject.

Examples

In the following examples, the term denoting time is given in italics.
  (1) Description of education in India in *1954*.
  (2) Description of education in India in the *nineteenth century*.
  (3) History of education in India from the *Vedic period to the present day*.

Time flows uniformly, it is said. It is taken to flow along one direction only. We can speak only of " portion " of time. We really call it " duration." All time isolates formed by the duration measured from a specified epoch will together form a facet. It is Time Facet.

3511   CHARACTERISTIC

To form arrays in such a facet, the only characteristic available for dividing time is " duration." This gives the measure of time. To measure duration, we need a starting point and a unit of duration.

With the first choice of " unit of duration," an infinite array of the first order is formed. With a smaller " unit of duration " applied to any isolate in the first order array, an array of the second order is formed. And so on. In any array, the isolates are arranged by the Principle of Later in Time.

Example

The conventional origin for measuring public time is the birth of Christ. We may use " Century " as the first choice of the unit of duration. Each isolate in the first order array will then be a century. Let us use " Decade " as the second choice of the unit of duration. Each isolate in a second order array will then be a decade. Let us use " Year " as the third choice of the unit of duration. Each isolate in a third order array will then be a year. And so on.

C.C. No.	Time Isolate	U.D.C. No.
N	1900-1999	19
N5	1950-1959	195
N54	1954	1954

3512 CHANGE OF ORIGIN

We can get a different set of time isolates by changing the origin. In this way, time isolates according to any era may be formed. But it is desirable to use one and the same era as far as practicable. For a classificatory language is an international language.

3513 CHANGE OF UNIT OF DURATION

It is not necessary to have the same unit of time for the first order array for all periods. To maintain balance in memory-perspective, larger units may be used for far-off periods.

Period	Unit of Time for First Order Array	C.C. Isolate No.
First millennium A.D.	1,000 years	D
First millennium B.C.	1,000 years	C
Second to tenth millennium B.C.	9,000 years	B
Before tenth millennium B.C.	Geological age	A

352 Space

The surface of the earth is a manifestation of the fundamental category " Space." It occurs in every subject forming a local description or local history of any subject.

Examples

In the following examples, the term denoting space is given in italics.

(1) Descriptive account of education in *Italy* in 1954.

(2) History of education in *India* from the Vedic period to the present day.

(3) History of education in *Japan* from the early Buddhistic days to the Russo-Japanese War.

In a local description of this kind, the surface of the earth is taken to be without any organ or constituent. We can only speak of a portion of the earth's surface. Therefore space isolates of the kind considered will together form a facet.

3521   FIRST LEVEL SPACE FACET

Earth's surface is unbounded finite space of two dimensions. Any portion of it will also be of two dimensions. That is, it will be an area. The choice of the unit of area may be made in several ways. In hardly any case in use will it depend on the measure of extent. In other words, a quantitative unit is seldom found helpful. We have to use a qualitative unit. Many qualities are available for use in the choice of unit. For the first choice, the " occupant " of the area is taken as the quality. The occupant may be land or water.

35211   Canonical Isolates

The quality relevant for most purposes is the political and administrative group of people occupying them. To make this quality the first choice is not, however, helpful. We therefore first divide the surface of the earth by the "physical occupant"—land or sea. We divide each of these total areas into canonical sub-areas. This gives the continents and oceans as the classes in the first order array of the surface of the earth taken as a unit. We arrange the resulting areas according to the Principle of Spatial Contiguity.

Example

C.C. No.	Area	U.D.C. No.
4	Asia	5
5	Europe	4
6	Africa	6
7	America	7/8
8	Australia	94
	Land within	
91	Indian Ocean	
92	Atlantic Ocean	
93	Pacific Ocean	95/96
943	Antarctic Ocean	99
947	Arctic Ocean	98
	Ocean qua Ocean	
95	Indian Ocean	267
96	Atlantic Ocean	261/264
97	Pacific Ocean	265/266
983	Antarctic Ocean	269
987	Arctic Ocean	268

35212   Political Characteristic

The second order array of classes is formed on the basis of political characteristic. The Principle of Spatial Contiguity is used for arranging the classes. This characteristic violates the Canon of Permanence. But it is made obligatory by the Canon of Relevance. It has not been possible to resolve this conflict between these two canons in the idea plane. The only course appears to be to have different systems of space isolates for different political periods. This throws extra strain on the notational plane.

35213   Administrative Characteristic

Political characteristic may have to be repeated to arrive at arrays of higher orders. Then will come the use of administrative characteristic. These two characteristics are indistinguishable at the point of their separation. For the basis of their distinction is the extent of sovereign power and legislative power. Political science postulates gradations of these powers. The difference between political and administrative areas is made to depend on convention or statute. Neither of these is permanent. Even in an array made of clearly administrative divisions, the characteristic does not obey the Canon of Permanence. Change is often made for administrative convenience. But the characteristic is made obligatory by the Canon of Relevance.

35214   Intension

The first train of characteristics can be continued as far as necessary. In other words, the number of First Level Space Arrays can be increased as much as necessary. In other words again, any First Level Space Chain can be lengthened as much as necessary. In still other words, the intension in the First Level Space Isolate can be increased as much as necessary. The Canon of Hospitality in Chain can thus be satisfied to the necessary extent.

3522   SECOND LEVEL SPACE ISOLATE AND POSTULATE 5

In Indian tradition, the physiographical features of the surface of the earth are taken as analogues to the organs of a person. This anthropomorphic tradition gives a clue to the solution of a difficult problem encountered in the division of the surface of the earth. This difficulty has been brought out in my *Optional facets in library classification* (3), (4) and (5), appearing in pages 73-83, 97-107 and 140-147 of the *Annals* part of the *Abgila*, Vol. 1, 1950. At that time these problems baffled us. They looked insoluble. The conception of " Level," taken along with the above-mentioned anthropomorphic tradition, opens out a line for pursuing this problem. Our using this tradition does not amount to swearing our faith in that tradition for all purposes. It should not be so mistaken. For example, in this tradition a serpent-hill is the analogue for ear. Whispering into this ear of the earth with our lips touching it will lead to death by serpent-bite! We really convert this anthropomorphic tradition into a convenient postulate, enabling us to solve an insoluble problem in the classification of the fundamental category Space manifesting itself as Geographical Space. This is postulate 5.

3523   PHYSIOGRAPHIC (FEATURE) ISOLATE

The following is an illustrative schedule of Second Level Space Facet:

C.C. No.	Isolate	U.D.C. No.
1	Land (Geosphere)	
11	Subterranean	24
115	Submerged	?
12	Surface	25
121	Desert	252
122	Prairie	251.3
123	Cultivated	254
124	Forest	253
13	In relation to sea	
131	Coastland	210.5
132	Peninsula	210.1
133	Cape	210.2
134	Isthmus	210.4
135	Inland	
137	Delta	282.6
14	Island	22
15	Marsh	285.3
16	Valley	23
165	River valley	282.4
17	Plateau	23
175	Watershed	
2	Mountain	23
3	City	26.03
5	Water (Hydrosphere)	
51	Underground	
53	In relation to land (Salt water)	26
531	Coastal sea	
532	Bay	26.04
533	Gulf	26.04
534	Strait	26.04
535	High sea	26.02
536	Land-sea	26.05
537	Estuary	282.6
54	Lake. Fresh water	285
6	River	282.2
8	Atmosphere	

The different arrangements of the isolates in C.C. and U.D.C. show the uncertainty of hitting upon any universally acceptable principle, in the idea plane, for securing "more or less" helpful sequence of physiographical features. In the C.C. sequence, there is progression in a vertical direction from below the earth's surface through the geosphere and hydrosphere to the atmosphere.

3524 RIGIDITY OF NOTATION

In U.D.C. the concept of two levels of space facet has not been developed. The peculiar distribution of the numbers of the first order array in the main class " 9 History " is putting a restriction on the notation giving freedom to the idea plane. This makes the sequence [Physiographical Division; Continental and Political Division] obligatory. The idea plane appears to have no freedom to consider the advantages of reversing the sequence. In C.C. physiographical divisions are made into a separate facet. This gives freedom for both the facets to grow independently of each other. The advantage of having this freedom will be seen in part 4, " Depth Classification."

353 Energy

Both C.C. and U.D.C. postulate Time and Space Facets. Therefore there is some material for a comparative study. On the basis of comparative study, it has been possible to build up the region of classificatory discipline belonging to the fundamental categories Time and Space. But no such help is available for the regions belonging to the other three fundamental categories. Energy, Matter and Personality Facets have been, till now, postulated extensively only by C.C. There are, however, a few Energy Facets provided by U.D.C. in a few places under the name " Special Analytic Divisions." But these are too casual to admit of use in a systematic comparative study. In the circumstances, the only course is to use the different editions of C.C. as basis for comparative study. The third and fourth editions offer materials for illustrating the ideas developed in this chapter. The first edition, also, may have to be used for illustrating a few of the ideas.

3531 MANIFESTATION

In the third edition of C.C., the term " Problem " has been used to denote a manifestation of energy. In edition 4, also, the very same term is used in the tabular statements at the beginning of chapters in part 1 against the manifestation E. A perusal of the problem schedules of different basic classes in the fourth edition throws some light on the nature of Energy-Manifestation. They include categories of the following:

(1) Action by human agent (such as exploration, designing, construction, repair, generalisation, abstraction, enunciation, verification, criticism, grading, etc.);
(2) Reciprocal action and/or relation (other than phase relation) among:
  (i) Concrete entities (such as physical and biological); and
  (ii) Quasi-concrete entities (such as natural groups in biological sciences) and social groups in social sciences;
(3) Method used in action or involved in reciprocal action; and
(4) An array of categories such as structure, normal functioning, abnormal functioning, evolution from one form to another, and development of one and the same form.

I am not able to find a single label to cover the fourth set of categories mentioned above. Perhaps it may be called Auto-Action of entity.

3532   ROUND AND POSTULATE 6

We often come across the need for a succession of Energy Manifestations, each depending on the preceding one. In other words, a focus in Energy Facet calls for a second Energy Facet to be set up. For example, in " J Agriculture " the Energy Focus " Manuring " needs to be followed by another Energy Facet consisting of foci such as Collection, Grading and Application. Again, the Energy Focus " Harvesting " needs to be followed by another Energy Facet consisting of foci such as Recovery, Grading, Disease, Yield and Storage. A third example is taken from " Medicine." The Energy Focus " 4 Disease " needs to be followed by another Energy Facet consisting of foci such as Etiology, Diagnosis, Pathology, Prevention, Treatment, Surgery, Diet Regulation and After-Care. In " History " and " Political Science " the Energy Focus " 91 Election " needs to be followed by an Energy Facet consisting of foci such as Nomination, Polling, Counting, Declaration and Objection. In " Sociology " each of the Energy Foci Activity, Personality and Equipment needs to be followed by another Energy Facet consisting of foci such as Influence, Evolution and Improvement. These are depending upon the occurrence of the First Focus of Energy.

The first manifestation of energy in a basic class gives its First Round Energy Isolates. The facet of First Round Energy Isolates of a basic class is its First Round Energy Facet. The second manifestation of energy in a subject, i.e. the one depending on a First Round Energy Isolate, gives its Second Round Energy Isolates. The facet of Second Round Energy Isolates of a basic class, i.e. the one dependent on the First Round Energy Facet, is its Second Round Energy Facet. And so on. The concept of Round and its hierarchy is the sixth postulate.

3533   SEPARATION OF CATEGORIES

Let us compare the following schedules occurring in third and fourth editions of C.C. They belong to the basic class " L Medicine." They cover the same idea.

Edition 3		Edition 4				Com-bined C.C. No.
Problem Facet		Energy Facet		Personality Facet		
C.C. No.	Isolate	C.C. No.	Isolate	C.C. No.	Isolate	
4	Disease	4	Disease			4
42	Infectious	4	Disease	2	Infection	42
43	Parasitic	4	Disease	3	Parasite	43
44	Poison	4	Disease	4	Poison	44
46	Metabolistic	4	Disease	6	Metabolism	46

During the time of the earlier editions of C.C., the separation of characteristics according to the fundamental categories manifesting themselves as these characteristics had not been thought of. In the fourth edition such separation is made. The result is seen above. The final C.C. number is the same according to both editions. This is due to the prescription for the omission of connecting symbol between Energy Isolate Number and the succeeding Personality Isolate Number. In spite of no change in the appearance of the isolate numbers given by the two editions, there is a fundamental difference in the idea plane. The fourth edition recognises " Disease " only, as manifestation of the fundamental category Energy. It regards " Infection," etc., as manifestations of Personality. " Infection " is really used in the sense of " Protista." Protista, Parasite, Poison and Metabolism are factors causing " Disease." They are the agencies by which " Disease " is caused. These causal factors or agencies are not manifestations of action or interaction. They are not therefore taken as manifestations of Energy. On the other hand, they are taken as manifestations of Personality. The fourth edition thus separated the fundamental categories in the idea plane.

3534 PERSONALITY AND ROUND

" Personality " may manifest immediately after the First Round Energy; this is the Second Round Personality. Similarly, a " Personality " manifestation immediately after the Second Round Energy is the Third Round Personality. And so on.

3535 POSTULATE OF A SINGLE DIGIT (POSTULATE 7)

The following provisional postulate has been made. An Energy Isolate Number can have only one significant digit. In other words, an Energy Facet can have only one array. As in the example given in section 3533, every energy isolate number shown with two or more digits in the third edition is separable into a single-digited Energy Isolate Number and a personality isolate number of one or more digits. This is the seventh postulate. It works well in many cases.

3536 ALTERNATIVE

However, there are likely to be cases asking for two or three significant digits in the energy isolate number. This will be so if the number of energy isolates in an array is greater than twenty-four. If in these cases all the isolate numbers in a facet are of the same number of digits, there will be no difficulty. Otherwise, the postulate of single digit must be given up; and the connecting symbol should be inserted between the energy isolate number and the succeeding personality facet. Sufficient experience has not been gained to decide this issue. This problem should be kept in the list of problems for further research.

3537 Number of Rounds

Any basic class may throw forth subjects involving many Rounds of Energy. Within each round there may be Manifestations of Personality and Matter. To provide for these is the crux of the problem in classification. This will be examined in part 4, " Depth Classification."

354 Matter

In the fourth edition of C.C., Matter Facets have been postulated only in a few cases. Some of these are:

In 2   Library science: Reading materials
In D   Engineering: Construction materials
In ND   Sculpture: Materials forming the medium
In NQ   Painting: Materials used for painting
In NR   Music: Musical instruments

Economics and Sociology await revision in the light of the new analysis in progress. They are likely to present material facets. Material facets will be frequent in the diverse canonical divisions of M Useful Arts. But there are few industries with industrial libraries in India. Consequently, general libraries too do not have varieties of books on arts and crafts. Experience with reading materials in those subjects is meagre. Therefore the facet-analysis of those applied subjects has not yet been made. Experience in arts, crafts and technologies is essential to understand the manifestations of Matter. This is now possible only in the long-industrialised countries of the West.

3541 Attribute

Till now attributes—such as density, elasticity, specific heat and other physical attributes; valency, affinity, atomic weight, bond, taste and other chemical attributes—have been treated as manifestations of energy. This has not been found satisfactory. Such an attribute is an abstract part of a whole. It is distinguishable from its whole, though not separable. An attribute-part is obviously not a portion of the whole according to the definition of " portion " given in section 3502. Nor can it be taken to be an organ of the whole. For an attribute may occur in the members of many different universes, even as iron may occur as a constituent in the members of many different universes. Can we then regard attributes as constituents of wholes? If so, can we treat them as if they are matter? If we use " matter " according to its common usage, we cannot do so. But what we do is to postulate " matter " as a fundamental category capable of manifesting itself as the " constituent of a whole." We have to test the helpfulness of such a postulate in meeting problems in classification. If it proves helpful, we can admit it.

355 Personality
3550 Basic Personality

One set of compulsory manifestations of the fundamental category Personality is that of Basic Classes, i.e. main classes and canonical classes. Without personality there can be no organ, constituent, attribute, action, reaction, or incidence in space or time. Personality forms the basis, the host, the locus of all other fundamental categories. These are various ways of emphasising the necessity for any class, subject or class number beginning with a basic class as the initial component. This essential manifestation of personality is Basic Personality. The level of its manifestation is Basic Level.

35501 Amplified Basic Personality

The exposition of each basic subject will have to be according to some system of thought. Let us take medicine. " Medicine " has to be expounded according to some system such as Ayurveda, Siddha, Unani, Allopathy, Homoeopathy and Naturopathy. It is not possible to expound " medicine " independently of any " System " whatever. Similarly, " Psychology " cannot be expounded except according to some system such as Classical, Psycho-analysis and Behaviourism. So also " Economics " cannot be expounded except according to some system such as Capitalism, Socialism and Communism. As in " Psychology," a system may not have a name of its own. Then it is called by a term such as classical or canonical. A system of a basic class does not cover the whole of the basic class. It covers only a part of it. A system has no significance apart from its being a part of the basic class. At any rate this is postulated. Thus a " System " becomes an " Organ " of its Basic Class. It therefore belongs to another level of " Personality." The level of a " System " is Amplifying Level. Amplifying level may also be called " System Level." The manifestation of Personality in Basic and Amplifying levels taken together is Amplified Basic Personality. The combined level of manifestation is Amplified Level. The class itself is Amplified Basic Class. Unamplified Basic Class is ineffable. This concept of the ineffability of unamplified basic class is important.

35502 Favoured System

In any Knowledge-Epoch, one of the many systems of a basic class attracts more literature than the others. It also attracts more readers. Such a system is the Favoured System. Literary warrant decides the favoured system.

35503 Usage

For all practical purposes, we shall have to consider only Amplified Basic Classes. For brevity, however, it has become a habit to speak of the Favoured System as the Basic Class. This usage has potentiality to create fallacy in further thinking. But it can be adopted with sufficient awareness and agility to replace it by the full term " Favoured Amplified Basic Class," whenever necessary.

3551 FIRST LEVEL

In the fourth edition of C.C., every basic class is provided with a schedule for Personality Facet. This is called First Level Personality, in spite of the Basic Level and Amplifying Level having occurred earlier. This is a matter of conventional usage. " First Level " may be interpreted to mean " First among Levels not having the special names Basic or Amplifying or System."

3552   Second Level

The following is a selection from the basic classes for which the fourth edition of C.C. has given schedules in Second Level Personality.

Basic Class		Personality Level	
C.C. No.	Subject	First	Second
B25	Higher algebras	Form	Degree
R3	Metaphysics	View	Subject
R4	Ethics	Topic	Controlling Principle
V	History	Community	Organ
W	Political science	Type of State	Organ
Z	Law	Community	Law

These second levels of personality occur commonly. Therefore they are enumerated in the book. Second levels of personality may occur in other subjects also. Schedules will have to be provided for them as and when need arises.

3553   Third Level

The following is a selection of the basic classes for which the fourth edition of C.C. provides schedules for three levels of Personality Facet.

Basic Class		Personality Level		
C.C. No.	Subject	First	Second	Third
B33	Differential equation	Equation	Degree	Order
P	Linguistics	Language	Stage	Element

Other subjects also may call for schedules for Third Level Personality.

3554   Fourth Level

The fourth edition of C.C. provides the following four levels of Personality Facet for the basic class " O Literature ":

Personality Level			
First	Second	Third	Fourth
Language	Form	Author	Work

In any basic class, subjects may arise calling for any number of Levels of Personality Manifestation. To provide for these is the crux of the problem in classification.

3555 Packing of Levels

The facets of the different levels of personality follow consecutively without a facet of any other fundamental category intervening. These form a hierarchy of levels, each level dependent on the preceding one. Each Personality Level of such a hierarchy coming immediately after Basic or Amplified Basic Personality is a First Round Personality Level. Similarly, there can be a packing of Personality Levels in the second round. If so, each of them is a Second Round Personality Level. And so on.

356 Sequence of the Five Categories

Seven postulates have been stated already. The postulates in this and later sections are numbered serially in continuation of these seven.

3561 First Set of Postulates

(8) The first round is started by the basic class.

(9) Energy can start a new round.

(10) In each round, any number of levels of personality may occur in succession closely packed.

(11) In each round, any number of levels of matter may occur in succession closely packed.

(12) There is no level for energy. For personality and matter facets can occur between two consecutive energy facets. We have only round.

(13) The fundamental categories occurring in a round stand arranged in the sequence " Personality, Matter, Energy."

(14) The fundamental categories Space and Time can occur only in the last round.

(15) The fundamental categories Space and Time stand arranged in the sequence " Space, Time."

The following can be inferred from the above postulates:

The number of facets of a class may be anything from zero upwards. No facet is compulsory. Facets are all optional.

3562 Second Set of Postulates

(16) A Common Personality or a Common Matter Isolate may initiate a new round.

A round started by energy is an Energy Round.

A round initiated by a Common Personality or Common Matter Isolate is a Common Isolate Round.

(17) Common Personality Facet or Common Matter Facet may be prescribed to be after-space or after-time.

(18) The round preceding a Common Isolate Round may end with a space facet or with space and time facets, according to the nature of the isolate initiating the common isolate round.

3563   Master Facet Formula

The postulate of Five Fundamental Categories and the later postulates have settled the sequence of facets or dimensions, irrespective of the basic class to which a subject may belong. The facets of any subject should be arranged according to the two sets of postulates mentioned above. These postulates really amount to a Master Facet Formula to fit all subjects. This Master Facet Formula will be given in symbols in section 875.

357   **Impersonation**

Before leaving the chapter on Fundamental Categories it must be repeated that there can be impersonation among fundamental categories.

3571   Personality
35711   Time

The foci in a personality facet may be fixed by chronological device. This does not mean that the resulting focus ceases to be a personality focus and becomes a time focus. For example, the first round, third level, personality focus in Literature in the C.C. is got by chronological device. We get J64 for Shakespeare. Here J64 and Shakespeare are not time foci. They are personality foci.

35712   Space

The foci in a personality facet may be fixed by geographical device. This does not mean that the resulting focus ceases to be a personality focus and becomes a space focus. For example, the first round, first level, personality focus in History is got by geographical device. We get V44 for History of India. Here 44 and India are not space foci. They are personality foci. They represent the " Community of India."

35713   Matter

The focus in a personality facet may be what looks like matter. In Chemistry and Technology the first round, first level, personality schedule lists substances. In the context of chemistry and technology these are personality foci.

3572   Matter

Many commodities may have to be individualised by Chronological Device. This does not mean that the resulting focus ceases to be a matter focus and becomes a time focus.

3573   Energy

A focus in an energy facet may be fixed by Chronological Device or Subject Device. This does not mean that the resulting focus ceases to be energy focus and becomes time focus or personality focus.

358 General Principles

Before turning the discussion on to the notational plane, it will be of help to state two principles of a general nature belonging to the idea plane. These concern the sequence of classes—whole classes, basic, compound or complex—and not isolates in an array or within a facet. Therefore these are different from the principles set out in sections 1431 to 1438 to secure helpful sequence within an array.

3581 INCREASING CONCRETENESS

If two classes are such that one can be said to be more abstract and less concrete than the other, the former should precede the latter.

This is the Principle of Increasing Concreteness.

35811 Examples

Here are a few examples:

(1) Mathematics precedes Physics; Physics precedes Engineering; Pure Science precedes Applied Science.

(2) General Physiology precedes Animal Physiology; Animal Physiology in general precedes Vertebrate Physiology; Vertebrate Physiology in general precedes Bird Physiology.

(3) General Psychology precedes Psychology of Child or of Woman or of the Old.

(4) Education in general precedes Descriptive Account of Education in a particular country or at a particular time.

(5) Price theory precedes Price of a particular commodity or of a particular service.

An implication of this is that any Methodology precedes its Application. Another implication is that theoretical account of a subject precedes local description of it.

35812 C.C.

C.C. follows this principle more or less consistently both in the sequence of its main classes and in the sequence of the sub-classes of a basic class. A review of C.C. from the angle of this general principle will be found in sections 7176 to 71763, and 7177.

35813 Other Schemes

In the other schemes, the adherence to this principle may not be equally visible in the array of main classes. But it is more easily visible in the sequence of the sub-classes of a main class.

35814 Adult

Adherence to this principle is helpful because in intellectual activity methodology in abstract is generally learned before it is applied to concrete cases. As the intellect develops, the number of sensory experiences, concrete things and concrete concepts mounts to a burdensome level. Consequently, generalisation begins very early. Abstraction follows side by side. Laws of a subject, hypotheses, normative principles and methodology form the basic stuff first sought by a person with some intellectual development. Once familiarity with these is acquired, their application to particular concrete contexts becomes easier. Reading is essentially an intellectual activity. Therefore the sequence from abstract to concrete is more helpful to the majority of readers than the opposite one.

35815   Child

But an adult's method of approach to recorded materials should not be confused with a child's method of learning. The latter is no doubt from the concrete to the abstract. The recognition of this is vital in teaching method. The chief implication of this in the universe of books is that a book intended for children should begin with concrete facts and situations, and progress towards and, when possible, culminate in generalisation and abstraction. The implication in library work is that a children's library should have such books with concrete backgrounds rather than theoretical ones. Even an abstract subject like Arithmetic should be presented in a realistic way. Granting that every subject in a children's library is treated that way, the sequence of the subjects may well be as in an adult library. It has also to be remembered that the child of today will be the adult of tomorrow and that the child should be prepared for that status even in relation to library matters.

35816   Non-intellectual Adult

The non-intellectual adult raises problems in library service, which are more or less similar to the child's. The problem to be solved is the production of books with a concrete approach. This problem has been fully described in my *Social education literature for authors, artists, publishers, teachers, librarians, and governments* (1952). The adult should no doubt be slowly inducted to an appreciation and use of generalisations and abstractions. But it should be through Craft-Centred books such as those described in section 245 and its subdivisions in that book. The crucial factor in the library service to the labouring class, as part of the recently developing Productivity Drive, is the production of books with flair and concrete approach, centred round the various crafts and industrial processes. The implication of the requirements of non-intellectuals in library service is the acquisition of such books in the library. The Laws of Library Science will indicate the formation of special collections of such books in general libraries, as a help to attract such readers and retain their custom. But, since all the books will be of a concrete make-up, their arrangement in the ascending sequence of the subjects dealt with will not be a hindrance.

35817 Same Classification

This problem has been gone into in some detail to emphasise that the use of the Principle of Increasing Concreteness in a scheme of library classification does not mean that it is unsuited for use in a school or public library. The same classification will serve all kinds of libraries. The standard and make-up of the presentation are the only factors that distinguish them.

3582 INCREASING ARTIFICIALITY

If two classes are such that one can be said to be nearer to the " thing-in-itself " or naturalness and farther from artificiality than the other, the former should precede the other.

This is the Principle of Increasing Artificiality.

35821 Needs Investigation

For example, Law is more artificial than Sociology. The principle is not consciously applied in any scheme. Nor is it as widely implied in schemes as the Principle of Increasing Concreteness. It is perhaps more applicable to the sequence of main classes than to the sub-classes of a basic class. Something of it is implied in the sequence of the main classes of C.C. An elucidation of it will be found in section 71764. But a full elucidation of the related terms " naturalness " and " artificiality " and a wide experiment on the usefulness of this principle in classification are yet to be made.

3583 INVERSION

In an analytico-synthetic classification, the implementation of the Principle of Increasing Concreteness requires that the facets in the facet formula of a basic class should be in the decreasing sequence of concreteness. If the scheme has rounds of facets, the facets in each round should be in the decreasing sequence of concreteness.

This is the Principle of Inversion.

This is a consequence of the ordinal value of a connecting symbol being less than that of any substantive digit.

CHAPTER 36

NOTATIONAL PLANE AND ZONE ANALYSIS

361 Notational Organisation

IN THE LAST CHAPTER, work was done in great detail in the idea plane, uninfluenced by the notational plane. This chapter will be devoted to the notational plane. Notation should be so organised as to carry out the findings and the implications of the idea plane, and the maximum benefit should be obtained from the digits used by a scheme without any of their potential uses being allowed to run to waste. No new species of digits should be introduced without an essential functional need, which could not be met with the already existing species. The Law of Parsimony has its eye not only on the length of class number, but also on the number of species of digits and the number of digits brought into use in each species.

3611 PURE NOTATION

The D.C. used a pure notation of Arabic numerals with considerable success. It increased its potentiality greatly by organising its class numbers as pure decimal fractions, and it has established the superiority of the decimal fractional organisation of notation over the integral organisation. The C.C. established the advantage of setting apart the last of the digits in the species as a mere octavising digit without being used as a significant digit to represent an isolate idea or part of an isolate idea. This is called Octave Device, and it is described in section 2232. The U.D.C. also has recently adopted this feature in the organisation of the digits of a species.

3612 MIXED NOTATION

The Expansive Classification realised the need to lengthen the number for a main class by one digit, as a result of the base of Arabic numerals being too short for the number of main classes recogniesd in its time. To avoid this lengthening, it chose the more capacious base of Roman capitals. But it soon found out that the use of the same long base in later arrays was not necessary. A succession of capital letters was found to be difficult to use both for the eye and for memory, and it therefore brought in the use of Arabic numerals in the later arrays. This mixed notation was adopted by the L.C., S.C. and C.C.; the B.C. alone persisted in using Roman capitals in later arrays. The use of the alphabetical device mixed up Arabic numerals and Roman letters in the later arrays of the U.D.C., L.C., and C.C. Such an organisation, in one and the same array, of two different species of digits on a functional basis, was a forward step.

3613   CONNECTING SYMBOL

An even deeper functional organisation of notation was made by the U.D.C. when it introduced a distinct species of digits to serve merely as connecting symbols, using them to connect the facets in a class number. The C.C. did the same, and has carried out this organisation more thoroughly during the last five years. This new organisation of the connecting symbols in the notational plane was necessary to implement the findings in the idea plane given in chapter 35. The essence of those findings is analysis in the idea plane, which has separated out five fundamental categories; the facets of a subject fall into five corresponding groups. This analysis has also separated out rounds and levels of facets. There is also the phase-analysis developed in section 236. To connect and show forth the phases and the different kinds of facets is the function of the connecting symbols. Here is the table of connecting symbols in U.D.C. and the C.C.:

For	U.D.C. Symbol	C.C. Symbol
Time Facet	" . . . "	.
Space Facet	(. . .)	.
Energy Facet	either - or :	:
Matter Facet	either - or :	:
Personality Facet	either - or :	,
Phase	:	o
Auto-bias		-
Approach Material	(o . . .)	Anteriorising value of Roman small, but no symbol.

36131   U.D.C.

The U.D.C. gives distinctive connecting symbols only for the categories of Time and Space, but even here it has not given a general specification for the sequence of these two categories, so that their sequence will have to be thought out for each subject, in the idea plane. This is usually tantalising. Further, U.D.C. does not distinguish the fundamental categories Energy, Matter and Personality, nor does it give them distinctive connecting symbols. This is due to some of the facets lying already hidden in its D.C. core. It is able to apply facet analysis only in the cases in which the D.C. number does not have hidden facets. Thus U.D.C. has not had the occasion to go the whole way with facet analysis, and it uses the same connecting symbol for all facets other than Time and Space. When the D.C. core gives co-ordinate numbers in the same array for Energy, Matter, and Personality facets, the U.D.C. is obliged to use phase device to represent a subject having two or more of these facets. Thus, the common connecting symbol for these three facets is sometimes " - " and sometimes " : ", as shown in the table.

36132   Colon Classification

On the other hand, the C.C. has laid its very foundation on facet analysis, though it was more or less unconscious, and it therefore easily lends itself to implementing the new development emanating from the postulate of five fundamental categories. To implement the results in the notational plane, the fourth edition (1952) provides different connecting symbols for the different categories, and while it prescribes the same connecting symbol for Time and Space, the possibility of ambiguity is avoided by the way in which the first order array after the connecting symbol is organised: the Time Isolate number is a Roman capital, while the Space Isolate number is an Arabic numeral. Moreover, the Time Facet does not arise unless Space Facet precedes it, in local descriptions and histories, where these facets usually occur.

36133   Connecting Symbol for Round and Level

There is another peculiarity to be noted. Even the C.C. does not provide any connecting symbol that can distinguish rounds or levels, as it is believed that they are not necessary. This belief is based, first, on the assumption that a level in a hierarchy of levels will not occur unless all the earlier levels have occurred, and second, on the conjecture that the assignment of a Matter facet or a Personality facet to a round preceding or succeeding the relevant Energy focus can be uniquely determined in the idea plane in each case. We have not had sufficient experience in assessing the validity of this assumption and conjecture; if they prove to be invalid, a difficult problem will have to be faced in the notational plane. However, see end of section 3692.

36134   Bibliographic Classification

The B.C. does not provide for facets as much as U.D.C. or the C.C., though it uses a comma as a connecting symbol for common isolates, and also for the isolates enumerated in its schedule 8 to 20. Each of these schedules is a mixture of Energy and Matter or Personality isolates. It also uses the same connecting symbol for language and time isolates, and in still another connection, as illustrated by the following:

ACES   = Spinoza
ACESA   = Criticism
ACESA,J = Joachim's criticism

For phase-connecting symbol, the B.C. uses a hyphen.

36135   Sufficiency of Connecting Symbols

B. C. Vickery has suggested that it may be necessary to postulate more connecting symbols, because of the need to distinguish two or more kinds of Energy manifestation. In section 3531, four kinds of manifestation of energy were mentioned—Action, Reciprocal Action, Method of Action and Auto-Action. These four kinds of energy are arranged in the C.C. in one and the same array and the result is the same sort of blocking of hospitality in chain as the arrangement of isolates based on different trains of characteristics in the same array in the D.C. or U.D.C. Moreover, in the current edition of the C.C., the isolates belonging to different kinds of manifestation of energy are not even separated from one another when they occur in the same array. The present belief is that there will be no need to adopt Vickery's suggestion of introducing more connecting symbols such as the division sign. Perhaps the number of cases in which two or more kinds of manifestation will occur together will be small, and in these few cases the auto-bias device will prove sufficient. To make this give helpful results, the different kinds of manifestations of Energy should be arranged in separate groups, or zones in an array. However, if experience demands the introduction of more kinds of connecting symbols, so as to provide a distinct one for each kind of manifestation of Energy, there should be no hesitation in providing them.

3614   Packet Notation

Mixed notation is made necessary by subject device also. This may be illustrated as follows. Consider the U.D.C. number 026:61 (44). It is two-phased. The number in the second phase — 61 — is got by subject device. Let us interpret the two-phased number. It can mean either (1) Medical libraries in France or (2) Libraries of materials on the French medical system. Thus the number is homonymous, and homonyms are fatal in a system of class numbers. This difficulty is not peculiar to U.D.C.; and it will occur in any analytico-synthetic scheme using facet and phase devices. It occurs in the C.C. Consider the C.C. number T:3,U.44. It can mean either (1) Teaching of geography in India or (2) Teaching of the geography of India. The C.C. number is a homonym. The fact is this: in the U.D.C. and C.C. there is no means of indicating whether the last facet—Space facet—belongs to the entire number preceding it or to its later part got by the subject device. This kind of homonym has been challenging us all for the last thirty years, and although various makeshifts were made in the C.C., in every case the cure appeared worse than the disease. In a deep discussion with S. Parthasarathy one summer night in 1950, the idea occurred that the subject device part of a class number might be enclosed or " packeted " within circular brackets, which we decided to call Packet Notation. But there was mental resistance to the adoption of that notation, part of which was due to the unexpressed, subconscious question, " Are we to add further to the mixedness of the notation? " There were also a few other difficulties. The question was taken up again and again in the Library Research Circle in Delhi, and every time it was abandoned without coming to a firm decision.

36141   Ultimate Acceptance

In June, 1954, an occasion came to see its value, in spite of all the difficulties. It was at a meeting of the Classification Research Group in London, where experienced business librarians, working in libraries of industrial concerns and Government departments, brought up a number of problems, many of which admitted of a neat solution with packet notation. The brackets do the same work here as they do in mathematical language, where, as well as in classificatory language, they transform a complex of two or more digits into a single digit, for the purposes on hand. This is indeed a very helpful transformation, called " Association " in mathematics. Whatever be the number of digits, including connecting symbols, whatever be the number of facets or phases in the number within the brackets, it has only the status of a single-digited isolate number in the entire class number. It has actually only the status of a part of an isolate number, that is, the status of a focal number in an array, not necessarily amounting to a complete isolate number.

36142   Effect of Acceptance

The relative ordinal values of two packets are determined by those of the numbers within the respective brackets, and the resolution of the homonym by the adoption of packet notation can now be illustrated as follows:

T:3,(U).44 = Teaching of geography in India
T:3,(U.44) = Teaching of the geography of India

The above gives also the sequence of the two numbers, which satisfies the Canon of Decreasing Extension in respect of the packeted numbers. Comparing the two subjects got by going to the end of the respective third isolates, the former gives " Teaching of geography " and the latter gives " Teaching of the geography of India," the former being of greater extension than the latter. It must be remembered that the subjects got by going only to the end of the respective second isolates are indistinguishable; distinction becomes possible only when the respective third isolates are brought into the picture. It is only at this stage that the Canon of Decreasing Extension becomes applicable.

A similar resolution of homonym is possible in U.D.C. also. As it is already using circular brackets as the connecting symbol for Space facet, square brackets may be used for packeting the part of a class number got by subject device, so that the resolution of the homonym mentioned in section 3614 will be as follows:

026:61 (44)   = Medical libraries in France
026:[61(44)] = Libraries of materials on the French System of medicine

36143   Law of Parsimony

The above proposal was brought up for discussion, by incorporation in Ranganathan's *Annual report* 5 to the F.I.D., as Rapporteur-General to its Committee on the General Theory of Classification F.I.D./C.A., in a document issued by the F.I.D. on May 24th, 1955. In his commentary of August 6th, 1955, on this document, S. Parthasarathy wrote, " Though the Packet Notation resolves the homonym wherever it arises in the application of subject device, it has to be applied even in cases not giving rise to homonyms. In other words, it has to be used in all cases where subject device is used. It would mean an addition of two extra digits in using subject device. This throws a challenge to notation," from the angle of the Law of Parsimony.

36144   Starter and Arrester

To meet this valid criticism, the following definitions and postulates have been proposed, along with the necessary terminology: The Starter is the first of the circular bracket pair, inserted before the first digit of the part of the number derived by subject device. The Arrester is the second of the circular bracket pair, inserted after the last digit of the part of the number derived by subject device.

It is postulated that the Starter should be omitted if either (1) the subject device number starts a phase, or (2) all the foci in an array are got by subject device. The Arrester should be omitted if the subject device number is not followed by a facet belonging to the whole of the class number ending with the subject device number.

The above postulates should be applied and experimented upon to test their consistency with the other postulates and the essential qualities of classificatory language and also its usefulness.

3615   ORDINAL VALUES OF DIGITS
36151   Substantive and Octavising Digits

The digits of Arabic numerals have their ordinal values determined by the commonly current convention. Similarly, the ordinal values of Roman capitals are determined by the commonly current convention. So it is with Roman smalls. If either all three of these species of digits or any two of them are to be used in one and the same array, a new convention should be established. The simplest method is to keep the different species distinct from one another, and to fix the ordinal scale for the species themselves. For example, the rule 025 of colon classification fixes the following ascending ordinal scale: Roman smalls, Arabic numerals, Roman capitals. In the B.C. the ascending scale is: Arabic numerals, Roman capitals. The usage of L.C. also implies this, though it does not seem to be explicitly fixed by rule. It is doubtful if the Arabic numerals and Roman capitals occur in the same array, calling for a ruling on the relative ordinal values of the species.

36152   Connecting Symbols

The digits used as connecting symbols do not form a species about which there is a similar current convention to determine the relative ordinal values of the digits, and their scale of ordinal values has therefore to be fixed by rule. The ordinal scale as between the species of connecting symbols and the other species of symbols has also to be fixed by rule.

36153   Colon Classification

The C.C. settles all the questions connected with the ordinal values of connecting symbols by rule 025, according to which the digits fall in the following ascending scale: zero, full stop, colon, semicolon, comma, hyphen, roman smalls, Arabic numerals and Roman capitals. This scale of the connecting symbols is not fixed arbitrarily; on the contrary, it is a necessary implication of the Principle of Increasing Concreteness, and the postulate that, when arranged in increasing concreteness, the five fundamental categories fall in the sequence Time, Space, Energy, Matter and Personality.

This implication can be demonstrated by particular example. Consider the two classes,

    2:1   Book-selection
    2;12:1   Selection of manuscripts

The first is of a more general and abstract nature; the second is more specialised and concrete. Therefore, in the idea plane, the first class should precede the second. In the notational plane, it is the second digit that has to decide their relative position, and in order to fix it as determined in the idea plane, the second digit of the first class number should have a smaller ordinal value than the second digit of the second class number. This means that the colon should have a smaller ordinal value than the semi-colon. The relative ordinal values of each consecutive pair of connecting symbols can be fixed in a similar way.

That the ordinal position of the species of connecting symbols should be lower than that of the other species is a necessary implication of the Principle of Increasing Concreteness, and it can be demonstrated by particular examples. In doing so, it is sufficient to show that the largest of the connecting symbols should be smaller than the smallest of the other digits. In C.C. this means that it is sufficient to consider the relative ordinal values of hyphen and the Arabic numeral 1. The Roman smalls need not be considered, because they have anteriorising quality, and the need for knowing the relative ordinal values of that species and the species of connecting symbols will not arise. Let us now consider the two classes,

    L21-73:2 Anatomy of the nerves of the mouth; and
    L211:2   Anatomy of the lip

Lip is part of the mouth, and it is helpful to put all the literature on mouth as a whole together and bring in the literature on parts of mouth later. This is in the idea plane; to implement it in the notational plane, the hyphen should be less than 1 in its ordinal value.

36154   The U.D.C.

The U.D.C. does not appear to give an explicit rule either about the ordinal values of its connecting symbols relative to another, or of their species in relation to the other species of digits. However, subsection E and the examples in subsection G of the section " Auxiliary tables " imply the following ascending ordinal scale: colon (o . . .), (. . .), " . . ", Roman capitals, hyphen, o and the other Arabic numerals.

Fixing the ordinal value of the species of connecting symbols lower than the smallest of the other digits is a necessary implication of any scheme adopting the facet device and satisfying the canons and principles enunciated in parts 1 and 2. The U.D.C. is such a scheme, but the " Auxiliary Tables " imply that Roman capitals are of lower ordinal value than the hyphen. This is a fault, and it is recommended to the F.I.D. that this matter should be rectified.

3616 Arrester and Starter Digits

The ordinal value of the arrester digit ")" used in subject device should be smaller than the smallest of the connecting symbols. To demonstrate this, consider the two classes,

T:3,Uo*b*S Teaching of geography from the point of view of psychology

T:3,U):4 Faults in the teaching of psychology

The instruction of the idea plane is that the first of the above classes should precede the second. It is their respective digits O and) that decide the ordinal values of their class numbers in the notational plane, and it follows, therefore, that O should precede the arrester digit. Although this demonstration used the C.C. for definiteness, the result is true for any scheme using the facet device and conforming to the canons and principles enunciated in parts 1 and 2. In particular, the result holds good in U.D.C.

In the C.C. it is proposed to fix the ordinal value of the starter digit "(" of the subject device to be greater than the greatest of the digits used in the scheme, that is, greater than Z. The considerations leading to this decision will be given in section 3622.

3617 Implications of the Notational Organisation

The implications of the proposed notational organisation in the C.C. can be seen by taking an example. Consider the following subjects:

C.C. No.	Subject
2	Library science
20*b*T	Library science expounded for teachers
2.4	Library in Asia
2:1	Book selection
2:1.4	Book selection in Asia
2;44	Periodicals in a library
2;44.4	Periodicals in a library in Asia
2;44:1	Selection of periodicals
2:44:1.4	Selection of periodicals in Asia
2,1	Book selection section

C.C. No.	Subject
2,1.4	Book selection section in Asia
2,1;44	Periodicals for book selection section
2,1;44.4	Periodicals for book selection in Asia
2,1;44:1	Selection of periodicals for book selection section
2,1;44:1.4	Selection of periodicals for book selection section in Asia
23	Academic library
23*ob*T	Academic library expounded for teachers
23.4	Academic library in Asia
23:1	Book selection in academic library
23:1.4	Book selection in academic library in Asia
23;44	Periodicals in academic library
23;44.4	Periodicals in academic library in Asia
23;44:1	Selection of periodicals in academic library
23;44:1.4	Selection of periodicals in academic library in Asia
23,1	Book selection section in academic library
23,1.4	Book selection section in academic library in Asia
23,1;44	Periodicals for book selection section in academic library
23,1;44.4	Periodicals for book selection section in academic library in Asia
23,1;44:1	Selection of periodicals for book selection section in academic library
23,1;44:1.4	Selection of periodicals for book selection section in academic library in Asia
23-7	Private academic library

(Formation of fifteen classes on the whole as in the case of 2 and 23)

| 233 | University library |

(Formation of fifteen classes on the whole as in the case of 2 and 23)

36171   Mechanising Pattern-Production

The above sixty classes stand arranged in the ascending sequence of their class numbers. This is one of the "more or less" helpful sequences of the 60! (= factorial 60 = 1 × 2 × 3 × ... 58 × 59 × 60) ways of arranging them—a fabulously large number. The postulates will produce this pattern of sequence in all subjects, and it will be difficult to describe the detailed qualities of this pattern in words. It is difficult even to keep them in mind. It will be still more difficult to reproduce the exact pattern in all subjects without mechanisation, without the aid of the artificial language of ordinal numbers. For the number of "more or less" helpful sequences is bound to be very large. The pattern is postulated in the idea plane, in terms of the postulated fundamental categories and their connecting symbols, without reference to any subject in particular. Thereafter the notation takes care of the work of throwing the subjects within any main class in the postulated pattern.

The crux of the matter in the mechanisation of the postulated pattern is in the assignment of each facet of a subject to the appropriate fundamental category, and no general help is available in this important work in the idea plane. Some models alone can be given. The models are in the form of the expressed facet-formulae and the expressed schedules for the isolates in the respective facets. Applying these to actual subjects sufficiently often will develop a sense of feel about the fundamental categories, rounds and levels in any subject. There is nothing unusual or mystical in this; it is the way in which all our knowledge and skills are acquired and developed. There is hardly any royal road to it.

3618   LENGTHENING OF ARRAY
36181   Bibliographic Classification

In practically all arrays of order 1—be it the array of main classes, or the first order array of a facet introduced by the connecting symbol comma—the B.C. uses the two species of digits, Arabic numerals and Roman capitals, so that the length of array is of forty-five places. Failure to use the octave device restricts the length to this measure.

36182   The U.D.C.

The U.D.C. uses only either Arabic numerals or Roman capitals to form an array of order 1. Thus basically the length of a first order array can be made only of ten or twenty-six places. But with Arabic numerals, the U.D.C. is now using the octave device, and therefore its arrays made of Arabic numerals are theoretically of infinite length. In practice, however, not more than three octaves are used. Such a lengthening of array is not, however, made in an array of Roman capitals.

36183   First Octaves in the C.C.

The C.C. has been all along using three species of digits in an array. These are, in ascending sequence, Roman smalls, Arabic numerals and Roman capitals, generally excluding I, *i*, *l*, O, and *o*, so that basically the length of array can be 56. In fact, it is only 55, because 9 is made a non-significant octavising digit. Strictly speaking, z and Z should also be set apart as non-significant octave digits. Then, basically, the length of an array would only be 53. But as we saw in the preceding section, sacrificing the last digit of a species from its use as a significant digit makes the corresponding zone of the array theoretically of infinite length. In practice, however, it is not convenient to have more than two consecutive octavising digits at the beginning of an isolate number. In other words, as in U.D.C., in the C.C. also the first three octaves alone are used. This would contribute twenty-four places to the zone of an array where an isolate number has an Arabic numeral as the first significant digit. For convenience of reference, the zone of an array where the first significant digit is an Arabic numeral shall be called the First Octaves. Using this term, we may say that the first octaves contain an infinity of octaves, but that we use, in practice, only the first three of them.

36184 Last Octaves in the C.C.

Let us next examine the zone of an array in the C.C. occupied by Roman capitals, which will have twenty-four places. Consider next the numbers beginning with one octavising 9 and having a Roman capital as the first significant digit. These numbers give twenty-four more places. We may call the former set of places in the array the Last Octave, and similarly we may call the latter set of places the second last octave or the Penultimate Octave of the array. Again, the set of twenty-four numbers beginning with two octavising 9's and having a Roman capital as the first significant digit may be called the Second Last Octave. This process of prefixing octaves to the last octave can be continued *ad infinitum*. The totality of these will, for convenience of reference, be called Last Octaves. The last octaves, too, contain, theoretically speaking, an infinity of octaves, each with twenty-four places, but in practice we seldom use more than the last three of these.

36185 Result of Two Species

An important result of using the eight Arabic numerals and twenty-four Roman capitals with 9 as octavising digit is that we get ninety-six places in an array in the C.C., whereas we had got only twenty-four places in the U.D.C. for convenient practical use—viz. those of the first three octaves. This is a considerable advantage got by the mixed notation in question.

36186 Further Lengthening of Array

To the ninety-six places arrived at in the preceding section, we should add for the C.C. the twenty-three places given by the Roman smalls in array. These twenty-three, of course, precede the other ninety-six places. This brings the total number of places in array to 119.

The proposed packet notation increases the length of an array still further. It must be remembered that the brackets used as starter and arrester are not significant digits, but that any number enclosed between them is virtually equivalent to a single digit. Each packeted number is, therefore, an additional place in the array. Obviously there can be as many packeted numbers as there can be class numbers, so that, theoretically, the packet notation adds an infinity of places in the array. Since the starter bracket is greater in value than Z, these places come after the last octave. We may call it Extra Last Octave of infinite length.

362 Zone Analysis

The last few sections have brought out a result of using two or more species of digits in an array; it enables the recognition of Zones in an array. Apart from the increase in the number of places in the array, the formation of zones can be put to other uses. This is not merely fortuitous, nor is it a phenomenon merely in the notational plane. It has a correlate in the idea plane. This is one of the instances where a notational system of great potency makes it possible for the notational plane to direct attention to phenomena in the idea plane, which are otherwise overlooked.

3621 IDEA PLANE

The isolates in an array fall into two major groups:

(1) Common Isolates, hereafter denoted by (CI); and
(2) Special Isolates, hereafter denoted by (SI).

(CI) fall into two groups in their turn:

(1) Common isolates got by enumeration, hereafter denoted by (ECI); and
(2) Common isolates got by a device, viz. subject device in this case, hereafter denoted by (DCI).

(SI) also fall into two groups in their turn:

(1) Special isolates got by enumeration, hereafter denoted by (ESI); and
(2) Special isolates got by a device, viz. alphabetical device or chronological device in this case, hereafter denoted by (DSI).

(ESI) are based on a characteristic special to the immediate universe classified. On the other hand, (DSI) are based on a general characteristic, such as the alphabetical make-up of the name of the isolate, or its time of origin, which can be used as the basis for classifying any immediate universe. It may be remarked that general-characteristic-isolates do not need enumeration, but that the special-characteristic-isolates need independent enumeration practically for every host-class. Thus the isolate ideas in an array fall into four kinds—(ECI), (ESI), (DSI) and (DCI). Each kind gives a zone of its own in the array.

36211 Sequence of the Four Zones

The next problem in the idea plane is to determine the sequence in which the four kinds of isolates should be arranged in the array, so as to satisfy the Canon of Helpful Sequence. There are twenty-four possible sequences for the four kinds of isolates, which is simply the number of permutations of four things taken four at a time. It may be held that the two kinds of enumerated isolates should come together, and that the two kinds of isolates got by devices should come together. Then the number of choices available is reduced from twenty-four to six. For we have to decide only whether it should be

(1) Enumerated set first or device set first (two possible choices);
(2) (ECI) first or (ESI) first, among the enumerated set (two possible choices); and
(3) (DSI) first or (DCI) first, among the device set (two possible choices).

Now some of the (ECI) stand for approach materials, and therefore (ECI) should come before (ESI). It also follows that (ECI) should come at the very beginning. We have yet to determine only between the two choices given in category 3 mentioned above. Alphabetical and chronological devices are used more often than the subject device; in fact, in many cases the subject device is used only as a temporary measure, till the flow of literature has become sufficient to assign a more helpful place for an isolate. Therefore it is desirable to give the last place to (DCI). Thus, one line of thinking in the idea plane suggests for helpful sequence (ECI), (ESI), (DSI), (DCI).

3622 NOTATIONAL PLANE

The notational system should be so organised as to implement in the notational plane the above-mentioned findings of the idea plane. The implementation is illustrated below with the C.C., because this is the only scheme today using four species of symbols to form places in an array. But the use of the C.C. for illustration does not take away from the general validity of the results; other schemes may well work out ways of utilising the results of zone analysis. The U.D.C., for example, may not find it difficult to introduce zone analysis.

We must recall that, in the C.C.,

(1) Roman smalls are used to represent (ECI);
(2) Arabic numerals form the first significant digits of (ESI);
(3) Roman capitals form the first significant digits of (DSI); and
(4) Packeted numbers are generally used to represent (DCI).

It should also be recalled that Roman smalls have lower ordinal values than Arabic numerals, and that Arabic numerals have lower ordinal values than Roman capitals. These two prescriptions, already made by rule 025 of part 1 of the C.C., implement the sequence (ECI), (ESI), (DSI). This was not predesigned in 1925 to serve the purpose of zone analysis conceived in 1955. But happily the design of 1925 happens to be of use now, in a way not then thought of, to implement the results of zone analysis. Finally, the value of the starter bracket should be determined so as to make (DCI) the fourth zone. This requires that the starter should have a greater ordinal value than Z. This was the result stated without proof in section 3616.

3623 ALTERNATIVE DETERMINATION

The argument of section 3621 may be taken along another line, leading to a different ordinal value for the starter bracket. We may begin with the assumption that the two kinds of (CI) should come together and that similarly the two kinds of (SI) should come together; then it can be proved that the starter bracket should lie between z and 1. But the other value has been preferred, provisionally, because the subject device is used usually to represent newcomer subjects which, after their filiations are made clear, are absorbed into the second or third zone. Of course, helpfulness will require leaving some of them permanently in the fourth zone itself. More experience should be gained before the preferred choice can be made firm.

3624 New Problems

The idea of zone analysis raises a number of problems for investigation. Some general observations may be made. The isolates in the zones 1, 3 and 4 are unitary. That is, they do not admit of second order arrays being added to them, in the idea plane. Even if the number of digits in the isolate number is greater than one, we should not deem the second or later digits to belong to different arrays in reality. But this does not prevent facets being attached to them. The isolates in zone 2 are, in general, groups, i.e. multiple universes, and they therefore admit of second and higher orders of arrays being derived from them, in addition to the freedom to add further facets after them. All the zones in all the arrays are not now being used at present. The reasons for this should be found out. It may be that in certain arrays, certain zones will always have to be kept barren. But the Law of Parsimony would keep us ever on the alert to find uses for them for it would not like any zone in any array left fallow. According to this law, the additional versatility added to the notational system by the idea of zone analysis may open our eyes to certain types of isolate, which we had hitherto overlooked in the idea plane, or set aside as beyond the capacity of classification, for the very reason of the inability of the notational system to implement them. Therefore, an ever-continuing task will be to examine every array brought into use from time to time and to investigate the possibility of bringing all its zones into use. Immediately, all the arrays already in current use should be examined. For this purpose, the concept of Efficiency Table, described in Vol. 3 of the *Annals of library science* may be of use.

363 Array of Main Classes

As an example, we shall examine the array of the very first order in the division of the universe of knowledge. For convenience of reference, we shall call it the Main Array. We shall begin with the Colon Classification.

3631 Zone 3

Zone 3 was the first to be occupied, by certain traditional main classes. Some commentary on the filling up of the third zone with these main classes will be given in sections 7174 to 71764. But these classes were not got by alphabetical or by chronological device. Obviously, alphabetical arrangement would have nullified filiatory or helpful arrangement, and chronological arrangement would be impossible, since most of the main classes date from prehistoric periods and their years of origin would not be ascertainable. Therefore, the method used in filling up the third zone was to arrange the main classes in a more or less helpful sequence and assign the digits of the Roman capitals in succession, with certain adjustments. These occupied the last octave in zone 3. Nothing has been done to occupy the penultimate octave or the octave before it. It is a reserve region for main classes likely to emerge in future, and at present it is difficult to say what criterion will have to be used to admit a new main class into either of these two octaves.

3632 Zone 2

In the first edition of the C.C., zone 2 was filled up in sheer imitation of class zero of the D.C. The only true main class was " 2 Library Science." The other classes were mainly used for generalia approach materials, such as bibliography, encyclopaedia, learned society, periodical, yearbook, etc. As in the D.C., these numbers were used to represent not only the approach materials themselves, but also the methodology of preparing such materials, which was unhelpful, as the readers of approach materials are usually different from those interested in the materials describing their production. This was realised in the idea plane within a few years, but the lack of versatility of the notational system at that time led to the implementation of this being set aside. The fourth edition of C.C. retained, in zone 2, only materials on the technique of production. But it was felt that Library Science could not go with them. In fact, no criterion was found for the kind of subjects to be accommodated in the second zone. Now it is realised that this zone should have only subjects which have to do more or less with the entire range of main classes assigned to zone 3, so that Library Science alone deserved to be retained in zone 2. A search was then made for other main classes satisfying this test, and the following subjects appear to be fit to go into that zone:

(1) Universe of knowledge—structure and development
(2) Library science
(3) Book science—authorship
(4) Journalism

The rest of the places in the first octave and the places in the later octaves are available for occupation by other main classes satisfying the prescribed test.

3633 Zone 1

In zone 1, z has been used to represent Generalia proper, which is more comprehensive than the partially comprehensive sub-generalias provided for in zone 3, as described in section 22311. Obviously there can be only one Generalia class. How are the other Roman smalls in zone 1 to be utilised? They should not be left fallow. The C.C. brings them into use by a trick, so to speak. To see how, we should consider the second order array with z as the immediate universe in the first order array.

36331 Zone 3 of Second Order Array

The C.C. has prescribed, in rule 9z3, the use of zone 3 of the second order array to represent materials centring round any person who has been encyclopaedic in his range of influence and contribution to recorded thought, and attracts contributions on himself from the angle of most of the main classes. The part of the isolate number lying in the second order is to be got by the alphabetical device. Example: zG = Gandhism.

36332   Zone 2 of Second Order Array

The C.C. has also prescribed, in rule 9z2, the use of zone 2 of the second order array to represent materials of an encyclopaedic nature centring round a geographical area or entity. Examples:

z4 Orientalia	z441 Dravidology	z57 Scandinavianology	
z41 Sinology	z4497 Ceylonology	z67 Egyptology (in	
z42 Nipponology	z5 Occidentalia	generalia sense)	
z44 Indology	z51 Greekology	z73 Americanology	
		z79 Hispanology	

There are usually periodicals demanding such generalia classes. In some cases there are also books of such a nature. Their utility and the need for the recognition of them as distinctive generalia classes and for having distinctive and expressive class numbers for them was brought home while compiling the *Retrospective directory of Asian learned periodicals,* which was finalised and sent to Unesco in March, 1955.

36333   Zone 4 of Second Order Array

The same directory brought up also periodicals on generalia centring round particular subjects. Jainology, Catholicology and Islamology are examples. They are not merely on the religions concerned. Nor are they on the sociology of the community following the religion concerned. They are generalia in every sense of the word. The last zone of the second order array with z as the immediate universe easily gave place to such classes. Example: z(Q3 Jainology.

36334   Zone 1 of Second Order Array

Let us now consider approach materials on generalia, unrestricted in any of the ways mentioned in the three preceding sections. We shall get a schedule such as the following:

za General bibliography		zn General directory	
zk General encyclopaedia		zp General conference	
zm General periodical		zw Generalia biography	

Obviously, there is nothing gained by repeating z in each of the above numbers. The Law of Parsimony will be pleased if it is omitted. The arrangement will still be the same as if z were written. In the notational plane, it will result in apparently filling up the first zone in the main array. Of course, this is only a notational illusion, because the first zone in the notational plane is really formed by the telescoping of z, a number of order 1, and *a* to *y*, which are in reality—that is, in the idea plane—numbers of order 2.

3634   Zone 4

Zone 4 of the main array is being brought into use only now. In fact, it is only created now as a result of the adoption of the starter bracket and the arrester bracket as digits; its formation is due to the ordinal value of the starter bracket being fixed as greater than Z. This is in the notational plane. We have to examine the idea plane to find out if there are any main classes needing representation and admitting of being accommodated in Zone 4.

36341   Displaced Main Classes

In section 3632 we saw that the main classes forming the respective techniques of making approach materials, such as bibliography, encyclopaedia and biography, were displaced from zone 2. They were separated from the classes formed by the corresponding approach materials in the second edition of C.C. in 1942. While the approach materials were accommodated in zone 1, the main classes forming the techniques were left in zone 2 itself. In paper 1.18 " Prels," included in the symposium *Depth classification* (1953), edited by S. R. Ranganathan, these newly emerging main classes were called Preliminary Main Classes or Prels; and in contradistinction, the traditional main classes were called Positive Main Classes. This early attempt to make a distinction among main classes has now been extended to a considerable degree, since it is now realised that the newly emerging main classes are far too many to be accommodated in zone 2. Moreover, as stated in section 3632, these newly emerging main classes do not satisfy the criterion set up to admit a main class into zone 2, viz. having to do more or less with the entire range of main classes.

36342   Genesis of New Main Classes

An examination of the genesis of the displaced new main classes gives us some insight into the possible genesis and number of new main classes already emerging or likely to emerge. Bibliographology, encyclopaediology, biographology and all such new main classes, described as displaced ones, are methodologies. They have evolved in course of time—most of them only in recent years—from the systematisation of the method of preparing the respective approach materials. They have been distilled out, so to speak, from long-continued rule-of-thumb methods, as distinct disciplines. These disciplines were first embodied in a sparse way in articles only, and therefore figured only as micro-thought. Till very recently, classification schemes did not attempt to classify micro-thought to the point of individualising them. Therefore the need for finding places for the science and art forming the discipline was not felt. But some of these disciplines have now been cultivated with sufficient elaboration and have even approached the status of macro-thought embodied in books, and they have therefore to be numbered as main classes. These new main classes have mnemonic affinity to the corresponding approach materials. It is therefore proposed that they can be accommodated in the fourth zone of the main array in the way indicated below:

(*a*)   Bibliographology (art and science of preparing of bibliography)

(*f*)   Festschriftology (art and science of preparing festschrift) (*k*)   Encyclopaedology (art and science of preparing encyclopaedia)

(*m*)   Periodicalism (art and science of preparing periodical)

(*n*)   Serialism (art and science of preparing a serial such as yearbook and directory)

(*p*)   Conference technique

(*r*)   Technique of writing report

(*t*)   Commission technique

(*t*4)   Survey technique

(*t*5)   Planning technique

(*wn*)   Who's who technique

(*w*)   Biographology

(*w*1)   Autobiographology

(*y*7)   Case study technique

36343   Analogy

As already stated, these new main classes are stemming in our own days from common isolates, which are anteriorising. By analogy we should expect other new main classes to stem from the posteriorising common isolates also. In the C.C., these also are represented by Roman smalls. Moreover, there are posteriorising common isolates which are manifestations of each of the fundamental categories Energy, Matter and Personality. It will not be helpful to design numbers for all these main classes by merely packeting the mnemonic Roman smalls. In the first place, it will create many homonyms, a fatal fault in classificatory language. Secondly, the resulting sequence of the new main classes will not be helpful. We should therefore find some way of distinguishing the numbers for the main classes stemming from the different kinds of posteriorising common isolates, both among themselves and from those stemming from the anteriorising common isolates for which we have constructed numbers in section 36342. There is another complication also. It will be seen in part 4 that there is need for two or more schedules for the posteriorising common isolates of each of the three fundamental categories Energy, Matter and Personality. In view of this, it is suggested that, within the packet, the Roman small may be prefixed with an indicator number to show the schedule of posteriorising common isolates from which the new main class concerned stems. The following schedule of indicator numbers is suggested:

z1 for posteriorising energy common isolate of kind 1.

z2 for posteriorising energy common isolate of kind 2.

z3 for posteriorising energy common isolate of kind 3.

    ***   ***   ***   ***

z5 for posteriorising matter common isolate of kind 1.

z6 for posteriorising matter common isolate of kind 2.

z7 for posteriorising personality common isolate of kind 1.

z8 for posteriorising personality common isolate of kind 2.

Here are some provisional main class numbers, by way of illustration.
They are based on the tentative schedule of posteriorising common
isolates, with which we are experimenting.

Main Class	C.C. No.	U.D.C. No.
Art and science of making hypothesis	$(z1a)$	167.5
Technique of criticism	$(z1g)$	165.65
Scientific method	$(z1y)$	?
Technique of production planning	$(z2a)$	.001.14
Waste utilisation	$(z2w)$	.004.8
Secretariat work	$(z3b)$	?
Conduct of meeting	$(z3k)$	06.053.5
Museology	$(z7e)$	?
Laboratory organisation	$(z7g3)$	?

36344   Further Use of Analogy

We may similarly provide, in zone 4 of the main array, for main
classes likely to stem from or have affinity with any of the main classes
of zones 2 and 3 or any of their sub-classes. For example, the distinctly
human medium for communication is language. We may therefore
represent the newly emerging main class "Art and science of
communication, in general terms" by the number (P). Perhaps, we
may represent the newly emerging main class "General theory of
organisation" by (X), and the "General theory of public relation"
by (Y).

3635   FUTURE WORK

Many new main classes may take shape from time to time in future,
in response to accumulating literary warrant, which should be provided
with numbers in the main array. The creation of zone 4 has provided
an infinity of places for new main classes. The new main classes will
seldom spring from the waves like the goddess Venus, as Bliss puts it
on page 32 of *Bibliographic classification*, Vol. 1, 1940. They are likely
to be generated by the process of distillation mentioned in section
36342, with some mnemonic affinity to an already existing and
cultivated class. At any rate, many of the newly emerging main classes
will be of this kind. We have demonstrated a method of constructing
numbers for them in zone 4 of the main array. Each of the new main
classes will have to be facet-analysed, and the necessary schedules for
the various facets in the different levels in the different rounds will have
to be constructed. None of these can be constructed in anticipation,
but only as and when their proliferations are disclosed by the literature
produced. Work in the idea plane should thus wait. But the work in
the notational plane has fitted the notational system to meet any
emergency, to acquire adequate hospitality and to receive any number
of main classes of pure methodology in a more or less helpful sequence
in zone 4 of the main array. The work on schedules, which
comprehends all the three planes—idea, notational and verbal—will
have to be an ever-continuing affair. This is an inevitable consequence
of the perpetual dynanism of the universe of knowledge.

3636 Main Class Array in B.C.

The Bibliographic Classification has two species of digits for use in the main array, viz. Arabic numerals and Roman capitals, so that it has two zones to accommodate main classes. The traditional main classes are accommodated in zone 2, formed by Roman capitals. Zone 1, formed by Arabic numerals, mixes up approach materials and the main classes stemming from them. This mixing up cannot have been a conscious or unconscious imitation of D.C. tradition, because it introduces into zone 1 categories which do not at all belong to the thought-content or the subject of the materials.

Examples

1 Reading room collections.
3 Select or special collections, or segregated books.
4 Departmental or special collections.
5 Documents or archives of governments, institutions, etc.
7 Miscellanea (includes encyclopaedias not selected for reference, pamphlets, photographs, cinema films, phonograph records).
9 Antiquated books.

Surely these should be looked after by the collection-number part of the call number, described in section 67 and its subdivisions. There is no indication as to how new main classes of general methodology are to be accommodated; on the contrary, there is a naïve assumption that new main classes will not arise at all in future. This is stated in page 32 of Vol. 1 of the B.C. in the following categorical words: " Classifications develop by adjustment, or adaptation, and by branching, rather than by addition of new insular, self-contained specialities; they grow by division and subordination rather than by difference and co-ordination." This is not true. The development of the universe of knowledge is not merely like the development of an ordinary tree, all of whose branches lean for ever and subordinate themselves to the stem. On the contrary, as in a banyan tree, some of the tentacles, stemming no doubt from a branch, reach down to earth, strike root, and begin to function as a new stem—as a main class.

3637 Main Class Array in U.D.C.

The U.D.C. uses only one species of digits in the main array, which would make one expect that there can be no zones in its main array. However, the zone idea appears to be inexorable, for U.D.C. has, in fact, improvised three zones in the main array. It uses initial zeros or their absence to implement the zone-formation needed by the idea plane: a main class number in zone 1 begins with two zeros; that in zone 2 with one zero; and that in zone 3 begins straight away with a digit other than zero—the traditional or positive main classes are enumerated in zone 3.

36371   Zone 2

The D.C. itself had formed zone 2. It labelled it by the generic name
" Generalia." This does not, however, tell the right tale, if we take
generalia to mean either a total or a nearly full comprehension of all
the main classes in zone 3. For zone 2 includes 02 Library Economy.
Surely this is itself a main class and not a comprehension of others.
The U.D.C., therefore, abandoned the label Generalia. However, it
uses a longer descriptive term which is equally bad. It reads,
" Generalities: Information, Persons, Organisations, Activities, Documents and Publications in general." How can " Library Economy "
be brought under this label? This is not only a difficulty in the verbal
plane, for it has its roots in the idea plane. The main classes
accommodated are too heterogeneous. The adoption of packet
notation, using square brackets, will remove the true main classes
stemming from approach materials into a new zone—zone 4.

36372   Zone 1

Zone 1 of the main array of U.D.C. is occupied by such main classes
as

001 Science and knowledge in General. Organisation of
     Intellectual Work.
002 Documentation. Books. Manuscripts and authorship.
003 Writing. Graphic characters.
007 Action and Organisation in General. Human Work.

Some of these are made necessary by literary warrant. They are
disciplines independent of and co-ordinate with the traditional or
positive main classes. They are distillates of certain imponderables all
along applied and inherent in many of the main classes, and nowadays
distilled out as methodologies. But it is doubtful if " 003 Writing and
graphic characters " cannot go with Linguistics. Apart from this, the
zone accommodating such newly emerging main classes should be
extensive enough to receive a very large number of them. It is therefore
a recommendation to the F.I.D. that the formation of zone 4 with
packet notation may be considered.

364   Canonical Class Array

By the very definition given in section 345, canonical classes can
occur only in arrays of order 2 or of higher orders. Mathematics,
Physics, perhaps Engineering, Geology and Philosophy form one
group of main classes calling for canonical classes to be enumerated as
the first step, before facet analysis can be applied for further
classification. In these cases, the main class is more like a bundle
holding several canonical classes. Tradition has found such bundles
to be convenient, but as there is also some intimate filiation among the
canonical classes in some main classes, there is therefore some intrinsic
justification also for grouping them under a label denoting the main
class. Fine arts is another main class holding several canonical classes

with some mutual filiation. But this differs from the first group in one essential respect, in that the main class admits of style facets, as much as its canonical divisions do. Useful Arts is a third variety of main class. It is a bundle of classes, created by an exigency in classification itself, and there is hardly any filiation among the classes included under this label. It is largely a heterogeneous collection of classes based on the application of sciences to the production of commodities and services of particular kinds, not provided for among the other main classes in a scheme. In each of the three groups, zone 1 of array of order 2 is reserved for accommodating approach materials. The other zones alone need study.

3641 Group 1

In studying the notational organisation for canonical classes of main classes of group 1, we shall use array of order 2 as the type. Zone 2 only is used to represent canonical classes. Zone 3 is reserved for the specials and the systems of the main class. Zone 4 has not yet been brought to use. Is there any chance for the formation of canonical classes by subject device? Or is there any other way of forming canonical classes with the aid of packet notation? These questions need investigation, and their answers will show a way of utilising zone 4. At present, the notational system of C.C. alone poses such questions to the idea plane. If the idea plane furnishes answers in the affirmative to either of them, the other schemes too may realise the advantage of using packet notation in arrays of second and higher orders accommodating canonical classes.

3642 Fine Arts

The number of Fine Arts, whose literary warrant demands a place among canonical classes, is now not more than sixteen. This had led the C.C. to accommodate them in zone 2, which has landed it in a difficult situation. The Style of Fine Arts in general, as well as each of the individual arts, has to be individualised by geographical device followed by chronological device. Consequently, the style number has two facets, viz. geographical and chronological facets. The style is a manifestation of the fundamental category Personality. The geographical facet being of level 1, the geographical number need not be preceded by a comma. But a comma should come before the chronological number, as it is of level 2.

36421 Creation of Homonyms

The creation of homonyms is easily illustrated by one example. N5 can mean either " European Style of Fine Arts " or the canonical class " Painting." A method used till now for the resolution of this kind of homonym is to insert a comma before the geographical facet of the style number, if it is applied to the main class number N.

Zone analysis suggests a better solution. Zone 2 may be reserved solely for style. The canonical classes may be accommodated in the last octave of zone 3. This will not call for the special rule involved in the solution mentioned in the preceding section.

36422 Greater Hospitality

Incidentally, the above solution secures for the canonical classes the greater hospitality of zone 3. More canonical classes can be accommodated with a single digit. Literary warrant is calling for more of them. The Indian Shadow Play is an example. The C.C. may very well incorporate this suggestion in its future editions. Section 52 of Ranganathan's *Depth classification* (15) in *Annals of library science,* Vol. 2, 1955, page 97 et. seq. has redrafted the schedule of Fine Arts along these lines.

No use has so far been found for zone 4. All the remarks in the latter part of section 3641 are applicable to this section also.

3643 USEFUL ARTS

In the past, literary warrant has turned most of classificatory thought towards pure—or fundamental—sciences, natural as well as social, and the humanities. Engineering, chemical technology, agriculture and medicine were the chief branches of applied science, whose classification had been cultivated to a considerable extent. But today there is an ever-increasing number of arts and crafts with more or less affinity to natural sciences, and of certain techniques with more or less affinity to social sciences, all of which need attention, since they give rise to myriads of basic classes. Literary warrant demands the inclusion of all of them in the schedules of classification. They are too many to be accommodated in the main array as main classes, and in practice every scheme accommodates them in arrays of second or higher orders, as canonical classes. The label " Useful Arts " or something similar is used to denote the main class covering them.

36431 U.D.C.

The short base of Arabic numerals has made the U.D.C. include even the old and well-cultivated applied sciences in the improvised main class " Useful Arts " represented by 6. Apart from the four major applied sciences, U.D.C. uses 64, 65, 67, 68 and 69 to represent all the rest. The last three have a generic label—Manufactures and Trades. Many trades are listed, but even they are not exhaustive, neither is there any indication about the way in which others are to be accommodated, either in the idea plane or in the notational plane.

36432 Library of Congress

The L.C. gives a place to agriculture and medicine in the main array. It includes all the other applications of natural sciences in the main class T Technology. It divides this main class into the four groups,

TA to TH   Engineering and Building Group.
TJ to TL   Mechanical Group.

TN to TR   Chemical Group.
TS to TX   Composite Group, which are detailed into
TS Manufactures; TT Mechanic trades, arts and crafts; TX Domestic Science.

It is difficult to know the denotation of the last three, except with the aid of the Canon of Enumeration. Domestic Science includes catering. Mechanic Trades include woodworking, metalworking, leatherwork, painting, etc., drapery, hairdressing and laundry work. Manufactures include metal manufacture, covering also watches and clocks, woodwork, leather industry, paper manufacture, textiles, and rubber. Then follows " Miscellaneous Industries (Alphabetically)." Under this are enumerated animal products, carriage and wagon making, celluloid, flour industry, gloves, hats, and tobacco industry. Then comes " 2302 Various minor industries," giving the following illustrative alphabetical subdivisions:

.C7 Copying Presses .P3 Phonographs   .U5 Undertakers'
.M8 Monuments   .T7 Toys   supplies
.N5 Notions   .T9 Transfer-pictures

The above demonstrates the struggle involved in making a schedule of arts and crafts and the justifiable hesitancy to have recourse to alphabetical device.

36433   Bibliographic Classification

The B.C. distributes " Chemical Technology " as subdivisions of the main class " C Chemistry " and includes all other applications under " U Useful and Industrial Arts, including Special Technology." The following groups occur in this main class:

UA to UB Agriculture   US Mechanic Arts and Trades
UC Animal Industry   UT Manual Arts and Trades
UD Mining   UU Handicrafts and textile industries
UE to UR Engineering   UV (Residual) Industries

Then comes, UW " Alphabetical arrangement of industries etc." This is the place " For the alphabetical arrangement, more or less complete, of the residual industries," not enumerated under UV. Here are some illustrative classes:

UEB2 Hair-cutting UWD7 Doors   UWG7 Milling
                                            Grains
UWB4 Hair-dressing UWE5 Embroidery UWL7 Lock-smithy
UWB7 Bottle-   UWG3 Gasoline   UWT6 Tin-plate
      industry   supply stations
UWC9 Cutlery

36434   Reluctance to Alphabetise

The reluctance to resort to alphabetisation is caused by two factors. In the first place, alphabetical scattering is unhelpful, and secondly, none of the arts and crafts has an international name. There cannot be an international nomenclature for them as in the fundamental sciences. Nevertheless, it is not practicable to avoid alphabetisation at some stage or other, on account of the enormous number of arts and crafts. A parallel problem will arise also in Economics in classifying the economics of the several industries.

36435   Colon Classification

In the C.C., Engineering, Chemical Technology, Mining, Agriculture, Animal husbandry and Medicine are made main classes. All other arts and crafts with filiation to natural sciences are accommodated in the formal main class M. Unlike N Fine Arts, there is no need to forgo zone 2 for enumerating the subdivisions. Even in the fourth edition of C.C., the utilisation of zones 2 and 3 is not satisfactory. It will be helpful if the eighteen places in the first three octaves of zone 2 are given to eighteen canonical classes in the light of the literary warrant, actual and anticipated. The residual subjects should be divided into twenty-four groups, on the basis of the super-characteristic " Utility." Each of these may be divided perhaps on the basis of utility once more or some other super-characteristic. Then comes the problem of finding use for zone 4. Some work along these lines has been started in sections 58 to 72 of Ranganathan's *Depth classification* (5) in the *Annals of library science,* Vol. 2, 1955, page 97 et seq. This schedule will also be of use in the subdivision of " Industries " in Economics.

365   Zone 2 in a Facet

The isolates of zone 1, being common isolates, can be enumerated more or less exhaustively; at any rate, the occasions for listing new isolates will be few and far between. The isolates in zones 3 and 4 are easily formed by definite devices. But the isolates of zone 2 are not only based on characteristics special to the host-class, but have also to be enumerated *ad hoc* for each host-class. In personality and matter facets, we can have a succession of arrays based on a train of characteristics—indeed, there may be an infinity of characteristics to choose from. But it is a matter of convenience to reach individualisation within a facet in a few steps—that is, with a few characteristics. The optimum number of characteristics is three and six is the maximum number to be used.

3651   Finding in the Idea Plane

The following are the findings in the idea plane. Incidentally, the findings introduce some additional terminology.

(1) There are many claimants to the privilege of being chosen as characteristic.

(2) In a train of characteristics, each characteristic is, in a sense, dependent on the preceding one; in other words, each First Characteristic carries its own train.

(3) With an optimum of three characteristics and with a maximum of six, a train of characteristics in a facet should nearly reach individualisation.

(4) The efficiency of a scheme depends on the selection of the most helpful first characteristic and its train; this may be called the Favoured First Characteristic and its train the Favoured Train of Characteristics. Literary warrant determines them.

(5) Literary warrant of less intensity may call for the choice of some other first characteristic and its train also as the basis of classification.

(6) It may happen that no characteristic can be singled out as the favoured first characteristic.

Determination of the First Characteristic of a train and of the Favoured First Characteristic in the light of literary warrant is now left to unaided flair. Can any guiding principles be laid down?

3652 IMPLEMENTATION IN THE NOTATIONAL PLANE

A method of implementing these findings is as follows. It is sufficient if the implementation in the first order array is shown. This method would satisfy the Law of Parsimony.

(1) When there is a Favoured First Characteristic, the first octave is used to accommodate the isolates based on the favoured first characteristic. The second octave is used to accommodate the remaining non-favoured first characteristics themselves, instead of the isolates based on them. Their isolates will be accommodated in their respective arrays of second order. If the number of isolates based on the favoured characteristic is greater than eight, the second octave also is used for them; and the non-favoured first characteristics are accommodated in the later octaves.

(2) When there is no favoured first characteristic, the first octave is filled with the first characteristics themselves; if necessary, the second and later octaves also may be used for them. Their isolates will be accommodated in their respective arrays of second order.

Examples of the first kind occur in the Natural Group facets of Botany and Zoology, given in section 3667. An example of the second kind occurs in the Library facet of Library Science, given in section 3662.

3653 CROSS-CLASSIFICATION

The use of two or more characteristics in one and the same array violates the Canon of Consistency, and will lead also to the violation of the Canon of Exclusiveness. An obvious result of this will be cross-classification, a serious fault. For example, a specific family of plants like Water Lily will call for a place under the subgroup Renalls on the basis of the favoured train of characteristics; it will also call for a place under Water Plants, which is a division based on the non-favoured first characteristic Ecology. The fault is remedied by the following convention: Division on the basis of successive characteristics in the favoured train of characteristics can be continued without restriction; but division on the basis of a characteristic belonging to a non-favoured train of characteristics should be stopped at the point where it reaches an isolate arising out of the favoured train of characteristics. For example, let us go down the chain in Botany that belongs to the non-favoured train of characteristics based on the ecological characteristic:

C.C. Number	Plant Group	U.D.C. Number
195	Ecological groups	581.526
1955	Water plant	581.526.3
19551	Fresh water plant	581.526.323.2

Probably, the next link in the chain will be Lily. If so, the chain should be sealed before Lily is reached. This convention permits the inclusion of divisions based on different first characteristics in one and the same array. Such an organisation of notation in zone 3 is needed to meet the literary warrant that exists.

366 Terminology

For the further study of the organisation of notation in zone 2 of an array, it is helpful to introduce a few additional concepts. These are:

1 True Isolate 3 Pure Array   5 Pure Octave   7 Telescoped Array
2 Quasi Isolate 4 Mixed Array 6 Mixed Octave 8 Disjunctive
                                                  Incidence

In pursuing these concepts in the succeeding sections, the following symbols will be used for the sake of brevity.

$[1P1]$ = Personality facet of first level in first round

$[1P1](2Z)$ = Zone 2 of $[1P1]$
$[1P1](2Z)(1\,O)$ = Octave 1 of $[1P1](2Z)$
$[1P1](2Z)(1\,O)(fF)$ = Focus f in $[1P1](2Z)(1\,O)$
$[1P1](1A)$ = Array 1 in $[1P1]$

Further we shall confine ourselves only to zone 2 in all our discussions in this chapter, and so we shall effect a further economy by dropping $(2Z)$ in all the symbols.

Thus we shall have only

$[1P1]$ in the place of $[1P1](2Z)$
$[1P1](1\,O)$ in the place of $[1P1](2Z)(1\,O)$
$[1P1](1\,O)(fF)$ in the place of $[1P1](2Z)(1\,O)(fF)$

3661 True Isolate

Let us consider the isolates enumerated in $[1P1]$ of " B6 Geometry." They are:

1 Line   3 Solid (of three dimensions)   5 Five dimensions
2 Plane   4 Four dimensions   7 n dimensions

These isolates are all based on Dimension as characteristic. Each of the isolates is a space of just a single measure of dimensions. Each is an entity forming a subject of study. None of them is a group of two or more of such entities. An isolate like this will be called a True Isolate. Here is a table of some other facets with true isolates:

Basic Class Number	Number of Round	Number of Level	Descriptive Name of Facet
B13	1	1	Number
B23	1	1	Equation
B33	1	1	Equation
B33	1	2	Degree
B33	1	3	Order
B7	1	1	Matter
B9	1	1	Body
O	1	2	Form
U	1	1	Geography
V	1	2	Organ
W	1	1	Type of State
W	1	2	Organ
X	1	1	Business
Z	1	2	Law

3662 QUASI ISOLATE

Next let us consider the isolates enumerated in [1P1] of " 2 Library Science." Here they are:

1 Trans-local	3 Academic	5 Subscription	7 Private	95 Contact
2 Local	4 Business	6 Special class	8 Governmental

Each of these isolates is really a characteristic which can be used to classify libraries. None of them denotes a library as an entity by itself, but each denotes a group. A group as an isolate, i.e. a characteristic enumerated as an isolate, is not a true isolate. Let us call it a Quasi Isolate. Here are two other examples of facets made entirely of quasi isolates:

Basic Class Number	Number of Round	Number of Level	Descriptive Name of Facet
J	1	1	Utility
Y	1	1	Group

When there is a name for a facet of quasi isolates, as in the above two cases, we may use it also to name the characteristic on the basis of which the characteristics forming the quasi isolates are themselves derived. To distinguish the former characteristic from the latter ones, we may call the former a super-characteristic, in this particular kind of context.

3663 PURE ARRAY

All the isolates in each [1P1] mentioned in section 3661 are true isolates. Each such array will be called a Pure Array. Each is a pure array of true isolates. Again, all the isolates in each [1P1] mentioned in section 3662 are quasi isolates. Each such array will also be called a Pure Array. Each is a pure array of quasi isolates. It may be repeated here that this distinction is applicable only in (2Z).

3664 MIXED ARRAY

Let us consider the isolates enumerated in [1P1] of the basic class " M(J7) Rope-making " (as in the fourth edition of C.C.) and in [1P2] of " P Linguistics." They are as follows:

Isolates in [1P1] of M(J7) (Material Facet)	Isolates in [1P2] of P (Element Facet)
1 Cotton	1 Phoneme
2 Coir	2 Syllable
3 Hemp	3 Word
4 Flax	4 Phrase
5 Jute	5 Clause
6 Sisal	6 Sentence
8 Other vegetable fibres	7 Piece of composition
94 Artificial fibres	8 Punctuation
98 Metal fibres	9 Practising materials
	91 Grade 1
	92 Grade 2

In M(J7), [1P1](1 O)(1F) to [1P1](1 O)(6F) are all true isolates but [1P1](1 O)(8F) to [1P1](2 O)(8F) are quasi isolates. In P, all the isolates in [1P1](1 O) are true isolates, but those of (2 O) admit of a common label, viz. " practising materials." This fact should not mislead us to import the idea of quasi isolate into this array. It must be remembered that 9 is not an isolate number; it is only an octavising digit, which happens to admit of a label being attached to it in the verbal plane in this particular case. Each array like the one in M(J7), containing both true and quasi isolates, will be called a Mixed Array. It may be repeated here that this definition is applicable only to (2Z).

3665 PURE OCTAVE

In M(J7), all the isolates of [1P1](2 O) are quasi isolates. An octave like that having only quasi isolates will be called a Pure Octave. Here, it is a pure octave of quasi isolates. In the personality facets mentioned in section 3661, all the octaves are Pure Octaves of true isolates. In those of section 3662, all the octaves are Pure Octaves of quasi isolates.

3666 MIXED OCTAVE

On the other hand, in M(J7), [1P1](1 O)(8F) is a quasi isolate. But all the other isolates are true isolates. An octave like that having both true and quasi isolates will be called a Mixed Octave.

3667 TELESCOPED ARRAY

It can be seen easily that the whole of the earth's surface, and the several subdivisions of it into continents and oceanic regions, have been put in one and the same array, in C.C. as well as U.D.C. Such a phenomenon happens in other arrays also. Here are two more examples. They occur in [1P1](1A) of " I Botany " and " K Zoology."

[1P1](1A) of I Botany			[1P1](1A) of K Zoology		
C.C. No.	Isolate Term	U.D.C. No.	C.C. No.	Isolate Term	U.D.C. No.
1	Cryptogam	21	1	Invertebrate	2
2	Thallophyta	22	2	Protozoa	31
3	Bryophyta	32	3	Porifera	34
4	Pteridophyta	35	4	Coelenterata	33
5	Phanerogam	41	5	Echinodermata	39
6	Gymnosperm	42	6	Vermes	51
7	Monocotyledon	52	7	Mollusca	4
8	Dicotyledon	61	8	Arthropoda	52
95	Ecological groups	152.6	9	Prochordata and vertebrate	6
951	Land plant		91	Prochordata	
952	Creeper		92	Fish	7
953	Climber	152.643	93	Amphibia	76
954	Insectivore	152.415	94	Reptile	81
955	Water plant	152.63	96	Bird	82
9551	Fresh water	152.632.32	97	Mammal	9
9555	Marine	152.632.33	995	Ecological groups	15
			9955	Water animal	
			99551	Fresh water	19(28)
			99555	Marine	19(26)

For the purpose of this section, we shall confine ourselves to (1 O) in Botany and (1 O) and (2 O) in Zoology. Viewed from the idea plane, (1 O)(1F) and (1 O)(5F) of Botany are isolates of order 1, while the remaining foci are isolates of order 2. In fact, isolates 2, 3 and 4 are subdivisions of isolate 1; and isolates 6, 7 and 8 are subdivisions of isolate 5. But from the notational plane, they all appear to be of the same order and to be co-ordinate isolates. This illusion in the notational plane is due to two arrays of the idea plane having been telescoped and presented as a single array in the notational plane. Similarly, in Zoology, (1 O)(1F) and (1 O)(9F) belong to array of order 1, and the remaining isolates in the first two octaves of (1A) belong to array of order 2, as viewed from the idea plane. But these two arrays of the idea plane have been telescoped into a single array, as viewed from the notational plane. This notational exigency arises to prevent the isolate numbers of an array from running to waste in cases where the number of isolates in the array is too small—say, one or two.

3668   VACANT FACET

Section 241 of Ranganathan's *Library classification: Fundamentals and procedure* (1944) reads as follows: " The class number of a book will translate only those facets of a specific subject in which it is unifocal, and generally leave untranslated those in which it is multifocal or diffuse, and those that are absent." This triple use of Vacant Facet introduces the fatal fault of homonym into the notational language, and it should be avoided. It may be that diffuseness need not necessarily be distinguished from absence, as the boundary line between them is not sharp enough for the Canon of Ascertainability. We may therefore give the same treatment to them. Common sense would suggest absence being indicated by the omission, i.e. vacancy of the facet. Literary warrant too will support this. In the universe of macro-thought embodied in books, it is conjectured that there are more books with absent or diffuse facet than multifocal books. If this be true, it is even more appropriate to indicate absence or diffusion by omission of the facet.

36681   Multifocalness

Multifocalness means a disjunctive treatment of the isolates. In its geographical schedule, the C.C. uses the isolate number 1-1 to denote disjunctive incidence of " 1 World " and the bare digit 1 only to denote integral incidence. In disjunctive incidence, the subject matter of the books deals severally with each of the continents, regions or countries. In integral treatment, the world is treated as a whole. A similar notational distinction is applicable also to continents, countries, etc. Here are examples:

C.C. Number	Geographical Isolate	U.D.C. Number
1	World (integral)	100.2
1-1	World (disjunctive)	100.3
4	Asia (integral)	500.2
4-1	Asia (disjunctive)	500.3
44	India (integral)	540.02
44-1	India (disjunctive)	540.03

In *Depth classification* (6) of Ranganathan appearing in the *Annals of library science*, Vol. 1, 1954, pages 193-201, the use of the same notational device in the case of every other kind of facet was considered, but it leads to such inconvenient combinations of digits such as ",-".

36682   New Suggestion

The concept of telescoped array gives another suggestion for indicating disjunctive treatment. We use z to represent Generalia in the main array. Disjunctive treatment is equivalent to generalia, in relation to the foci in an array, and therefore z may be used to re-present disjunctive treatment. In the array of the first order of any facet, other than the first level personality facet in any round, it will place disjunctive treatment just before the first focus of zone 2—the correct helpful position. But in the case of the first level personality facet, the anteriorising quality of z will take effect. To nullify this, z must be preceded by the connecting symbol (comma) wherever it stands for disjunctive treatment of isolates in a first level personality facet. The appropriate connecting symbol should also be added in the case of all arrays of order higher than 1 in all facets.

36683 Examples

The result of the above suggestion is illustrated by the following examples:

C.C. Number	Class
T	Education (integral, i.e. with absent or diffuse facets)
ToaS	Education from the angle of psychologist
T.44	Education in India (integral)
T.44-1	Education in India (disjunctive, i.e. State by State treatment)
T:z	Educational problems (disjunctive in energy facet and absent or diffuse in personality facet)
T:3	Teaching technique (unifocal in energy facet and absent or diffuse in personality facet)
T ,z	Education (disjunctive in personality facet and absent or diffuse in energy facet)
T ,z:z	Education (disjunctive in personality and energy facets)
T1	Education of children (unifocal in array of order 1 of personality facet, but absent or diffuse in array of order 2 of personality facet and in energy facet)
T1:z	Education of children (unifocal in array of order 1 in personality facet, absent or diffuse in array of order 2 and disjunctive in energy facet)
T1 ,z	Education of children (unifocal in array of order 1 and disjunctive in array of order 2 of personality facet)
T1 ,z:z	Education of children (unifocal in array of order 1 of personality facet and disjunctive in array of order 2 of personality facet and in energy facet)
T13	Nursery education (unifocal in personality facet and absent or diffuse in energy facet)
T13:z	Nursery education (unifocal in personality facet and disjunctive in energy facet)
T13:3	Teaching technique for nursery schools (unifocal in personality and energy facets)

367 Telescoped Facet

In the C.C., we have also the phenomenon of telescoped facets. This arises out of the concepts of Systems and Specials. The generic name for both is Amplified Basic Class. Here are examples taken from the main class " L Medicine."

Specials		Systems	
L9C	Child	LB	Ayurveda
L9E	Old age	LC	Siddha
L9F	Female		
L9H	Tropical	LD	Unani
L9U8	Aviation	LL	Homoeopathy
L9V	War	LM	Naturopathy
L9X	Industry		

The idea of " system " had been recognised in the idea plane and provided for in the notational plane, even in the first edition of C.C. It was denoted by the term " School of thought." But it was only in

1952 that the idea of " special " was conceived. The idea of " system " and " special " was first applied in the following articles in the series *Optional facets* in the *Annals* part of the *Abgila: System of physics and special physics* by S. Parthasarathy in Vol. 2, 1952, pages 265-267, *Specials in economics* by K. D. Puranik in Vol. 2, 1952, pages 268-272, and *System and special in agriculture* by D. B. Krishna Rao in Vol. 3, 1953, pages 25-29.

3671 SYSTEM

Systems of a basic class are distinguished from one another by the chronological device; the chronological number is added to the basic class number. The epoch used is the year chosen as the one in which the system was first expounded. It is, of course, difficult to get the exact year, and even historical research into this problem may not be able to assert a particular year. But systems are not invented every year or even every decade, and so it is sufficient if the approximate century is represented in the class number. Indeed, in regard to the ancient Indian systems of medicine Ayurveda and Siddha even the century could not be asserted. The chronological numbers shown against them in the above schedule are therefore simply those representing two of the divisions of the pre-Christian era. Such liberties are possible.

Viewed as a class, a system is called an Amplified Basic Class. The chronological isolates attached to a basic class to denote systems are said to constitute an Amplifying Facet. We may also state that

Basic Class + Amplifying Isolate = Amplified Basic Class;
Basic Class Number + Amplifying Isolate Number = Amplified Basic Class Number.

36711 Favoured System

Any exposition of a subject will have to be according to some system. In other words, there can be no document in a basic class *qua* basic class. The ideas in a basic class are ineffable, unless it is amplified to represent a system. In the notational plane, this means that no document can have an unamplified basic class number to begin its class number. However, in practice, one of the systems of a basic class is taken as the Favoured System. The favoured system is determined by literary warrant, or, rather, by the current tendency in literary warrant. Allopathy, for example, is taken as the favoured system in Medicine. To satisfy the Law of Parsimony, the amplifying facet is omitted in the class number of the favoured system. If a document deals disjunctively with many systems, its basic class number is amplified by the digit A.

36712 Non-Favoured System

All the facets which can be added to the favoured system may be added to a non-favoured system also. But an implication of rule 6503 of the C.C. requires that the isolate number in [1P1] should be preceded by its own connecting symbol (comma) if an amplifying facet precedes it. Generally, the same schedules of the various facets may be suitable for use in the favoured system as well as in the other systems. But it is not obligatory. Each system may call for a different schedule with different isolates in one or more facets. These may have to be worked out separately for each system. To make depth classification efficient in the service of micro-thought, such differing schedules may be needed. This is a piece of work that yet remains to be done. Intensive progress in the ancient history of a subject will produce documents making this piece of work urgent. Ancient chemistry, usually referred to as alchemy, may need problem schedules different from those of modern chemistry. So also, Ayurveda may need at least a few extra problem divisions.

3672 Specials

In a Special, there is restriction in the universe of the basic class. Specials arise out of such a restriction, unlike systems which arise from differences in hypothesis, postulates, etc. For example, in Medicine, Child Medicine and Old Age Medicine restricts the universe of the living body of man to that of one within certain age limits. The field of study of each of these is confined to those problems that are peculiar to the restricted age group concerned. Similarly, Industrial Medicine denotes the study of the medical problems peculiarly incident to industrial workers. So also, Aviation Medicine stands for the study of medical problems peculiar to flying, usually at speeds far in excess of the one normally experienced in motion on surface, and also usually at high altitudes—with centrifugal accelerations, atmospherical bumps and so on. Specials in Physics would mean the study of physical phenomena, such as properties of matter, coefficient of thermal expansion, electrical conductivity and every other problem, when some of the factors are abnormal, such as high pressure, low temperature, high voltage, infinitesimal dimensions, astronomical dimensions and so on. In Agriculture, soilless cultivation, dry cultivation, arctic cultivation, etc., are specials, with abnormal restrictions in soil, water supply, temperature, etc., respectively.

36721 Idea Plane

The possibility of such specials was not foreseen thirty years ago when the C.C. was designed, because in those days there were few books on such specials coming into our experience. But the universe of micro-thought, met with in documentation, brings them up fairly often. There was at first difficulty in the idea plane itself. It was finally decided about the end of 1951 that the literature on each special should all be kept together to satisfy the Canon of Helpful Sequence. The Canon for Filiatory Sequence requires that documents on a special, i.e. embodying results of study within an abnormal or restricted range of some of the factors, should not be mixed up with the documents of some other special or of any normal system, favoured or not. This means that as each system creates a parallel sequence within a basic class, each special also will create a parallel sequence of its own.

36722 Notational Plane

The above indication of the idea plane was utilised in the notational plane, and it was decided that the specials also should be individualised by the device of Amplification. Amplification really amounts to accommodation in zone 3. The last octave of zone 3 having been reserved for systems, it was easily decided that the specials should be accommodated in the penultimate octave of zone 3. The next problem was the choice of the device for getting the first significant digit in the number of a special, which can be either by alphabetical device or by chronological device. The specials did not always have an internationally accepted standard name, and therefore alphabetical device was not available. But neither is it easy to determine the year of the beginning of each special. Moreover, it is only in recent years that research has been intensified sufficiently, and therefore a crop of specials comes up more or less at the same time. For all these reasons, chronological device also had to be abandoned. Finally, we had to land on enumeration, with Roman capitals as base.

36723 Objective Principles

Some tentative guides in the allocation of the twenty-four Roman capitals have been proposed. We can (1) follow mnemonics—literal or scheduled; or (2) divide the twenty-four letters among the fundamental categories, in respect of which the special range of study gets restricted or is likely to get restricted. Which of the categories may be safely ignored, in which sequence the categories should be arranged in the array, and in what proportion the twenty-four letters should be divided among the categories—these issues have now to be decided *ad hoc* for each basic class, according to actual or potential literary warrant. Again, whether the first alternative or the second alternative should be followed also depends on the peculiarity of the basic class concerned. There may even be need to combine the various alternatives. This is what has happened in the sample schedule of specials of Medicine, given in section 3675. The first four specials have been numbered on the basis of verbal mnemonics, using English terms as a basis, while the last three have been numbered on the basis of scheduled mnemonics in an oblique form; it is not, however, a subject device. The formulation of more definite objective principles for the use of the digits in the array of specials is one of the problems for investigation in the notational plane—i.e. in the organisation of notation to meet the requirements of literary warrant.

3673 EXAMPLES OF CLASS NUMBERS

Let us consider a few select classes in Medicine involving the ideas developed in the two preceding sections.

L	Medicine	L9C	Child Medicine	LA	Medical Systems
L:3	Physiology	L9C:214	Dentistry	LB	Ayurveda
L214	Dentistry	L9F	Female Medicine	LB:3	Physiology
L214:54	Prevention of dental disease	L9F:4	Gynaecology	LB,214: 54	Prevention of dental disease
L82	Orthopaedics	L9F,553	Uterus	LB,82: 478:7	Orthopaedic Surgery
L82:478	Fracture	L9F,553: 4713	Wrong Position		
L82: 478:7	Surgery	L9F,553: 4713:7	Surgery	LL	Homoeopathy
		L9V	War Medicine	LL,44: 453:6	Treatment for Asthma
		L9V,82: 478:7	Orthopaedic Surgery	LM	Naturopathy
				LM,44: 453:6	Treatment for Asthma

In reading the isolate terms in the schedule, one must apply the Canon of Context. For example, the last subject in the first column should be read as Orthopaedic Surgery (in Allopathy, the favoured system). The last-but-two subject in the second column should be read as Surgical Correction of the Position of Uterus (in the favoured system). Similarly, the fourth subject in the first column should be read as Prevention of Dental Disease in Allopathy (the favoured system); while the fourth subject in the third column should be read as Prevention of Dental Disease in Ayurveda. The above twenty-five subjects were enumerated to demonstrate the way in which the different amplifying facets and the ordinary facets can be combined to get expressive, co-extensive class numbers. It will be of use to add one more subject to the list to demonstrate the combination of a system as well as a special in one and the same subject. Here it is:

LB,9C,214:54 Prevention of dental disease in children according to Ayurveda.

3674 LEVELS OF PERSONALITY

We find in general that the System Isolate and the Specials Isolate figure as Personality Facets. They are, indeed, treated as different levels of personality facet. A Special is [1P0]. A System is [1P(-1)]. In words, a Special is a personality of level " zero " in the first round; while a System is a personality of level " minus one " in the first round.

3675 CONSEQUENCES OF SYSTEMS AND SPECIALS

To bring out the consequence of the recognition of Systems and Specials in the idea plane and their accommodation in the notational plane, we shall consider the following sequence of classes:

L   Medicine   L9A Specials
L1   Regional Systems   L9C Child Medicine

L2	Digestive System	L9F	Female Medicine
L3	Circulatory System		
		L9X	Industrial Medicine
L7	Nervous System	LB	Ayurveda
L8	Co-axial Systems	LC	Siddha

Let us overlook the first digit L denoting the basic class Medicine. What remains constitutes the Array of Order 1 as viewed from the angle of the notational plane. But, as viewed from the angle of the idea plane, it is not so. Not only do they not all belong to the same array, they do not even belong to the same facet. We saw in the preceding section that they belong to different facets, forming different levels of the fundamental category Personality. (1F) to (8F) belong to [1P1], (9AF) to (9XF) belong to [1Po], (BF) to (CF) belong to [1P(-1)]. Thus three different facets stand telescoped into a single array in the notational plane. We may call it a Telescoped Facet. However, the facets stand separated in the class number of a subject presenting two or all three of these facets. This was illustrated amply in section 3673. This kind of Telescoped Facet is made possible by the zones and octaves created by mixed notation.

3676 LAW OF PARSIMONY

The notational adjustment implied in the bringing about of such a telescoping of facets satisfies the Law of Parsimony to a considerable degree. It does so with due regard to literary warrant. In the universe of books embodying macro-thought, books on allopathy will form the bulk, except in specialised libraries. Still, there may be a few books on the allopathic treatment of some specials. They all get short class numbers—only two or three digits in most cases. There may also be a few books on the other systems of medicine. Their class numbers too are short—only two digits in most cases. As the intension increases, the length of class number increases. As we enter the universe of articles in periodicals, embodying micro-thought, the first octaves and the last octaves of the telescoped facet and many other facets appear all combined in one and the same class number. In the design described, the length of the schedule is increased only by the addition of a few specials and fewer systems. But the number of depth classes that can be given individualising class numbers increases many-fold.

3677 OTHER USES

A very helpful use of telescoped array, which can be spread out into different facets of diverse levels as and when needed by a document, has been experimented upon in Ranganathan's *Depth classification 19; classification of management, Annals of library science*, Vol 3, 1956, pages 33-72.

368 **Group Notation**

Octave notation uses one and only one significant digit to denote the isolates in an array. On the other hand, the number of isolates to be accommodated in zone 2 of the array may be far too many to be conveniently denoted by a single significant digit. Use of 2, 3, 4, etc., significant digits may be necessary in order to shorten isolate numbers. Then we say that we use Group Notation. The choice between octave notation and group notation is determined mainly by the Law of Parsimony. The number of isolates in the array is determined only in the idea plane. The Law of Parsimony has no sway over the idea plane. It has sway only over the notational plane.

3681   One Significant Digit

Let us allow ourselves only one significant digit in the isolate number. Then three octaves are needed to accommodate twenty-four isolates. The average number of digits for an isolate number will then be two. If the number of isolates is less than twenty-four, the average will be less than two. Of course, the average will be one if the number of isolates is not more than eight. If the number of isolates is more than twenty-four, the average will be greater than two. Let us next allow ourselves two significant digits in each isolate number. But let us not exercise the freedom to use the octavising digit. Then one octave-block of two-digited numbers will accommodate sixty-four isolates. The average number of digits will be two. Even if the number of isolates is less than sixty-four—even if it is one only—the average will continue to be two. Thus it is seen that (1) octave notation is economical if the number of isolates in zone 2 of the array is not greater than twenty-four; and (2) group notation of two significant digits is more economical if the number of isolates is greater than twenty-four.

36811   Critical Number

A general mathematical equation has been derived in the *Optional facets* (11) of Ranganathan, published in the *Annals* part of the *Abgila*, Vol. 2, 1952, page 249. It is as follows:

$$2 (\log_B M) = M\text{-}1$$

where (K) = integer equal to or greater than K, B = number of significant digits in use, M = (number of isolates)/B, and BM is the critical number. In the particular case where B = 8, the critical number is 24, as the solution of the above equation is M = 3.

3682   Two Significant Digits

Let us allow ourselves two significant digits in each isolate number. Let us also have the freedom to use the octavising digit. We can have sixty-four isolate numbers of two digits, sixty-four of three digits with 9 as first digit, sixty-four of three digits with 9 as second digit, and sixty-four of four digits with two 9's. Thus with an average of three digits, 256 isolates can be accommodated. If the number of isolates is less than 256, the average will be less than three. If the number of isolates is greater than 256, the average will be greater than three.

Let us next allow ourselves three significant digits, but no octavising digit, in each isolate number. Then one octave-block of three-digited numbers will accommodate 512 isolates. The average number of digits will be three. Even if the number of isolates is less than 512, even if it is one only, the average will continue to be three. Thus it is seen that (1) group notation of two significant digits is economical if the number of isolates in zone 2 of the array is not greater than 256; and (2) group notation of three significant digits is more economical if the number of isolates is greater than 256. Thus 256 is the critical number.

3683   THREE SIGNIFICANT DIGITS

Let us allow ourselves three significant digits in each isolate number. Let us also take the freedom to use the octavising digit. We can have 512 isolate numbers of three significant digits only, 512 with 9 as the first digit and three additional digits each being a significant one, 512 with 9 as the second digit and three additional digits each being a significant one, 512 with 9 as the third digit and three additional digits each being a significant one, and we may choose to have any 512 isolate numbers with three significants and 9 inserted twice among them. The average number of digits per isolate number, when we use all the resulting 2,560 isolate numbers, will be four. With an average of four digits of which three and only three digits are significant, 2,560 is the maximum number of isolate numbers that can be accommodated. If the number of isolates is less than 2,560, the average can be made less than four. If the number of isolates is greater than 2,560, the average will become greater than four.

Let us next allow ourselves four significant digits, but no octavising digit, in each isolate number. Then one octave block of four-digited numbers will accommodate 4,096 isolates. The average number of digits per isolate number is obviously four. The average will continue to be four, even if the number of isolates is less than 4,096—even if there be only one isolate. Thus it is seen that (1) group notation of three significant digits is economical if the number of isolates in zone 2 of the array is not greater than 2,560; and (2) group notation of four significant digits is more economical if the number of isolates is greater than 2,560. Thus 2,560 is the critical number.

3684   FOUR SIGNIFICANT DIGITS

Similarly, let us allow ourselves four significant digits in each isolate number. Let us also take the freedom to use the octavising digit. We can insert just one 9 either as the first or as the second or as the third or as the fourth digit. Then with all the four digits as significant ones, we can have 4,096 isolate numbers. With four significant digits and one 9 only we can have 4 × 4,096, i.e. 16,384 isolate numbers. If we put in 4,096 more isolate numbers with two 9's inserted among the four significant digits, we shall have on the whole 24,576 isolate numbers giving an average of five digits per isolate number. We can also state that (1) group notation of four significant digits is economical if the number of isolates in zone 2 of the array is not greater than 24,576; and (2) group notation of five significant digits is more economical if the number of isolates is greater than 24,576. Thus 24,576 is the critical number. The next critical number is 229,376.

3685   General Formula

We can arrive at a general formula for the critical number in the following way. Let us allow ourselves n significant digits in each isolate number. Then one octave block of n-digited numbers will accommodate 8^n isolates. We can get a number containing $(n + 1)$ digits by inserting the digit 9 as the first, or the second, ... or the nth digit in a number of n significant digits. Thus we can have $n8^n$ isolate numbers of $n + 1$ digits, each of which has n significant digits and just one 9. In taking the average, we must balance the 8^n numbers of n digits by an equal number of $(n + 2)$-digited numbers. These we get by inserting two 9's in the 8^n numbers with all the digits significant. Thus the total number of isolate numbers taken for averaging will be $(n + 2)8^n$; and the average number of digits per isolate number will be $(n + 1)$. Thus $(n + 2)8^n$ is the critical number. If the number of isolates is less than this critical number, the average will become smaller than $(n + 1)$. If the number of isolates is greater than the critical number, the average will be greater than $(n + 1)$; and a group notation with $(n + 1)$ significant digits will become more economical.

3686   Table of Critical Numbers

The following table will be of use for ready reference in the choice between octave notation with one significant digit only and group notation with different numbers of significant digits, for use in zone 2 of an array so as to satisfy the Law of Parsimony.

When the Number of Isolates in the Zone 2 is		Economic Number of Significant Digits for Group Notation
Greater than	but Not Greater than	
	24	1
24	256	2
256	2,560	3
2,560	24,576	4
24,576	229,376	5
$(n + 1)8^{(n-1)}$	$(n + 2)^n$	n

3687   Degenerate Case

In the degenerate case, when the number of significant digits in the group notation is one, the formula for critical number gives 2 as the lower limit for the number of isolates admitting the use of one significant digit in the isolate number. In other words, 2 is the critical number deciding the choice between the use of one significant digit or none at all to represent the isolate(s). This is got by putting 1 for n in

225

the formula in column 1. This means that no significant digit is necessary when there is only one isolate in the zone, and either one or no significant digit may be used when there are two isolates. This needs examination.

36871   Only One Isolate

When there is only one isolate, our impulse will be to represent it by a digit, say 1. But this would be contrary to the indication of the critical number. A little reflection will show that the indication of the critical number is right. For if a universe contains one and only one entity, it admits of no division. Its unique entity needs no name or number to denote it. Indeed, we have no bother of naming or classification. We need not worry ourselves about its attributes. It may be attributeless, or it may have an infinity of attributes. It makes no difference. This concurs with the saying of the Vedic mystics that *Brahmam,* the (monistic) Absolute, is at once of infinite attributes and of no attribute. It also accords with the recognition of two kinds of monism in the Vedantic School of Indian philosophy, viz. *Advaita,* monism proper, postulating *Nirguna-Brahmam,* attributeless Absolute, and *Visishta-Advaita,* modified monism, postulating *Saguna-Brahmam,* attributeful Absolute. In the notational plane, there is no need for a schedule or an isolate number when the universe itself is unitary.

36872   Two and only Two Isolates

When the number of isolates is just two—that is the critical number —the analogy of the non-degenerate cases suggests that we may use either no significant digit or one. If the former alternative is adopted, the two isolates will have to be represented by 9 and 99 respectively. Then the average number of digits will be one and a half. On the other hand, if the latter alternative is adopted, the two isolates may be represented by 1 and 2 respectively. Then the average number of digits will be one only. The latter is therefore to be preferred on the grounds of economy. Thus in the degenerate case when the number of isolates is two, the critical number should not be taken, as in the other cases, to give us an option.

369   Criterion for Telescoping

The telescoping in the notational plane, mentioned in section 367, is in a sense the opposite of the group notation mentioned in section 368. The former leads to economy in isolate number. The latter increases the length of the isolate number. The former is applicable when the number of isolates in an array is below a prescribed limit. The latter becomes necessary when the number of isolates in an array is above a prescribed limit.

3691   TELESCOPING OF ARRAYS

Let a = number of isolates in an array;
    b = number of isolates in the succeeding array;
      (both of the above as viewed from the idea plane);

$c =$ length of the base of the notation in the zones concerned within either array.

If we can assert that $a + b$ will be always less than c in respect of the arrays in question, then the two arrays may be telescoped in the notational plane.

The telescoping may, if necessary, be confined to a particular zone or even to a particular octave.

3692 TELESCOPING OF FACETS

In some arrays, it may be possible to form the isolates in zone 2 on the basis of one characteristic and those in zone 3 on the basis of another characteristic. We use for zone 3 that one of these two characteristics which gives the isolates of greater extension or greater concreteness. If the subject of a document calls for the use of both of these characteristics, the isolates of zone 2 are deemed to be isolates in a facet of the level next to that of the isolates of zone 3.

When the isolates of zone 3 are of greater extension than those of zone 2, the former have been called " specials " and " systems " in section 367.

Cases of isolates of zone 3 being of greater concreteness than those of zone 2 were recently experienced in designing the classification of " Management." Here is an example taken from [P1] applied to the " Management of a factory ":

9V	Purchase
9V1	Indent
9V2	Source
9V7	Voucher
9VB	Raw materials
9VD	Intermediate commodities
9VE	Commodities (Finished products)
9VY	Materials for the maintenance of factory
9VY6	Electric current
X9:89VY6,2	Source for purchase of electric current for a factory

As viewed from the notational plane, the schedule presents in the same array foci 1 to 8 based on one characteristic, and foci B to Y based on another characteristic; and the latter foci are more concrete than the former. This mode of telescoping facets gives a solution to the problem stated in section 36133. Examples will be found in section X2 of Part 1 of the fifth edition of the Colon classification (1957).

CHAPTER 37

ANALYTICO-SYNTHETIC PROCESS

370 Standard Procedure to Classify

THE POSTULATES EXPLAINED IN the preceding chapters of this part make classification analytico-synthetic. Chapter 33 analysed the process of knowledge-classification for library purposes, and emphasised the need for distinguishing between work in the idea plane from work in the notational plane. Chapter 35 stated several postulates in the idea plane. These provided for:

(1) Fundamental-category-analysis
(2) Phase-analysis
(3) Facet-analysis involving
(4) Round-analysis and
(5) Level-analysis

Chapter 36 postulated a set of connecting symbols for phases and facets of different kinds, and also postulated their ordinal values. These postulates regarding the idea and notational planes were shown to imply a unique pattern in the arrangement of diverse subjects belonging to a main class. Chapter 36 laid down also some general principles to organise work in the notational plane, and provided for Zone-Analysis. The utilisation of the zones of different arrays was more or less standardised. This provides a standard procedure for constructing schedules of isolates belonging to different facets. The work of classifying any subject, expounded and embodied in any graphical form for communication, has been thus reduced to five stages:

(1) Analysing the subject into its ultimate phases and the facets in the different phases, and naming the isolates in each facet.
(2) Rearranging the names of the isolates so as to conform to the syntax of the classificatory language adopted, i.e. to the postulates regarding the sequences of phases, rounds, levels and all the facets arising therefrom.
(3) Changing the name of each isolate into the standard terminology found in the Scheme of Classification adopted.
(4) Translating the name of the isolate in each facet into isolate number with the aid of the schedule for the facet and the devices applicable to it.
(5) Synthesising the basic class number and the different isolate numbers into the class number with the aid of the connecting symbols.

228

A scheme of classification calling for conscious work in these five stages is Analytico-Synthetic Classification. Work in the first two stages is entirely in the idea plane. Work in the third stage is in the verbal plane. Work in the fourth stage embraces both the verbal and the notational plane. In contradistinction, a scheme of classification giving ready-made class numbers more or less to all the conceivable subjects is an Enumerative Classification. Even in enumerative classification, some analysis in the idea plane is no doubt necessary, but it is not guided by any standardised procedure. The second, third and fourth stages are not distinguishable. Perhaps they may be said not to occur at all. Having formulated the subject in some way, it is merely a question of " hit or miss " with the aid of the systematic schedule and the alphabetical index. In an analytico-synthetic classification, stages 1 and 2 implement the postulates in the idea plane. These stages are of use not merely for the primary purpose for which classification was originally thought of, but for several other purposes. It may be worth while to consider the various uses to which the analytico-synthetic process of classification can be applied. These were first set forth in Ranganathan's *Library Classification: its added uses*, published in *Libri*, Vol. 2, 1951, pages 31-36.

371 First Use—Arrangement

The first use for which library classification was designed was to preserve a preferred helpful sequence among known specific subjects without the necessity for re-examining them every now and then and re-determining their sequence. In other words, the first use was mechanisation of arrangement.

372 Second Use—Exploration

A properly designed classification should be able to assign to a newly formed specific subject such a class number as would place it among the already known specific subjects, in a tolerably helpful position. This implies firstly the existence of appropriate vacant numbers for the reception of new subjects, and secondly the vacant numbers suggest the creation of the corresponding new subjects. Library classification can thus be of use in pioneering work and creative exploration. Facet and phase analysis, including fundamental category, round, level and zone analysis, and the use of seminal mnemonics, should be practised intensively to get the fullest benefit of this, the second use of library classification.

373 Third Use—Help to Classifier

An analytico-synthetic classification will be of immense help to the classifier in determining the focus of a piece of writing, be it simple, compound or complex. In other words, it will enable him to determine the specific subject of the piece of writing exactly, however complex and involved it might be, so that the work of classifying will not be merely a matter of hit or miss, with the aid of an alphabetical index. The only situation in which unaided flair would be the sole guide will be the initial one of determining the Basic Class of knowledge to which the piece of writing belongs. Even here, if flair fails and a start is made with a wrong basic class, further work with the prescribed analysis in the idea plane will lead to an impasse; this will make the classifier wise, and he will start with another basic class.

The analysis will then play the part of a diffraction grating or prism in spectrum analysis. With its aid the classifier can unerringly and almost mechanically break the content of the piece of writing into its ultimates and spread them out into a spectrum. The class number which is finally constructed by synthesising the ultimates will be permanently expressive of the features of the spectrum of the subject classified.

374   Fourth Use—Help to Reference Librarian

But we have to remember that the ultimate purpose of a library is neither arrangement nor classifying, nor even exploration *qua* exploration. Its ultimate purpose is the expeditious establishment of contact between a reader and the exact reading material pertaining to his field of interest at the moment. This fitting of the right reader and the right piece of expressed thought will depend upon a prior assessment of the exact requirement of the reader on the one hand, and on the other of the exact focus of each of the pieces of expressed, embodied and socialised thought available in the holdings of the library system. The latter work would have been already done by the classifier using an analytico-synthetic scheme of classification. Its analytico-synthetic process will also be of help to the reference librarian in ascertaining the requirements of the reader in exact terms. It will be an effective guide for the reference librarian to probe into the mind of the reader. Often a creative reader has the bulk of his mind tied up, as it were, with his own creative thinking while coming to the library, and in this state of inevitable absent-mindedness he should be helped, with sympathy and delicacy of a high order, by the reference librarian. If he has a good discipline in the use of the apparatus of a library classification of the analytico-synthetic type, he will be eminently fitted to elicit the needs of the reader unobtrusively for the purpose of helping him with his reading material. As the reference librarian proceeds along the prescribed lines of analysis, the reader too will feel more at home; he will participate with the reference librarian with confidence and openness. The classified panorama of specific subjects, with their names in the natural language and their equivalent class numbers fully expressive of all their foci, facets and phases spread before the reader, and interpreted and pointed to by the reference librarian, will achieve this result.

375   Fifth Use—International Communication

In 1950 my attention was invited by Dr. Bernard, President of the Rockefeller Foundation, and his co-workers to a possible fifth use of an analytico-synthetic classification. This has been analysed in Ranganathan's *Classification and communication* (1951). The question is: Can such a classification scheme be of help in the promotion of international communication unvitiated by inexactness in expression and translation from one natural language to another? If so, to what extent can it help? What are the lines along which the foundations of analytico-synthetic classification should be strengthened or relaid in order to fit it for its fifth use?

3751 EMOTIONAL SPHERE

In his letters to me from 1950 to 1952, Mr. Rusk of Baltimore had been emphasising the potentiality of the Colon Classification for development into a universal language for international communication. In his paper *Resolution of cultural conflicts*, presented at the Eighth All India Library Conference convened by the Indian Library Association in January, 1948, he suggested the promotion of a " master system of classification " as a means of resolving cultural conflicts in the world. This may perhaps be beyond the bounds of a scheme of knowledge classification. Conflicts may stem from wrong knowledge or bad emotions such as fear, avarice, envy, hatred and anger. Classification belongs to the intellectual plane, and it cannot directly eliminate bad emotion of any kind. Nor can classification help in the international communication of emotions!

3752 TRANS-INTELLECTUAL SPHERE

There are certain ineffable elements in the experiences and thought of men, which cannot be communicated by any external means, but can only be experienced by each one independently. Poetry, painting, sculpture, music and other fine arts and symbolism of all kinds can only communicate it partially. According to a well-known dictum current in literary criticism in Sanskrit, there is more in what is suppressed than in what is expressed. Mahamahopadhyaya Professor S. Kuppuswami Sastriar used to emphasise this with the words, " There is more in suppression than in expression." A fathomless poem like the premier poem, the *Ramayana* of Valmiki, illustrates this unmistakably. The ineffability of experience in this sphere is traceable to its being trans-intellectual. Classification should abstain from analysing such ineffable elements of trans-intellectual experience. It should treat them as wholes. This is the purpose of Classic Device in classification, which is explained in chapter 62.

3753 INTELLECTUAL SPHERE

But unequivocal communication is practicable in experiences falling solely within the intellectual sphere. It is so, as much in the social sciences and even in the disciplines of philosophy, aesthetics and literary criticism usually labelled " humanities," as in the physical and biological sciences. Today, new thought is being created by several communities having diverse languages as media of expression. International economy requires that the output of research should be promptly served to all concerned, even when it is in its nascent state. The diversity of languages militates against this. Even within the same language it often happens that a newly created thought calls for new terminology, and in the first stages the different creators of it use different terms to denote it. It will be a long time before the terminology can be made uniform. A term in the natural language, used by the creator of the thought, usually produces in the minds of others several unintended associations and thus blurs the image of the thought.

3754 TRANSFORMER-LANGUAGE

It is here that a well-designed, scientifically constructed, analytico-synthetic classification can be of considerable help in international communication and in the communication of nascent thought within a language. If the scheme of classification is sufficiently equipped with mnemonics of high potency to form foci, facet-formulae with provision for optional facets to express all possible manifestations of the chosen fundamental categories as facets, and phase-formulae with distinctive symbols for all possible relations between different subjects, every new specific subject will be born with its own class number in its pocket as it were. This will enable us to place it in an appropriate place amidst the older subjects so that it will be correctly understood by the Gestalt pressure produced by the context in the arrangement. Class numbers formed in this manner will constitute also a Transformer-Language. This means that when a new specific subject is named in one natural language, it can be translated into the correct class number which will be international, and this can again be re-translated into any other natural language. Incidentally, universal bibliography can throw into one classified sequence all the records, irrespective of the natural language in which they may be expressed. The class number will indicate to an inquirer what entry can be of value to him; and he may ask for that alone to be translated into his own language.

I think that an analytico-synthetic classification has a great potentiality as a Transformer-Language; and therefore it becomes a fit subject for research and continuous improvement to effect economy in international effort, to promote international understanding and team-work, and thus to help in the promotion of international peace. I further believe that the use of machinery for bibliographical search will demand an ever-increasingly minute breakdown of subjects. This, in its turn, will stimulate research into the deeper foundations of a truly individualising and expressive analytico-synthetic classification.

CHAPTER 38

STRUCTURE AND DEVELOPMENT

381 Banyan Tree Analogy

THE STRUCTURE OF AN analytico-synthetic scheme of classification is different from that of an enumerative one. The former is comparable to a banyan tree with innumerable branches and sub-branches (facets) shooting forth in different directions, and with some branches shooting downwards and striking roots (phases) and themselves becoming secondary stems. On the other hand the enumerative scheme is like a palmyra tree with a single branchless stem. The structure of the schedule of an analytico-synthetic scheme of classification is also different from that of an enumerative one. The former consists of several independent schedules, while the latter has virtually one single schedule. Several analogies have been used to bring out the difference between the two types of classification.

382 Meccano Analogy

Paragraph 6 of the conspectus of the fourth edition of the Colon Classification compares the standard unit schedules of an analytico-synthetic scheme of classification to the standard pieces of strips, wheels, etc., in a Meccano set. By combining these standard pieces in different ways, many different objects can be constructed. So also by combining the isolates in the different unit schedules in a prescribed manner, the class numbers for all possible subjects can be constructed. The function of the connecting symbols is like that of the bolts and nuts in the Meccano set.

383 Medicine Analogy

Some have compared an enumerative scheme of classification to patent medicine. The doctor has no doubt to make some little diagnosis, but then he has to choose the medicine from among the ready-made patent ones. So also the classifier has no doubt to make some analysis in the idea plane even in an enumerative scheme of classification, in order to find out the thought-content of a document. But his freedom of prescription is restricted to the choice available in the list of patent medicines. On the other hand, an analytico-synthetic scheme of classification has been compared to compounded medicine. The doctor diagnoses each patient thoroughly, and then writes out a prescription choosing the chemicals needed to meet the diverse indications of the diagnosis, and also fixing their proportion to suit each individual case. The prescription then goes to the apothecary, who has a stock of different elemental medical substances. He weighs and measures each elemental drug according to the prescription, and then synthesises them with the necessary secondary substances, such as water, adhesive and other neutral stuff, to give the resulting medicine the proper consistency. So it is in classification. The analysis in idea plane corresponds to diagnosis. The synthesis in the notational plane corresponds to the compounding. Each subject gets its own individualising class number, as each patient gets his individual medicine.

384 Language Analogy

Again, the enumerative classification has been compared to a tourist's vocabulary book. It anticipates the sentences likely to be needed by a tourist in a country with a language alien to his own. He has just to point to the appropriate sentences or speak them out. The other side has only to point out the relevant answer from among those given against the question. Similarly an enumerative classification anticipates the subjects likely to turn up for classification. It provides class numbers for each of them. But with a tourist's vocabulary, one cannot express ideas not scheduled in it. So it is with classification. For subjects not enumerated, a class number cannot be devised. On the other hand, an analytico-synthetic classification is like a dictionary of words taken along with grammar of the language. No doubt the use of such a linguistic equipment requires more familiarity than in the case of a tourist's vocabulary. But it enables the tourist to express any idea as and when it occurs to him. With the words in the dictionary, he can compose sentences to express any idea. So it is with an analytico-synthetic scheme. It is possible to construct the class number for any subject by analysing it into its ultimate phases, facets and foci, translating each of these with the dictionary, and then forming the class numbers by synthesis. Of course, as for the use of a rushing tourist, a schedule of ready-made class numbers may be published for the use of school and public libraries, even of an analytico-synthetic scheme of classification.

385 Structure of Schedule

The structure of the schedule of an analytico-synthetic classification is thus not monolithic as the enumerative classification. It is polylithic, and consists of hundreds of schedules, some common to all subjects, some common to some subjects, some special to individual subjects. Some are even special to individual isolates in the different facets of one and the same subject. Such a structure naturally results in considerable economy in schedule-space to the satisfaction of the Law of Parsimony. For an analytico-synthetic classification does not construct a schedule of ready-made class numbers for every subject. It constructs a few hundred short schedules of isolates, in addition to a short schedule of basic classes.

386 Constituent versus Composite Terms

An analytico-synthetic classification is able to evade the responsibility to fix the name of a class in a natural language. It restricts itself to the task of naming the isolates in the various facets. This may be put in the following way. An analytico-synthetic scheme confines itself to the Fundamental Constituent Terms. It leaves the Derived Composite Terms to the care of individual classifiers and reference books.

3861 LAW OF PARSIMONY

Take a subject like Medicine. Is it necessary to load the schedule or the index with the names of diseases like the following?

(1)

Nephradenoma	Nephrolith
Nephralgia	Nephrolysis
Nephrapostasis	Nephromalacia
Nephratonia	Nephromegaly
Nephrauxe	Nephroparalysis
Nephrectasia	Nephropathy
Nephrectomy	Nephrophthisis
Nephrelcosis	Nephroptosia
Nephremia	Nephropyelitis
Nephremphraxis	Nephropyosis
Nephria	Nephrorrhagia
Nephritis	Nephrosclerosis
Nephrocele	Nephrosis
Nephrocolic	Nephrospasia
Nephrocystosis	Nephrotuberculosis
Nephroerysipelas	Nephrotyphoid
Nephrohydrosis	Nephrotyphus
Nephrohypertrophy	Nephrozymosis

(2)

Adrenalitis	Antiaditis
Alveolitis	Aortitis
Amniotitis	Aponeurositis
Angitis	Apophysitis
Angiocarditis	Appendicitis
Angiocholitis	Arthritis
Angiodermatitis	Gastritis
Annexitis	Tonsillitis

Is the classification schedule to ignore the presence of dictionaries and reproduce large slices of dictionaries? Does not the Law of Parsimony imply that such a course is wasteful and that it is desirable to recognise the existence of other informative books and to economise the schedule and the index by providing the necessary apparatus for drawing the maximum possible help from such books?

To show how the classification schedule of an analytico-synthetic scheme of classification can take advantage of the existence of dictionaries and other reference books to construct the class numbers of derived composite terms from out of fundamental constituent terms which alone are to be specified in the schedule, we shall illustrate from the Colon Classification.

Taking Nephrauxe, we find from the dictionary that it is hypertrophy of kidneys. In the schedule for L Medicine, we find, under the divisions based on Organ Characteristic, 51 Kidneys and, under the division based on Problem Characteristic, 412 Hypertrophy. Thus we get the number L51:412 for Nephrauxe.

To take another example, we find from the dictionary that Aortitis is inflammation of aorta. From the divisions based on the Organ Characteristic in L Medicine, we get 34 Aorta and from the divisions based on Problem Characteristic we get 415 Inflammation. Thus we construct the number L34:415 for Aortitis.

3862 Extent of Saving

As these examples show, an analytico-synthetic scheme gives the maximum possible satisfaction to the Law of Parsimony in the matter of Terminology. The saving can be explained symbolically as follows:

Suppose there are a divisions in facet A, b divisions in facet B, and c divisions in facet C in any subject. Then it is possible to form abc classes by combining them in all possible ways. As the schedules give the fundamental constituent terms of the subject and as the meaning of any derived composite term can be got from a good dictionary, there is no need to load the schedule or the index with the abc derived composite terms indicated by the $a\,b\,c$ classes. The enumeration of the $a+b+c$ fundamental constituent terms is sufficient. Now it is a matter of elementary algebra that $a+b+c$ is considerably smaller than $a\,b\,c$.

3863 A Numerical Example

To realise how much saving this implies in the actual length of the schedule and in the shifting of a large part of the burden of terms to the dictionary or other appropriate reference book which already exists, let us take, for example, that there are 100 divisions on the basis in the first facet, 200 divisions in the second facet, and 300 divisions in the third facet. In an analytico-synthetic scheme, only 600 fundamental constituent terms need figure in the schedule and in the index. The 6,000,000 derived composite terms need not figure there. The classifier should use the schedule along with a good dictionary or other suitable reference book to construct the class numbers to represent any of these 6,000,000 derived composite terms as and when need arises. There is surely a great difference between 600 and 6,000,000! In a two-columned book of normal format, the former will require only twenty pages. But the latter will require 200,000 pages or 400 volumes of 500 pages each.

Surely it is impossible to put in all the terms of the infinite universe of knowledge in the schedule. The only sensible course is to confine ourselves to the fundamental constituent terms and leave the derived composite terms to be managed by individual classifiers with the aid of reference books, as and when need arises.

3864 PRESCRIPTION OF APPARATUS

If a new composite term gets coined in any field of knowledge demanding a new class, firstly, the meaning of that term is to be got from the books concerned; and next, that meaning is to be expressed in terms of the fundamental constituent terms occurring in the schedules of classification applicable to the field of knowledge concerned; and lastly, the expression so formed is to be represented by the appropriate class number from the schedules concerned with the aid of the appropriate devices or apparatus prescribed in the scheme.

3865 EVASION

Such a provision by an analytico-synthetic scheme of classification invests it with an element of evasion. This is an advantage to the scheme without any disadvantage to the users of the scheme. The derived composite terms are likely to take time to get settled and may also be unsettled and changed from time to time by usage and by the committees on terminology in different subjects. But the fundamental constituent terms will be relatively more stable. Hence, by mooring itself to the fundamental constituent terms and by merely providing the necessary apparatus to express derived composite terms, a synthetic scheme of classification escapes many of the ordeals of terminological flickerings and fights, leaving them to be negotiated by and reflected in the catalogues of individual libraries just to the extent warranted by the books on the shelves. The scheme can say " Terms may come and terms may go. But my representation of the classes behind them goes on for ever, even without my naming them."

387 Development

The development of an enumerative scheme consists in adding to its monolithic schedule. But the development of an analytico-synthetic scheme consists in adding to the number of its schedules and to the number of isolates in the schedules. New schedules will be called for by the new rounds and new levels of the fundamental categories involved in new micro-thought getting embodied from time to time. Its schedules will no doubt be ever growing; but it will be at a much smaller rate than the monolithic schedule of an enumerative scheme. The growth of the schedule length will be linear in an analytico-synthetic scheme of classification; but it will be exponential in an enumerative scheme of classification.

388 Autonomy of Classifier

In chapter 21, we described the peculiarities of the infinite universe of knowledge. Many classes, now unknown and unknowable, will be known and will call for a helpful place and an appropriate class number from time to time in the future. A new class may present a new facet, not found scheduled in the scheme. Or a facet of it, though already found scheduled, may present a focus not listed in the schedule. Then, one of two things may happen. It may call for a new focus in an array already scheduled, or it may call for a new array to be formed. In an enumerative scheme, the classifier has to depend on the classificationist to find the number for the new class. He cannot create it by himself. Until he gets the number from the classificationist, he will have to give it a temporary number, more extensive than the one which would closely fit the new class. But in an analytico-synthetic scheme, the classificationist would have given rules of procedure to analyse the subject in the idea plane, to arrange the resulting facets in a definite sequence, and then to look up the schedule for translation into numbers. The further rules implementing the canons of classification, particularly those relating to mnemonics, will help in the putting up of a new schedule, or the extension of an existing array in the schedule, or the lengthening of an existing chain in the schedule— whatever is demanded by the new class. The classifier need not wait for the number to be given by the classificationist. He can create the number by himself. This will be demonstrated in chapter 57. An analytico-synthetic scheme gives this much of autonomy to the classifier, in the classification of books embodying macro-thought. The Colon Classification gives this autonomy to the classifier in an appreciable measure. It is this fact that is brought out so pointedly by the following observation made in the *Library Association record,* 1934, page 98, in regard to the C.C. " A new subject creates its own number in the notation."

PART 4

THEORY OF KNOWLEDGE CLASSIFICATION
Third Approximation
DEPTH CLASSIFICATION

CHAPTER 41

WHAT, WHY, HOW

411 **What**

DEPTH CLASSIFICATION is a scheme of classification fitted to reach coextensiveness and expressiveness in the classification of micro-thought having many rounds and levels of facets, and isolates of high orders in any or all of them.

A scheme of depth classification cannot conveniently be enumerative. Perhaps it will have necessarily to be analytico-synthetic. It should have the capacity to represent as many facets as any micro-thought of any degree of intension may present. It must also have the capacity to sharpen any isolate in any facet to the degree found in the micro-thought. The assignment of each facet to the helpful round and level will require considerable judgment. Depth classification should be backed by sufficient hints to arrive at the right result. This is all work in the idea plane. Either schedules should be provided, or rules should be laid down to construct them, for several facets not needed in the classification of macro-thought. This has to be done jointly in the idea and notational planes. Isolate numbers should be worked out to a far greater number of digits than in classification for macro-thought. The resulting class number will be long. The Canon of Relativity would make us expect this. In contradistinction to depth classification needed by micro-thought, the classification that is sufficient for macro-thought may be called Superficial Classification. It must be remembered, however, that the terms micro-thought and macro-thought are relative; the boundary line between them is not sharp; it is very hazy. Accordingly, the transition from superficial to depth classification has to be as arbitrary as that from, say, the Indian Ocean to the Bay of Bengal, or high sea to coastal waters.

412 **Why**

Depth classification is a challenge thrown up by the universe of knowledge to the classificationist and the classifier. Perhaps wrestling with it may give joy to the former. It is a duty to the latter engaged in documentation work. But it should not be taken to be their own creation, or of their own seeking for the sheer joy of it. It is a demand of micro-thought; and micro-thought occurs in the universe of knowledge quite independently of the classificationist and classifier. It is the creation of the thinkers specialising in the various subjects.

This in its turn is made possible by the inherent quality of the human intellect, which makes it atomise experience and thought. Apart from this creation of micro-thought by the human intellect, material to be woven into micro-thought is also furnished directly by the auto-record, made by phenomena, through self-recording instruments such as the photographing spectroscope and the optical or electronic microscope, the cloud chamber, radar, and a host of electronic instruments. This is one of the concomitants of intensive team-research, being organised today on a national and international basis. Such an organisation of research is not a fortuitous happening. It has become a social necessity. These factors in the why of depth classification will be examined in greater detail in chapters 42, 43 and 44.

413 How

It will not be possible for a classificationist to work out all by himself a scheme of depth classification down to every facet and every isolate for all micro-thought. It may be possible for him to do so for macro-thought. But for micro-thought, he can only provide the methodology. For the enumeration of schedules, he will have to take the help of the subject-specialist concerned. Nor can the subject-specialist do it all by himself. The specialised knowledge of the classificationist is equally essential. A proper organisation for co-operative work of these two parties is necessary. At present, the Working Parties of the F.I.D. appear to be lacking in a proper balance in this respect. The problems to be faced will be illustrated in chapters 45 to 47, and the problem of organisation will be considered in chapter 48.

CHAPTER 42

SOCIAL PRESSURE

421 Chart of Human Needs

A LIBRARY IS ESSENTIALLY a social institution. Its techniques are therefore conditioned by social pressure. The need for depth classification
is certainly due to this. The social pressure can be traced down to
human needs. Man has several wants. Some of them are compelling
or essential needs for one and all. Some others are desirable wants in
the interest of social advancement and well-being. Both of these kinds
of wants can be met by voluntary effort by individuals or by collective
effort backed by political, economic and legal organisation. A few of
the wants are felt only by some individuals; and their satisfaction too
is largely to be found by action emanating from their inner urge. No
doubt the results of such action by the few may be beneficial to society.
But they are largely involuntary. Organisation can only collect,
conserve and make the results of such action available to society. In
the following chart of human wants, the satisfaction of group 1 is
essential to one and all; that of groups 2 to 4 is desirable for all; but
that of groups 5 and 6 is the privilege of a few only.

Group 1. Bodily Needs (Essential): 11 Food, 12 Clothing, 13
Shelter.

Group 2. Emotional Needs (Desirable): 21 Entertainment, 22
Private Festivity, 23 Public Festivals.

Group 3. Intellectual Needs (Desirable): 31 Basic Education, 32 All-
through Further Intellectual Development, 33 Contact with one's
Peers.

Group 4. Social Needs (Desirable): 41 Organised Life, 42 Communication, 43 Peace.

Group 5. Intuitional Urge (Privilege of a Few): 51 Art, 52 Literature,
53 Creative Work in other Fields.

Group 6. Spiritual Urge (Privilege of Occasional Few): Delight of
Self-Realisation.

Of these, groups 5 and 6 are not amenable to much social manipulation. Nor can they be suppressed. A genius will sprout even in a
dunghill. We shall therefore consider only the other four groups.
Among these, the first group appears to be a spring-board for the
others; while the fulfilment of the needs in all the groups depends
eventually on the cultivation of the intellectual resources of humanity.

Stated in terms of society, the maintenance of balance between population pressure and the bodily needs of the community on the one hand and of the materials available to satisfy the needs on the other, determines the intensity of the other needs. Further, when the population pressure reaches beyond saturation point, the restoration of the balance has to depend on and to begin with an intensive, organised and universal cultivation of the intellect. Increase of research man-power and the co-ordination of research work form the only means.

422 The Past and Nature's Gift

In the past, near-natural commodities have been in excess of the needs of population pressure. Satisfaction of bodily wants was got without much intellectual effort. Social formations too were on a small scale. Therefore much intellectual work was not necessary to fulfil social needs. The creative work of the occasional man of genius was sufficient. From about A.D. 1600, the population pressure began to exceed the capacity of little-aided Nature's gift, in certain areas of the earth. But migration to other areas of low pressure, such as America, Australia and parts of Africa, was possible. The state of cultural exhaustion and apathy of the communities living in the fertile areas in Asia and Africa made it possible to get relief through colonial exploitation. For this purpose, industrial venture by private men with ambition proved sufficient. The result was poor cultivation of the universe of knowledge in an organised manner.

423 The Present and Population Pressure

At present, the countries of Asia and Africa have shaken off their sleep. They are all bursting into irrepressible new life. They are pushing aside the hand of colonial powers. Their own population pressure has begun to cross the saturation point. The regions of low pressure, such as America and Australia, are more or less tightly fenced against immigration. Therefore, Europe and Asia are alike facing the crisis due to population pressure upsetting the balance.

424 Supplementing Nature's Gift

To restore the balance and meet the crisis, Nature's near-free gift has to be supplemented by human invention. Artificial building, clothing and food materials have to be fabricated from raw materials never before connected with food, clothing or shelter. Reinforced concrete and chemically impregnated timber have been produced. Textiles have been spun out of coal tar and petroleum. Plastics technology has had to be developed. Even artificial rice has been prepared from hitherto inedible vegetable matter. All this means increased intensity in intellectual work. This means intensive cultivation of the universe of knowledge.

425 Enlargement of Economic Sphere

National boundaries continue to be impenetrable barriers in the political sphere, but they admit penetration in the economic sphere. Though they prevent migration of human beings, they allow exchange of raw materials and manufactured commodities. The futility, if not the folly and danger, of a low-pressure area fattening itself alone while high-pressure areas are famishing, is being increasingly realised. The distribution of natural resources and fertility on the face of the earth is quite different from the distribution of population pressure. This difference in distribution persists also between the points of production of industrial commodities and the points of their consumption. All commodities—natural as well as manufactured—have to be transported from places of production to the places of consumption, scattered all over the world. The perishable commodities have to be transported within a short time, before they lose their value in the state of nascence. World-wide commerce demands also world-wide travel. These are now more in demand among free nations than they were in the colonial age. This enlargement of the economic sphere, so as to envelop the entire surface of the earth, creates gigantic problems in transport, commercial management and international relations. Their solution calls for intensive and continuous cultivation of the universe of knowledge.

426 Advent of Democracy

The advent of democracy and its universal spread since the last century have aggravated the problem of satisfying human wants. It is adding to social pressure. The material needs of all strata of society are getting equalised. The same is being attempted in regard to the emotional and intellectual needs also. More food, more clothing, more houses, more public entertainment, more schools and libraries and more transport facilities have to be found, as democracy means equality of opportunity for all—not merely for the upper classes but for the masses as well. With the irresistible march of socialism, human needs will increase a hundredfold. Therefore the supplementing of Nature's gifts by human invention and industry will have to be on an ever-increasing scale. It is inhuman to depend on war and pestilence to reduce the social pressure now being stepped up by democracy. Many view with revulsion the recourse to birth control. At any rate, it is more human and wise to meet the social pressure first by an intensive cultivation of the universe of knowledge.

427 Large-Scale Work

The pressure of population and democracy calls for large-scale work in every sphere. Large-scale work creates its own problems. It is one thing to put up a hut for a small family; it is quite another affair to erect a skyscraper for occupation by fifty thousand persons. It is one thing to communicate with the immediate neighbourhood; it is quite another affair to reach entire humanity through the Press and the radio. It is one thing to organise a village community or a city state; it is quite another matter to organise and manage affairs of state in a nation of a few millions, or of a near-world-state, such as the Commonwealth or the United Nations. So it is in the supply of every commodity and of every service. Such large-scale work in any sphere creates colossal problems in the social sciences. Their solution leads to further intensification of the cultivation of the universe of knowledge.

CHAPTER 43

DEVELOPMENT OF THE UNIVERSE OF KNOWLEDGE

431   The Past and Casual Development

IN THE PAST, WHEN population pressure and social pressure were low, there was no incentive for organised or co-operative development of the universe of knowledge. Creation of new knowledge was due mostly to the irrepressible inner urge to create, found in a few men of genius appearing on occasions and found scattered here or there. It was a casual affair. A genius creates because he cannot help creating, even as a flower cannot help blossoming.

432   Research in Parallel

There was no seeking of co-operation among the scattered men of genius. On the contrary, there was considerable secrecy and even antagonism. Each one did his work without informing himself of what had been done or was being done in other parts of the world. Consequently, the research potential was often wasted by the same results being reached at different places and by different persons. The history of the differential calculus illustrates this. It was not till the last century that Cambridge voted in favour of changing over from the " Newtonian Dot-(age) to the Leibnitzian D-(ei)-t-(y)." Population pressure was too small to correct the tendency to work in parallel. The result was slowness in the development of the universe of knowledge.

433   Time-Lag

Again, in the past, sparseness of population and low social pressure were not able to create the incentive for quick exploitation, for social use, of new developments in the fundamental regions of knowledge. There was a time-lag of more than a century before the discovery of the electrical form of energy led to its extensive exploitation. The DDT discovered in 1874 came to be put to practical use as an economical insecticide only as late as 1939. Thus development of the applied field in the universe of knowledge was also a slow and casual affair.

434   The Present and Organised Development

On the other hand, at the present time, when the essential needs have been shot up by population pressure to a high level, and even desirable needs are drawn by the spread of democracy to the level of essential needs, social pressure is leading to a conscious, organised and even State-planned development of the universe of knowledge, both in the fundamental and in the applied regions. The involuntary work of the stray genius is supplemented by the work of a hierarchy of persons of successive removes in the intellectual scale. With each man of genius is associated, directly or indirectly, an army of persons drawn from various intellectual strata, to complete the task by a large volume of routine research and pedestrian work. Taking Great Britain, for example, organised research man-power is said to be nearly fifty thousand strong and to include about ten thousand university graduates. And yet not a week passes without vehement protest against the perpetuation of the social prejudices of old, which keep away the abler brains from the research grid, set up for the development of the universe of knowledge in order to provide for essential and desirable human needs. The present awareness of the need to get the best out of even the lower quartiles in the intellectual scale is evidenced by the recent Productivity Drive. It seeks to improve efficiency even in the mechanical, repetitive sectors of the applied region by aggressive reference service and the production of new literature, written down to the level of the semi-intellectual technician and the non-intellectual common labourer, on every simple process in manufacturing work.

435 Research in Series

Further, wastage incidental to " Research in Parallel " is sought to be eliminated by organising " Research in Series." In spite of political barriers, except in the sector of Defence Science, there is a tendency to allow the research grid engaged on any subject to extend over the whole world. Recently, even nuclear physics is being brought into this category of subjects. Prompt communication of new thought through thousands of periodicals, hundreds of abstracting periodicals, and myriads of more rapid index-services almost abreast of the appearance of the original periodicals themselves, make it almost impossible to repeat any investigation needlessly, unless it is done deliberately for confirmation. The more radical results are even flashed round the world through the wireless.

I remember the immediate cabling, by an international news agency in 1928, of the discovery of a " New Radiation " by Raman announced by him in a public lecture at Bangalore. Several other scientists immediately turned their thought on the new radiation, which soon received the appropriate name of " Raman Effect." A few months later, Raman gave a course of lectures at the Madras University under the muffled title " Properties of Liquids." I obtained a preview of its subject-matter from Raman, and learned that it was to be on the application of Raman Effect. This made me prepare and mimeograph an exhaustive bibliography on the Raman Effect. About sixty papers had accumulated within a few weeks of its discovery, produced in different countries.

4351 SPEED OF DEVELOPMENT

During the last few decades research has been planned and arranged in series more consciously and thoroughly. As a result, research potential is less exposed to wastage. It is being used mainly for carrying development continuously ahead. Time-lag is reduced considerably in the application of new discoveries and inventions to beneficial social use. We see it illustrated in the rapid progress being made in the application of nuclear physics to nuclear engineering. Social pressure is causing the establishment, both at national and international levels, of a mixed agency for the promotion of research in series, financed and sponsored jointly by the State and private enterprise. Such an agency is intended to have at once the benefit of the resources, stability and freedom from profit motive characteristic of the State, and of the capacity to harness initiative, sensitiveness to success and failure, and persistence of effort characteristic of private enterprise. A case for this type of organisation to carry forward from fundamental research to the production of commodity or service has been made out in chapter 7 of Ranganathan's *Social education literature* (1952). The result of such strict organisation of research in series is considerable increase in the speed of development of the universe of knowledge.

436 Cycle of Development

Research in series, organised on a national or international basis, is leading to a cyclic movement of short period in the development of the universe of knowledge. As the movement is cyclic, we can begin its description at any point. Here is a description of the chief stages:

(1) Research in pure science—Fundamental Research,
(2) Application of the findings of fundamental research to a specific utility-field—Applied Research,
(3) Establishment of new process of production of an already known commodity or of a new commodity—Pilot Project,
(4) Design and production of new machinery;
(5) New material,
(6) New product,
(7) Using the new product—either an intermediate or an ultimate commodity,
(8) New problems created by the new product sooner or later,
(9) Fundamental research again to solve the new problems, and repetition of the cycle *ad infinitum*.

The above is presented schematically in the accompanying diagram. In the past, the period of the cycle was large—extending over centuries. But social urge caused by population pressure is progressively shortening its period. For example, within the last ten years nearly half the commodities in the chemical, textile and metal range have come to involve materials and processes developed since World War II. This war gave an extraordinary acceleration to this cyclic movement in the development of the universe of knowledge.

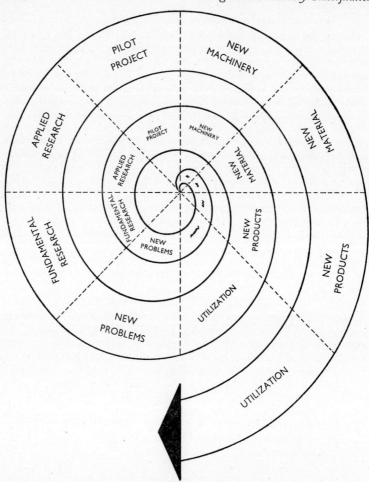

437 Dynamic Continuum

The Vedic Seers emphasised the inherent, though hidden, unity of the phenomenal world. This mystic experience had been re-lived and uttered by Francis Thompson in the rapturous lines of stanza 21 of his *Mistress of vision*:

> " All things by immortal power
> Near or far,
> Hiddenly
> To each other linked are,
> That thou canst not stir a flower
> Without troubling of a star."

In the intellectual recorded universe of knowledge, this phenomenon of inextricable interrelation is denoted by the term *Ekavakyata*. It emphasises that whatever the atomising mind might do, no subject can be developed without its calling for some development in every other subject sooner or later; in other words, the universe of knowledge is a continuum. In the past, at long intervals, the work of a powerful genius used to throw it into a state of turbulence. But the state of turbulence gave place to one of placidity in a fairly short time, and during long periods the universe of knowledge was mostly static; of course, it was a static continuum. But at present, organised research in series is producing a continuous cascade of new micro-thoughts, each stimulating another in succession in every region of knowledge. This cascade makes the universe of knowledge a dynamic continuum. Depth classification of micro-thought stems as a link in the chain of communication needed to prevent the reversion of research in series into research in parallel. This will be examined in the next chapter.

CHAPTER 44

CALL OF COMMUNICATION

441 Role of Communication in Research

IN THE DISTANT PAST, the rate of research was low. It was mostly isolated. The quantity of new thought to be absorbed by a research worker was small. As research work was largely confined to persons of great ability, practically every research worker could help himself by correspondence or personal contact. Socialised communication—that is, communication through print, available to any interested—was not much in demand for new micro-thought. Books were produced only for communication of macro-thought got by the accumulation and integration of micro-thought formed over several years. But the role of communication in the prompt dissemination of all nascent micro-thought becomes vital in the organisation of research in series. There should be no time-lag. Nor can there be any restriction in the flow of the results of research into any part of the world. Communication has, therefore, worked out for its channel thousands of periodicals, reports and pamphlets, produced either by conventional printing or by the quicker and cheaper near-printing processes. In *Abstracting services in medical sciences,* published in *Annals of library science,* Vol. 2, 1955, pages 89-96, Neelameghan estimates the number of medical periodicals to be 4,000. Even a subdivision like Ophthalmology has about 100 periodicals of its own. Through such channels, embodied micro-thought is flooding the world of research at the rate of nearly a hundred thousand papers a week. These large numbers have created new problems in making communication efficient. The workers get drowned, as it were, in this flood. A detailed discussion of the various factors in the efficient maintenance of communication will be found in chapters 31 and 32 of Ranganathan's *Classification and communication* (1951). We shall examine here only the factors of documentation and classification.

442 Role of Documentation in Communication

4421 DOCUMENTATION SERVICE

It has become impossible for each worker in a research team to scan all the recorded micro-thought, in order to spot out just those having a direct or indirect bearing on the specific subject of his pursuit. From the point of view of organisation also, it is uneconomical for each worker in a team to cut down his time from the positive pursuit of his subject and turn it on literature-search. Conservation of research-power, within a nation or in the world at large, calls for division of labour. It is more economical to set apart a special squad of persons for the sole work of literature-search. This is now being done in country after country, and in subject after subject on an international basis. The function of this squad is to scan all the current records of new micro-thought and to feed each research worker with appropriate documents on demand certainly, and in anticipation as well. This form of intensive reference service, with emphasis on micro-thought and even there on nascent thought, is called Documentation Service. Many business houses have established it, and Government departments have also begun to establish it. Curiously, it has been late in getting established in universities.

4422 Documentation Work

Experience has shown the value of a further division of labour among the members of the squad set apart for literature-search. There is found to be greater saving of man-hours and greater efficiency in the ultimate stage of reference service, if the articles, etc., are indexed as rapidly as they appear and a periodical list of them is produced for use in reference service and for circulation to the research workers and others interested. The release of the list should be nearly abreast of the release of most of the host periodicals. This preparatory work for documentation service is called Anticipatory Documentation Work. The list itself is called a Documentation List. Each entry may merely give the title and its location; or it may be annotated; or it may give an abstract. Such a list can be an economical proposition only if it has a large circulation. The present tendency is therefore to have National Documentation Centres—particularly for anticipatory documentation work on current publications. Its work has necessarily to be impersonal. The more intimate and personal documentation work made on demand, and/or more closely attuned to the investigation in progress—tailored documentation—is left to the care of the local library concerned.

4423 The Saving

An idea of the saving effected by documentation work can be got as follows. Let us assume that the average number of words in an article is 2,000. Let us also assume that the average number of words in its entry in a documentation list is twenty. Then, the extent of scanning to be done by a research worker or by the reference librarian on his behalf is reduced to $1/100$ by the establishment of documentation list.

443 Role of Classification in Documentation

The above figure gives the saving, when the documentation list is in dictionary form. If the list is in a broadly classified form, the saving will be greater. For definiteness, let us assume that the documentation list is thrown into 100 subject groups. Then, the extent of scanning to be done may be further reduced to 1/100 of what was reached in section 4423. This would mean $1/10^4$ of the extent needed for scanning the original articles. By increasing the minuteness of classification, the saving can be increased further. The saving will be not only in time but also in the cheer of the worker.

444 Apupa Pattern and the Ideal

The saving will be greatest if the classification is so detailed as to pin-point the very region of the list, presenting in continuous succession all the entries relevant to the work being pursued at the moment. Here we have to remember that picking out what is relevant in the universe of thought is often like pulling up grass by the roots. Though the stem looks unitary, the root has several ramifications and comes out of a scattered area as a complicated structure. It is not sufficient to present only the articles directly expounding the specific subject of pursuit. Let us call the specific subject the Umbral Region of the universe of knowledge, from the point of view of a particular seeker. Let us also call the region of the documentation list covered by the class number of that subject his Umbral Region of the list. He will be better helped if the list fans out on either side of the umbral region entries having successively a decreasing bearing on the specific subject. The two regions—on either side of the umbral region—may be called the Penumbral Regions of the list from the point of the seeker considered. The sequence of the class numbers covering the two penumbral regions may be said to be his Penumbral Class Numbers. The penumbral regions will ultimately thin out into Alien Regions in the list—that is, none of the entries in them will have any bearing whatever on the specific subject by the seeker under consideration. As he glances from one end to the other of the documentation list, he will pass successively through Alien, Penumbral, Umbral and again Penumbral and Alien regions. We may say that the list will present to him an " Apupa " Pattern. The ideal arrangement for the entries in a documentation list is the Everywhere-Apupa-Pattern. In other words, whatever specific subject is brought up as his umbral region by any worker, the list should present an apupa pattern to him.

445 Symbiosis with Catalogue and the Practicable

But the ideal of everywhere-apupa-pattern is not reachable in practice. For the universe of knowledge is multi-dimensional, whereas the universe of class numbers is one-dimensional. To use mathematical terminology, a space of many dimensions has to be mapped on, or transformed into, a space of one dimension. In any mapping, all the relations in the original configuration cannot be preserved; only a few can be kept as the invariant of the transformation. So it is in classification. The design of a scheme of classification depends on what is regarded as the minimum, essential invariant. The successive isolates in a chain within a facet, considered from the angle of the idea

plane, form a Nest of Cells in many dimensions. Viewed from the angle
of the notational plane, the nest gets transformed into a Nest of
Intervals on a line, lying one within another. A Nest of Isolates is kept
invariant in most of the known schemes of classification. In the
universe of knowledge—in a multi-dimensional space—a facet can
have many facets touching it—that is, contiguous to it. But when
transformed into the universe of class numbers—in the transformed
one-dimensional space—it can have only two facets contiguous to it.
The others will be separated from it. But no facet, not contiguous to
it in the original, will intervene between it and the transforms of the
other contiguous ones in the universe of class numbers. This is the
invariant property implied in the Canons for Filiatory Sequence. The
mathematics of this mapping has not yet been worked out in detail by
anybody. But what little has been said above is sufficient to show that
a set of class numbers cannot present an everywhere-apupa-pattern, for
all kinds of subject-approach. Therefore a scheme is obliged to do so
only for the most widely used approach. To satisfy the needs of the
other approaches, classification has to take the aid of the catalogue.
The approach not provided for by the classified part has to be provided
for in the second best way by the alphabetical part of the catalogue
giving class index entries according to the Chain Procedure based on
the class number. This is described in Ranganathan's *Classified
catalogue code,* ed. 3, 1951. Chain procedure has been found to be a
source of reciprocal help between classification and cataloguing. It is
therefore regarded as effecting symbiosis between classification and
cataloguing. This appears to be the only practical way of compensating
for the inevitable failure of everywhere-apupa-pattern.

446 Search by Machinery and Its Limitations

Much of the difficulty, due to classification being equivalent to the
mapping of a multi-dimensional space over a one-dimensional one,
arises in the synthesis of the facets. If there are n facets in a micro-
thought, a scheme has to chose forcedly one of the $n!$ ways of arranging
them in the class number. For those seeking the documents on it, *via*
the chosen sequence of facets, the classified part of the catalogue gives
exhaustive help immediately. But, if the approach is *via* any other
permutation of the facets, all the documents will not be found entered
in consecutive entries. The different places where the entries will be
found should be first located with the aid of a few class index entries.
But if machinery is used—be it anything from a hand-sorted punched
card to an electronic rapid selector—the entries are picked out
exhaustively with equal facility whatever be the sequence of the facets
used in the approach. This is so because search by machinery bypasses
the need for the synthesis of the facets. The irrelevant entries that
happen to be picked up are negligibly few. But the entries will fail to
give a panoramic view of the distinctive apupa pattern of the seeker.
It is known that such a view is convenient, if not essential, in the

determination and formulation of the exact requirement of the seeker, jointly by the reference librarian and the seeker. This has been shown by a number of case studies in Ranganathan's *Reference service and bibliography* (1939). Moreover in a documentation list for circulation, the machinery for search cannot be of avail; and a classified arrangement is essential; this means that the forced choice of one of the many possible sequences of the facets is inevitable.

447 Role of Depth Classification

Thus all the steps of the procedure prescribed for an analytico-synthetic classification, including the step of synthesis, are necessary in the preparation of a documentation list. In the case of machinery for search also, the steps of facet analysis and determination of the isolate number in each facet are necessary. For any machinery needs these isolate numbers to be determined, before they can be coded on the binary or any other scale needed by it. The sharpness of the focus in each facet should be fully reached both in the idea and in the notational planes. Thus depth classification has a definite role to play in the effective communication of micro-thought in an organisation for research in series, whether the tool for search be the catalogue or some machinery.

CHAPTER 45

ARRAYS AND CHAINS

451 Arrays

IN DEPTH CLASSIFICATION, there is need for a far greater number of foci in the arrays of main classes and canonical classes than in superficial classification. The emergence of new main classes and canonical classes has been caused by literary warrant from time to time, in past ages. It will be so in the future also. This has been explained and illustrated in sections 3634 and 3645. We have not yet got any definite guiding principles to help us in finding a more or less helpful place for a new class in such arrays. Moreover, the devices available now in the notational plane are not sufficient to implement the findings of the idea plane. But the breakdown of a scheme on this ground will not occur often. There are two reasons for this. Firstly, one need not be as meticulous in the arrangement of basic classes as in that of isolates in an array of a facet. Secondly, new basic classes emerge only at long intervals. We are now in an epoch of their emergence. The formation of a new zone to accommodate them, with the aid of the simple notational device of packeted notation, has been suggested in sections 3634 and 3635.

452 Chains

The choice of relevant characteristics for classification has been systematised to some extent by the postulate of the five Fundamental Categories. The sequence of relevant characteristics also has been systematised, though to a less extent, by another set of postulates. But the choice of the characteristics for division within a facet is now left to unaided judgment. It is so with the sequence of the chosen characteristics also. In spite of this, the chains in the earlier facets are easily hit upon so as to be helpful. In other words, the formation of chains in superficial classification has not given much difficulty. This is due to two reasons. Firstly, literary warrant is plentiful to guide judgment. Secondly, the chains in the earlier facets are usually worked out by the classificationist. These are not left to the ordinary classifier in any scheme. As stated in the subsections of section 1288, the classificationist works largely through intuition. Both of these favourable factors fail progressively with the depth at which the chain in a facet has to be designed. Perhaps continued experience, gained by

257

trial and error, in depth classification may in course of time give enough facts, from which some helpful principles of guidance can be generalised.

453 Time Facet

4531 BOUNDED DURATION

In the classification of Time, the C.C. enumerates in each array only a particular unit of time—be it a geological age, a millennium, a century or a decade or a year. The U.D.C. does similarly. In superficial classification, as needed for macro-thought, it is found sufficient to represent in the time isolate number the latest point of time touched in the subject. But in depth classification, it is found necessary to represent both the beginning and the end of a stretch of time. In other words, a bounded duration should be truly represented.

The U.D.C. uses the inclusive notation for the purpose. The isolate number is formed out of the beginning point and the end point of the stretch of time by connecting them with a slant stroke. Classes with such a notation will get arranged by the beginning point in the stretch of time represented. Classes with the same beginning point of time will get arranged by the ordinal value of the representative of the end point.

U.D.C. No.	Isolate	U.D.C. No.	Isolate
15/17	16th to 18th century	16/18	17th to 19th century
15/18	16th to 19th century	160/165	1600-1650
16	17th century	17/18	18th and 19th century

The arrangement of the second to the sixth isolates in the above table violates the Canon of Decreasing Extension. Moreover, the majority of readers will find it more helpful if isolates with the same end points of time are arranged together. Such an arrangement is seen in the Colon Classification.

The C.C. uses the symbol " ← " as the digit to connect the end points of time. The end point of time comes to the left of the arrow. The beginning point of time comes to the right of the arrow.

C.C. No.	Isolate	C.C. No.	Isolate
K	17th century	M←J	16th to 19th century
K5←Ko	1600-1650	M←K	17th to 19th century
L←J	16th to 18th century	M←L	18th and 19th century

The notational system of the C.C. secures the sequence preferred in the earlier paragraph. It satisfies the Canon of Decreasing Extension. The relative helpfulness of the sequences in the examples of this section needs study.

4532   Past and Future

In depth classification there is need to represent " past " and " future." The U.D.C. makes the following provision for this.

311   Past (bygone times, once).
312   Present (actual times, now).
313   Future (Forecast, predictions, prophecy, later on).

The provision of a special number for Present appears to be redundant. The present can be represented by the actual number arrived at as for public time. Again, Past and Future are relative terms. They do not become precise unless they are used in relation to a particular point of time. Thus the above specification becomes ineffective.

The prescription of the C.C. avoids these faults. It uses the symbols " ← " and " → " as the digits to show past and future. Either of these symbols should be preceded by the point of time used as reference. If 1954 is the year of reference, we have

N54← Past
N54→ Future

4533   Private Time

Public time is generally measured from the date of birth of Jesus Christ as origin. But this may be too cumbersome in fixing the time isolate in certain subjects. It may be useful to measure time from an epoch inherent to the subject itself. The unit of time for forming isolates in the first order array will also have to be fixed differently for different subjects. Both public and private time will be necessary in depth classification.

45331   Origin

In the biography of a person, it is more convenient to use his year of birth as origin. We speak of the first twenty years, the last ten years and so on. In speaking of the reign of a British monarch, we use the year of his ascending the throne. We speak of the twentieth year of the reign and so on. Similarly in the history of an institution, it is convenient to take the year of its foundation as the origin. In the case of history of the foetus, it is convenient to take the approximate time of fertilisation as the origin. In the natural history of bacteria, the hour of starting a culture is a more convenient origin. In the study of experimental pharmacology, the time of the intake or injection of the drug is the helpful origin for measuring time. In the study of fundamental particles in physics, the time of fission or formation of the particle is the natural origin of time in the study of its life-period.

45332   Unit

In private time, the helpful unit of duration to form the isolates will not be the same in all cases. It may vary from as small as a microsecond in the case of fundamental particles to as much as a geological age in the case of the formation of mineral oil. It is therefore necessary to make the first order array of private time facet consist of isolates made of units of time. Perhaps these may be arranged in the ascending sequence of their size. In fact both ascending and descending sequences are equally helpful. In the C.C., zone 1 of array of order 1 is partly used to accommodate these units of time. In U.D.C., the isolate number 4 is used to represent the quasi characteristic " Duration of Time," which is used in the sense of " Unit of Time."

C.C. No.	Isolate (Unit of Time)	U.D.C. No.	C.C. No.	Isolate (Unit of Time)	U.D.C. No.
a	Period		*h*	Month	44
b	Microsecond	411	*j*	Year	45
c	Second	412	*k*	Century	47
d	Minute	413	*m*	Millennium	48
e	Hour	414	*n*	Geological age	49
f	Day	414.2			
g	Week	43			

The number of units of duration should be added after the digit denoting the unit of duration.

4534   Featured Time

Time is punctuated by the movement of earth and moon. These movements are periodical. Day is the period of rotation of the earth on its axis. Lunar month is the period of one perambulation of the moon on its ecliptic. Year is the period of one perambulation of the earth on its ecliptic. These are the three primary periods of time. The very astronomical factors causing these periods cause also some climatic correlates. These concern heat, light, atmospheric movement, humidity variation, cloud, fog, rain, dust, etc. The total effect of these correlates divide each natural period of time into more or less distinct parts. Most activities—in the physical, plant, animal, human and social world—are correlated to these parts of each kind of period of time. These form important isolate ideas in the time facet of many subjects. Depth classification should take them into consideration. It will be an advantage to provide a schedule for them. In the C.C., the unoccupied later part of zone 1 of array of order 1 in the time facet is used for the purpose. In U.D.C., the array derived from the quasi isolates " 3 Subdivision of time from different points of view " and " 4 Duration of time " are used for the purpose. In depth classification, occasion may arise also for other natural periods, such as those associated with the other heavenly bodies, the precession of the axis of the earth, and other cosmic phenomena.

In some subjects, featured time may have to be used as a second level of time.

C.C. No.	Isolate	U.D.C. No.	C.C. No.	Isolate	U.D.C. No.
p	Day	414.2	t	Solar month	33
q	Day-time	414.21	t_1	January	330.1
q_1	Morning twi-light		t_2	February	330.2
q_2	Sunrise	414.211		*** *** ***	
q_3	Morning	414.211	t_8	August	330.8
q_4	Forenoon	414.211	t_{91}	September	330.9
q_5	Noon	414.212	t_{92}	October	331.0
q_6	Afternoon	414.213	t_{92}	November	33.11
q_7	Evening	414.221	t_{93}	December	33.12
r	Night	414.2	u	Season	32
r_1	Sunset		u_1	Spring	321
r_2	Evening twi-light		u_3	Summer	322
r_3	Early night	414.221	u_5	Autumn	323
r_4	Fore-midnight	414.221	u_7	Winter	324
r_5	Midnight	414.22	u_{91}	Dry season	
r_6	After-midnight	414.223	u_{95}	Wet season	
r_7	Late night	414.223	w	Periods relative to other heavenly bodies	
s	Lunar month		w_1	Mercury	
s_1	Waxing moon		w_2	Venus	
s_2	New moon		w_3	Mars	
s_3	First half		w_4	Jupiter	
s_4	Second half		w_5	Saturn	
s_5	Waning moon		w_6	Uranus	
s_6	Full moon		w_7	Neptune	
s_7	First half		w_8	Solar pheno-mena	
s_8	Second half		w_{91}	Ascending node of ecliptic	
			w_{92}	Descending node	
			x	Precession period	
			y	Other cosmic periods	
			z	(Octavising digit)	

454 Space Facet

4541 WORLD

In superficial classification adequate for macro-thought embodied in books, the conventional division of the world into continents, countries and constituent states is usually sufficient. These divisions occupy zone 2 of their respective arrays in the notational plane. In particular, the array of continents stands telescoped into the same array as "World," since the latter needs only one place in its own array. In depth classification, need will often arise for divisions of the world on the basis of other characteristics, such as orientation, near-world-state formation, minerals, crops, and political, economic and social and other similar factors.

In the C.C., zones 3 and 4 are used for the purpose in the array of order 2 having "1 World" as its immediate universe. The following schedule is illustrative, and the U.D.C. number also is given wherever possible.

C.C. No.	Isolate	U.D.C. No.	C.C. No.	Isolate	U.D.C. No.
11	Eastern hemisphere *** *** ***		1N	League of Nations Countries	100″19″
14	Northern hemisphere		1N4	United Nations Countries	100″194″
16	Atlantic countries	100:261/264	1N48	The Commonwealth Countries	100″1948″
17	Pacific countries	100:265/266	1(F	Industrialised Countries	
192	Tropical zone	213	1(H7160	Uranium Areas	
195	Temperate zone	212	1(J381	Rice Belt	
198	Arctic zone	211.1	1(JA	Forest Areas	
19B	East *** *** ***	100-11	1(P23	Spanish-speaking Countries	100=60
19W	North East	100-18	1(Q7	Islamic Countries	
19X	Inside	100-191	1(W87	Colonies	100-52 (?)
19Y	Surrounding	100-192	1(Y:41	Under-developed Countries	
19Z	Outside	100-194			

Examples of the use of this schedule follow.

C.C. No.	Subject	U.D.C. No.
L57.195	Personal hygiene in temperate region	613(212)
T.1N48.N5	Education in the Commonwealth up to 1950's	37(100-41 " 1948 ") " 195 "
T.1(W87).N5	Education in colonies, up to 1950's	37(100-52) " 195 "
T.1(Y:41).N5	Education in under-developed countries up to 1950's	
V1N48:55. N5	Franchise in the Commonwealth, up to 1950's	324(100-41 " 1948 ") " 195″
V1(W87):55. N5	Franchise in colonies, up to 1950's	324(100-52) " 195 "
X:5.1(X6.73) 9Z.N5	Commerce of non-dollar areas, up to 1950's	
X:6.1(Y:41). N5	Capital in under-developed countries, up to 1950's	
Y:71.1(J381	Vitality of the community in the rice belt	

4542 COUNTRY

Any continent, country or any geographical area may be divided on the basis of diverse characteristics, such as those indicated above for the world. But in the notational plane, zone 2 is not available for such divisions. It is proposed to make the divisions of 9A in zone 3 take as subdivisions any of the categories corresponding to the divisions in zone 2 of the world given in the above section. But the occasion for their use may be little. Another way of dividing a country or a constituent state is likely to arise for administrative purposes, e.g. Fifth Engineering Circle; North-East Railway Zone; and North Revenue Division. The U.D.C. has provided a schedule of hyphenated numbers to be used as special analytical divisions in the space facet to meet such problems in depth classification. In the C.C. it is proposed to make the divisions of 9A in zone 3 take as subdivisions any such special administrative divisions. It is believed that no case will arise when both of the uses of 9A proposed in this section will occur in the same host class.

Examples

C.C. No.	Subject	U.D.C. No.
JB.4411	Forest in Madras State	634.9(5481)
JB.44119A5	Forest in the Fifth Forest Circle of Madras State	634.9(5481-035)
X415.449A8	Railway in the North-West Railway Zone of India	656.2(54-038)

455 Energy Facet

According to the postulate 7 given in section 3535, there will be no chain in an Energy facet. Therefore the only problem to be considered is that of array. The occupation of an Energy array has been prescribed by schedule for the superficial classification of many of the basic classes. Zone 2 proves sufficient in most cases. But in depth classification there will be need to occupy all the other zones also.

4551 ZONE 1: POSTERIORISING COMMON ENERGY ISOLATE

According to the finding in section 3622, zone 1 should be given over to (ECI), that is Enumerated Common Isolates. In this case, they become Common Energy Isolates. In C.C. their isolate numbers will begin with a Roman small, but the Roman small's anteriorising quality is inoperative, as it will be preceded by the connecting symbol colon and a number ending with a connecting symbol cannot be a class number by itself. Thus a common energy isolate is a posteriorising one. In depth classification, there will be need to occupy zone 1 more fully than in superficial classification. In the latter, it is only the isolate " Criticism " that is usually incident. Therefore, the other isolates have not been scheduled fully. In Ranganathan's *Depth classification* (5), published in *Annals of library science*, Vol. 1, 1954, pages

129-136, it has been conjectured that there may be need for different schedules suited to three kinds of activity, viz. intellectual procedure, commodity production and organisational work. It needs investigation how many isolates will recur in all the three schedules. "Criticism," for example, is likely to be one of them. If such recurring isolates are only a few, the isolates for each kind of activity may occupy the whole of zone 1, providing the same digit for a recurring isolate. On the other hand, if all the isolates will be demanded by one and the same host-class, the digits in zone 1 will have to be divided among them, and the base of the Roman smalls will be too small. In that case, there will be need for the numbers of the zone to be constructed on a two-digit basis. These possible alternatives are yet to be examined.

4552   Zones 2, 3 and 4

Postulate 7 of section 3535 implies that the octave device should be used in zone 2, if the number of (ESI)—that is, Enumerated Special Isolates—exceeds eight. If their number exceeds twenty-four, the octave device is uneconomical, but postulate 7 prevents the use of group notation.

It is possible to use zone 3 also for (ESI), because an energy isolate is not likely to be formed by alphabetical or chronological device. This possibility gives rise to a suggestion. There will be on the whole five octaves for the accommodation of (ESI) in an energy array. Can we specialise each of these octaves for isolates of particular kinds—say, 1 for preliminary operations in general and the other seven places in octave 1 for the individual preliminary operations; octave 2 for the primary operations; octave 3 for the secondary operations; penultimate octave for the finishing operations; and last octave for adaptations to specialised uses? These terms are meaningful in the case of commodity production; but corresponding terms can be found to represent the seminal ideas behind them, when they are applied to the other two kinds of activities. This suggestion needs to be experimented upon in the basic classes not yet fitted with energy schedules and presenting too many isolates for the three octaves of zone 2 and the two of zone 3.

Zone 4 may have to be reserved for the normal use of accommodating (DCI), that is, common isolates to be got by subject device.

456   Matter Facet

The Matter facet is not much in use in superficial classification, but it is bound to be much in demand in depth classification. A profitable utilisation of all the four zones needs examination.

4561   Zone 1: Posteriorising Common Matter Isolate

The suggestion made in section 3541 leads to the proposal that attributes of a physical, chemical or biological nature, and of the nature of value, may be looked upon as common matter isolates and accommodated in zone 1 of array 1 of the Matter facet. These will, of course, be posteriorising common isolates, even as common energy isolates are and for reasons similar to those given in section 4551. The isolates in this zone will be very large in number, therefore several arrays may be necessary. Each letter in the array of order 1 may represent a group of attributes or values which can be correlated more or less to the traditional main classes. Each of these may be subdivided on the basis of some suitable characteristic. Such a comprehensive schedule is yet to be constructed, but here is a short illustrative schedule of that kind.

c	Physical properties	$r4$	Ethical value
$c4$	Thermal properties	$r5$	Aesthetic value
$c433$	Specific heat	s	Psychological value
$c47$	Thermodynamic properties	t	Educational value
$c475$	Free energy	y	Social value

When applied to materials, these isolates will occur in the second level of the Matter facet.

4562 Zones 2, 3 and 4

The number of materials figuring in depth classification will be very large. But in a particular basic or host class, only a limited number of materials will be relevant. It is only these that will have great literary warrant. The number of such may not exceed the capacity of the three octaves of zone 2. Therefore they may be numbered by the favoured category device. This schedule has yet to be constructed for various host-classes.

Many artificial materials may figure in certain host-classes. Such artificial materials will appear from time to time and also disappear from use similarly. It is likely that they have international trade names. If so, they may be given isolate numbers by the alphabetical device. If not, they may be given isolate numbers by the chronological device. The former class of materials will be accommodated in the last octave of zone 3; and the latter in the penultimate octave of the same zone.

Occasionally, certain materials not chosen for zone 2 or 3 may figure in any host subject. It will be a convenience to have, for this purpose, a more or less exhaustive schedule of materials. It will be an advantage to make this schedule correspond to the schedule of Useful Arts suggested in section 36435. Then, the number for any additional unusual material of a host-class may be enclosed within brackets and accommodated in zone 4.

457 Personality Facet

The personality facet has been worked out fairly fully for superficial classification. The only additional work to be done is to lengthen the chain whenever depth classification needs it, in zone 2. Zone 3 of the first round first level of the personality facet has been put to another use—accommodation of systems and specials, which are of help in depth classification. The chief work to be done is to work out a schedule for zone 1—in other words, for posteriorising common personality isolates. The C.C. has worked out a schedule for institutions. These isolates are to come only after space facet. We have yet to construct a schedule for use in zone 1 of array of order 1 in the second and later personality facets in a round.

458 Common Isolate

A blind tradition has persisted through several decades in regard to the schedule of common subdivisions, also called form divisions. This schedule has all along been a hotchpotch. The development of depth classification of micro-thought for documentation purposes has high-lighted the irrationality of it. It has been critically examined in the following papers of Ranganathan:

Optional facets (6), published in *Abgila*, Vol. 1, 1950, page 161 *et seq.*

Annual report (4) to F.I.D./C.A., published by the F.I.D. as its documentat F54-40.

Depth classification (3), published in the *Annals of library science,* Vol. 1, 1954, pages 65-80.

Depth classification (5), published in the *Annals of library science,* Vol. 1, 1954, pages 129-136.

Common isolates in documentation, published in the *Review of documentation,* Vol. 22, 1955, pages 18-25.

The last of these is expected to be continued in a few more articles. These studies show that a heterogeneous set of categories has been generally billeted in one schedule. The remarks against some of the form divisions of U.D.C., given below, will make this statement clear.

U.D.C. No.	Name of Form Division	Remarks
22	Books of intermediate range	This does not relate to subject-matter, but the extent of coverage
247	Books for children	This relates to the standard of treatment
3	Encyclopaedia	Reference book, which is helpfully kept before ordinary books on the subject concerned
41	Pamphlet	This does not relate to the subject matter, but to the physical size of the book
42	Lecture	This relates to the form of exposition
43	Newspaper article	This refers to the place of occurrence
486	Abridged edition	This amounts to a related book
5	Periodical	A type of publication, which is looked up but not continuously read
58	Year book	Reference book, which is helpfully kept before the ordinary books on the subject concerned
592	Tear-off calendar	Is this to be classified as a book?
6	Publication of society	This relates to authorship or sponsoring. Is it necessary to classify by author or sponsor?
753	School books for inter-mediate classes	This relates to standard

U.D.C. No.	Name of Form Division	Remarks
841.22	Cinema film	This relates to the physical form and not to the subject
841.7	Block for printing	This relates to the physical form of the document. Is it to be treated as a document at all?
844	Atlas	Reference book
861	Gummed document	This relates to the physical form of the document
867	Gramophone record	This relates to the physical form of the document
891	Artificially formed collection	This relates only to the assembly of documents into a collection, and not to subject-content

4581 TYPES OF COMMON SUBDIVISIONS

It is convenient to recognise four kinds of common subdivisions and to have each kind scheduled separately. These have been discussed in several sections of this book as shown below:

Schedule of subdivisions concerning the	To be called Schedule of	And discussed in this book in section or chapter
(1) Physical form of document	Collection Number	67
(2) Language, form of exposition, mutual relation, etc. of documents	Book Number	66
(3) Documents which it is helpful to arrange anterior to ordinary ones on the subject concerned	Anterior Common Isolates	4582
(4) Thought-content of documents, not needing anterior position	Posterior Common Isolates	Several chapters of Parts 2 to 4

Kinds 3 and 4 belong to class number. A combination of class number, book number and collection number is called call number. This is discussed in detail in chapter 68. The terms Isolate and Common Isolate have been defined in section 345, and the latter may be repeated here for ready reference: if the same isolate number represents the same isolate term and denotes the same isolate idea, in its occurrence as or in a facet of all or at least many host-classes, the isolate is a Common Isolate.

4582 ANTERIOR COMMON ISOLATE

We may use the significant term " Approach Materials " to denote the documents which it is helpful to place anterior to the ordinary reading materials on the subject contained. These are: bibliography, cyclopaedia, directory and all other kinds of ready-reference materials; periodical, report of conference and other quasi reference materials; and biography, anthology, syllabus and other materials which are also looked up and not continuously read, even as in the case of the above-mentioned two kinds.

45821   Colon Classification

As stated in section 3322, the C.C. secures anterior position to approach material by representing the anteriorising isolate in its class number by a Roman small and postulating that a Roman small has anteriorising value. Thus B9*a* " Bibliography of astronomy " has precedence over B9 " Astronomy," L:4:6*k* " Cyclopaedia of thera-peutics " has precedence over L:4:6 " Therapeutics," and SO*b*Z*m* " Periodical on legal psychology " has precedence over So*b*Z " Legal psychology." This neat and economical notational device is a valuable contribution of the C.C. It avoids the use of a connecting symbol.

45822   Bibliographic Classification

The B.C. represents a common subdivision by an Arabic numeral and invests it with anteriorising value. But it is halting in this pres-cription, for we read in page 49 of Vol. 1, " But this disposition is not required by rule. If the classifier should disagree, if the readers should disapprove, the strict logical subordination is alternative . . . the numerical subdivisions would then not be anterior but posterior like the other subdivisions." In this respect, the B.C. does not want to give a firm decision in the idea plane. However, it has provided for the implementing of a decision prescribing anterior position to approach material.

45823   U.D.C.

The U.D.C. does not now have a notational device to secure anterior position for approach material. However, its notation is easily adapted for the purpose. It uses bracket zero (0 . . .) as connecting symbol for a common isolate number. Accordingly, the following recommendation was made to F.I.D./C.C., the Committee of F.I.D. on U.D.C., by F.I.D./C.A., the Committee on General Theory of Classification:

(1) It is helpful to secure that the approach materials—such as bibliography, encyclopaedia, yearbook—on any class precede the general works on the class.

(2) This will be of help in (1) shelf arrangement, (2) arrangement of documents in vertical files and (3) arrangement of entries in catalogues and bibliographies.

(3) If (1) and (2) are approved, it is necessary for the notation of a scheme of classification to secure the sequence mentioned in (1).

(4) This is secured by the Bibliographic Classification and the Colon Classification, by giving " anteriorising quality " to the digit rep-resenting a common isolate (=common subdivision).

(5) A similar implementation of the idea mentioned in (1) can be secured in U.D.C. by giving the connecting symbol (0 . . .) anteriorising quality.

(6) The adoption of the suggestion contained in (5) will not affect any of the existing U.D.C. numbers; nor will it be a handicap to the progressive amplification of the U.D.C. schedules.

4583 POSTERIOR COMMON ISOLATE
45831 Space and Time Isolates

All the space and time isolates in C.C. and U.D.C. satisfy the definition of common isolate. The addition of such isolates to a class gives a local or an historical treatment of the class. The resulting class should therefore come only after the host-class itself. Therefore, space and time isolates are posteriorising common isolates. The insertion of a connecting symbol between the host-class number and the space or time isolate number secures for the resulting class number a position posterior to the host-number. In the B.C., the space isolate gets this treatment, but the time isolate is not made a common isolate. For each subject, a separate time schedule has to be constructed, and special time schedules must be constructed for the history of each country. For it is stated, " History of each country has its own periods, and these are often incommensurate with centuries." By providing a separate schedule for each country and for each subject, the time isolate number is made of one digit in most cases. In the C.C. and U.D.C., it needs a minimum of three digits. Is it worth seeking economy in the number of digits in this case, or is it better to reduce schedule length by making the time isolate a common isolate? This is a moot point. Further, the former course puts too much responsibility on the classificationist and takes away from the autonomy of the classifier.

45832 Energy, Matter, and Personality Common Isolates

The facets of the fundamental categories Energy, Matter and Personality present both common and special isolates. The former are posteriorising ones for reasons similar to those mentioned in section 45832. These have been discussed in sections 362, 455, 456 and 457. Considerable work remains to be done on these schedules.

CHAPTER 46

ROUNDS, LEVELS, AND PHASES

461 Rounds

IN SUPERFICIAL CLASSIFICATION, found sufficient for books embodying macro-thought, only a few basic classes present more than one round. Agriculture, Animal Husbandry, Medicine, Sociology and Law are these subjects. But this is not sufficient for depth classification of micro-thought. According to postulate 9, given in section 3561, a new round is started by an Energy isolate. It is with such a round that we are concerned in this chapter. The chief problem in the theory of rounds concerns the round to which a personality or a matter facet should be assigned—the round preceding or succeeding the energy isolate starting the latter.

4611 POSTULATE 19

One set of these facets is subjected to the action represented by the energy isolate; we shall call any such facet an Actand. The other set consists of the actor or the instrument used in the action. Experience with the rounds occurring in superficial classification suggests the following postulate:

Postulate 19.—An Actand facet should precede, and an Actor or Instrument facet should succeed, the Energy (Action) isolate concerned.

For example, when " Weaving " or " Spinning " is the energy isolate, " Cotton " is the actand; it should therefore precede the isolate " Weaving " or " Spinning." But the " Loom " or the " Spindle " is the instrument; therefore either of these should come after the energy isolate concerned. Again, in Tuberculosis of the lungs, "(production of) disease" is the action; "Lungs" are the actand; and the " tubercular micro-organism " is the actor; therefore " Lungs " precedes " Disease," and the " Micro-organism " succeeds it.

4612 POSTULATE 20

There is also another kind of experience. One set of facets is the result of the action; we shall call any such facet a Product. Another set of facets is the instrument with which the product is made. Experience with such cases, in superficial classification, suggests the following postulate:

Postulate 20.—The Product facet should precede, and the Instrument facets should succeed, the Energy (Action) isolate concerned, when the Product is an ultimate commodity.

For example, Bread precedes Baking, while the utensil, fire, etc., succeed it.

4613 Convention

The fields of application of postulates 19 and 20 have to be distinguished by convention. Postulate 20 is to be applied only when an ultimate commodity is the product. When no commodity is the result of action or the product is only an intermediate commodity, postulate 19 is to be applied. Let us illustrate. In spinning, " Yarn " is the product. It is only an intermediate commodity, therefore " Cotton," the actand, will come in the round preceding the energy isolate " Spinning." The instrument " Spindle " will come in the succeeding round. " Yarn " itself will come only in the later round started by the energy isolate " Recovery of product." So also with the energy isolate " Weaving " and the resulting intermediate commodity " Cloth." But in " Tailoring," " Clothes " is the ultimate commodity. Therefore, the " Clothes " produced, say Coat, will come in the round preceding the energy isolate—be it " Cutting " or " Stitching " or any other operation. Let us next consider " Tuberculosis of lungs." Here, there is no commodity resulting from the action. The action is " causing of Disease." The actand is " Lungs." The actor is the " Micro-organism " concerned. Therefore the personality isolate " Lungs " precedes the energy isolate " Disease," and the personality isolate " Micro-organism " succeeds the energy isolate. Postulate 20 is not applicable, and only postulate 19 is applicable.

462 Levels

In superficial classification, found sufficient for books embodying macro-thought, only a few basic classes present more than one level. Even that is only in round 1. Literature present four levels of personality, viz. language, form, author and work. But this is not sufficient for the depth classification of micro-thought. Criteria or conventions have to be established to utilise the concept of levels, as applied to the different fundamental categories in different rounds. Some results have been so far obtained about time and space levels, and much less about matter and personality levels in round 1.

463 Time Levels

It is possible for featured time, scheduled in section 4534, to occur in the second level of time, apart from its appearing in the first level itself. The following examples will show it.

C.C. No.	Subject	U.D.C. No.	No. of Time-Level
U2855.4411	Rainfall in Madras	551.578(548.1)	nil
U2855.4411.q6	Afternoon shower in Madras	551.578(548.1)"414.213"	1
U2855.4411.u3	Summer shower in Madras	551.578(548.1)"322"	1
U2855.4411.u3.q6	Afternoon summer shower in Madras	551.578(548.1)"322:414.213"	2
U2855.4411.N56	Rainfall in Madras in 1956	551.578(548.1)"1956"	1
U2855.4411.N56.u3	Summer shower in Madras in 1956	551.578(548.1)"1956:322"	2
U2855.4411.N56.u3.q6	Afternoon summer shower in Madras in 1956	551.578(548.1)"1956:322:414.213"	3

The Principle of Decreasing Extension is applied to determine the sequence in which the different time levels should be packed—or, in other words, in determining the syntactical arrangement of the different levels of time facet.

464 Space Levels

Depth classification will have to draw upon the second level of space facet described and called physiographic or featured space in sections 3522 and 3523.

The following schedule of assorted isolates will show the difference between C.C. and U.D.C. in the sequence in which space levels are packed.

C.C. No.	Category	U.D.C. No.	U.D.C. No.	Category	C.C. No.
4.2	Mountains of Asia	235	234	Mountains of Europe	5.2
4.6	Rivers of Asia	282.25	235	Mountains of Asia	4.2
5.2	Mountains of Europe	234	252.3:6	Deserts of Africa	6.121
5.6	Rivers of Europe	282.24	282.24	Rivers of Europe	5.6
6.121	Deserts of Africa	252.3:6	282.25	Rivers of Asia	4.6

The above examples show that physiographical divisions are put in level 2 in C.C., but in level 1 in U.D.C. The left half of the table shows the sequence of the categories formed in C.C. The right half of the table shows the sequence according to U.D.C. In the latter, the sequence has been determined by the notational exigency created by its D.C. core in dividing the main class " History ". Digits 3 to 9 have been used for regional divisions. The digit 2 only is available to represent physiographic features. In C.C., the sequence of the levels has been decided in the idea plane itself. A mountain is a part of a continent, while a continent is not a part of a mountain. The notational plane has merely implemented the decision made in the idea plane.

4641 ZONES IN ARRAY OF NEXT ORDER

In depth classification, there will be need to further subdivide the physiographic divisions enumerated in section 3523, on the basis of diverse characteristics. For example, mountains may have to be divided on the basis of height as hillocks, hills, medium high, high, and so on. They may have to be divided also on the basis of their length, geological formation, and other characteristics. Moreover, individual mountains should be given distinctive numbers. In the C.C., all these are provided for in the array following the isolate " Mountain." Zone 2 of this array accommodates quasi isolates such as height, length and geological feature. The last octave in zone 3 individualises particular mountains by the alphabetical device. In the U.D.C., kinds of mountains are differentiated by the addition of another facet made of the " Special analytical subdivisions applicable throughout (23) " given in page 22 of U.D.C., English edition, 1943, Vol. 1, page 1. The different kinds of mountains consist of " wholes of mountains." Therefore, the formation of a new facet to represent them is not in accordance with the general criterion laid down in section 3507 and its subdivisions for change of facet. Further, the enumeration of individual mountains with *ad hoc* numbers makes it impracticable to provide numbers for all mountains. These differences between the C.C. and U.D.C. occur also in regard to every other physiographic division.

C.C. No.	Category	U.D.C. No.
4.213	Low mountains of Asia	235.01
4.218	High mountains of Asia	235.03
4.2A	Altai	235.22
4.2H	Himalaya	235.248
44.2	Mountains of India	235.5
44.213	Low mountains of India	235.5.01
44.218	High mountains of India	235.5.03
44.2A	Aravalli mountains	?
44.2V	Vindhya mountains	?
4411.2	Mountains of Madras	?
4411.2K	Kolli hill	?
4411.2	Servarai hill	?

The use of alphabetical device enables the classifier to construct the number for any mountain, big or small, without the need for their being enumerated in the schedule by the classificationist. Neither this hospitality nor this autonomy of the classifier is possible in U.D.C. The C.C. numbers imply a prescription of the idea plane—viz. the extension of the isolate in the first level facet of a mountain should be the minimum consistent with the isolate in the second level facet falling more or less entirely within the former. It may be a continent, a country, a constituent state, a district, or a division of a district, etc. The isolate numbers in the first level facet are merely those in the commonly used geographical schedule. But in the U.D.C., special divisions are enumerated for each continent, in the case of each physiographic feature. For examples, in 234.65 Mountains of Scotland, 465 is Scotland, but in 287.242.1 Rivers of Scotland, 421 is Scotland, and in 4/9 Places in the modern world, 411 is Scotland. It is doubtful if there is sufficient advantage in such a deviation from the Canon of Scheduled Mnemonics in this respect.

4642   THIRD LEVEL SPACE FACET

In depth classification, there may be need to add one more level in the case of certain physiographic formations like mountain and river. The array of order 1 in this facet may have its zone 2 occupied by quasi isolates such as vertical zones, longitudinal zones, transverse zones and other appropriate ones. The C.C. would use a third level space schedule for the purpose. The U.D.C. does so in the case of mountain only. In the case of river, it merely adds another array as shown in the schedule given below. As the different parts of a river do not each form the whole river, the use of another array in this case is at variance with the criterion given in section 3505 for the addition of an array instead of a facet.

C.C. No.	Category	U.D.C. No.	C.C. No.	Category	U.D.C. No.
4.2H	Himalaya	235.248	5.6D	Danube	282.243.7
4.2H.12	Tree zone	235.248.071	5.6D.21	Source	282.243.71
4.2H.15	Treeless zone	235.248.073	5.6D.22	Upper I	282.243.72
4.2H.18	Snow zone	235.248.075	5.6D.25	Lower I	282.243.75
5.2A	Alps	234.3	5.6R	Rhine	282.243.1
5.2A.21	Eastern Alps	234.32	5.6R.21	Source	282.243.11
5.2A.23	Southern Alps	234.323	5.6R.22	Swiss Rhine	282.243.12
5.2A.25	Western Alps	234.31	5.6R.25	Middle Rhine	282.243.15
5.2A.27	Northern Alps	234.322	5.6R.28	Rhine estuary	282.243.17

The C.C. numbers in the third level facet are got by mnemonics. They do not therefore need a schedule. The U.D.C. on the other hand provides a separate schedule in each case.

465   Energy Levels

In the case of the fundamental category Energy, level cannot be distinguished from round. For its first level in round 1 starts round 2, so that the next energy facet appears only in round 2. This is true of every round. A modulated change-over from one round to another of Energy is now left to flair unaided by any objective rule. Of course, it depends on the sequence in which different kinds of action are taken. In most cases, the sequence is unique.

466   Matter Levels

We have had very little experience in dealing with the Matter facet. A possible second level of the matter facet is the one made of the zone 1, containing isolates of attributes as described in section 4561 for matter facet of level 1. We have not yet found use for the other zones of level 2. It is for examination if the zones 2 and 3 of successive levels may be used to represent the different materials which go into the make-up of the category forming the host personality isolate. Even if this is possible, the sequence of the levels will give difficulty. This problem persists with even greater difficulty in the later rounds.

467 Personality Levels

In the case of subjects dealing with physical and biological entities, the concept of organ, defined in section 3503, is of help in deciding change-over from one level to another among the personality facets in round 1. The unsolved question in modulation, made in section 152 in connection with the links in a chain within a facet, reappears here in regard to the successive levels of personality levels within a round. The degree to which resolving power should be used to pick out the organs to be put into a particular level of personality has now to be left to flair. This becomes very difficult when the object of study has many parts. A cycle for example is said to have over a thousand parts; a motor car, over 3,000; and an aeroplane, over 130,000. Each part has some literary warrant; each may also have many brands or makes. Each set of co-ordinate organs should be put into a separate level of facet. The number of levels may be very large in an entity like the aeroplane. This is about personality level in round 1.

Even less is known about the levels in later rounds. Equally little is known about the utilisation of levels of personality in any round, when the basic subject belongs to the domain of social science or is an abstract one. With more practice in applying depth classification to micro-thought, it should be possible to arrive at helpful results.

468 Phases

4681 PHASE RELATION

Even superficial classification of macro-thought embodied in books has to provide for phase relations. The value of the phase device has been explained in section 236 and its subsections. The connecting symbol for phase is o in the C.C. and : in the U.D.C. The latter does not distinguish between different kinds of phase relations, but the C.C. distinguishes between three of them. There is need to isolate more of them. In the first edition, the C.C. recognised only one relation. It recognised two in the third edition. Experience with micro-thought, gained since then, suggests the following schedule of phase relations.

C.C. No.	Phase Relation	C.C. No.	Phase Relation
a	General	*e*	
b	Biasing	*f*	
c	Comparison	*g*	Influencing
d	Difference	*h*	

In the case of biasing, environmental and influencing relations, the first phase is the actand, and the second phase is the actor. The sequence of the subjects forming phases is uniquely determined. But in the case of the general and comparison relations, there is no inherent criterion to determine the sequence, which has to be determined arbitrarily. For definiteness and consistency in practice, the following convention may be adopted. The class which comes earlier in the classification scheme may be made the first phase. This has been discussed by T. N. Koranne in the *Abgila*, Vol. 1, 1949, pages 37-39.

4682   COMPLEX CLASS

In superficial classification, we seldom come across a complex class, formed by any kind of phase relation, presenting facets peculiar to itself. But with the advance of research, it is likely that this will happen. " WOgU Geopolitics," for example, may call for techniques peculiar to itself. Perhaps, SObT Educational psychology, in the sense of psychology for educationists, as the class number indicates, may call for its own schedule of energy and even matter facets. When more intensive investigations are made in the history of various subjects, a complex class with influencing phase may demand facets of its own. These are some of the directions for the development of study about phase relation.

4683   INTRA-FACET RELATION

Depth classification may have to deal with a subject which involves relation among the isolates of a single facet of it, similar to the phase relations enumerated in section 4681. We may denote such a relation by Intra-Facet Relation. " Comparison of rural folk and city folk," in general or in respect of, say, social festivals, is an example, and " Teaching technique as influenced by Curriculum " is another. Physiological anatomy, in the sense of an exposition of anatomy from the angle of physiologists, is a third example. In the present practice, the C.C. treats them as phased complex classes. The C.C. numbers have to repeat the basic class numbers in both the phases, which makes the numbers long. It could be avoided if there were a schedule of Intra-Facet Relations for application between isolates in one and the same facet. This schedule may be parallel to that of phase relations given in section 4681, somewhat as follows :

C.C. No.	Intra-Facet Relation	C.C. No.	Intra-Facet Relation
j	General	n	Difference
k	Biasing	r	Influencing
m	Comparison		

The effect of the proposal on the length of class number can be seen by the following :

Old C.C. No.	New C.C. No.	Subject	Number of Digits saved
Y310*c*Y35	Y310*m*35	Comparison of village folk and city folk	1
Y31:30*c*Y35:3	Y310*m*35:3	Comparison of the social practices ditto	3
T:30*g*T;4	T:30*r*4	Teaching technique as influenced by curriculum	2
L:20*b*L:3	L:20*k*3	Physiological anatomy	2

In the U.D.C., the different relations cannot be distinguished in the notational plane, and the full class number will have to be repeated on both sides of the colon, the connecting symbol. The F.I.D. may well consider introducing a schedule for phase relations and for intra-facet relations, and thus relieve depth classification of the fault of homonyms and make it conform to the demands of the Law of Parsimony.

The schedule of intra-facet relations will be of frequent use in the space facet in Economics, when trade and other mutual relations, comparisons and influences between countries are studied.

CHAPTER 47

PROGRESS IN DEPTH CLASSIFICATION

471 Limitation of Enumerative Classification

AN ENUMERATIVE CLASSIFICATION HAS to confine itself virtually to
known classes. At best, it can anticipate a few probable new classes in
the making. The organisation of its notation has been till now
determined by the needs of current publications embodying macro-
thought. The B.C., for example, closely packs up the whole array in
each case without sufficient provision for interpolation or extrapolation.
The isolates of each of its arrays are arranged more helpfully than in
the D.C., but the provision to receive new proliferations is as
inadequate as in the D.C. An enumerative classification is not suited
to the work of the depth classification needed in documentation of
micro-thought.

472 Freedom of Analytico-Synthetic Classification

An analytico-synthetic classification is equipped to receive any new
formation in the universe of knowledge. It lays down a procedure to
analyse a new formation in a systematic way. The results of analysis
will be the phases, rounds, levels, fundamental categories, facets,
arrays, zones and isolates, involved in the new formation. The
schedules of the scheme are then to be looked up. It might have
schedules for all the facets of the fundamental categories occurring in
the different rounds and levels. It is then merely a question of picking
up from the schedules the isolate numbers of each of the isolates
occurring in the new formation. Thus, the classification will be able
to provide an expressive and coextensive class number for the new
formation. It might not have been anticipated at the time of the
building of the schedules. All the same, it can be analysed in the idea
plane, and its class number can be got by synthesis.

4721 U.D.C.

The U.D.C. has this freedom to some extent. It derives it mostly
from its enumeration of time and space isolates as universally common
isolates. It derives some small additional freedom from the tiny
schedules of special analytic divisions scattered here and there in the
main enumeration of its classes. With the aid of these, U.D.C. numbers
can be constructed for some subjects not anticipated at the time of the
building of the schedules.

4722 BIBLIOGRAPHIC CLASSIFICATION

The B.C. also has freedom to some extent, a little less than that of U.D.C. For it too has a space schedule enumerated independently of any subject, so that its space isolates are common isolates. Its time isolates are not equally common, but lend themselves to be forcedly treated as common. In addition the B.C. has provided special auxiliary schedules applicable to special groups of subjects. There are thirteen of them. These enable the construction of B.C. numbers for some new formations in the universe of knowledge not anticipated at the time of the construction of the schedules. B.C.'s own estimate is that it has capacity to provide distinctive class numbers for ten million classes.

4723 COLON CLASSIFICATION

The freedom going with an analytico-synthetic classification is at its greatest in the C.C. This is due to its reducing enumeration to the level of basic classes and isolates only. Among the isolates there are more schedules of common isolates than in any other scheme. Time and space isolates are no doubt common, and C.C. has already provided for levels in space and time. Further, it has enumerated common isolates recognisable as manifestations of Energy, Matter and Personality. It has also provision for common isolate numbers by subject device. It gives enumerated schedules for the special manifestation of Energy, Matter and Personality specific to each particular basic class. It enumerates such special isolates for different rounds and for different levels in each round likely to inhere in various subjects belonging to each basic class. These schedules are all short. There is lastly the enumerated schedule of phase relations and intrafacet relations. Thus the number of combinations that can be formed from the short enumerated isolates is many many times greater than in any other scheme. It is this feature of the C.C. that makes it derive, far more than any other existing scheme, the freedom going with an analytico-synthetic scheme of classification. With an optimum of three digits per isolate number, it can individualise 10^{14} subjects. With a maximum of six digits for isolate number, it can individualise 10^{21} subjects.

4724 LIMITATION OF C.C.

Every new formation in the universe of knowledge may not be expressible in terms of the isolates in the facets scheduled in the C.C. It may present extra facets. Each of them should be assigned to the appropriate fundamental category, round and level, and the isolates in the second zone of each of them should be determined. The position, among the other likely isolates of the new facet, of the isolate manifest in the new formation of knowledge should be fixed so as to be helpful. In some cases, each new facet may be uniquely determinable, but in other cases it may not be so. Then different classifiers will arrive at different class numbers. This inconsistency can be eliminated only by the classificationist himself prescribing the new facets and enumerating the isolates in them. This means taking away the autonomy of the classifier, which is a limitation of the C.C.

473 Limitation of Analytico-Synthetic Classification

Is this limitation peculiar to the C.C.? Or will it be a limitation of any analytico-synthetic scheme? Our experience with analytico-synthetic schemes is too meagre to answer these questions. A conjecture alone is possible. If the limitation is due to causes in the notational plane, they can be removed. If, on the other hand, the limitation is due to causes in the idea plane, that removal may not be equally easy. Some deeper analysis in the idea plane will have to be set up. This is work for the future. It will amount to standardisation of modulation and of the resolving power appropriate to each of its stages.

474 Causes in the Idea Plane

There are two factors in the idea plane which may limit the freedom of an analytico-synthetic scheme to provide unique class numbers to any new formation in the universe of knowledge. They are (1) the degree of resolving power to be used at each stage, and (2) the assignment of a personality or matter facet associated with an energy focus to the round preceding it or following it.

Resolving Power, a term suggested by Ramabhadran, is the power of recognising the isolates appropriate to the next later level of personality or matter facet. This may be described as the flair to fix the correct degree of modulation appropriate to the first order array of a new level of personality or matter to be set up. When the object of knowledge is concrete, i.e. when it is amenable to sensory experience, this flair may perhaps be acquired by practice. It may even give the same result whoever does the work. But when the object is abstract, i.e. when it is a creation of the intellect, it may not be equally easy to acquire such a flair.

Assignment of a new personality or matter facet to the appropriate round should be reduced to an objective mechanical process, and the following objective criterion is postulated. Let us call an Energy focus an Action. An Actand, an Actor and a Tool can go with it. The actand isolate should precede the action isolate. The actor isolate should succeed the action facet. The tool isolate should come still later. This is the opposite of the syntax of the English language. For in that language the sequence is Actor, Action, Actand and then Tool. Sufficient experience has not been gained to test the helpfulness of this postulate.

475 Ideal

The ideal for depth classification is to have a scheme of classification capable of providing an expressive, individualising, unique class number to any micro-thought, with any number of facets and phases—i.e. of any degree of intension or depth whatever. An analytico-synthetic classification can be made to approximate as closely as possible to this ideal. There is no doubt that the class number will be long and apparently cumbersome and complicated in some cases. When as many as 10^{21} subjects are to be individualised, we cannot help having twenty-two digits in some of the class numbers. If the subjects should be thrown into a more or less helpful filiatory sequence and new subjects should be similarly provided for, the class numbers must be expressive. They should be faceted and phased. They should have connecting symbols. An optimum of three digits for a facet will imply about seven connecting symbols in the longest class number. Its length will therefore tend to be about thirty digits. This cannot be attributed to a fault in the scheme used. It is intrinsic to the subjects calling for depth classification in documentation work. Can it be said that documentation need not be so meticulous in keeping close to the ideal?

476 Too Complicated?

Here is such a view expressed by Henry Evelyn Bliss on page 70 of his *Bibliographic classification,* Vol. 1 (1940). "Documentation, according to the documentalists, should provide for a hundred thousand subjects—any conceivable subject in any conceivable relation or aspect. This could be undertaken thru complex, supplementary classification and notation. The millions of subdivisions would not all be real or requisite, but they should be provided for in the system, in so far as they are 'conceivable.' Thus the documentalists would justify their complicated notations. For bibliographic citations on cards, for immense depositories of documents, for archives, for special collections, for pamphlets, excerpts, clippings, etc., such extensions of bibliographic classifications may perhaps be more requisite and serviceable than they are in *bibliography* in our more limited scope.

"As studies have become more specialised and interests more diverse, the relations have become more intricate. To classify all these subject matters and relations coherently and synthetically and so as to serve all the analytical and purposive interests, and then to index them consistently and efficiently has become increasingly problematical. To some extent this service is feasible. But beyond limits it ceases to be economical or serviceable. The classifications become too cumbersome, the notations too complicated."

477 Aeroplane Analogy

The above view stems from the basic assumption that there is an economical limit to the length of a class number. This appears to be an unwarranted assumption. Notation is a tool, a machine, a mechanism, designed to do a job—the job of mechanising the throwing of subjects in a preferred helpful sequence. The beneficiaries of classification are concerned only with the helpfulness of the sequence of subjects secured by it. They are not worried by the nature of the mechanism securing it. A passenger in an aeroplane is interested in his being carried to his destination. He does not worry himself about the mechanism of the aeroplane or its engine. So it is with classificatory mechanism. Its cumbersomeness and complication affect only the members of the library profession, even as the cumbersomeness and complication of an aeroplane affect only the crew and the designers of the aeroplane. What is feasible to make service efficient should of course be done. What is necessary for service should also be done. The specialist reader needs it. He can also understand the need for complicated class number. He will not be repelled by it.

478 Non-Specialist Reader

It may be argued that the non-specialist, less gifted reader will be baffled, if not scared, by the cumbersomeness of the classification and complication of the notation. This is only an imaginary fear. The non-specialist reader will go in only for macro-thought. Macro-thought gets only a simple short class number. This is a consequence of the Canon of Decreasing Extension and the Canon of Expressiveness. Thus the non-specialist reader will not face a long, complicated, class number. Indeed, he may never come across it. For he will get his reading materials in a general library. This will contain only books embodying macro-thought and therefore carrying only simple short class numbers.

479 Future

When the D.C. was forged, a class number of three digits was opposed as being too cumbersome and complicated. The B.C. now regards seven digits as permissible. It considers that documentation should be satisfied with it. But fourteen digits occur quite frequently among class numbers appearing in abstracting periodicals. Specialist users are getting accustomed to them. As proliferation increases in the universe of knowledge, the number of digits will have to increase, if we still continue to use analytico-synthetic schemes of the kind now in vogue. Depth classification will have to put up with them. But by putting up with them it will prompt the creation of some other kind of scheme which can reach the ideal of depth classification with shorter class numbers. The future will thus be kept ever-productive in serving documentation needs with schemes of depth classification of ever-increasing efficiency.

CHAPTER 48

ORGANISATION

481   Need

THE DESIGNING OR MAINTENANCE of a scheme of superficial classification does not need much of an organisation. The basic designing is best done by a single classificationist with a fair gift of intuition. The additions needed will be few and far between, if the basic design is sound. The general principles laid down by the classificationist will prove sufficient to enable any trained classifier to add to the schedule more or less in a unique way. Any little discrepancy that may arise between the findings of different classifiers can be reconciled through a library periodical and in periodical conferences which are bound to be convened for clearance work of various kinds in the library field. But it is unlikely that any classificationist will be versatile enough or have sufficient familiarity with literature to provide all the schedules needed for depth classification of diverse subjects. To construct detailed schedules in later rounds, and even in the first round in applied fields just gaining literary warrant, concerted team-work in the intellectual plane is essential. This needs a well-planned organisation.

482   Structure

The organisation for the schedules needed in depth classification should draw its sustenance through roots permeating the several institutions in the different nations, consuming and serving micro-thought in their daily work. For this purpose, it should have a structure spread over each nation and over the international plane. Within each nation and in the international plane, it should have three tiers. These may be respectively called Working Party (WP), Co-ordinating Group (CG), and Central Committee (CC). The primary work should be done by the tiers in each nation. The finalisation should be on the international plane.

There should be a National WP (NWP) for each subject field being actively cultivated within the nation. Each NWP should have either three or six members, depending upon the number of institutions cultivating the subject field of the party.

There should be a National CG (NCG) for each group of allied subject fields. Each NCG should have one representative of the NWP's federating into it. An NWP may federate, if necessary, into more than one NCG.

There should be one National CC (NCC). It should have one representative of each NCG. Each NWP and each NCG should be federated into it. It will be convenient for the NCC to have a panel of Research Consultants, whose help may be sought in ascertaining the trend of development in different fields of knowledge.

There should be an International WP (IWP) for each subject field being cultivated actively in any part of the world. It should have six members. To facilitate holding of meetings, it is desirable that all the members of an IWP should be from one country. In fact, the NWP of the country chosen for the purpose may function as the IWP. In this way, the International Working Parties will be distributed over different nations.

There should be an International CG (ICG) for each group of allied subject fields. This body may have to do its work largely by correspondence. Nor will its work be as heavy or as frequent as that of an IWP. It may therefore have one representative from each corresponding NCG.

There should be an International CC (ICC) to co-ordinate the work of the entire structure. It should have a representative of each ICG. It should further have a panel of Research Consultants. This body also will have to do most of its work by correspondence. It should use the occasion of the annual conference of FID to have personal discussion among its members.

4821 PERSONNEL

Considerable spade-work will have to be done by each NWP. It is desirable that it should be strong in experts in its subject field. It should also have in it an expert or two in the discipline of classification. Perhaps the proportion of subject to classification experts may be as two to one. On the other hand, it is desirable that the proportion may be reversed in an NCG or an ICG. Each NCC and the ICC should have even a larger proportion of classification experts. In fact, there is hardly need for more than one subject expert for each of the two regions of the universe of knowledge, viz. natural and social sciences respectively. The secretary of each body should be a classification expert.

In a field of this kind, most of the intellectual contribution has to be made by honorary members. But to keep each constituent body in full steam is beyond the capacity of an honorary person. There should therefore be adequate secretarial help available. The success of the organisation will depend on the provision for it. The particular institution from which the classification expert of an NWP is taken should be one willing to give him the necessary secretarial help and other facilities, for the NWP, which is in the lowest tier, will have considerable correspondence and paper work. It will be much more so in the case of an NWP, which has also to function as an IWP. The secretarial work may not be heavy in an NCG or an ICG. But it will be very heavy in an NCC and in the ICC. It is therefore desirable that the secretary of an NCC should be a classification expert working in the National Documentation Centre. So also the secretary of the ICC should work in the headquarters of the F.I.D.

483 Function

The function of each member of the federal structure proposed is easily inferred from its name. Some essential details and the procedure in regard to them will be explained in the following subsections.

4831 National Bodies

The classification expert of an NWP should watch the flow of literature in the periodicals in its subject field. As and when a new proliferation gains appreciable literary warrant, he should put it down for consideration by the NWP. At suitable intervals, the NWP should meet. The originals embodying the new proliferation should be studied at the meeting. The most helpful place for it should first be determined in the idea plane, without any influence from the notational plane. Then the findings should be implemented in the notational plane. At this stage, any suggestion emerging in the notational plane should be taken back to the idea plane and the isolate number should be decided upon. This number should be communicated to the other classifiers likely to be interested in them, for experiment and report. It should also be sent to the NCG concerned for remarks. The final number, arrived at by the NWP in the light of the criticism received, should be sent to the NCC.

At stated intervals, the secretary of an NCG should collate all the new isolate numbers received from the different NWPs federating in it. Any conflict revealed by the collation should be brought up for consideration by its members. The findings should be communicated to the federating NWPs.

At stated intervals, the secretary of an NCC should collate all the proposals received from the different NWPs. If necessary, the panel of Research Consultants or the NCGs may be consulted. The final results should be sent by it to the ICC. The ICC should distribute to the various NWPs the proposals concerning their respective subject fields.

4832 International Bodies

The secretary of an IWP will receive at stated intervals the remarks of its corresponding NWPs on the proposals received by them. He should collate these remarks. The IWP should consider the isolate numbers, arrive at a provisional decision, and send the same to the ICG concerned and the corresponding NWPs. A final decision should be made on the replies of these bodies and communicated to the ICC.

The secretary of an ICG should collate all the proposals received from the IWPs federating in it. At stated intervals, it should consider the discrepancies, if any, and send its suggestions to the IWPs concerned.

Some routine distribution work to be done by the secretary of the ICC has been already mentioned in section 4831. His substantive work commences when the IWPs send their decisions. These should be collated and put up for consideration by the ICC. The ICC may have to seek the advice of ICGs, the panel of Research Consultants, and the Theory of Classification Committee mentioned in section 485. After taking all the advice into consideration, the ICC should include the emerging isolate number in the schedule concerned. It may also have to initiate general problems and methodology for consideration, at the request of the Theory of Classification Committee.

4833 TIME FACTOR

The progress of a proposal through the various tiers at the national and international levels will be necessarily slow. It may take about two years to reach the final stage. But this is inevitable. Nor will there be need to arrive at results more speedily—it may not even be safe to do it speedily, for it takes about two years at least for a new proliferation in the universe of knowledge to mature and get itself crystallised.

484 Elimination of Waste

The present organisation set up by the F.I.D. is moving in this direction. It is not easy to make so many bodies work in unison. The subject experts are unfamiliar with the discipline of classification. The classification experts are not familiar with the highways, byways and the latest developments in the various subject-fields. The defects due to this inevitable cause can be reduced to some extent if the subject experts of a WP are persons who have a personal liking for classification problems, and if its classification expert is one who has had opportunity to specialise to some extent in the subject field concerned, either in his university course or in his career as librarian and classifier. Another necessary means to reduce defects still further is to publish a *Manual of instructions* for the guidance of all the members in all the bodies in the organisation.

4841 F.I.D.'s ATTEMPT

About 1950, the F.I.D. realised the need for such a manual, and therefore worked on a draft for some years. It brought out in 1953 its *Guiding principles* of twenty-six pages (publication 268), and a revised edition in October, 1955 (twenty-eight pages, publication 283). This contains only eight general principles for guidance of work in the idea plane, and five relating to the notational plane. This is far too meagre. It is not sufficient to help the subject experts to realise in what direction their contribution should be. It is not sufficient even for classification experts, either to secure helpful places for new isolates, or to construct their numbers consistently. The rules of procedure are twenty-four in number, and are perhaps sufficient.

4842 More Detailed Guidance

The *Manual of instructions* should give more detailed guidance. To make communication precise, a section on terminology should be put at the beginning. Then should follow the Canons of Classification, the principles for securing helpful sequence in array and chain respectively, and the postulates to be used as guidance in establishing the new arrays or facets demanded by new proliferations in any subject field.

485 Theory of Classification Committee

The suggestions of the preceding section imply that a consistent theory of classification be used as the basis. No theory can hold good eternally. On the other hand, great vigilance is necessary to keep it abreast of the new happenings in the universe of knowledge. The postulates should be constantly tested against those happenings. This should be a continuing process. Further, the formulated propositions in the theory will need interpretation in being applied to new situations. This too will be a continuing process. The decisions brought up by the various NWPs should be critically examined in the light of the formulated canons, principles and postulates. This is quite apart from securing conformity to the rules of procedure, which can be left to the sole care of the ICC or even its secretary. But the other technical controls mentioned in this section cannot be done in a routine or administrative way. Nor can the emergence of a context calling for change in the theory be sensed by administrative approach. Corresponding to the judiciary in a political organisation, there should be a Theory of Classification Committee (TCC) in the organisation set up to keep a scheme of classification alive and growing. The TCC may be a small committee of experienced classificationists and classifiers. The IWPs should keep feeding the TCC with refractory cases turning up in their respective subject fields from time to time. Apart from the scrutiny of all new proposals just before they are finalised, the work of the TCC should be two-pronged. It should, as it were, distil out of the refractory cases new abstractions with which the methodology of classification can be improved. It should also do theoretical work beginning with the canons, principles and postulates, and embody all their latent implications in the form of easily applicable methodology. By these two methods, the TCC should keep the apical bud of classificatory discipline ever active and growing. This will amount to work on the Theory of Abstract Classification described in part 8.

486 Media for Communication

To keep the various parts of the organisation informed mutually, there is need for systematic circulars to be published. This should be one of the functions of the ICC. The F.I.D. is now doing this in a helpful way, through its *PE-notes* for proposed extensions, *PP-notes* for provisional proposals, *Extensions and corrections to the UDC*, and authorised editions of U.D.C., brought out at convenient intervals.

487 **Periodical Seminar**

The universe of knowledge is an ever-turbulent dynamic continuum. Its proliferations will now and again outwit classification. The small adjustments made from time to time will sooner or later call for substantial changes in methodology. I estimate that this may happen almost every decade. By this time, a new set of people will come to many of the WPs. The problems created by both of these factors can be met best by a decennial Seminar on Depth Classification. The decennial seminar will also be of help in bringing out a revised edition of the *Manual of instructions*.

PART 5

THEORY OF KNOWLEDGE CLASSIFICATION
DEMONSTRATION

CHAPTER 51

ARRAY OF MAIN CLASSES

510 Introduction

THE SUBJECT OF STUDY in this chapter is the array of Main Classes in each of seven schemes, the Decimal, Expansive, Universal Decimal, Library of Congress, Subject, Colon and Bibliographic classifications. These arrays are given in sections 729, 735, 745, 755, 765, 778 and 785. The Canon of Enumeration is used to make clear the denotation of the main classes that have unusual or ambiguous names.

511 Decimal Classification

(1) o Generalia includes 010 Bibliography and 020 Library Economy.

(2) 3 Sociology comprises 310 Statistics, 320 Political Science, 330 Political Economy, 340 Law, 350 Administration, 360 Associations, 370 Education, 380 Commerce and 390 Customs.

(3) 5 Pure Science comprises 510 Mathematics, 520 Astronomy, 530 Physics, 540 Chemistry, 550 Geology, 560 Palaeontology, 570 Biology, 580 Botany and 590 Zoology.

(4) 6 Useful Arts comprises all the applications of sciences.

(5) 9 History comprises 910 Geography, 920 Biography and 930-990 History.

512 U.D.C.

The U.D.C. differs from the D.C. in the following two important features:

(1) Statistics (Theory) is transferred from 310 to 519.2; and

(2) Atomic Physics is transferred from 54 Chemistry to 53 Physics.

513 Colon Classification

(1) New formations comprise the newly emerging main classes other than the traditional ones.

(2) F Technology comprises only Chemical Technology.

(3) G Biology serves also as a generalia class for all the Biological Sciences.

(4) M Useful Arts includes Recreative Arts and all applications of science except Engineering, Technology, Mining, Agriculture, Animal Husbandry and Medicine.

(5) U Geography includes U28 Meteorology.

514 Subject Classification

(1) A   Generalia comprises AO Generalia, A1 Education, A3 Logic, A4 Mathematics, A6 Graphic and Plastic Arts and A9 General Science.

(2) B, C, D, Physical Science includes among other things Engineering, Music, Astronomy, Meteorology, Geology, Chemistry and some Useful Arts.

(3) G, H Ethnology and Medicine includes Recreative Arts.

(4) I   Economic Biology includes most of the Useful Arts.

(5) L   Social and Political Science includes Economics.

(6) M Language and Literature includes Bibliography, Book Production and Library Economy.

(7) X   Biography includes Heraldry.

515 Library of Congress Classification

(1) B   Philosophy includes BL Religion.

(2) G   Geography includes GN Anthropology and GV Sports and Amusements.

(3) H   Social Sciences comprises HA Statistics, HB-HJ and HX Economics, and HM-HY Sociology.

(4) J   Political Science includes JF-JQ Constitutional History·and JX International Law.

(5) Q   Science includes QM Human Anatomy, QP Physiology and QR Bacteriology.

(6) T   Technology includes all applied sciences.

516 Expansive Classification

(1) B   Philosophy includes BR Religion.

(2) M Natural History includes Geology and Biology.

(3) V   Athletic and Recreative Arts includes Vv Music.

517 Bibliographic Classification

All the main classes except the following 13 require explanatory notes, which are added in the Table of Main Classes itself.

I   Psychology
J   Education
L   to O History
R   Political Science
S   Law
T   Economics
U   Useful Arts
W   to Y Linguistics and Literature.

518 Comparison

The following table gives the percentage of the classes in the array of main classes, that are self-explanatory and do not require any special elucidation with the aid of the Canon of Enumeration:

S.C.	D.C.	U.D.C.	B.C.	C.C.	L.C.	E.C.
36%	40%	40%	50%	70%	71%	80%

519 **Helpful Sequence**

The sequence of main classes in each of the seven schemes of classification is more or less helpful. There is not much to choose between them from the point of view of the Canon of Helpful Sequence. A good deal of time is spent in finding fault with each scheme in this respect, but, as is shown in section 718, this is futile. On the other hand, time may usefully be spent in assisting beginners to appreciate the helpfulness of the sequence of main classes in each scheme. It will be a good exercise to find out the reasons for the preferred sequence of each scheme, and this has indeed been attempted in section 71 and its subdivisions.

CHAPTER 52

ARRAY OF ORDER 2

520 Clarification

THE LIMITED BASE OF Arabic numerals makes the D.C. and U.D.C. introduce a difference between classes in the idea plane and in the notational plane. In the notational plane, they are obliged to show, as sub-classes, some of the classes currently taken to be main classes in the idea plane. A similar exigency arises also in the E.C., L.C., S.C. and B.C., but for another reason. They all use the more capacious base of Roman capitals, yet they do not derive the fullest benefit from it, in this particular matter, for they allocate more than one letter to a single main class like History or Literature. Therefore in the notational plane they too are obliged to show, as sub-classes, some of the classes currently taken as main classes in the idea plane. This exigency is avoided by the C.C. Therefore, and for definiteness in terminology, we shall hereafter use the term First Order Array to mean the Array of Main Classes in the C.C. Consequently, when we speak of Array of First Order, Array of Second Order, etc. we shall take them in the sense in which they will be according to the C.C. This clarification should be remembered in understanding these terms in the remaining chapters of this part.

5201 SECOND ORDER ARRAY DERIVED THROUGH MATHEMATICS

The number of arrays of order 2 runs to a few hundreds in most of the schemes. It is, therefore, not practicable to include in this book a comparative study of all the arrays of order 2. We shall make a comparative study of only one array of order 2, as a sample. We shall choose the array of order 2 having Mathematics as its Immediate Universe. We shall first extract the schedule of this second order array from each scheme, and then make a systematic comparison of them, with the aid of the canons of classification. Five schedules are given below.

521 U.D.C.

511 Arithmetic and Theory of Numbers
512 Algebra
513 Geometry
514 Trigonometry, Polygonometry
515 Descriptive Geometry. Projections. Perspective

516 Analytical Geometry. Co-ordinates
517 Analysis
518 Methods of Calculation. Nomography. Tables. Graphic
Calculation. Mathematical Games and Recreations
519 Combinatory Analysis. Calculus of Probabilities. General
Theory of Groups of Transformation. Theory of Aggregates.
Geometry of Position

522 Colon Classification

B1 Arithmetic
B2 Algebra
B3 Analysis
B4 Other methods of Analysis
B5 Trigonometry
B6 Geometry
B7 Mechanics
B8 Physico-Mathematics
B9 Astronomy

523 Subject Classification

A401-425 Arithmetic
A430-443 Algebra
A450-456 Weights and Measures
A460-461 Statistics
A470-489 Book-keeping
A500-515 Geometry
A520-525 Calculus
A530-532 Trigonometry
A540 Mensuration

524 Library of Congress

QA101-145 Arithmetic
QA152-295 Algebra
QA300-431 Analysis
QA445-699 Geometry
QA802-930 Analytical Mechanics
QA931-935 Elasticity

525 Bibliographic Classification

AN Arithmetic, elementary and general
AO Algebra: Elementary. Arithmetic and Algebra. Higher
Arithmetic
AP Equations
AQ Higher Algebra
AR Analysis
AS Functions
AT Geometry

AU   Analytical Geometry
AV   Descriptive Geometry
AW Mensuration, including Trigonometry and Surveying
AX   Metrology
AY   Statistics

526 Canon of Enumeration

(1) Applying the Canon of Enumeration, we find that the connotation of the term " Mathematics " varies from scheme to scheme. The S.C. and B.C. deviate most from enumeration.

(2) The apparent common factors are Arithmetic, Algebra, Analysis and Geometry. Trigonometry and Probability are also common, though not apparent, as they are comprised in Geometry and Algebra (or Statistics) respectively.

(3) One major variation consists in the U.D.C. and B.C. restricting the range of the term " Mathematics " to " Pure Mathematics," while the C.C. and L.C. use it in the wider sense to include " Applied Mathematics."

(4) The two latter schemes, however, do not agree in the branches of Applied Mathematics included. The C.C. omits Elasticity and assigns it to Physics; the L.C. omits Astronomy and makes it an independent class.

(5) The C.C. includes also Physico-Mathematics to accommodate Potentials, Wave-Geometry and other specialities in Mathematics to face problems in Physics. This is no different from the practice of the L.C., in which it is comprised under Analysis.

(6) Inclusion of Weights and Measures and Book-keeping in the array derived from Mathematics in the S.C. is utterly repugnant to accepted practice. This is only one of the many instances of flouting of convention out of extreme deference to its principle of " placing all topics in logical sequence . . . in a systematic order of scientific progression." The B.C. too includes Metrology. Its inclusion of Surveying is not quite happy, as it implies techniques outside Mathematics, which comes into relation with it only as an intellectual tool.

(7) It may also be remarked that the whole subject of Statistics (as a mathematical method) is accommodated in the class Mathematics explicitly by the U.D.C., S.C. and B.C., and implicitly (in Algebra) by the C.C. But the subject is dismembered by the L.C., where Probability alone is put under Mathematics. The other parts of Statistics are considered as a class of Social Sciences, along with the statistical data of the social variety. This is a practice of doubtful value, which crept in at the initial stages, before the real mathematical nature of statistical methods and the almost universal range of their application were realised, and which has since been given up by the learned world. The C.C. will do well to transfer Statistics from Algebra to Other Methods of Analysis, because it has now reached such a co-ordinate status.

(8) The term " Calculus " has been rightly replaced by " Analysis " in the U.D.C., C.C., L.C. and B.C.

(9) The term " Polygonometry " in the U.D.C. is not happy, if it is its own invention. It is defined in the schedule itself as " extension of goniometry to multi-dimensional geometry." But the term sets up strong associations with the term " Polygon," which belongs to two-dimensional geometry.

(10) The inclusion of " Higher Arithmetic " in Algebra, by the B.C., is evidently the prolongation of the old tradition of textbooks in algebra including an elementary chapter on the subject; the L.C. does similarly. But Higher Arithmetic is concerned with the properties of integers and analogues of it, and uses as a tool not only Algebra but also Analysis. The subject studied is Arithmetic, and it should therefore be included in that.

(11) The terminology is verbose and crowded in the U.D.C. and B.C. This is the result of not using the Canon of Enumeration. To give a telling example, U.D.C. need not mention 519 at all, because the isolates 5191, 5192, 5193, etc., are sufficient by themselves. There is nothing gained by repeating against 519 all the isolate terms found at 5191, 5192, 5193, etc. The terminology is crisp and precise in the C.C., L.C. and S.C.

527 Hospitality in Array

The Canon of Exhaustiveness and the Canon of Hospitality in Array are satisfied fully by the U.D.C., C.C. and B.C., but the S.C. and L.C. satisfy them only to the extent allowed by the gaps in their notation.

In the U.D.C., three of its ten places are given to one and the same subject—Geometry. This is its inheritance from the D.C., but it has improved on the latter by adopting octave notation. The digit 9 was Probability in the D.C., but is made the octavising digit in U.D.C. This classification, however, is filling up the second octave with classes which are properly sub-classes of classes in the first octave, e.g. Combinatory Analysis can go with Algebra, and Geometry of Position with Geometry.

In the C.C. there is apparently no room for new classes, since all the nine divisions have already been used up in violation of its much-vaunted Octave Principle. But this is only apparent. Mathematics is essentially a tool or method, and its future developments can consist only of the development of new methods. The divisions 3 Analysis and 4 Other Methods of Analysis form the real core of Mathematics as method. Of these, 4 Other Methods of Analysis has been duly classified on the octave principle, thus ensuring Hospitality in Array to any desired extent. The isolate 8 Physico-Mathematics also provides hospitality in its array.

The S.C. has thirty-nine vacant numbers in the array, and can thus accommodate a possible maximum of thirty-nine new co-ordinate branches of Mathematics. But the numbers available will really be much less, because each new branch will need more than one number to accommodate its sub-classes.

The L.C. has 115 vacant numbers. But since each newcomer will demand considerably more than one number, the scheme still does not ensure Hospitality in Array to *any* desired extent, as do the U.D.C. and C.C.

The B.C. imitates U.D.C. in throwing away three places to Geometry, and it also gives three places to Algebra. And yet it does not suffer in hospitality. This is due to class AR taking charge of all Methods of Analysis. In fact, the symbol ARY functions merely as an octavising number.

528 Helpful Sequence

The Canon of Helpful Sequence is well satisfied by the C.C., L.C. and B.C., but not so well by the U.D.C. and S.C. In both the latter, the position of Analysis and Calculus respectively would be happier if they had priority over Geometry, since Algebra and Analysis are pure methods and should be contiguous. Geometry has a large element of application in it as well as its " pure " element, so that it should not come between Algebra and Analysis. The position of Trigonometry in U.D.C., between two branches of Geometry, is quite anomalous and difficult to justify on any grounds. This is another inheritance from the D.C.

CHAPTER 53

ARRAY OF ORDER 4

530 Clarification

IF ARRAYS OF ORDER 2 are counted in hundreds, arrays of order 4 have to be counted in tens of thousands. We shall therefore consider only one array of order 4 as a sample. We shall choose the array of order 4 which has Analysis as its Immediate Universe. First, we shall extract the schedule of the fourth order array from each scheme, and then make a systematic comparison of them, with the aid of the Canons of Classification.

531 D.C. and U.D.C.

	D.C.	U.D.C.
517.1	Infinitesimal Calculus	General Principles
517.2	Differential Calculus	Differential Calculus
517.3	Integral Calculus	Integral Calculus
517.4	Calculus of Variations	Functional Determinants. Differential Forms. Differential and Integral Operators
517.5	Functions	General Theory of Functions
517.6	Calculus of Finite Differences	Definite Integrals
517.7	Calculus of Operations	Elliptic Functions and Their Applications
517.8	Complex Variables	Hyper-elliptic Functions
517.9	Problems	Differential Equations. Functional Equations. Finite Difference Equations

The schedules have been given in parallel columns to show the extent of modification of D.C. by U.D.C. As will be seen in the later sections of this chapter, the freedom of reconditioning has not been used to the best advantage.

532 Colon Classification

B31 Foundation .
B32 Calculus
B33 Differential Equations
B34 Continuous Groups
B35 Differential Forms

B36   Infinite Series
B37-39   Functions
B41   Calculus of Finite Differences
B42   Calculus of Variations
B43   Calculus of Functional Analysis
B44   Graphical Calculus and Nomography
B45   Quaternions
B46   Vector Analysis
B48   Operational Calculus

533 Subject Classification

A521   Differential Calculus
A522   Integral Calculus
A523   Quaternions
A524   Functions
A525   Finite Differences

534 Library of Congress Classification

QA303-316   Calculus
QA331-351   Theory of Functions
QA371-381   Differential Equations
QA38   Continuous Groups
QA401-431   Analytical methods connected with physical problems

535 Bibliographic Classification

ARA   Foundations
ARB   Problems
ARC   Numerical Calculus
ARD   Differential Calculus
ARE   Special subjects, concepts
ARF   Fluxions
ARG   Maxima and Minima
ARH   Taylor's Series
ARI   Calculus of Finite Differences
ARJ   Integral Calculus
ARK   Methods of Integration
ARL   Indefinite Integrals
ARM   Definite Integrals
ARN   Infinite Integrals
ARO   Riemann, Lebesgue, etc.
ARP   Differential Equations
ARQ   Ordinary Differential Equations
ARR   Partial Differential Equations
ARS   Linear Differential Equations
ART   Special Differential Equations
ARU   Integral Equations
ARV   Calculus of Variations

ARW	General Analysis (Moore's and others)
ARY	Special subjects relative to Analysis
AS	Functions. Theory of Function
ASR	Calculus of Functions
ASS	Functionals

The above is a telescoped array. Classes of orders 4 and 5 are telescoped into a single array. It has been reproduced to demonstrate how class numbers may be shortened by telescoping, which has been made possible because the B.C. uses the more capacious base of Roman capitals even in arrays of higher order.

5351 TRUE ARRAY OF ORDER 4

The following is the true array of order 4 lying telescoped in the array given in section 535.

ARA	Foundation
ARD	Differential Calculus
ARI	Calculus of Finite Differences
ARJ	Integral Calculus
ARP	Differential Equations
ARY	Other methods of Analysis
AS	Functions

536 Hospitality in Array

With regard to the Canon of Exhaustiveness and the Canon of Hospitality in Array, the C.C. retains its infinite hospitality; the L.C. satisfies the canons to a very limited extent; the U.D.C. and S.C. have become rigid and petrified, with no places to offer; the B.C. has left ARZ and ASU to ASZ free.

With their customary hasty prodigality, the D.C. and U.D.C. have squandered away all ten places. They have given three places (517.1 Infinitesimal, 517.2 Differential, 517.3 Integral) to Calculus proper, instead of one. Even in the revision of the array to meet modern requirements, U.D.C. has not been prudent in regard to Hospitality in Array. For example, it has no place for Infinite Series, and has to billet it in 517.2 Differential Calculus, which could have been avoided by merging the more related subjects Differential Calculus and Integral Calculus in one number representing Calculus, used in the traditional restricted sense.

The C.C. has accommodated all the newcomers already, and has in reserve any number of places as a result of its octave principle. The second octave 49 and all the later octaves are kept free, so that it can cope with the situation, no matter what magnitude the number of new subjects eventually attains.

The S.C. had set apart only six inexpansible places for Analysis, and all six have been occupied. Even by putting the fullest possible load on its categorical tables, it cannot accommodate even one additional class of a co-ordinate status.

The L.C. has fifty-one free places, and so can house a few more new classes; but a time will soon come when more places will be needed.

The B.C. has secured hospitality in array by setting apart ARY virtually for " Other Methods of Analysis," though the term used against it, " Special subjects relative to Analysis," does not explicitly indicate it.

537 Canon of Exclusiveness

The Canon of Exclusiveness is not properly satisfied by the D.C. and B.C., but well satisfied in all the other schemes.

(1) The improvised classes, 517.9 Problems in the D.C. and ARB in the B.C., are prominent offenders. How can this class be prevented from overlapping with the other classes? If there is a method, it should have been explicitly stated. In the C.C., " Problem " will be indicated by v in the form facet of book number.

(2) The class 517.8 Complex Variable in the D.C. is also a source of trouble. The class 517.3 Integral Calculus comprises 517.36 Abelian Functions. Have they not a natural place under 517.8 Complex Variable?

(3) Although it is not quite relevant, another extraordinary deviation from the Canon of Exclusiveness may be brought to light here, as there may not be a more suitable occasion to deal with such cases. Under 517.2 Differential Calculus, we find the classes 517.24 Theory of Plane Curves and 517.26 Theory of Curved Surfaces. But under 513.2 Curves we also find 513.26 Higher Plane Curves, and under 513.5 Modern Geometry we find 513.59 Surfaces of Higher Order. Similar divisions are also repeated under 516 Analytical Geometry. But there is no explanatory note in any of the overlapping places as to how the situation is to be reconciled with the Canon of Exclusiveness. My fairly intimate knowledge of the subject shows me, as a matter of fact, that it is not easy to effect any reconciliation in the universe of books.

(4) Such offences against the Canon of Exclusiveness are found in large numbers when we dive deep and compare arrays of higher and higher orders of U.D.C., though they are absent on the surface, i.e. in the arrays of the first, second and third orders. It would be a good exercise for a student to make an exhaustive list of such deep-lying cases of overlapping (i.e. offences against the Canon of Exclusiveness) in all the arrays of all the orders.

538 Helpful Sequence
5381 Decimal Classification

Incidentally, this last feature in the D.C. also violates the Canon of Helpful Sequence. If we have books which deal, say, with curved surfaces, exclusively by pure methods, by analytical methods, and by differential methods, separating such books from one another, and assigning the groups to different classes which are not contiguous—in fact are far from one another—offends against the Canon of Helpful Sequence. It happens because the D.C. divides first by the methods of study and then by the kind of spatial configuration. But experience shows that division first by spatial configuration and then by the method would be more helpful to readers, that is, would be a satisfactory relevant sequence. This fault is due to neglect of the Principle of Decreasing Concreteness in arranging the facets which are manifestations of the fundamental characteristics Personality and Energy.

5382   U.D.C.

(1) The U.D.C. avoids this error by transferring all the above-mentioned classes to 513.6 under 513 Geometry. This is proper, because calculus is only the method used in the study of curves and surfaces. For in this context, curves and surfaces are manifestations of the fundamental category Personality, and calculus, of the fundamental category Energy.

(2) The U.D.C., however, ignores this salutary way of arranging facets, when it is at the class 517 Elliptic Functions and Their Applications. It commits the same mistake as the D.C. did in regard to the applications of 517.2 Differential Calculus. To lay this bare, we may extract some of the subdivisions of 517.78 Applications of Elliptic Functions.

517.781 **Algebraic applications**
517.781.2 Gauss's arithmetico-geometrical mean
517.782 Solution of the equation of the fifth degree
See also 512.41 Group of an equation (in 512 Algebra)

517.783 **Arithmetical applications**
517.783.2 To the partition of numbers
See also 511.29 Partition of numbers (in 511 Arithmetic)

517.784 To the decomposition of numbers into sums
517.784.2 Of three squares
517.784.3 Of four squares
517.784.4 Of more than four squares
See also 511.46 Representation of numbers by quadratic forms (in 511 Arithmetic)

517.786 **Geometrical applications**
517.786.2 To spherical trigonometry
See also 514.6   Spherical trigonometry
517.786.3 To Poncelet's and analogous theorems
See also 513.274 Polygons inscribed in and circumscribed about two circles
513.541 Properties relative to two or more conics
513.543 Confocal conics (all in 513 Geometry)

517.787	Geometrical applications to curves of genus one
	See also 513.614.2 Curves of genus one
	513.634.2 Curves of genus one
517.788	**Mechanical and physical applications**
517.788.2	Conical pendulum
517.788.3	Elastic curve
517.788.4	Herpolhode
517.788.5	Motion of a body in liquid
517.788.6	Movement of a point attracted to two centres
	See also 531.8 Dynamics

53821   Remedy

The *see also* cross-references tell the tale of cross-classification brought about by U.D.C. They openly declare that the Canon of Exclusiveness is violated. At bottom, drifting into such a situation is traceable to failure to found the work of designing the scheme on a clear statement of objectives and directives, formulated at the very beginning. One of the essential qualities of a classificatory language of ordinal numbers is that it should have no synonyms in it. Cross-references of the nature mentioned in section 5382 amount to admission of synonyms. This error should be corrected. To correct it, the subjects mentioned in the extract should be removed from one or the other of the alternative places mentioned. " From which," is the question. This is best answered on the basis of the hypothesis of Fundamental Categories. In the subjects enumerated under the class number 517.78 Elliptic Function stands only for the method of study. In them, therefore, it forms the focus in the energy facet. That is its status in the context of 517.78, though it has the status of personality in the contexts of 517.71 to 517.77. On the other hand, the personality facets in the subjects mentioned under 517.78 are, respectively, Arithmetico-Geometric Mean, Algebraic Equations, Integers, Systems of Circles and Conics, Algebraic Plane and Skew Curves, and Dynamics. These form the proper hosts for the subjects under consideration, and not Elliptic Functions. Therefore all these subjects should be removed from 517.78 and distributed in the places of the respective host-subjects. It may be asked, " How is the specialist in Elliptic Functions to be helped to get at these subjects?" This is an oft-recurring question. The help should be provided by giving the class index entry, in the alphabetical part of the catalogue, the main heading " Elliptic Functions." Chain Procedure will furnish there all the classes where Elliptic Function has been used as a tool, by entries such as " Elliptic Function, Partition, Integer, *see* 511.29:517.7." If the C.C. were used, the index number would have been B135:393L8.

53822   Terminology

Incidentally, the extracts in section 5382 illustrate the looseness and verbosity occurring all though the schedules of the U.D.C. It uses " motion " in one line and " movement " in the next. When 517 is

Elliptic Functions, 517.8 need not show " Application of Elliptic Functions " against itself: " Application " is sufficient. Similarly, when 517.8 is Application, 517.781 need not carry " Algebraic Applications " against itself: " Algebra " is sufficient. These faults could be avoided automatically if the Canon of Context is respected. Failure to use crisp one-worded terms wherever possible makes the schedules of U.D.C. unserviceable in the rendering of headings of class index entries and subject entries in the catalogue. At bottom, this is due to failure to regard Classification and Cataloguing in a holistic setting. If it is done, Chain Procedure will make the catalogue exercise a wholesome effect on the scheme of classification in the choice of its terminology.

5383 Colon Classification

To go back to the incidence of cross-classification and of inconsistency in placing " Application " with the class applied in one case and with the class to which applied in another case, the C.C. escapes all such faults. This is due to its loyalty to the postulates about fundamental categories. It does not need to think about the problem of priority among facets on each individual occasion on the particular merits of the subject-complex under consideration. To do this is usually perplexing, and leads to inconsistent decisions. On the other hand, as between two consecutive facets, it is easier to decide which is more concrete and which more abstract; which is the object studied and which the method of study; which is personality and which energy. This secures conformity to the Canon of Consistent Sequence in an easier way. It would be a good subject for investigation for a student to examine the schedules of U.D.C. from the angle described above.

53831 Additional Gain

The gain of the C.C. is even greater, as a result of loyalty to the postulates. It is not necessary to repeat each energy focus in each case. A general remark that the foci in an energy facet are to be got by the subject device, or by a specified modification of it, is quite sufficient. The schedules are thereby made slimmer. Incidentally, it secures a somewhat prophetic provision for foci not in use at the moment of the design of the scheme of classification. For example, the number for " Application of elliptic functions to partition of numbers " given in 53821 need not be given in the schedule. The same benefit will also be of avail in U.D.C., and the Law of Parsimony can thus be satisfied.

CHAPTER 54

CHAIN IN THREE DIMENSIONS

540 A Chain in Mathematics

THE TERM DIMENSION WAS introduced and illustrated in section 315, and the term Facet was defined in section 3505. The two terms are equivalent. In considering a chain of classes, the term " dimension " is more helpful; we can speak of the parts of the chain or of the links in the chain, lying in dimension 1, 2, 3, etc. In considering a class number, the term " facet " is more helpful; we can speak of the isolate numbers in facet 1, 2, 3, etc. Indeed, each facet in a class number belongs to a dimension differing from that of any other; reciprocally, each dimension in a chain gives rise to a facet in a class number. The number of chains arising in a scheme of classification is very large. Some chains lie entirely within the Basic Dimension itself; in other words, the digits in the entire class number taken together denote only a basic class without any facet attached to it. The following chain in mathematics is an example:

Order	Subject	U.D.C.	C.C.	S.C.	L.C.	B.C.	No. of the Link
1	Mathematics ↓	51	B	A401 to A546	QA	AM to AY	1
2	Analysis ↓	517	B3	A520 to A525	QA300 to QA431	AR to AS	2
3	Function	517.5	B37 to B39	A524	QA331 to QA351	AS	3

The last subject in the above table is a basic class. It has no facet attached to it. The chain of which it is the last link lies entirely in the basic dimension. It does not extend into any other dimension. By convention, we do not take a basic dimension into the count of the dimensions of a subject. The number of chains lying in many dimensions will be very large in any scheme of classification. We shall study in this chapter one sample chain lying in three dimensions. It is a chain starting from Mathematics. We shall first give this chain in each of five schemes, before comparing them.

541 **Sample Chain**

Order	Subject	U.D.C.	C.C.	S.C.	L.C.	B.C.	Dimension
1	Mathematics	51	B	A401 to A546	QA	AM to Ay	Basic
2	Analysis	517	B3 to B4	A520 to A525	QA300 to QA431	AR to AS	Basic
3	Function	517.5	B37 to B39	A524	QA331 to QA351	AS	Basic
4	Real variable	517.51	B37		QA331.5	ASA	1
5	Analytic representation	517.512	B37:2				2
6	Infinite series		B37:26				3
7	Fourier series	517.512.2	B37:26M				3

542 Hospitality in Chain

The U.D.C. and C.C. have equal hospitality in chain, the greatest of the five schemes. They are able to reach up to order 7, and their chains extend to three dimensions. Their notation can take them to higher orders also. The S.C. has the least hospitality, as its chain stands arrested even in the basic dimension. It does not reach beyond order 3. The L.C. and B.C. have equal hospitality in chain, coming midway between the S.C. on the one side and the U.D.C. and C.C. on the other. They are able to reach up to order 4 only, and their chains are arrested in the first dimension. The B.C. has a class called Special Methods, numbered ASB. It is difficult to guess its contents, though it may be taken to carry its chain into the second dimension. But it is too general to be of much help.

543 Comparison of Notation

The following table gives the number of digits in the class numbers of successive orders in the different schemes:

Order	Number of Digits in the class number of				
	U.D.C.	C.C.	S.C.	L.C.	B.C.
1	2	1	4	2	2
2	3	2	4	5	2
3	5	3	4	5	2
4	6	3		7	3
5	7	5			
6		6			
7	9	7			
Average for orders 1 to 4	4	2.25	4	4.75	2.25
Average for orders 1 to 7	5.4	3.86			

544 Relativity and Expressiveness

The table shows the extent to which the Canon of Relativity is satisfied by the different schemes. The U.D.C. and C.C. conform to the canon, but S.C., L.C. and B.C. do not. The Canon of Expressiveness is satisfied only by the C.C. The beginning of the energy facet is indicated in the C.C. by the presence of the connecting symbol (colon).

545 Length

Class for class, the B.C. number is the shortest, and the C.C. comes next in order. The U.D.C. occupies the next rank up to order 2 only, and thereafter it goes down to the last rank. The S.C. and L.C. occupy, generally speaking, the third and the fourth ranks respectively. In comparing average length for the whole chain, all five chains can be brought in only if we stop with order 4. Then C.C. and B.C. stand bracketed in the first rank, followed by the S.C., U.D.C. and L.C. in succession. The average for all the seven orders can be compared only for U.D.C. and C.C. The extra length in U.D.C. does not reflect more expressiveness, but is due only to the presence of the two dummy dots, introduced to give relief to breath and to the eye. The C.C. has saved one digit in order 4 by telescoping it into order 3. The U.D.C. has saved one digit in order 7 by violating the Canon of Modulation and skipping order 6. This is not right, since documents do exist expounding the representation of a function in different kinds of series. The B.C. has saved digits, as usual, by using the more capacious base of Roman capitals in all the arrays, and telescoping arrays of orders 2 and 3 into the array of order 1.

CHAPTER 55

CHAIN IN MANY DIMENSIONS

550 Chains in Economics

THEORETICALLY, THERE CAN BE no end to a chain. This is a consequence of the universe of knowledge being infinite, ever developing, ever adding to its structure. Again theoretically, there can be no limit to the number of dimensions in which a chain may lie. But in practice few documents have hitherto demanded a chain lying in more than a dozen dimensions. In facet-terminology, theoretically there can be no limit to the number of facets presented by a subject, but in practice it seldom exceeds a dozen. Again theoretically, there can be no limit to the number of the order of a class, but in practice it seldom exceeds twenty. This is according to the literary warrant of today. We shall consider in this chapter a few chains of the main class Economics, lying in many dimensions. To demonstrate the branching of new chains from any link whatever in any chain, we shall take for the sample a bunch of chains, all having Economics as the common universe. This bunch is given in the two succeeding pairs of mutually-facing pages (section 5502).

5501 EXPLANATION

Column 1 gives the serial number of the classes occurring in the bunch. To make reference easy, this number is repeated in the verso as well as the recto of the double page. The table is intended to contain 280 classes, marked off into fourteen blocks, and to save space some of the blocks are not fully filled up. The classes in blocks 1 to 4 are all printed in full, and together contain the first twenty-eight classes of the bunch. Blocks 5 and 6 are each to contain twenty-one classes, but only the first and last classes are printed in each of them. The remaining nineteen classes of each should be filled in by the reader, parallel to the classes in blocks 2 to 4. Blocks 7 to 10 are each to contain seven classes, but again only the first and last classes are printed in each, and the remaining five classes of each should be filled by the reader, parallel to the classes in blocks 1 to 4 respectively. Similarly, blocks 11 and 12 should be filled like blocks 5 and 6. Lastly, each of the blocks 13 and 14 are to contain seventy classes, filled parallel to the classes 1 to 70.

The 280 classes in the tables are arranged according to the sequence of their C.C. numbers.

Column 2 gives the names of the subjects classified. They are arranged as successive links in their respective chains. In each subject, only the name of the last link in it is printed. The Canon of Context should be used to fill up the full name of the subject. For example: the name of subject 28 is " Lockouts in India in 1955 "; the name of subject 49 is " Lockouts in child labour in India in 1955 "; and the name of subject 280 is " Lockouts in girl labour in common-salt industry in India in 1955."

Column 3 gives the facet formulae appropriate to the subjects in column 2. The following symbols have been used in stating the facet formulae.

(BC)	= Basic class	[2P3]	= Second round third level personality
[E]	= First round energy	[2P4]	= Second round fourth level personality
[P]	= First round personality	[S]	= Space
[2P1]	= Second round first level personality	[T]	= Time

Column 4 gives the number of dimensions through which the chain of the subject in column 2 extends.

Column 5 gives the order of the class of the subject in column 2, as measured with 0 for the Universe of Knowledge and 1 for Economics.

Columns 6 to 9 give the class numbers of the subjects in column 2, according to the C.C., U.D.C., L.C. and B.C. respectively. The C.C. numbers are taken from the forthcoming fifth edition. They are based on the further investigations made and clarified since 1950 and incorporated in Ranganathan's "Depth classification (19): Classification of Management," appearing in the *Annals of library science,* Vol. 3, 1956, pages 33-72.

5502 SAMPLE BUNCH OF CHAINS

1 Ser. No.	2 Subject	3 Facet Formula	4 No. of Dimen- sions	5 Order No.
1	Economics	(BC)	0	1
2	Asia	(BC).[S]	1	2
3	up to 1920's	(BC).[S].[T]	2	4
4	India	(BC).[S]	1	3
5	up to 1950's	(BC).[S].[T]	2	5
6	from 1919 to 1955	(BC).[S].[T]	2	9
7	in 1955	(BC).[S].[T]	2	6
8	Labour	(BC):[E]	1	2
9	Asia	(BC):[E].[S]	2	3
10	up to 1920's	(BC):[E].[S].[T]	3	5
11	India	(BC):[E].[S]	2	4
12	up to 1950's	(BC):[E].[S].[T]	3	6
13	from 1919 to 1955	(BC):[E].[S].[T]	3	10
14	in 1955	(BC):[E].[S].[T]	3	7
15	Industrial relation	(BC):[E] [2P4]	2	3
16	Collective agreement	(BC):[E] [2P4]	2	4
17	Dispute	(BC):[E] [2P3]	2	4
18	Conciliation	(BC):[E] [2P3],[2P4]	3	5
19	Adjudication	(BC):[E] [2P3],[2P4]	3	5
20	Settlement	(BC):[E] [2P3],[2P4]	3	5
21	Strike	(BC): E [2P3]	2	4
22	Lock-out	(BC): E [2P3]	2	4
23	Asia	(BC): E [2P3].[S]	3	5
24	up to 1920's	(BC): E [2P3].[S].[T]	4	7
25	India	(BC): E [2P3].[S]	3	6
26	up to 1950's	(BC): E [2P3].[S].[T]	4	8
27	from 1919 to 1955	(BC): E [2P3].[S].[T]	4	12
28	in 1955	(BC): E [2P3].[S].[T]	4	9

5502 SAMPLE BUNCH OF CHAINS (*continued*)

Ser. No.	C.C. Number	U.D.C. Number	L.C. Number	B.C. Number
1	X	33	HB151	T
2	X.4	33(5)	HC411	T,8
3	X.4.N2	33(5)"192"	HC414.3	T,8,T
4	X.44	33(54)	HC431	T,87
5	X.44.N5	33(54)"195"	HC436.4	T,87,V
6	X.44.N55←N19	33(54)"1919/1955"	HC436.3/4	T,87,R
7	X.44.N55	33(54)"1955"	HC436.5	T,87,U
8	X:9	331	HD4901	TH
9	X:9.4	331(5)	HD8564	TH,8
10	X:9.4.N2	331(5)"192"	HD8565/6	TH,8,T
11	X:9.44	331(54)	HD8584	TH,87
12	X:9.44.N5	331(54)"195"	HD8585/6	TH,87,V
13	X:9.44.N55←N19	331(54)"1919/1955"	HD8586	TH,87,R
14	X:9.44.N55	331(54)"1955"	HD8586	TH,87,U
15	X:97	331.1	HD6971	TDB
16	X:972	331.116.3	HD6483	TDS
17	X:979C	331.89	HD5306	TDC
18	X:979C,4	331.153	HD5481	THW
19	X:979C,7	331.16	HD5485	THW
20	X:979C,8	331.15	HD5481	THW
21	X:979D	331.892	HD5307	THT
22	X:979W	331.895	HD5471	THT
23	X:979W.4	331.895(5)	HD5471.A6	THT,8
24	X:979W.4.N2	331.895(5)"192"	HD5471.A6.1920	THT,8,T
25	X:979W.44	331.895(54)	HD5471.I4	THT,87
26	X:979W.44.N55	331.895(54)"195"	HD5471.I4.1950	THT,87,V
27	X:979W.44.N55← N19	331.895(54)"1919/1955"	HD5471.I4.1919/1955	THT,87,R
28	X:979W.44.N55	331.895(54)"1955"	HD5471.I4.1955	THT,87,U

5502 SAMPLE BUNCH OF CHAINS (*continued*)

1 Ser. No.	2 Subject	3 Facet Formula	4 No. of Dimensions	5 Order No.
29 ***	Econ. Lab. Child *** ***	(BC):[E] [2P1] ***	2 ***	3 ***
49	Lock-out. India. 1955	(BC):[E] [2P1],[2P3].[S].[T]	5	10
50 ***	Girl *** ***	(BC):[E] [2P1] ***	2 ***	4 ***
70	Lock-out. India. 1955	(BC):[E] [2P1],[2P3].[S].[T]	5	11
71 ***	Econ. Chemical Industry *** ***	(BC) [P] ***	1 ***	2 ***
77	India. 1955	(BC) [P].[S].[T]	3	7
78 ***	Labour *** ***	(BC) [P]:[E] ***	2 ***	3 ***
84	India. 1955	(BC) [P]:[E].[S].[T]	4	8
85	Industrial relation	(BC) [P]:[E] [2P4]	3	4
***	*** ***	***	***	***
91	Strike	(BC) [P]:[E] [2P3]	3	5
92 ***	Lock-out *** ***	(BC) [P]:[E] [2P3] ***	3 ***	5 ***
98	India. 1955	(BC) [P]:[E] [2P3].[S].[T]	5	10
99 ***	Child *** ***	(BC) [P]:[E] [2P1] ***	3 ***	4 ***
119	Lock-out. India. 1955	(BC)[P]:[E][2P1],[2P3].[S].[T]	6	11
120 ***	Girl *** ***	(BC) [P]:[E] [2P1] ***	3 ***	5 ***
140	Lock-out. India. 1955	(BC) [P]:[E] [2P1],[2P3].[S].[T]	6	12
141 ***	Econ. Salt industry *** ***	(BC) [P] ***	1 ***	3 ***
210	Lab. Girl. Lock-out. India. 1955	(BC) [P]:[E] [2P1],[2P3].[S].[T]	6	13
211	Econ. Common salt industry	(BC) [P]	1	5
***	*** ***	***	***	***
280	Lab. Girl. Lock-out. India. 1955	(BC) [P]:[E] [2P1],[2P3].[S].[T]	6	15

5502   SAMPLE BUNCH OF CHAINS (*continued*)

Ser. No.	C.C. No.	U.D.C. No.	L.C. No.	B.C. No.
29 ***	X:9B ***	331.3 ***	HD6231 ***	QVK ***
49	X:9B,79W.44.N55	331.3:331.895(54) "1955"	?	QVK-THT,87, U
50 ***	X:9B-F ***	331.44 ***	? ***	QVK-QW ***
70	X:9B-F,79W.44.N55	331.44:331.895(54) "1955"	?	QVK-QW-THT,87, U
71 ***	X9(F) ***	33:66 ***	HD9650.5 ***	CUB-T ***
77	X9(F).44.N55	33:66(54)"1955"	HD9657.I4.1955	CUB-T,87, U
78 ***	X9(F):9 ***	331.66 ***	HD8039.C451 ***	CUB-TH ***
84	X9(F):9.44.N55	331:66(54)"1955"	HD8039.C451.I4. 1955	CUB-TH, 87,U
85 ***	X9(F):97 ***	331.1:66 ***	HD6976.C451 ***	CUB-TDB ***
91	X9(F):979D	331.892:66	HD5392.C451	CUB-THT
92 ***	X9(F):979W ***	331.895:66 ***	HD5471.C451 ***	CUB-THT ***
98	X9(F):979W.44.N55	331.895:66(54) "1955"	HD5471.C451.I4. 1955	CUB-THT, 87,U
99 ***	X9(F):9B ***	331.3:66 ***	HD6247.C451 ***	CUB-QVK ***
119	X9(F):9B,79W.44.N55	331.3:331.895:66 (54)"1955"	HD6247.C451.I4. 1955	CUB-QVK-THT,87, U
120	X9(F):9B-F	331.44:66	?	CUB-QVK-QW
***	***	***	***	***
140	X9(F):9B-F,79W.44.N55	331.44:331.895:66 (54)"1955"	?	CUB-QVK-QW-THT,87, U
141 ***	X9(F4) ***	33:661.8 ***	HD9660.S1 ***	CUF-T ***
210	X9(F4):9B-F,79W.44.N55	331.44:331.895: 661.8(54)"1955"	?	CUF-QVK-QW-THT,87, U
211 ***	X9(F44171) ***	33:661.42 ***	HD9213 ***	CUG ***
280	X9(F44171):9B-F, 79W.44.N55	331.44:331.895: 661.42(54) "1955"	?	CUG-QVK-QW-THT,87, U

5503 GENERAL OBSERVATIONS

The sample bunch of chains, belonging to the main class Economics and given in the four preceding pages, brings out the relative versatility of the C.C., U.D.C., and B.C. in securing individualisation (i.e. coextensiveness with the subject) by their respective notational systems. The L.C. keeps step with them, except in its inability to provide for " girl-labour." Perhaps this can be easily rectified. The sequence of classes is not the same in all the schemes. Some of the differences are due to differences in the idea plane itself, which is understandable; it is for consideration which sequence is more helpful than which. But some of the differences are due to difficulties in the notational plane. Others are due to a combination of the differences in both the planes. For example, consider " Labour in chemical industries." In U.D.C., this has to be treated as a subject of two phases, therefore 331, the number for Labour, and 67, the number for Chemical industries, have to be combined by a colon. The notational convention in colon combination is that the smaller ordinal number is put before the bigger one, giving the number 331:67. But this is the result in the idea plane, of the system of knowledge, forming the basis of U.D.C., having put Economics before Technology. Thus U.D.C.'s sequence of classes differs from that of the C.C. as shown below.

Sequence in C.C.	Sequence in U.D.C.
Labour: General account	Labour: General account
Chemical industry: All problems	Chemical industry: Labour problem
Chemical industry: Labour problem	Chemical industry: All problems

In B.C., the sequence is still another. It is: 1 Chemical industry: All problems. 2 Chemical industry: Labour problem. 3 Labour: General Account.

551 Time Facet

In the C.C. and U.D.C., the isolate number in the time facet can be made coextensive with the time isolate in the subject, in all cases. The notational device provided by these two schemes gives autonomy to the classifier to construct exactly fitting isolate numbers of time, whatever the country or subject studied. But in the L.C. and B.C. there is no similar provision. In the L.C. certain periods are mentioned in certain subject schedules. In some cases, the period is denoted by a single digit; in others, the full number of the year has to be written. In the B.C. there is a common schedule of time isolates, but this has been avowedly constructed for a particular subject in a particular country. Again, both in the L.C. and B.C. there is notation only for certain traditional epochs. Any interval of time, starting with any year and ending with any other year, cannot be denoted with precision, as is possible in the C.C. and U.D.C.

552 Space Facet

In all the schemes, the isolate number in the space facet is coextensive with the space isolate in the subject. The Canon of Scheduled Mnemonics is satisfied in the C.C., U.D.C. and B.C., but not in the L.C. In the latter, different digits represent the same geographical area in different classes. There is therefore need to look up tables I to X to pick up the space isolate number, according to the prescription given in each class. But the design of the ten tables for the space isolate number, so as to fill up the gaps in the gap-notation of L.C., is clever. In all the schemes, the space facet is the penultimate one.

553 Rounds and Levels

In the C.C. alone, different rounds and levels of facets are used. This enables the C.C. to arrange the classes in a more helpful sequence and in better conformity to the Canons for Filiatory Sequence. This is seen in blocks 2 to 5—i.e. in classes 8 to 28. The absence of such a provision scatters filiatory classes in the U.D.C., L.C. and B.C., as is well brought out by classes 15 to 22. The scattering is less in the B.C. than in the other two schemes. In all probability, the scattering in all these three schemes is due to difficulties in the notational plane caused by the non-recognition of rounds, rather than to a deliberate choice of the sequence in the system of knowledge used as basis, in the idea plane.

554 Personality Facet

In the C.C. and B.C., the personality facet precedes the energy facet, in accordance with the Principle of Decreasing Concreteness prescribed for a facet formula. In the C.C. this happens in each of the rounds and deliberately so. In the B.C. this does not arise as there are no rounds. In the U.D.C. and L.C., the energy facet precedes the personality facet —i.e. the facet with the industry as focus. In the U.D.C. this happens because of the fact that among the main classes Economics precedes Chemical Technology. In the L.C. the reversal of the sequence is due merely to causes in the notational plane.

555 Expressiveness

In the C.C. and U.D.C. the class number is expressive: the different facets inherent in the subject are thrown in relief by the connecting symbols, which is a help for one searching for literature. This is only done to the greatest possible extent in the forthcoming fifth edition of Colon. In the earlier editions, the expressiveness was blurred towards the latter half of class number, which has caused dissatisfaction, and in fact it was this dissatisfaction that ultimately led to the postulate of rounds.

In the B.C. expressiveness is ordinarily secured only for the time and space facets. In other facets, the urge for shorter notation has led to the adoption of the species of Roman capitals in all the arrays. This leads to the telescoping not only of arrays, but even of facets. Thus expressiveness is sacrificed at the altar of the " economic limit in the length of number." However, in many cases, phase relation has to be used. This secures expressiveness automatically, as the phases have to be separated by a connecting symbol. This is what has happened in classes 71 to 280.

In the L.C., the class number is severely unipartite in most cases—even much more than in B.C. But notational exigency sometimes brings about some expressiveness. This happens often when the geographical tables I to X are brought into use. Sometimes, phase relation too produces a similar effect, as is seen in classes 78 onwards, where a particular industry comes up for study.

556　Over-all Coextensiveness

In the C.C. and U.D.C., the class numbers attain over-all coextensiveness with the subjects represented. In the B.C., they fail in two respects. All the modes of settlement of industrial disputes are represented by the same number, as seen in class 18 to 20. Again, " lockout " and " strike " are represented by the same numbers, as seen in classes 21 and 22. This happens also in L.C., which in addition makes no provision to distinguish " Girl labour " from " Child labour." It is difficult, of course, to provide for everything possible in sheer anticipation in an enumerative classification. It is here that an analytico-synthetic classification scores. It gives schedules only for fundamental constituent isolates, and by prescribing suitable notational devices, it enables a classifier to analyse an unscheduled composite isolate into its component elements and then construct by synthesis the coextensive class number.

557　Over-all Length

In class numbers of up to three or four orders, the over-all length of class number is more or less the same in C.C., U.D.C. and B.C. But the L.C. number is usually longer. To have shorter numbers for classes of earlier orders is a help. The books in a public library, and in any library the books sought by non-specialist readers, will belong only to the earlier orders. This means that such readers may not have much occasion to face long numbers.

The B.C. has the shortest class numbers in the later orders. This is due, as has been repeatedly pointed out, to the adoption of the more capacious species of Roman capitals practically in all arrays. Sacrifice of mnemonics also contributes to shortness. As shown in section 555, expressiveness and coextensiveness also are sacrificed in the higher orders.

In most cases, the U.D.C. has the longest class number. This is due to its seeking to do the work of facet notation by phase notation; to the presence of dummy dots to give relief to breath and eyes; and to the use of double digits—brackets and quotation marks—as connecting symbols. Elimination of these factors in the notational plane would shorten U.D.C. numbers considerably. This is a piece of work awaiting to be done, which I commend to the F.I.D. Committee on U.D.C.

The C.C. numbers are shorter than U.D.C. numbers. This is due to the use of the more capacious species of Roman capitals for the array of main classes; to the use of the more compact facet notation; and to the use of single-digited connecting symbols. The C.C. number is, however, lengthened by two digits, in some cases, by the use of packet notation for subject device. At present no shorter notational device is seen. Another factor leading to longer notation is connected with auto-bias device. The entire isolate number has to be repeated in both the components of the auto-bias. The C.C. should endeavour to effect economy of digits in this matter.

The over-all class number of the L.C. is the longest in the first four or five orders. Thereafter, the L.C. number is usually shorter than the C.C. or U.D.C. number, but longer than the B.C. number. The shortness in higher orders is due to the use of gap notation, in spite of the risk involved; the sacrifice of expressiveness; the sacrifice of coextensiveness; and the sacrifice of scheduled mnemonics, causing undue strain to the classifier.

558 Relativity

The Canon of Relativity prevails in the C.C. and U.D.C. It fails in the L.C. on account of its gap notation. It fails in the B.C. on account of its telescoping of arrays and even of facets.

CHAPTER 56

DESIGN

561 Agriculture as Sample Basic Class

CHAPTERS 51 TO 55 demonstrated the application of the Canons of Classification to a critical and comparative study of known schemes of classification. Such a comparative study has also been made already in respect of each main class of C.C. and D.C., in the symposium *Colon classification vs. Decimal classification* presented to the Sixth All India Library Conference held at Jaipur in 1944. It was occasioned by the publication of the fourteenth edition of D.C. in 1943, and has been printed in full in the *Proceedings* of the Conference. The D.C. does not lend itself to depth classification, so it has been replaced in this edition by U.D.C. in the preceding chapters devoted to comparison. A more detailed comparative study of the C.C. and U.D.C. in respect of some of the features of an analytico-synthetic classification has also been made already in a symposium presented to the Tenth All India Library Conference held at Hyderabad in 1953. This has been printed as a book with the title *Depth classification, etc.* (1953), ed. by Ranganathan. Further, a systematic and critical comparison of C.C. and U.D.C. in respect of the auxiliary schedules and the main class Library Science has been appearing in the *Abgila*, Vols. 2 and 3, 1952-3, and thereafter in the *Annals of library science,* Vol. 1, 1954, in the series of articles entitled *Critique of UDC*. This chapter is turned on another demonstration. It is proposed to demonstrate here the application of the postulates and canons to the design of classification. Agriculture has been taken as the sample basic subject. This has been pursued by D. B. Krishna Rao in his doctorate thesis. One of the instalments of this thesis has been published in the *Annals of library science,* Vol. 2, 1955, pages 12-21, under the title *Depth classification* (9), *Agriculture* (5), *Species and cultivar*. In this article, Krishna Rao has assembled the necessary data. It demonstrates the important preliminary work to be done in the idea plane before work on the notational plane can be taken up. This chapter takes up for demonstration only the design of classification in the first level of the first round of the personality facet.

562 Symbols

For convenience and brevity, the following symbols will be used:

[P] = the fundamental category Personality
[1P1] = Personality facet of first level in first round

$$[1P1](aA) \qquad = \text{Array } a \text{ in } [1P1]$$
$$[1P1](aA)(fF) = \text{Focus } f \text{ in } [1P1](aA)$$

It should be remembered that we are confining our attention to the second zone only, which is why we use the symbol [1P1] instead of [1P1](2Z). In what follows, the first of these symbols stands for the latter; this is done for the sake of brevity.

563 [1P1]

All the cultivated varieties of plants form the universe of [1P1]. Not every genus and species distinguished in Botany contributes to the universe of plants forming the subject of study in Agriculture, for some may not include any cultivated plant whatever.

5631 CULTIVAR

A variety or strain of plant brought under cultivation is denoted by the term " cultivar." Not more than 5,000 botanical species are said to contribute to the universe of cultivars, and these belong to only about 500 genera. The number of cultivars, however, is very large. In wheat alone, 26,000 cultivars have been identified by N. I. Vavilov in *Chronica botanica*, Vol. 13, and there may be a similar number in rice also, and in many other cultivated species of plants. We may therefore safely say that the universe of cultivars is very large; in other words, the number of isolates found in [1P1] of Agriculture is very large, and it may run to many hundreds of thousands. Literary warrant demands that all of them should be recognised in designing [1P1] for the depth classification of micro-thought. The superficial classification needed for classifying macro-thought, however, may not demand more than a few hundred isolates to be recognised in [1P1]. But convenience suggests that the shorter schedule for the universe of macro-thought should be contained in the longer schedule for micro-thought.

5632 GROUP NOTATION

The existence of thousands of isolates calls for group notation in preference to octave notation. Reference to section 3686 will show that a group notation of five or more significant digits is needed for micro-thought and of not more than three digits for macro-thought. This indicates that, in the idea plane, we should try to form the groups at each stage, not arbitrarily, but in such a way that when we reach the subgroups at the third level, they include all the cultivars usually represented in documents embodying macro-thought. In other words, we should see if we can enumerate characteristics, i.e. quasi isolates, in what presents itself as first order array or second order array. It will be even more helpful if these characteristics themselves can be viewed as derived on the basis of some characteristic of a higher or more comprehensive nature—say a super-characteristic.

5633 SUPER-CHARACTERISTIC

In fact, each of the first two orders of groups do admit of being named after such a super-characteristic. In agriculture, Utility may well be used as the favoured first characteristic. The group of the first order, i.e. the quasi isolates in (1A), may be conveniently labelled " Utility," and the isolates based on the Utility characteristic may be formed out of the primary use of a cultivar. We have to adopt this convention because a plant can be put to many uses. For example, the possible uses of rice plant are (1) food made of the seed, (2) feed made of the straw, (3) roofing material made of the straw, and so on. It is a matter of judgment based on experience to choose the use of seed as food for the primary utility, i.e. include rice in the group of cultivars containing food-yielding cultivars, instead of, say, in the group of feed-yielding or building-material-yielding cultivars.

5634 SECOND SUPER-CHARACTERISTIC

Generally speaking, when the first characteristic of a train of characteristics is fixed, the succeeding characteristics are suggested almost uniquely. This is true of super-characteristics also. The illustrations used in the preceding section readily suggest that the second order group, i.e. the quasi isolate in (2A) derived from any focus in (1A), may be conveniently labelled " Organ." The isolates based on the Organ characteristic may be formed out of the organ of the cultivar, put to the primary use.

5635 UTILITY SCHEDULE

For definiteness of demonstration, we use the C.C. in the notational plane. The other schemes do not follow a definite analytical procedure to an equally unmistakable degree. Therefore, it is considered to be easier to demonstrate with C.C. in the notational plane. But the findings in the idea plane hold good for all schemes. The fourth edition of C.C. gives the following utility schedule:

1 Decoration	4 Stimulant	7 Fabric	92 Manure
2 Feed	5 Oil	8 Dye, tan	93 Vegetable
3 Food	6 Drug	91 Adhesive	98 Sugar

Most of these isolate numbers have been got by the application of scheduled mnemonics or seminal mnemonics. The last two isolates stand on a different footing from the others. They represent other first characteristics that can be used to form the first division of the universe of cultivars. Their use is justified by literary warrant at the level of macro-thought, for we have books on vegetables and on sugar-yielding plants. At the same time, we must beware of cross-classification. To avoid this, we should follow the usual convention that the train of characteristics initiated by any such other characteristic should be arrested or sealed just before it yields any particular cultivar derived by the application of a train of characteristics, got with any of the first ten characteristics as the first characteristic.

5636   ORGAN SCHEDULE

The fourth edition of C.C. gives the following organ schedule:

| 1 Sap | 3 Root | 5 Leaf | 7 Fruit | 91 Whole plant |
| 2 Bulb | 4 Stem | 6 Flower | 8 Seed | |

The isolate numbers are practically those already given in the organ schedule in Botany. In other words, it satisfies the Canon of Scheduled Mnemonics. In Botany itself, the organs are arranged so as to satisfy the Principle of Spatial Contiguity. Moreover, the convention of starting from the bottom and moving upwards is followed. Incidentally, this also satisfies to some extent the Principle of Later in Time.

564   **Further Digits**

We have already covered two arrays, i.e. we have formed group isolate numbers of two digits. For simplifying further discussion without loss of generality, we may ignore the two last utility divisions. The remaining ten isolates of the utility schedule and the nine isolates of the organ schedule can be combined in ninety possible ways. Thus, we get ninety " utility *cum* organ isolates " out of these two schedules. Krishna Rao has estimated that only fifty-two of these comprehend plants actually cultivated hitherto. Thus the 5,000 botanical species yielding cultivars fall into these fifty-two subgroups. This gives an average of 100 species to be represented in each utility *cum* organ subgroup. As shown in section 3686, this would indicate the need for the addition of a two-digited group notation to the two digits already used.

5641   CLOSER VIEW

This inference by average is, however, an over-simplification of the problem. It is a matter of experience that actuality is usually more complicated than the average. So it is here also. For Krishna Rao has shown the actual distribution of the 5,000 species among the utility *cum* organ subgroups to be quite askew. It is as shown in the following table:

Number of Subgroups	containing	Number of Species		Number of Significant digits needed
		Greater than	Not greater than	
43		0	24	1
5		24	256	2
3		256	2,560	3
1		2,560	20,465	4

The figures in the last column are taken from section 3686. Adding the two digits already needed to represent utility *cum* organ, we get the following results:

Number of Subgroups needing	Number of digits in the overall isolate number
43	3
5	4
3	5
1	6

5642 UNIVERSE OF MACRO-THOUGHT

Literary warrant indicates that nearly 90 per cent. of the books embodying macro-thought do not need to go beyond the utility number or the utility *cum* organ number. That is, in general agricultural collections and in public or popular libraries, the number of digits in [1P1] will be only one or two. Slightly more specialised documents may reach up to three digits at the most. It is only in the universe of articles embodying micro-thought that more digits will be needed. But from the way in which provision is made to add digits, it can be seen that the schedule for macro-thought is contained in the schedule for micro-thought.

5643 THE MOST NUMEROUS SUBGROUP

The most numerous subgroup needing six digits to represent a species is the one of Ornamental Flowers. It comprises about 3,000 species. We cannot help having six digits to individualise a species in this subgroup. The subgroups needing five digits are those of Ornamental Leaf, Ornamental Whole Plant, and Food Fruit. This means that horticultural plants need the longest numbers. The five subgroups needing four digits to individualise a species are those of Food Seed, Feed Leaf, Food Leaf, Dye-Tan Stem and Oil Leaf. Thus, the subgroup Food Seed, which usually attracts a considerable literature, needs at least four significant digits to individualise a species. In some cases, it is possible to use the third digit to represent the genus.

565 Species with Four Digits

Following is an extract from the schedule for a subgroup needing four significant digits. It is the Food Seed subgroup, represented by the isolate number 38.

The first of the underlined terms is the name of genus, and the second is the name of species. In deciding the first or second term, the Canon of Context must be borne in mind. In the case of rice, wheat and oat, the third digit denotes genus; and the fourth significant digit denotes species. In the case of millets, pulses and nuts, the third digit denotes only a favoured grouping. Such adjustments have to be made with

C.C. No.	Category	U.D.C. No.	C.C. No.	Category	U.D.C. No.
J381	**Rice.** *Oryza*	318	**J387**	**Millet**	633.17
J3811	*Sativa*	633.18	J3871	Grain sorghum. *Sorghum vulgare*	633.174
J3812	*Glabberima*		J3872	Pearl millet. *Pennisetum typhoides*	
***	*** ***		..	.. ..	
J382	**Wheat.** *Triticum*		J38791	Adlay. *Coix lachryma-jobi*	
J3821	*Vulgare*	633.11			
J3822	*Durum*		***	*** ***	
..	.. ..		**J388**	**Pulses**	63.65
J38291	*Turgudum*		J3881	Chick pea. *Cicer arietinum*	635.657
J38292	*Compactum*		J3882	Pigeon pea. *Cajanus cajan*	635.659
***	*** ***		J3883	*Phaseolous*	635.659
J383	**Oat.** *Auena*		J38831	Green gram. *Aureus*	635.659
J3831	*Sativa*	633.13	***	*** ***	
J3832	*Byzantina*		**J389**	**Nut**	634.5
..	.. ..		J3891	*Juglans*	634.51
J38391	*Strigosa*		J38911	Walnut. *Regia*	634.511
J38392	*Brevis*		J38912	Butternut. *Cineria*	634.518

care and with an eye on literary warrant. In the case of " grams," the exigency in the idea plane necessitates the use of five significant digits in [1P1] to denote a species. Such deviations from the normal do arise occasionally in any subject.

566 Universe of Micro-Thought

In section 5642, it was observed that 90 per cent. of the books in a general collection will demand only two digits in [1P1]. An appreciable number of articles may require the working out of [1P1] up to the stage of species only. In the notational plane, this would mean the addition to the basic two digits of one more significant digit in the case of forty-three of the two-digited subgroups, two more in the case of five, three more in the case of three and four more in the case of one subgroup. But most of the current investigations are on varieties and strains of each species, which are now called cultivars. For after all, the deeper aim in agriculture is to breed specialised cultivars to meet economic requirements. A place may have unusual climatic conditions or seasonal peculiarities, and there is then need to breed a strain to stand their pressure. There may be need to breed a strain of cotton with long lint. Or special breeds of rice may have to be produced to suit different modes of cooking or different kinds of dishes to be cooked. There can be no end to the special qualities that may be needed from time to time. Therefore new cultivars will be frequently established. It will also happen that fashion or custom changes and leaves some cultivars to go out of use and disappear altogether. This means that the cultivars will not satisfy the Canon of Permanence. Thus in the universe of micro-thought, which takes us into arrays of higher orders, further classification cannot proceed on normal lines.

Perhaps the large and ever-changing number of cultivar isolates would suggest the use of alphabetical device to construct their isolate numbers. Some cultivars have code names, each such name beginning with a letter of the alphabet. They thus lend themselves to use in alphabetical device. The fact that the later digits in the code names are usually numerals does not disqualify them for use in alphabetical device. Some cultivars have names in a natural language, but it is usually a local language. There are no names for them in a language like Latin used in international nomenclature. This fact may appear on the surface to militate against alphabetical device, but in most cases it will not be really so, for a cultivar tends to be localised. When it migrates to a nearby area, it carries its own name with it, even if the new area has a different language. The exceptions causing linguistic scattering, are believed to be few. Therefore alphabetical device may be used in the array following the array representing species.

Here are a few examples:

C.C. Number	Cultivar	U.D.C. Number
3	Food	
31	Sap	
311	Sugarcane. *Saccharum officianarum*	633.61
311B	Barbados	
311B85	B85	
311CO	CO (=Coimbatore)	
311CO213	CO213	
311COK	COK (=Coimbatore Karnal)	
311COK48	COK48	
311CP	CP (=Canal Point)	
311CP32/228	CP32/228	

There is another way of building cultivar numbers which deserves investigation. As stated in section 566, cultivars are established in order to secure in the organ of primary utility certain special qualities. The Canons for Filiatory Sequence will be better satisfied if all the cultivars having similar special qualities are brought together, instead of being scattered alphabetically. The special qualities may concern physical attributes, chemical attributes or ecological or any other attributes of the organ of primary utility. They may also concern biological attributes of the whole plant. Let us denote cultivars bred for a particular special quality a "Special." It is for consideration whether an Array of Specials may not be inserted immediately after the array of species and make the array of cultivar follow thereafter. Of course this means lengthening the isolate number by one more digit. It becomes a fight between the Law of Parsimony and the Canons for Filiatory Sequence backed by the Canon of Helpful Sequence. The F.I.D. should get this point thrashed out by specialists in agriculture —particularly in breeding. A similar point arises also in animal husbandry, and it may arise in other fields also. For example, in motor-car design, Specials may arise with reference to speed as in race cars, with reference to sturdiness as in cars for mountainous terrain, with reference to comfort as in luxury cars, or with reference to various other types of use.

5663   Suggestions for Design

If the specialist readers prefer the insertion of the array of specials, that would amount to a decision in the idea plane. We have next to find out methods of carrying out this decision in the notational plane. Then only will the design of classification be completed. One suggestion for investigation is that the array of specials should begin its numbers with a Roman capital, for the isolate number for species is made solely of Arabic numerals, and, further, the number of digits varies with the species. But a decision like this should be coupled with another prescription, viz. the cultivar number should never be added directly after the species number. Is this possible? In other words, will every cultivar lend itself to belong to one and only one " Special "? The specialist readers should be requested to answer this question. If the answer is affirmative, should we allocate the twenty-four Roman capitals to different groups of special qualities. Here is a tentative sample; C Physical qualities, E Chemical qualities, G Biological qualities, M Technological suitability, U Ecological qualities, and so on. Each of these should be further subdivided in the light of literary warrant.

5664   Alternative Design

If the answer of the specialist readers to the above question is negative, we should think of an alternative design in the notational plane. Here is a possible alternative for investigation. The numbers indicating Special Qualities may be made to occupy the second zone of the very array to which the cultivar belongs. In other words, the numbers for the specials may be packeted. In that case, we must adopt a convention. The numbers in the fourth zone should not be subdivided so as to arrive at a particular cultivar. They must be reserved to hold only documents dealing with the special qualities in general terms, or dealing at once with all the cultivars with the special quality in question. But any document dealing solely with one of these cultivars should be accommodated in the third zone under the cultivar number concerned.

567 Advantages of Present Approach

The advantages of the present analytico-synthetic approach in a conscious way can be seen by a comparison of the four editions of the C.C. In the first (1933), the third array was called " Crop Array." No distinction was made between a number in it representing a genus, a species, a variety or any popular grouping. The array had two zones.

The zone of Arabic numerals was filled up by the favoured category device; and the array of Roman capitals was left to accommodate all the other crops by the alphabetical device. Groups such as pulses and nuts, demanded by literary warrant, could not be formed in a helpful way. The second edition (1939) perpetuated this treatment, for none of the new ideas developed in the first edition of the *Prolegomena* was able to shed any light on the problem. Moreover, the agricultural collection of the Madras University Library was very poor. However, pamphlets received from the Agricultural Research Stations in the U.S.A. were disclosing the unhelpfulness of the schedule. But the absence of specialist readers of agricultural documents in the city of Madras did not allow any incentive to pursue the problem to a satisfactory end. The problem came to be faced persistently only after D. B. Krishna Rao took charge of the Library of the Agricultural College and Research Institute at Coimbatore. By 1949, he had gained considerable experience in regard to the difficulties. The Government of Madras deputed him to come to Delhi and work with me on these problems for about a month. He worked out a more detailed crop schedule, but it was too late for incorporation in the third edition (1950), and his expanded schedule was incorporated only in the fourth edition (1952). But even there, cultivars could not be individualised. The change-over from the second zone of the array to the third was haphazard, not based on any rational principles. It was only in 1953 that the concept of Whole and Organ was applied to distinguish the point at which array-formation should give place to facet-formation. Above all, the concept of Cultivar, which has clarified the problem, was finally adopted only in 1953 by the International Horticultural Congress. Their *International code of nomenclature for cultivated plants* (1953) came within our reach only in 1954. The clarification of the problem contained in this code led us forward. The analysis now pursued in the idea plane as well as the notational plane, in the light of this clarification, has given much better results. It has rigged up the C.C. for intensive depth classification in agriculture. It can now stand much more ably the onslaught of the universe of micro-thought in this field. Some of the problems still awaiting solution have been already indicated. Krishna Rao's thesis contains schedules worked out in great detail along the lines outlined in this chapter, and it is hoped to incorporate them in the fifth edition of the C.C.

CHAPTER 57

CLASSIFYING

570 Sample Micro-Thought

THE PROCEDURE FOR CLASSIFYING has been laid down in section 370. We shall demonstrate in this chapter the application of that procedure to micro-thought of considerable minuteness. We shall take an imaginary subject as sample:

" Statistics of the acetylene welding of broken steel shoulders of forks in Rudge cycles, as influenced by temperature conditions, during the period 1892 to 1955 in Greece."

We shall proceed to construct its class number, so as to satisfy the Canon of Expressiveness and so that it is coextensive with the subject. We shall use symbols like the following to secure brevity in expression. These are in addition to those given in section 562.

(BC)	=	Basic class
[P]	=	Fundamental category Personality
[mPn]	=	Personality facet at level n in round m
[mE]	=	Energy facet in round m
(P)	=	Phase
(P2)	=	Second phase
(P) (BC)	=	(BC) of (P)
(ACI)	=	Anteriorising common isolate

571 Analysis into Facets in Idea Plane

In separating out the basic class, facets and phases, we should fill up the ellipses in the name of the subject given in section 570. For example, the term " Rudge cycle " implies the basic class Engineering; this term should be supplied. Again, the term " Temperature conditions " implies the basic class Heat, belonging to the main class Physics. We get the following analysis in the idea plane. The terms got by filling up ellipses are in italics.

(BC)	*Engineering*	[3P1]	Welding
[1P1]	Rudge cycle	[3P2]	Acetylene
[1P2]	Fork	(P2)	Influence
[1P3]	Shoulder	(P2) (BC)	*Heat*
[1M1]	Steel	(P2) (BC) [1E]	Temperature
[1E]	*Disease*	[S]	Greece
[2P1]	Broken	[T]	Between 1892 and 1955
[2E]	*Cure*	(ACI)	Statistics

Notes

(1) It needs experience to put in the [1E] as Disease. This is in fact suggested by the term " broken."

(2) Breakage is the causal factor for the disease. It is therefore taken as [2P1].

(3) It also needs experience to put in the [2E] as Cure. This is in fact suggested by the term " welding."

(4) Welding is the causal factor or agency for cure. It is therefore taken as [3P1].

(5) For welding, heat is necessary. It can be supplied through various agencies. Acetylene is the one used here. It is therefore taken as [3P2]. Other possible agencies are any other gas such as natural gas, butane and hydrogen, or electric current.

572 Transformation to Suit the Syntax of Classificatory Language

In conformity with the assumptions and postulates about phase, round, level, manifestation of the five fundamental categories, their relative concreteness, and the resulting sequence for the facets, the syntax of the classificatory language gives the following rearrangement of the terms in the name of the subject along with those arrived at in section 571 by filling up ellipses: Engineering/Rudge cycle/Fork/ Shoulder/ Steel/ Disease/ Broken/ Cure/ Welding/ Acetylene/ Influence/ Heat/ Temperature/ Greece/ Between 1892 and 1955/ Statistics.

Notes

(1) Evidently, the imaginary document being considered is not a periodical for statistics. It is only a stray statistical document. Therefore, in accordance with the prescription in section 23 of part 2 of the C.C., the (ACI) " Statistics " should come only after the Time facet.

(2) It is evident that the statistics concern the complex class made up of both the phases, and not merely any one of them. Therefore [S] and [T] should come only after (2P).

(3) The notes in section 571 have indicated the reasons for the assignment of the various other terms to their respective facets and for the sequence of these facets. This is a matter of judgment. Considerable familiarity and experience is needed to arrive at the sequence. One should accustom oneself to the mode of thinking involved in the progression from the (1P)(BC) " Engineering " down the sequence of the facets to the (ACI) " Statistics."

573 Reduction to Standard Terms

The next step is to reduce the various terms in the transformed sequence of the words in the name of the subject to the corresponding standard terms as they are given in the schedules of the classification scheme in use. We get the following result: Engineering/Rudge

cycle/ Fork/ Shoulder/ Steel/ Disease/ Breakage/ Cure/ Welding/
Acetylene/ as influenced by / Heat/ Temperature/ Greece/ Between 1892
and 1955/ Statistics.

Notes

(1) In (1P), no term except Engineering, Cycle, and Steel occurs in
the schedule for Engineering.

(2) The terms Disease, Breakage, Cure, Welding, and Acetylene are
taken from schedules like those of Medicine which have analogous
isolate ideas.

(3) The other terms are taken from schedules appropriate to them.

(4) There is a total of sixteen items in the fully expressed name of the
subject, as given above. Two of these are (BC). One is a term indicating
phase relation. The others are all isolates.

(5) The scheme of classification in use is not responsible for this
large number of items. These are not the creation of the notational
plane.

(6) They all exist in the idea plane, quite independent of the scheme
of classification used.

(7) They are all necessary to express the subject unequivocally.

(8) The class number should express each one of them, in order to
secure for the subject a helpful, filiatory place among the other subjects
already existing and likely to take shape in future.

574 Translation into Numbers

The translation of each of the above basic classes, isolate ideas, and
phase relation into the corresponding Colon Numbers is given below.
The basic class numbers, isolate numbers and the relation number are
separated from one another by oblique strokes:

$$\text{D/5127RU/4/2/1/4/78/6/7/31/g/C4/2/51/N55} \leftarrow \text{M92/s}$$

Notes

(1) Of the sixteen numbers, the first and the last five alone are
taken from the schedules as they are. Of the remaining ten numbers,
eight have been left to be improvised totally by the classifier by the
exercise of the autonomy given to him, and two others need some
explanation. All these are covered by the succeeding notes.

(2) [1P1]. 5127RU (Rudge cycle). The C.C. gives 5125 for cycle.
Here, 5 represents Vehicle, 1 Land-vehicle, 2 Drawn by muscular
power. Since the muscular power of a person is used in a cycle, the
fourth digit 5 is replaced by 7 to secure conformity to seminal
mnemonics. In arranging different makes of cycles, alphabetical device
is used, because it gives as helpful a sequence as any other. Perhaps the
chronological device may suggest itself as slightly better, but the task
of finding the year of each make will involve much work. It is felt that
any greater helpfulness likely to result will be outweighed by the
trouble of getting the correct year. Raleigh is another make beginning
with R, so the first two letters are used to represent Rudge.

(3) [1P2]. 4 (Fork). In the first division of a cycle into its organs, we get, as we proceed systematically from bottom upwards, Tyre, Wheel, Axle, Fork, Handlebar. We start again along another vertical line in order to bring in the remaining organs as seen in the first division. We get in succession Pedal, Free-wheel mechanism, Frame, Seat. Then we list the remaining organs Brake, Bell, Light, Mudguard, Carrier. In the first division, we should not exercise our full resolving power and allow our eyes or mind to seize organs of these organs, such as Tube, Spokes, Hub and so on. We have not succeeded in designing a foolproof method to distinguish between the first level of organs and the second and later levels of organs. The necessary flair has to be acquired only by experience. Again, the shape of the cycle suggested scanning along three more or less parallel vertical lines. The premier importance of the organs appearing along it suggested our beginning with the frontmost vertical line. In each subject not fully scheduled in the scheme, the classifier will have to decide, in this way, a more or less helpful line of pursuit. It is believed that experience and the ideas implied in the tabulated schedules will accustom a classifier to arrive at it. It is further believed that there is a high probability for most of the properly trained and attuned classifiers to arrive at the same line of pursuit. Much work remains to be done to increase this probability with the aid of some objective directions. The sequence in which the organs are mentioned yields the isolate number 4 for the isolate idea Fork. Those spotted out along the second vertical may be put in the second octave. Similarly, the remaining auxiliaries like Brake and Bell may be put in the third octave, and so on.

(4) [1P3]. 2 (Shoulder). In dividing the Fork into its own organs, we adopt a similar procedure. Moving from bottom upwards, we get in succession Prongs, Shoulder, and Shaft. This yields the isolate number 2 for the third level personality facet.

(5) [1M1]. 1 (Steel). Shoulder does not admit of further division into organs for the purposes of the subject being considered. We have really to pass on to its constituent materials, which takes us to the material facet. Several materials can be used to make the shoulder, but the most commonly used is Steel. Therefore the Favoured Category Principle gives the isolate number 1 for the isolate idea Steel in this context.

(6) [1E]. 4 (Disease). The digit 4 is got by Seminal Mnemonics. It has occurred in the published schedules in Medicine and several other subjects.

(7) [2P1]. 78 (Breakage). Here we get help from Scheduled Mnemonics. Medicine is the main class in which Disease is worked out elaborately. There we find the digit 7 used to denote structural disease. But there is a serious omission there. Breakage is not included in the schedule of subdivisions of 7 Structural disease. Since breakage is mostly incident on bones, the digit 8 is suggested for breakage. It had been left unused in the schedule, so there is freedom to use it in this way. It is our general experience that needed digits are often found

unused. This is a result of following the Canons for Scheduled and Seminal Mnemonics.

(8) [2E]. 6 (Cure). The digit 6 is got by Seminal Mnemonics.

(9) [3P1]. 7 (Welding). There are various methods of repairing breakage of the Shoulder, which is made of metal. It can be mechanically tied together, braced, soldered, welded and so on. Of all the methods, welding restores the personality of the shoulder as closely as possible. Seminal Mnemonics, therefore, suggests the isolate number 7 for the isolate idea Welding.

(10) [3P2]. 31 (Acetylene). As stated in note (5) of section 571, Acetylene is a source of heat. It is a gas, and the scheduled mnemonic number for gas is either 3 or 8. Here, sources like electricity can be used, the scheduled mnemonic number for which is 6. Gas should go with the other states of matter, and should precede electricity. Therefore 3 is preferred. The Principle of Favoured Category gives the number 1 for Acetylene.

(11) g (Influence). The schedule for phase relations has not yet been worked out. The need for this was realised only four years ago. The digit c was provisionally used at the beginning, but after some more work had been done on the problem, it was replaced by g.

575 Synthesis in the Notational Plane

The last stage in classifying is to synthesise the basic numbers, the isolate numbers and the phases, by connecting them with the connecting symbols prescribed in the scheme. By doing so, we get the following class number for the imaginary subject used as a sample:

$$D5127RU,4,2;1:478:67,310g(C4:2).51.N55 \leftarrow M92s$$

Notes

(1) Rule 6503 of the C.C. prescribes the omission of the connecting symbol before [1P1], unless an amplifying facet precedes it. Again, recently another convention has been followed on account of the postulate that an energy isolate number will have only one significant digit. The convention is that the connecting symbol need not be inserted before the first level of personality in any round.

(2) The digit o is now used as the connecting symbol for any phase relation.

(3) C4:2 is got by subject device, and is therefore enclosed in circular brackets. It is converted into a packeted number.

(4) The focus in [T] is a definite time-interval bounded by the years 1892 and 1955. The rule for combining them by arrow is that the first member should be the later year and that the backward arrow should be used. Then only the Principle of Decreasing Extension will be satisfied. See section 4531.

576 Chain Procedure

The class number constructed in section 575 is coextensive with the subject classified, both in each facet and in the over-all. It is also expressive of all the relevant elements featuring in the subject. These qualities of coextensiveness and expressiveness secure the most helpful place for the subject among those already arranged and likely to be added in future. The main approach of the majority of readers to this subject is assumed to start from Cycle. Once we start with the Cycle as [P1] the other facets follow in a unique succession, as determined by the way in which we are accustomed to think. But there may be a few whose interest makes them start their approach to a document embodying this subject, from some other angle, say Welding. The Laws of Library Science require that they too should be helped. But classificatory language cannot give two different class numbers to one and the same subject. It cannot admit of synonyms. This is one of the attributes postulated for classificatory language. It means that we cannot start from two different facets. To reconcile this handicap and the demands of the Laws of Library Science, the help of the catalogue is invoked. The class index entries of the catalogue give the needed help.

Let us illustrate, by examining how a reader who starts the approach from Welding will be helped by the catalogue. The application of the chain procedure to the class number will give a class index entry with each of the links as the main heading. Welding is a link in the chain. Therefore, there will be a class index entry with Welding as the heading. Of course, Welding will occur as a link in many class numbers. To distinguish them from one another, different subheadings will follow the main heading Welding. The single heading Welding will give the number M4:7. Under this number will stand assembled all the basic literature on the process of welding without reference to any particular application of it. The class index entry, contributed by the link " Welding " in the class number constructed in this chapter, will have for its heading Welding. Steel. Shoulder. Rudge cycle. It will direct attention to the number D5127RU,4,2;1:478:67. When the user looks up this number in the classified part of the catalogue, he will find this document without much difficulty. There are, however, many difficulties awaiting solution in the application of chain procedure to the cataloguing of documents embodying micro-thought. They mostly centre round deciding which are sought links and which are not, and which are the minimum or the essential upper links to be represented as subheadings.

577 **Warning**

The class number arrived at in section 575 has forty-three digits. It is of order 21. This should not make one rush to the sweeping conclusion that class numbers are all long. Nor should it be allowed to induce in one a revulsion against classification itself. It must be remembered that macro-thought will only need a short class number. The Canon of Relativity will see to it that the number of digits in a class number is large only in the measure of the degree of intension of the thought-content of the document classified. As stated in section

571, the document chosen is an imaginary one. It was deliberately taken to embody thought of very great intension indeed. It was so taken to demonstrate the procedure for depth classification, based on an analytico-synthetic scheme giving considerable autonomy to the classifier to construct new isolate numbers and to add all the facets demanded by a document, and construct schedules for the facets not already provided with a schedule in the published scheme. The proposition sought to be demonstrated in this chapter is only a hypothetical one of the form:

" If such and such a subject of such and such depth, i.e. degree of intension, gets embodied in a document, we can get for it a unique, coextensive, and expressive class number in such and such a way."

Nothing more and nothing less. In practice, the probability is small that a subject, with as great an intension as the sample taken, will be embodied in a document. All the same a scheme of classification should be ever ready to meet any emergency. It should be ready with a definite procedure for analysis in the idea plane, with a method for constructing isolate numbers, and with the connecting symbols for synthesising them in the notational plane. For the universe of knowledge is dynamic; it is ever in a state of turbulence; and its demands are unpredictable.

578 Dynamic Turbulence

My attention was turned on this problem with some force about ten years ago. A few examples in the depth classification of micro-thought were studied in the *Library classification: Fundamentals and procedure* (1944). In September, 1948, the University Library Section of the British Library Association invited me to address their meeting in Birmingham. The subject chosen was *Challenge of the universe of knowledge*. This opened up a new outlook. About a month later, it was developed a little further in a talk in London under the joint auspices of the Aslib and the Society for Visiting Scientists. The substance of this talk was later written out and published as *Self-perpetuating classification* in the *Journal of documentation*, Vol. 4, 1949, pages 223-244. This experience lured me further and further into the pursuit of coextensiveness, expressiveness, and uniqueness of class number whatever be the intension of the micro-thought classified. This led to a drastic re-design of the foundations of classification. The advantage of the separation of work in the idea plane from that in the notational plane was seen gradually. Most of the difficulties in the depth classification needed by micro-thought are found to be in the idea plane. The notes in the sections 572 to 575 imply several assumptions. They indicate the regions to be investigated. They call for the exercise of flair. Some objective directions should be provided. The work in the notational plane is nearly mechanised by the concepts of the Five Fundamental Categories, Phase Analysis, Facet Analysis, and Zonal Analysis. The method of giving further help will be indicated in part 8, Abstract Classification.

CHAPTER 58

FALSE ALARM

581 Scepticism

THE DEMONSTRATIONS IN THE EARLIER chapters of this part, and particularly the provokingly immense schedule of micro-thought given in section 5502, may appear stupefying. Add to this the statement about the number of subjects capable of being individualised for depth classification in the different schemes: at the lower end we have 10^7 for the B.C.; and at the upper end 10^{21} for the C.C. What astronomical figures! Are there so many subjects? Will so many subjects ever take shape? Is it not all merely the conceit of notation-builders? Such is the scepticism of some librarians.

582 Recoil

On page 4 of Vol. 3 of the Bibliographic Classification, the description of such sceptics goes a step further. Bliss says with an implication of sympathy, " Bibliographers and librarians and especially cataloguers and classifiers of books and pamphlets recoil before this immense elaboration of subject-matter." I am now typing this, sitting in the balcony of my flat. It opens into the gardens at the back of the row of houses. There I see a demonstration of this species of recoil. A workman pulls out section after section of his ladder, until it reaches to a height of over fifty feet. He goes up the ladder. A lady has been watching it all along. As the ladder's length pushed up higher and higher, she was growing tenser and tenser. Now the workman is stepping on the tall roof. The lady recoils with a shriek. Does not unfamiliarity go a long way in explaining this recoil? Perhaps to this unfamiliarity is also coupled scepticism about the need to have such horribly long ladders. But is it within the province of roof-cleaners to fix a limit to the height of houses? Is it within the province of a scheme of classification to fix an " economic limit " to the order of micro-thought to be thrown forth by the universe of knowledge, or even to the number of its dimensions? To do so will be to play King Canute.

583 Derision

Of course, the B.C. itself does not " recoil before this immense elaboration of subject-matters." It provides class numbers long enough to nearly individualise them. It admits of numbers of ten digits and even a few more when necessary. It also rightly intersperses punctuation marks among the digits. With a ten-digit system of numbers, it can handle subjects to the order of 10^{10}. And yet it devotes the next sentence to derision: " But documentalists ambitiously in theory greatly exceed it and they even envisage unlimited analysis and specification. They even attempt systems and methods to render such elaboration feasible and available." The pith of this sentence is in the " it " of " greatly exceed it." The B.C. would much wish librarians and bibliographers to accept its 10^{10} subjects without recoil. It would set 10^{10} as the starting point of unacceptable and unwanted " immense elaboration of subject-matters." It would even dissociate itself with derision from " documentalists ambitiously in theory greatly exceeding it."

584 Nebulous Criticism

The nebulous criticism by the B.C. is all based on " economic length of notation." How it is arrived at has not been shown. By sheer repetition, it has been made a dogmatic creed. This creed reminds one of seeking the head to fit the cap. Surely, it is not the length that should decide the class number, but the subject.

A slant of—perhaps pardonable—pride in the shortness of its notation is betrayed by a footnote in page 8 of the third volume of B.C. published in 1953. It reads, " To exemplify the economy of our composite notation, three very special subjects follow here; and for comparison we add to these the supposed equivalent number-built notation of the expanded Decimal Classification. And how would the Colon Classification deal with these subjects and how long would its notations be? " Then follow the three subjects, each with its B.C. number and its U.D.C. number. I reproduce below these numbers as given in that book and add also the C.C. numbers.

(1) Development of radar in the French Navy

Scheme	Class Number	Number of digits
B.C.	BOW-RNf3	8
C.C.	D65,44(MV5.53	13
U.D.C.	621.396.9:359(44)	17

(2) Effect of heat treatment on the electrical properties of germanium

Scheme	Class Number	Number of digits
B.C.	CNGG,D,CH	9
C.C.	F143;*c*6oge4	11
U.D.C.	537.311.33:546.289:669-15	25

(3) Precise calibration of tuning forks in radio engineering

Scheme	Class Number	Number of digits
B.C.	BOS-BPF-BBTC	12
C.C.	D65,4;(C3*e*1:1	13
U.D.C.	621.317.755:534.321.7.08	24

The B.C. does score in all the cases. U.D.C.'s handicap is its D.C. core, clipping its versatility, when it might otherwise have shorter numbers. The average length in the C.C. is one and a quarter times that of the B.C.; and that in U.D.C. is slightly more than double.

But at what cost does the B.C. make this score in length? Its connecting symbols are all homonymous. Therefore its numbers cannot be translated backwards uniquely—i.e. into the name of one and only one subject. For example, the first B.C. number may mean any of the six subjects shown in the following table. The third column in the table gives the different C.C. numbers that the six different subjects get. The translation backwards of any of the C.C. numbers will lead only to one and the same unique subject.

	Name of Subject	B.C. Number	C.C. Number
(11)	Exposition, in France, of radar for students of naval science	BOW-RNf3	D65,440bMV5).53
(12)	Exposition of radar for the staff of the French Navy	BOW-RNf3	D65,440bMV5.53
(13)	Influence of naval science on radar, in France	BOW-RNf3	D65,440gMV5).53
(14)	Influence of the French Navy on radar	BOW-RNf3	D65,440gMV5.53
(15)	Development, in France, of the naval use of radar	BOW-RNf3	D65,44(MV5).53
(16)	Development of the use of radar within the French Navy	BOW-RNf3	D65,44(MV5.53

This means that the B.C. vitiates itself with the fault of homonyms —a fatal fault in a classificatory language of ordinal numbers, designed to mechanise the arrangement of documents, in a preferred sequence. It is the incidence of this fatal fault that led C.C. to the final adoption of packet notation for subject device in 1954. It is again the incidence of the same fatal fault that led C.C. in 1952 to the replacement of a bare zero by a zero followed by a lower-case letter, in order to distinguish the different kinds of possible phase relations such as bias, comparison, and influence. We do not know how the B.C. would add to its digits to differentiate the numbers for the six subjects mentioned above. But if we drop these essential corrective digits from the C.C., then the relative lengths of the B.C. and C.C. numbers will be as follows:

Subject Number	B.C. Number	C.C. Number
1	8	12
2	9	10
3	12	12

There is no appreciable difference in the length of the class numbers.

585 Scientific Approach

The scientific approach to the problem should not start with a prejudice against either an economic limit to the length of class number; or full expressiveness and coextensiveness of class number. Both are necessary. When the two cannot be secured in equal measure, the basic purpose of classification would make us uphold the latter, because the demand for expressiveness and coextensiveness is made by the universe of knowledge and belong to the idea plane, while economic limit to length of class number is made by the artificial universe of class numbers and belongs to the notational plane. A scheme of classification has no option but to accept the proliferations in the universe of knowledge as they are, and fully, and without any modification; while the universe of class numbers is its own creation. But we should always keep in mind the urge of the Law of Parsimony to shorten the notation; indeed, the very length of the notation will act as a constant reminder. It will keep alive the apical bud of research in library classification. It will continue as a persistent challenge to classificationists.

5851 Wrong Approach

It is wrong to uphold shortness of notation as against expressiveness and coextensiveness. To ignore the proliferations in the universe of knowledge calling for distinctive class numbers is like the cat closing its eyes and imagining the absence of any kind of danger. Progress in research in library classification will stop. But the proliferations of the universe of knowledge will not stop. The class number within economic limit will soon collect under it a hotchpotch of several subjects, defying the Canon of Helpful Sequence and the Canons for Filiatory Sequence. The arrangement of the documents having the same class number will form a pocket. It will be the very negation of classification. History repeats itself. The protest against three digits in the D.C. was no less vehement half a century ago than the protest against more than ten digits today. Protest of this kind is not legitimate in scientific method. Reconciliation and research into the problem should replace protests.

586 Rama versus Ravana

We should face the facts of the universe of knowledge—particularly of micro-thought. We should not black out any of the discomfitures in the notational plane. The dangers of the trickery of black-out and the benefits of keeping bare all the problems and all the discomfitures needing solution are well brought out in an episode in the exquisite epic, the *Ramayana* of the premier poet Valmiki. Rama the hero and Ravana the antihero are engaged in a war to the finish. Men die in numbers on both sides. Prompted by prestige and for propaganda, Ravana orders that all the dead bodies on his side should be promptly cleared and thrown into the sea, and that the battlefield should always show victory on his side. Rama does not do anything of this sort. He does not believe in hiding facts. The antihero is killed. The war ends. The gods come to felicitate the hero. They offer a boon to Rama. He uses it to ask for the resurrection of all those lying dead in the war theatre. They are all resurrected. Ravana's dead also would have been resurrected if their bodies were still there; but, alas, they had been devoured by the sharks of the sea. Ravana's body too had been cremated with all royal honours before the arrival of the gods. No, no, we should not hide the unsolved problems in getting coextensive and expressive class numbers, in order to show only short numbers.

587 Divide and Rule

There is another danger in the world of classification. The clever idle among librarians may use their cleverness to perpetuate their chance to continue idle and to add to their number. They may campaign, " Let the orthodox documentalists in business libraries do what they like with C.C., U.D.C., expressiveness, coextensiveness, depth classification, analytico-synthetic classification, and all such things. We shall grant that they want all such high-power schemes. But these are not suitable for our libraries—the hundreds of college libraries, the thousands of public libraries, and the tens of thousands of school libraries. We want only a very simple scheme of ready-made class numbers of not more than three or four digits—the abridged D.C. for example. No, even that uniformity is too soul-killing. We shall each modify it as we please. We can still call it D.C. Our managements will be silenced by that name."

5871 Ignorance or Mischief?

As political trickery, this is a clever move to divide the library world, and label the divisions with the usual slogans, " masses " and " classes." But it has no place in the world of scientific method. Let us expose the unexpressed suggestion in this trickery. It capitalises the following implication: " Analytico-synthetic schemes, such as B.C., C.C. and U.D.C., capable of handling depth classification and individualising micro-thought, will give long class numbers even to the simple popular books and textbooks in popular, school and college libraries. Let us therefore avoid such schemes, and further, give that as our expert opinion to all our managements and to the public also." The premises of this " expert opinion " are the very reverse of fact. The B.C., C.C. and U.D.C. give for such popular books and textbooks much shorter class numbers than D.C.—even U.D.C., because it drops the end zeros. The clever idlers are either ignorant of this fact, or, though aware of it, they are mischievously misleading the " masses " among librarians, the managements and the public.

588 Assurance

Section 424 has gone fully into this question. The " masses " among librarians may rest assured that the Canon of Relativity sees to it that they will not be bothered by long or complicated class numbers if they adopt a scheme that serves both macro- and micro-thought, that serves both popular or school libraries and business libraries.

Each book gets only what it deserves. The books used by public and college librarians will not need numbers of more than three or four digits. In U.D.C. they will often have only two digits, in B.C. and C.C. many will have only a single digit. To construct numbers of three or four digits will not be beyond the wit of even the least educated among the " masses " in the library profession. For their benefit, the cleverer ones may even bring out a schedule of about 10,000 often-used class numbers in about thirty pages. Probably they need not take even this trouble, since there are plenty of such reach-me-downs already in the field.

PART 6

THEORY OF BOOK CLASSIFICATION

CHAPTER 61

EMBODIED KNOWLEDGE

611 Introduction

IN PART 1 WE developed a general theory of classification, and arrived at twenty-two canons which it is desirable that any scheme of classification, applicable to any universe, should satisfy. In part 2, we studied the universe of knowledge as a preliminary to our chief objective—the elucidation of the special features of Book Classification. In discussing the universe of knowledge, we saw that classification of that universe had to face some special problems on account of (1) its being a universe with an infinity of classes, (2) many of its classes (pseudo-entities) being unknown at any moment, and (3) some of the unknown classes coming to be known from time to time.

A consideration of these features of the universe of knowledge led us to six additional canons, which are special to the theory of knowledge classification. It is desirable that every scheme of classification of the universe of knowledge should satisfy these six special canons in addition to the twenty-two general canons. We shall develop in this part 6 more canons to be satisfied in the classification of the universe of books *qua* books, apart from the universe of knowledge embodied therein.

612 Definitions concerning Book

We shall begin with establishing the terminology needed to denote the concepts in the universe of books. The need for this terminology is even more acute in the discipline of library catalogue. The definitions may with advantage be taken from that discipline. The following definitions, relevant to the discipline of library classification, are taken from Ranganathan's *Heading and canons: Comparative study of five catalogue codes* (1955).

613 Types of Work

6131 **Knowledge-Unit.**—Assumed term. It may extend to several volumes at one extreme, or only to a single sentence at the other extreme.

6132 **Thought.**—Knowledge-Unit. This term is introduced for brevity.

6133 **Expressed Thought.**—Thought expressed in language or symbols or in any other mode, and thereby made communicable.

6134 **Work.**—Expressed thought. This term is introduced for brevity.

6135   **Title.**—Name of work.

6136   **Sacred Work.**—Basic work of a religion, generally accepted as such among its followers. In most schemes of library classification, a sacred work is made a quasi class, i.e. a quasi subject (*see* 61391). Each part of it is made a sub-class. Chains of the sub-classes of a sacred book are usually enumerated in a system of classification.

6137   **Classic.**—Work embodied in several versions, adaptations and translations, attracting other works on itself, and coming out in print even long after its origin. A classic can be made a quasi class, i.e. a quasi subject in a scheme of classification, and is so made in the C.C. Some are so made in U.D.C. also. The B.C. makes the chief work of a classical author an independent class and puts all his other works together in another class (*see* schedule 6 of B.C.).

6138   **Work of Literature.**—Work in the form of poem, drama, fiction, prose or any other literary form, of which the outstanding qualities are taken to be beauty of form and emotional appeal, and/or which is of intuitive or trans-intellectual origin. A work of literature can be made a quasi class, i.e. a quasi subject in a scheme of classification, and is so made in C.C. Some are so made in U.D.C. also. The B.C. makes the chief work of an author an independent class, and puts all his other works together in another class (*see* schedule 6 of B.C.).

61391   **Quasi Class.**—Work made into a class in a scheme of classification or whose title is used as a subject heading in cataloguing practice. A quasi class thus become a quasi subject. In the C.C. a sacred work, or a classic, or a work of literature is made a quasi class. In most of the other schemes a sacred work is made a classic. But in U.D.C. a classic is made a quasi class in only a few cases; and work of literature is not so made. In the B.C. only one work, called the chief work, is made a classic in the case of each author (*see* schedule 6 of B.C.).

61392   **Pedestrian Work.**—Work not made into a quasi class or quasi subject by the scheme of classification or the cataloguing code in use.

61393   Micro-Thought and Macro-Thought are relative terms with meaning loosely fixed by convention. An article in a periodical or a chapter, a section or paragraph in a book or a pamphlet, may be said to embody micro-thought. In classificatory terminology, it forms a class of great intension. Macro-thought forms a class of great extension. It is usually embodied, all by itself, in a book of size greater than a pamphlet.

614   Document

6141   **Embodied Thought.**—Record of work on paper or other material, fit for physical handling, transport across space, and preservation through time. The recording may be done by hand, or printing process, or near-printing process, or typewriting, or any kindred process, or sound-recording machinery, or any other means. Record also denotes a record reproduced by photographic or other radiation process, or chemical process, or any other process, from a record already made. The material on which recording is made may be paper or any substitute for it, or gramophone disc, or sensitive paper, or any other material suitable for the recording process used.

6142 **Document.**—Embodied thought; or auto-record or direct record by instrument of natural phenomenon unmediated by primary senses or by intellect. This term is introduced for brevity. It was brought into use a few decades ago to emphasise embodied micro-thought. It is now used to include any embodied thought, micro or macro.

6143 **Volume.**—Several leaves of paper or units of other materials used for recording on, forming the whole of a part of a document, fastened together so as to be opened at any desired place.

6144 **Thought-Content.**—Expressed thought or recorded pheno-menon embodied in a document or a volume of it, is its thought-content.

615 Types of Document

6151 **Periodical Publication.**—Document with the following attributes:

(1) A volume or a small group of volumes of it is intended to be published or completed normally once in a year or at other intervals, though irregularity in period is not ruled out.

(2) Each successive volume or periodical group of volumes is usually distinguished by the year of publication and/or by a number belonging to a system of simple or complex ordinal numbers. Such a number is usually called a volume number.

(3) The intention had been to continue the publication of the volumes for ever, though not actually carried out.

(4) The intention had been to continue the same title in all the volumes, though not actually carried out.

(5) *Either,* (51) Each volume is made up of distinct and independent contributions, not forming a continuous exposition, normally by two or more personal authors, normally the specific subjects and the authors of the contributions in successive volumes are different; but all the subjects fall within one and the same region or class of knowledge, contemplated to be brought within its purview. *Or* (52) Each volume or each periodical group of volumes embodies mainly more or less similar information brought up to its year or other period of coverage.

The term " periodical publication " is also used to denote any volume of a periodical publication as defined above.

C.C. alone makes a periodical publication a quasi class.

61511 **Periodical.**—Periodical publication with attribute 51 mentioned in section 6151, or any volume of it.

61512 **Serial.**—Periodical publication with attribute 52 mentioned in section 6151, or any volume of it.

6152 **Book.**—Document other than a periodical publication. That is, it has been completed or had been intended to be completed in a finite number of volumes. It is generally in one volume. Some are in many volumes.

6153 **Composite Book.**—Book with two or more contributions, each with its own title, distinct and independent, not forming together a continuous exposition, and often, though not necessarily, by different authors.

61531 **Contribution.**—Work forming a part of a composite book or a periodical or a serial.

61532 **Article.**—Contribution in a periodical.

6154 **Simple Book.**—Book which is not composite, i.e. which embodies continuous exposition usually either by a single author, or by two or more joint authors. But it may be also anonymous.

6155 **Multi-Volumed Book.**—Book in two or more volumes, giving a continuous exposition of a subject, and for this or any other reason in the distribution of thought among the volumes, compelling all the volumes to be treated as an inseparable set, i.e. as if they take the place of a single volume.

6156 **Edition.**—*Either*, One of the different forms in which one and the same work is published and each form has a distinctive name such as Arden Edition, Variorum Edition, Standard Edition, Ananda Asrama Edition, Memorial Edition, Loeb Classics and so on; *Or*, One of the different printings or reproductions of a document with or without change in thought-content, and each being distinguished from others either numerically or by other equivalent term such as New, Revised, Enlarged, and so on. The change is not so serious as to change the character of the document. The title is not changed.

6157 **Related Books.**—Two or more books are said to be related books if the following conditions are satisfied: (1) none of the books is a classic; (2) the classes to which the books belong do not occur in one and the same chain of classes; and (3) it is possible to recognise one of the books of the set as the **Basic or Host Book.** It is also possible to coin a term to denote the relation of the basic book to the other books of the set and vice versa.

616 Equation of Book

A book is a concrete entity embodying expressed knowledge-unit or auto-record of phenomenon. We may say that a book is " embodied knowledge." We may also say that a book is a material transform of immaterial knowledge-unit. It is so transformed to facilitate (1) transport from any place to any other; (2) transmission from one generation to another; and (3) socialisation of knowledge.

We may set down the following equation of book:

Book (or document)
   = Work + Body
   = Thought + Subtle Body + Gross Body; or Phenomenon +
     Subtle Body + Gross Body
   = Thought + Expression + Physique; or Phenomenon +
     Recording + Physique.

617 **Consequence of the Equation**

Each term in the last step of the equation of book makes its contribution to the theory of book classification. In the first place, we should expect all the peculiarities of the universe of knowledge to be found reflected in the universe of books. Book classification should therefore include knowledge classification. Secondly, expression of one and the same knowledge-unit may be in different forms and media. Book classification should therefore treat each such form and medium as distinct. For this purpose, it should provide a Form Facet. Moreover many books can come out in the same knowledge-unit expounded in the same form or medium. More than one copy of the same book may come into the library. Book classification should therefore provide a facet to distinguish each such book and copy. There are also other matters to be cared for by book classification, which do not arise in knowledge classification. In short, book classification should also take into account the peculiar features of a book *qua* book, apart from the knowledge-unit embodied. To this extent, it may have to modify and supplement the scheme of knowledge classification adopted as basis.

618 **Seven Features**

The Universe of Books has seven features not found in the Universe of Knowledge. These derive from the subtle and gross embodiment involved in a book and from certain facilities to be given to readers, in order to fulfil the Five Laws of Library Science. The seven features are the following: 1 Quasi Class; 2 Local Variation; 3 Composite Book; 4 Partial Comprehension; 5 Form or Medium of Expression; 6 Related Book; and 7 Physique.

CHAPTER 62

QUASI CLASS

621 **Classics**

AN ADDITIONAL CANON NEEDED in the Theory of Book Classification, but not required in the Theory of Knowledge Classification, may be enunciated as follows:

A Scheme of Book Classification should have a device to bring together all the editions, translations, and adaptations of a classic, and next to them all the editions, etc., of the different commentaries on it, the editions, etc., of a particular commentary all coming together, and next to each commentary all the editions, etc., of the commentaries on itself in a similar manner (commentaries of the second order), and so on. This is the **Canon of Classics.**

The Canons of the General Theory of Classification imply that all the books on all the various schools of thought, deriving from a given enunciation of fundamentals in a basic text, should be arranged in a filiatory sequence. Thus the Canon of Classics is a corollary from the canons of the general theory of classification. The books relating to a class form a family—a hierarchy. The Canons for Filiatory Sequence should therefore be respected in arranging the books in such a family. The Canon of Classics merely spells out how it should be done in the case of the family of a classic.

622 **Colon Classification**

This canon has been fully recognised and observed only in the C.C. That the C.C. should have devised a special apparatus to fulfil this canon is due largely to its being of Indian origin. The universe of ancient Sanskrit books, belonging to any subject whatsoever, abounds in hierarchies of commentaries on a basic text (Classic). It was a common and accepted practice in Ancient India to start with the enunciation of the fundamentals of a subject in the most general terms in a basic text (Classic) and to elucidate the most far-reaching implications of the fundamentals along all possible—sometimes even opposite—directions, stage by stage, in a chain of commentaries and subcommentaries. Different new systems of thought have been formulated in different chains of commentaries and have become crystallised in course of time. Examples are given in the succeeding subsection.

6221   EXAMPLES

(1) A basic text for the grammar of classical Sanskrit is P15,C*x*1,1 Panini *Astadhyayi*. The following are three of the chains of commentaries depending upon it:

First chain
P15,C*x*1,1   Panini *Astadhyayi*
P15,C*x*1,1,2   Pantanjali *Mahabhasya*
P15,C*x*1,1,2,1   Kaiyyata *Mahabhasya-pradipa*

Sixth chain
P15,C*x*1,1   Panini *Astadhyayi*
P15,C*x*1,1,6   Bhattojidiksita *Siddhanta Kaumudi*
P15,C*x*1,1,6,1   Bhattojidiksita *Manorama*
P15,C*x*1,1,6,1,1 Haridiksita *Sabdaratna*
P15,C*x*1,1,6,1,1,1   Balambhatta *Bhavaprakasika*

A seventeenth-century chain
P15,C*x*1,1   Panini *Astadhyayi*
P15,C*x*1,1,K   Annambhatta *Vyakaranamitakshara*

(2) Another basic text for the grammar of classical Sanskrit is P15,C*x*7,1 Narendracarya *Sarasvata-sutras*. The following are two of the chains of commentaries depending upon it:

First chain
P15,C*x*7,1   Narendracarya *Sarasvata-sutras*
P15,C*x*7,1,1   Anubhutisvarupacarya *Sarasvata-prakriya*
P15,C*x*7,1,1,J   Kasinatha *Sarasvata-bhasya*

Second chain
P15,C*x*7,1   Narendracarya *Sarasvata-sutras*
P15,C*x*7,1,2   Ramacandrasrama *Siddhanta-candrika*
P15,C*x*7,1,2,1   Lokesakara *Tattvadipika*

(3) The basic text for the *Vedanta* philosophy is the classic R66:5 *Brahmasutras*. As is well known, six schools of Vedanta have branched off from this basic text.

(4) The R66 *Advaita* or Monistic school is developed in a number of chains of commentaries all of which have R66,5*x*1,1 Sankara *Brahmasutra-bhasya* as the first link. Here are two chains depending upon this first link.

First chain
R66,5*x*1,1   Sankara *Brahmasutra-bhasya*
R66,5*x*1,1,1   Padmapada *Pancapadika*
R66,5*x*1,1,1,1   Prakasatman *Pancapadiakavivarana*

Second chain
R66,5*x*1,1   Sankara *Brahmasutra-bhasya*
R66,5*x*1,1,2   Vacaspatimisra *Bhamati*
R66,5*x*1,1,2,1   Amalananda *Kalpataru*

(5) The R672 *Visistadvaita* or Modified Monistic school is developed in the following chain of commentaries.

R672,5×2,1   Ramanuja *Sribhasya*
R672,5×2,1,1   Sudarsana *Sribhasya-vyakhya*
R672,5×2,1,1,2 Laksmana *Gurubhavaprakasa*

(6) The R68 *Dvaita* or Dualistic school is developed in the following chain of commentaries.

R68,5×1,1   Anandatirtha *Brahmasutra-bhasya*
R68,5×1,1,1   Jayatirtha *Tattvaprakasika*
R68,5×1,1,1,1 Vyasatirtha *Tatparya-candrika*

(7) The R6892 *Dvaitadvaita* or Dualistic-Monistic school is developed in the following chain of commentaries.

R6892,5×1,1   Nimbarka *Vedantaparijata-saurabha*
R6892,5×1,1,1 Srinivasacarya *Vedanta-kaustubha*

(8) The R6891 *Bhedabheda* or Difference-Identity school is developed in the commentary:

R6891,5×1,1   Bhaskaracarya *Brahmasutra-bhasya*

(9) The R6893 *Suddhavaita* or Devotional-Monistic school has the following chain.

R6893,5×1,1   Vallabhacarya *Anubhasya*
R6893,5×1,1,1 Gosvami Sri-Purusottamjee *Bhasya Prakasa*

(10) Again, we have as a classic in Ayurvedic surgery LB:4:7×2,1 *Susrutasamhita.* A well-known commentary on it is:

LB:4:7×2,1,1 Chakrapanidatta *Bhanumati*

623 The Apparatus

The purpose of the Classic Device of the Colon Classification is simply to secure conformity to this Canon of Classics. The Device is enunciated as follows in chapter 7 of the fourth edition (1952):

" The Classic Device is employed for bringing together the different editions of a classic in a class, the different editions of each of its commentaries, the different editions of each of the subcommentaries of each of its commentaries and so on, and of securing that the group of subcommentaries of a commentary is in juxtaposition to the commentary, that the group of commentaries of a classic is in juxtaposition to the classic, and that the group formed of each classic and its associated commentaries is in juxtaposition to the groups of the other classics of the same class.

" The Classic Device consists of putting the digit x after the number representing the ultimate class to which the book would otherwise be assigned, and amplifying the digit x by the Favoured Category Device, or the Chronological Device to individualise the classic concerned. The amplified x may be termed the *Classic Number*. The commentaries are indicated by amplifying the corresponding classic number by the favoured category device or the chronological device. This amplifying number may be termed the *First-order Commentary Number*. The subcommentaries of a commentary are indicated by amplifying the corresponding first-order commentary number in a similar way. This amplifying number may be termed the *Second-order Commentary Number* and so on."

6231 CONVERSION INTO CLASS

One result of the application of the classic device is that the classic becomes a class by itself and hence its different editions come together, with the book number differentiating them. In the case of a classic, editions are likely to appear even at widely separated dates. But for this device, they would get scattered and mixed with other ordinary books in the same class. Such a mixing is likely to be disturbing to the minds of readers. It is certainly not desirable that Aristotle's *Poetics* or Dandin's *Kavyadarsa* should be indiscriminately lumped together with the ordinary modern books on literary criticism. Nor would it be happy to interpolate Sankaracarya's works on Indian philosophy with the modern textbooks on Indian philosophy. Similarly, it would be unhelpful to mix Karl Marx's *Capital* with the more pedestrian books on Communism.

6232 EVOLUTIONARY SEQUENCE

It not infrequently happens, particularly in works in Sanskrit, that a classic attracts many commentaries which themselves become classics and run through many editions, attracting to themselves sub-commentaries. All the Laws of Library Science will be best served if and only if the whole family of commentaries and sub-commentaries carry forward the theories contained in the classic. This carrying forward is done step by step in the hierarchy of commentaries and sub-commentaries. Hence the happy grouping of a classic with its commentaries and sub-commentaries brought about by the classic device incidentally arranges the books in the proper evolutionary order. This adds greatly to the convenience of the readers—nay, it is even educative.

6233 NO CONFLICT IN NOTATION

It may be stated here that the use of the digit x in the classic device is not in any way in conflict with the use of the same digit to indicate collected works. As a matter of fact, the one use is but a natural and consistent extension of the other.

A work attains the status of a classic and requires to be concerted into a class by itself by means of the classic device if (1) it has elements of permanent value, (2) it is saturated with the personality of the author, and/or (3) it stimulates other books on itself.

The examples already given illustrate the application of this device to Indian classics. There are also some occidental classics, such as Burke's writings in Politics, some of the classics of international law, the Greek and Latin classics, which may be most conveniently grouped by the classic device. Such a grouping is demanded by the Laws of Library Science.

624 Other Schemes

No other scheme appears to have gone into this problem of classics with any thoroughness. But it is an important problem to be attended to, if the Five Laws of Library Science are to be satisfied.

6241 BIBLIOGRAPHIC CLASSIFICATION

The B.C. is aware of the problem. But its insistence on " economic limit " to class number is perhaps responsible for a very poor provision to implement the canon of classics. Its schedule 6, appearing just after class WG Grammar, provides only the following isolates to individualise a classical work:

,K   Chief Work; Criticism, Interpretation, Appreciation.
,N   A Work of Secondary Importance.
,O   Other Works.

In the first place, this prescription violates the Canon of Reticence. Secondly, it satisfies the Canon of Classics only in the case of two works of an author. The others are all huddled together in one isolate number. Thirdly, it explicitly prescribes the use of these isolates only for classical works in philosophy. But perhaps it is not impossible to bring it into use in other subjects also, with some adjustments in the notation assigned in the different classes. See also the alternative prescription quoted in section 6262.

6242 U.D.C.

Perhaps the U.D.C. has not thought of this problem, since its attention has been largely turned on the natural sciences and their applications, and even there in providing isolate numbers for newly developing isolate ideas. But it will feel the need for the Canon of Classics when it turns its attention to the history of natural sciences, on which some work is being done of late. The need will be felt even greater when it turns equal attention on the humanities and social sciences. It should be possible to set up a simple notational device to implement the canon. I commend it to the F.I.D. Committee on U.D.C.

625 Sacred Work

Practically in every scheme, a sacred work is converted into a quasi class. Such a quasi class is also fitted with a schedule of sub-classes, or, at least, there is a notational mechanism for it.

626 **Work in Literature**
6261 COLON CLASSIFICATION

The C.C. provides for Work Facet in the main class Literature. This is deemed to be a personality facet of the fourth level in the third round. The first level is language; the second, form; and the third, author. This provision automatically converts every work of every author in literature into a quasi class. Thus all the editions, translations, adaptations, criticisms, and all other related works on a work in literature are all brought together.

6262 OTHER SCHEMES

The other schemes do not provide such a universally applicable device, no matter who the author is or what the work is.

The prescription of the B.C. to implement the Canon of Classics in literature is the same as the one described in 6241 for classics in philosophy. But there is also provision to individualise any work of an author by the alphabetical device. Here are examples taken from the illustrations found in Vol. 3 of the B.C.

YFYmv   *Merchant of Venice* of Shakespeare, where
         YF = Shakespeare; Y = Edition of a work; mv =
         Merchant of Venice.
YFTmv   Translation of *Merchant of Venice.*
YHP,B7w *Wuthering Heights* of Emily Brontë.

The authority for the use of Roman smalls to represent individual works is given as follows at the bottom of schedule 6:

" a-z The small letters should indicate the titles by their initials, which may have a numeral suffixed, if needed. Alternative to this arrangement is the arrangement under N and O."

In the U.D.C., the isolate number in the author facet is the whole name of the author. By the same analogy, one may perhaps think of adding a work facet after the author facet, and using the whole name of the work as the isolate number in it. But all this is rather carrying alphabetical device to an inordinate length. The F.I.D. may well consider the adoption of a device to make these specifications carry a small number of digits.

627 **Periodical Publication**
6271 COLON CLASSIFICATION

The C.C. is the only scheme converting a periodical publication into a quasi class. The need for doing so, the idea itself, and the convenience resulting from it arose in a particular circumstance. During the period 1926 to 1952, I acquired, for the Madras University Library, complete sets of many hundreds of learned periodicals. Research departments were established by the University practically for the first time. Open access was introduced for the first time. The current issues of about 2,000 periodicals had to be displayed in a helpful sequence, in the table-galleries in the periodicals room. This needed classification.

6272   Subject Grouping

The first step taken was to classify them by their specific subjects. This does not mean main classes only. If so, there would have been far too many in a class like medicine. The classification was taken to the ultimate subject, such as pathology, tuberculosis, therapeutics, physical therapy and X-ray therapy. The periodicals in each ultimate class were arranged alphabetically by title.

6273   Language Grouping

The reaction of readers was observed in the periodicals room. The mixing up of the periodicals in different languages, in one and the same specific subject, was not found to be helpful. First, we attached the language number as the first facet in the book number. Within each subject *cum* language group, the arrangement was by title. This was satisfactory for the display of the current issues in the periodicals room.

6274   Chronological Grouping

However, it did not work satisfactorily in the arrangement of the bound volumes in the stack room. The problem there was to keep together all the volumes of a long run of a periodical. But few periodicals continued to have the same title throughout their life. Thus alphabetical arrangement failed. The several idiosyncrasies of periodicals were studied and analysed. Eighteen of them were isolated and enumerated in chapter 8 of Ranganathan's *Classified catalogue code* (1934). Many of these brought chaos into alphabetical arrangement, because the title of a periodical is not a characteristic of it satisfying the Canon of Permanence. In fact everything about a periodical appeared to change. The subject alone held out to the last. So long as it held out, we had to keep all its volumes together. For this, we had to represent a periodical by an individualising number. For periodicals on the same subject, the only characteristic that satisfied the Canon of Permanence was found to be its year of commencement. It was resolved to use it.

6275   Transfer to Class Number

Using language facet and year facet in the book number, in order to individualise a periodical-set, caused difficulties in the use of the book number to individualise the volumes in the set. After three years of struggle, the transfer of the language number and the year number from the book number to the class number was hit upon. These were added as two facets after the Roman small representing the isolate idea " periodical publication." It was *m* for a periodical, *n, p, r,* etc., for a serial. The language facet and the time facet were later recognised to be different levels of personality in this context.

6276 GEOGRAPHICAL FACET

The experience of one more year showed that the replacement of the language facet by geographical facet gave better results. Thus the conversion of a periodical into a quasi class is done in the C.C. by the addition to the number of its specific subject a personality facet by geographical device using the country of origin as its focus, and thereafter another level of personality facet by chronological device using its year of commencement as its focus. In the case of a multi-lingual country, the constituent state or region is used as the focus in the geographical facet.

6277 ASSOCIATED PERIODICAL

Again, a periodical may put forth associated periodicals in the same specific subject. The Canon of Helpfulness requires their being kept adjacent to the host periodical. In a sense, such periodicals form a family; and therefore the Canons for Filiatory Sequence also would like to have them put together. This problem of associated periodicals was easily solved by the addition of a third level of personality facet. The focus in this facet is, with sufficient effectiveness and ease, fixed serially as 1, 2, etc. This device was hit upon only ten years ago, after the analysis on the basis of fundamental categories suggested itself. This completes the story of the conversion of a periodical publication into a quasi class in the C.C.

6278 U.D.C.

The problems that led to the conversion of a periodical publication into a quasi class are not created by the C.C. They are inherent in the publications themselves. Every scheme should face them to satisfy the Five Laws of Library Science. The practitioners of U.D.C. do not appear to have thought about this. But the notational system of U.D.C. has got all the elements necessary to implement the conversion of a periodical publication into a quasi class. I have experimented on it, and found it to be a success. Therefore, and in order to demonstrate it, I have given individualising U.D.C. numbers with space and time facets, and also association facet wherever found necessary, in the *Retrospective directory of Asian learned periodicals,* sent by me to Unesco in March, 1955, in fulfilment of an Asian Bibliographical Project entrusted to me. It avoids all the alphabetical scattering of a set and of associated sets inherent in the present practice of adding the title itself as part of the class number; this is the virtual implication of the present practice. No doubt, cross-reference is resorted to, to link up the various titles. But it does not give the reader the same benefit as presenting all the changes in titles in the same place in the correct chronological sequence. Nor is it of any avail in shelf-arrangement, as shown in section 6274. I commend this solution to the F.I.D. Committee on U.D.C.

Examples

C.C. Number	Subject or Periodical	Year of commence-ment	U.D.C. Number
B	**MATHEMATICS**		**51**
B*m*	„ PERIODICAL		51(05)
B*m*42	„ „ **Japan**		**51(05)(52)**
B*m*42,N	Tohoku math j	1911	51(05)(52)"19"
B*m*42,N2	Jap j math	1924	51(05)(52)"192"
B*m*42,N3	J math, Hokkaido Imp Univ	1930	51(05)(52)"193"
B*m*42,N33	Coll papers, Osaka Univ, s l, math *continued as* Osaka math j, from	1933 1949	51(05)(52)"1933"
B*m*44	**Mathematics. Periodical. India**		**51(05)(54)**
B*m*44,N	J, Ind Math Club *continued as*, J, Ind Math Soc, from	1909 1911	51(05)(54)"19"
B*m*44,N,1	Math student, (Ind Math Soc)	1933	51(05)(54)"19.1"
B*m*44,N1	J, Calcutta Math Soc	1912	51(05)(54)"191"
B*m*56	**Mathematics. Periodical. Great Britain**		**51(05)(41)**
B*m*56,M	Camb math j *continued as,* Camb Dublin math j, from *continued as,* Q j pure, app math, from *continued as,* Q j math, Oxford ser, from	1837 1845 1930 1930	51(05)(41)"18"
B*m*56,M6	Oxford, Camb, Dublin messenger math *continued as,* Messenger math, from	1861 1871	51(05)(41)"186"
B*m*56,M65	Proc, London Math Soc	1865	51(05)(41)"1865"
B*m*56,M65,1	J, London Math Soc	1926	51(05)(41) "1865.1"
B*m*73	**Mathematics. Periodical. U.S.A.**		**51(05)(73)**
B*m*73,M	Math m (U.S.A.)	1858	51(05)(73)"18"
B*m*73,M9	Bul, New York Math Soc *continued as,* Bul, Amer Math Soc, from	1891 1894	51(05)(73)"189"
B*m*73M9,1	Trans, Amer Math Soc	1900	51(05)(73)"189.1"
B*m*73,M9,2	Proc, Amer Math Soc	1950	51(05)(73)"189.2"

CHAPTER 63

LOCAL VARIATION

631 The Canon
THE NOTATIONAL SYSTEM OF a scheme of book classification should provide for variations due to special interests.

This is the **Canon of Local Variation.**

The aim of this canon is to secure priority in sequence for national or local documents and documents in favoured classes and to shorten class numbers in these cases. The need to consider local variation is not very pronounced in the universe of knowledge; but when it comes to the classing and arranging of actual books in a library to meet the requirements of the readers with the maximum possible conformity to the Laws of Library Science, the Canon of Local Variation is seen to be valuable.

632 Provision for Nationalities
The term " local " should be interpreted liberally so as to refer to a geographical area of any size. Thus this canon will provide, for example, for interests peculiar to the Americas, or New World interests, interests peculiar to a continent (such as European and Asian interests), interests peculiar to a country (such as English, Indian or Japanese interests), interests peculiar to a district or county, interests peculiar to a town or village, and even interests peculiar to the library of an institution or any other specialised library. In practice, however, except in what are known as " local collections " in local libraries, the special interests will be largely of a national nature. It is this fact that has led Bliss to say on page 8 of his *System of bibliographic classification* (1935), " Adaptation to nationality should in a standard system be liberal even to a radical alteration. This may in some cases be modified by alternative location reserved or provided. For history and literature these provisions are especially requisite. The ingeniously adaptable *Colon Classification* in its ' Geographical Divisions ' provides first for the ' Mother Country ' and next for the ' Favoured country ' . . . This exemplifies the need in an international standard for more extensive adaptability in providing for nationalities."

633 Colon Classification
6331 GEOGRAPHICAL AREA
In the C.C., the digit 2 is set apart for the " Mother country." But in practice, when a library specialises in local collections so far as they

are concerned 2 is used for the locality in question, whether it is a district, county, town or village. This results in considerable shortening of class numbers and gives priority to local collections in shelf-arrangement. In such cases, 3 may be used to represent the mother country. In the absence of a local collection of the kind mentioned, 3 is prescribed normally to represent "Favoured country," i.e. the country about which there are more documents in the library than about any other foreign country. This special use of 2 and 3 will provide for local variations in almost every subject and not merely in Geography and History, since the geographic characteristic figures as a basis of classification at some stage or other in most subjects as a means of amplifying a common subdivision digit, and in a few subjects even as a fundamental characteristic.

6332 FAVOURED LANGUAGE

The C.C. has also provided for local variation in the arrangement of books in Literature by defining "Favoured language" and by providing a special rule for literature in the favoured language. We have the following specification in the rules of *Colon classification*, fourth edition (1952). "0311 The favoured language of a library is the language in which the majority of the books of the library are written. Normally the language of the country is likely to be the favoured language; but under the peculiar conditions of India, and of Madras in particular, the favoured language of many libraries at present is likely to be English.

"0164 In the case of the literature in the favoured language, the Language Number should be replaced by a hyphen."

These two rules secure both saving of digits in class numbers and priority in shelf-arrangement for the literature in the favoured language.

6333 PHILOSOPHICAL SYSTEMS

The Canon of Local Variation is met by the Geographical Device and by the provision of special places for the favoured philosophical systems. We have in the array of the first order in Philosophy

R6 Indian Philosophy
R7 Greek Philosophy
R8 Other systems (To be divided by the geographical device).

Indian and Greek philosophies were given special places in the belief that they constitute the most elaborately worked-out systems.

In particular libraries, R6 or R7 may be used for their own favoured systems and the Indian or Greek system thus ousted may be accommodated in R8.

6334 FAVOURED HOST CLASS

A library may specialise in a particular subject—say cycle tyres, geological prospecting for gold, dairy products, cotton spinning, Indian constitutions, labour disputes, famine relief, income tax law. Let us call it the Favoured Host Class of the library. The library is bound to have books on other subjects too; but it will be an advantage to give priority in shelf-arrangement and in the catalogue to the documents on the favoured host class and its sub-classes. In the C.C. this is secured by replacing the class number of the favoured host class by a hyphen. The ordinal value of the hyphen is fixed by the rules to be just below that of *a*, the smallest of the substantive digits.

6335   SHORTENING OF THE CLASS NUMBER

Incidentally, the several digits in the normal class number of the favoured host class are replaced by a single digit. This is a welcome shortening of the class numbers of the documents in the subject in which the library specialises. It is of great help in documentation lists covering a very specialised field of narrow extension.

The C.C. is practically the first scheme to show such respect to the Canon of Local Variation. According to the *Library Association record,* 1934, page 98, " The supreme advantage of this synthetic type of classification scheme is that it may be utilised in various ways to suit the preferred principles of book classification. . . . Special collections can be formed at will at any point in the scheme."

634   Decimal Classification

Dewey himself had recognised that the D.C. paid little heed to the Canon of Local Variation. In a letter dated November 13th, 1930, he wrote to Ranganathan " Naturali the sistem 1st publisht in 1876 was from the standpoint of our American libraries. Thru the 12 editions it has constantli broadened. But we need speciali to cover *Asia* mor adequateli & hope we shal hav yur aktiv cooperation in making the decimal sistem stil mor wydli useful."

6341   EARLIER ATTEMPT

The following extract will show that even earlier an attempt had been made to get the D.C. to fulfil the Canon of Local Variation.

" In November 1929, correspondence with Dr. Dewey was initiated by Wm. Alanson Borden, who was engaged in library work in India from 1910-1913. Mr. Borden had evolved an outline classification by which the libraries of any country could give to that country the place of chief prominence under those subjects in which locality was a feature of special importance, i.e. religion, language, literature, history and geography. He wished, however, to take his subdivisions from D.C. and therefore laid the matter before Mr. Dewey. The D.C. having already been adopted on every continent and in many countries and being used more than all other systems combined, was obviously the vehicle by which Mr. Borden's idea could best be carried throughout the world and thereby accomplish his purpose. Before Mr. Borden's death in November 1931, the main features of the combination had been agreed upon and on Mr. Dewey's death the following month, the determination of minor details only was left to the D.C.

editor to bring about the most serviceable results possible for a world-wide constituency." The extract is from Grosvenor Dawe (comp.) *Melvil Dewey: seer, inspirer, doer, 1851-1931* (1932), pages 167-168.

6342 NO FRUCTIFICATION

Thus the wish to include Indology classes in the D.C. was not carried out. But Indology is only one of the many possible interests to be provided for. This will not be practicable by mere additions to the categories in the schedules. A suitable notational device is necessary to take charge of local variation; till that is done, the wish of Dewey will not fructify.

635 Universal Decimal Classification

The U.D.C. has inherited from D.C. the neglect of the Canon of Local Variation; but its notational system is not incapable of being adapted so as to respect that canon. The provision of a digit for favoured country, language or class is not beyond the capacity of U.D.C., and the attention of F.I.D. is invited to the need for implementing this suggestion.

636 Bibliographic Classification

The B.C. provides for local variation in the strict sense just in one place. It is in the main class Linguistics and Literature. Here W and X are used to represent the linguistics and literature of all languages, but Y is reserved for the favoured language. Actually, YA to YT are devoted to the English language. But in page 69 of the introduction to Vol. 3, the following permission is given: " Our classification is developed for English and American interests. For other nationalities the position may be transposed, if so desired." Again, there is similar permission in explicit language for further local variation in respect of authors: " To Chaucer and Shakespeare entire sections are assigned, YC and YF, in order to provide room for the extensive literature, much studied, and distinctive brief composite notation for the special subjects and topics. These sections might be assigned to other authors, but that would require changing other sections involved and their notation, with corresponding changes in the index." The last part of the last sentence in this quotation shows the awkwardness of filling the numbers, set apart for use in local variation for favoured categories, with the details of particular categories in the published scheme itself. It also throws light on the elegance of the C.C. including all the categories without exception in the general schedule and merely setting apart a few unoccupied digits—2 and 3 in space facet, and the hyphen for any isolate number in any array or for any class number whatever—to represent the favoured categories needed in local variation. This method of providing for local variation involves no " changing other sections and their notation, with corresponding changes in the index."

6360 BEYOND LOCAL VARIATION

But the B.C. goes beyond securing local variation. Its purpose is not merely to secure priority in position and shortness in notation for documents of dominant local interest and numerousness. In other words, it exceeds the requirements of the Canon of Local Variation as interpreted in this book. Four types of regions of " ex-territoriality " are mentioned in the four succeeding subsections.

6361 ALTERNATIVE FACET FORMULA

The B.C. often provides alternative sequences of facets in the facet formula of a basic class. This is implied in some of the illustrative class numbers given here and there in the scheme. For example, in the page of Vol. 2 beginning with the class number JS, the " Faculty of Ophthalmology in the New York Medical Centre " is given the following two numbers to be chosen according to one's interests: JTNbd,O6,L and JTNO6bd,L where JTN = Individual medical school; O6 = Ophthalmology; bd = New York; and L = Faculty. This is equivalent to the prescription that space facet and personality facet may be taken in any sequence one may like, and that the Principle of Decreasing Concreteness need not be followed in a facet formula. Is this freedom, involving a repermutation of many of the classes, really necessary to satisfy dominant local interests?

6362 OMISSION OF FACET

The B.C. provides also for alternative class numbers to be got by omission of facets. This is illustrated by the following example given in Vol. 3 in the page beginning with the class number YHR. " Novels of the Brontë sisters " is given the following three alternative numbers to be chosen according to one's interests:

	B.C. Number	Facets Included
	YHP,B76 YR,B76 YO,B76	Language, Period, Form, Author Language, Form, Author Language, Author
C.C. Number	O-,3	Language, Form, Author

In the C.C. the author number is got by chronological device; therefore the period is contained in the author number. Form is second level personality facet; and Author is third level personality facet. According to the Canon of Modulation, the third level can be specified only after the second level. Thus there is no freedom to drop a facet in a case like this. I believe that no local interest will require the alphabetical mix-up of poetry, drama, fiction, prose and other literary forms in a single array.

6363 ALTERNATIVE NUMBERS FOR SUB-CLASS

The B.C. provides also for alternative class numbers for some important sub-classes. In tables V and VI of Vol. 1, it mentions about forty sub-classes provided with alternative class numbers. Here are a few of them with remarks on each.

Category	Alternative Numbers or Places	Remarks
Constitutional Law	*Either* RC in Political Science *Or* Sc in Law	This is due to absence of clear rules on Phase-Analysis. Surely the primary main class studied is Pol. Sc. and not Law.
Microbiology	*Either* EY in Biology *Or* FLD in Cryptogamia *Or* FV in General Botany	This is due to failure to make a firm decision in the fight between tradition and scientific collocation.
Pamphlet	*Either* in respective subjects *Or* 5, *or* 7, *or* 8	This is a matter for collection number and not for class number.

A scheme of classification should take the responsibility of making a decision in the first two types of cases.

6364 ALTERNATIVE NUMBERS FOR MAIN CLASS

The B.C. evades the responsibility even in respect of some main classes themselves. Here are the cases:

Main Class	Alternative B.C. Numbers
Library Science	2. JV. Z.
Psychology	AI. I.
Religion	AJ. K. P. Z.
Social Sciences	K. P.

It would be more in the fitness of things for a scheme to provide unique number for each main class in accordance with a firm decision taken in regard to the sequence of main classes in the system of knowledge chosen as the basis, and to leave it for local convenience to decide the allocation of the gangways and tiers in the stack room for the several main classes. This convenience may change from time to time even in one and the same library. A library may have also to change occasionally the sequence of main classes in the stack room arrangement, to fulfil the Third Law of Library Science. This has been described in the *Five laws of library science* of Ranganathan.

637 Alternative Schemes

There are thus alternative numbers provided at all possible levels and orders of arrays. They are scattered all through the detailed schedules. To have such a plethora of alternatives is like hanging by too many ropes. In fact, the result is not so much providing for local variation as providing many alternative schemes of classification. All shown in section 718, the number of more or less equally helpful sequences, available for a linear arrangement of the classes in a system of knowledge, is large. This is due to the endless ramifications and their re-entrant quality in the universe of knowledge. It is necessary for a treatise on the theory of systems of knowledge to indicate all possible sequences. But a scheme of classification for the practical work of arranging documents and their entries should prefer one and only one of such sequences and prescribe it. The Canon of Local Variation does not mean an organic upsetting of the very system of knowledge chosen as the basis for the scheme of classification.

6371 Symbiosis

This does not mean, however, that the approach of readers interested in other sequences should be totally neglected. A compromise is possible. These other readers can be served by symbiosis between classification and cataloguing. The classified part of the catalogue leads a reader from the basic class successively through compound classes got by attaching facets to it in a prescribed sequence. On the other hand, if the headings of class index entries are chosen according to the Chain Procedure, the alphabetical part of the catalogue leads a reader from any isolate idea of his class he may think of, successively to compound classes got by attaching facets to it in the reverse sequence until the basic class is reached. Thus, whatever be the isolate brought up by a reader, he will be guided to the part of the catalogue that answers his needs.

638 International Documentation

Virtually giving alternative schemes in a published scheme of classification, may not be too serious a hindrance, in so far as an individual library is concerned, for it can choose one of the alternatives and stick to it permanently, neglecting the others. But if libraries in accessible neighbourhoods have chosen different alternatives, the readers happening to go to many of them for service will be put to an inconvenience, which it is worth avoiding. Moreover, a scheme offering virtually different schemes for choice disqualifies itself for use in international documentation. On the other hand, provision for local variation resulting merely in shifting the documents in a favoured class to the first position in the sequence and in providing shorter class numbers for them in a particular library or in a particular special bibliography does not disqualify a scheme for use in international documentation.

CHAPTER 64

COMPOSITE BOOK

641 Classificatory Trouble

COMPOSITE BOOKS ARE TROUBLESOME to a scheme of Book Classification. The problem does not arise in a Scheme of Knowledge Classification. This class of books can arise only at the stage of the physical embodiment of expressed thought.

A composite book includes within the same two cover pages two or more documents; usually, though not always, these documents are also by different authors. Each document has its own specific subject-matter, and therefore each admits of a different class number. At the same time, the component parts do not cohere and form a continuous exposition, therefore the different class numbers of the component parts do not have a common immediate universe. This is the cause of classificatory trouble in a composite book.

642 Frequency of Occurrence

Composite books are not frequently met with in the universe of the modern books of the West. They are quite common among Arabic, Persian and Urdu books. The centres of the pages may form one homogeneous work. The margins of the pages may be occupied by another homogeneous work. I described in the *Abgila*, Vol. 2, 1952, a Kanarese manuscript, in which reading the words in the normal sequence gave a work on one subject, reading together every alternative word gave a work on another subject, reading the words in the vertical order gave a work on still another subject, and so on. There are a few such freakish composite books, and they too need to be classified. Among books printed in India in Indian languages, composite books do come out appreciably often. To quote from the *Vagaries in Indian book production* of K. Natarajan, presented to the Second All India Library Conference and published in the *Modern librarian*, Vol. 5, 1935, page 141, " Such instances are very common in books belonging to certain series. For example, Brahmananda Sarasvati's *Advaita-siddhanta-vidyotana*, and Nrisimhasrama's *Nrisimha-vijnapana* have been issued as a single volume in the Princess of Wales Saraswati Bhavana Texts' Series, with distinct title-pages and sequences of pagination, and in addition a common title-page."

643   S O S to Library Catalogue

It is not fair to blame the library profession for failing to invent devices to make the notation stand the strain of such anomalous and freakish books. It is legitimate, and indeed proper and sensible, for the discipline of classification not to stand on prestige but to send an s o s to the catalogue. This is what it does. It assigns to such a composite book the class number appropriate to the first constituent work; and having given class numbers to each of the other constituent works, it passes the rest of the work on to the library catalogue. The catalogue provides cross-reference entries for the second and later constituent works. Details of this will be found in rules 621, 622, their subdivisions, 623 and 624, of Ranganathan's *Classified catalogue code*, third edition, 1952.

CHAPTER 65

PARTIAL COMPREHENSION

651 Concrete Example

WE SHALL BEGIN THE discussion of partial comprehension with a concrete example. Take Pure Mathematics as the immediate universe. Suppose its array of the first order to consist of the five classes: Arithmetic, Algebra, Analysis, Trigonometry and Geometry. So far as the universe of knowledge is concerned, it is sufficient if a scheme of knowledge classification specifies Pure Mathematics in the earlier order and the above-mentioned five classes in the next lower order, as forming the array derived from it. For we have only one of six possibilities: either the subject is Pure Mathematics or it is any one of its five subdivisions. It cannot be anything else in the subdivision of Pure Mathematics within the universe of knowledge. In other words, it is enough if the scheme provides for one all-comprehensive class and for each of the separate classes in the array as follows:

Pure Mathematics
Arithmetic
Algebra
Analysis
Trigonometry
Geometry

6511 POSSIBILITY IN THE UNIVERSE OF BOOKS

But this is not sufficient in the universe of books. For it is possible to have books on any combination of the five classes of the array taken any number at a time. In addition to a book on Pure Mathematics which comprehends all the five classes, we may have, theoretically speaking, books which deal with the many possible partial comprehensions of the five classes of the array. The possibilities are listed below.

6512 COMBINATIONS OF TWO CLASSES

1. Arithmetic and Algebra
2. Arithmetic and Analysis
3. Arithmetic and Trigonometry
4. Arithmetic and Geometry
5. Algebra and Analysis
6. Algebra and Trigonometry

366

7. Algebra and Geometry
8. Analysis and Trigonometry
9. Analysis and Geometry
10. Trigonometry and Geometry

6513 COMBINATIONS OF THREE CLASSES

11. Arithmetic, Algebra and Analysis
12. Arithmetic, Algebra and Trigonometry
13. Arithmetic, Algebra and Geometry
14. Arithmetic, Analysis and Trigonometry
15. Arithmetic, Analysis and Geometry
16. Arithmetic, Trigonometry and Geometry
17. Algebra, Analysis and Trigonometry
18. Algebra, Analysis and Geometry
19. Algebra, Trigonometry and Geometry
20. Analysis, Trigonometry and Geometry

6514 COMBINATIONS OF FOUR CLASSES

21. Arithmetic, Algebra, Analysis and Trigonometry
22. Arithmetic, Algebra, Analysis and Geometry
23. Arithmetic, Algebra, Trigonometry and Geometry
24. Arithmetic, Analysis, Trigonometry and Geometry
25. Algebra, Analysis, Trigonometry and Geometry

652 Formula

This enumeration of the twenty-five theoretical possibilities might be boring to those who know algebra. But it has been given in order to make the matter concrete for those who have had no algebraical discipline. Now the latter class of people may take the former on trust when they say " We knew that there would be twenty-five classes of partial comprehension, from the formula $(2^n - n - 2)$ for the number of partial comprehensions of n classes. If you care you may verify this formula in the particular case considered by substituting 5 for n. This gives us $2^5 - 5 - 2 = 25$. Q.E.D."

653 A Tall Order

If an array has n classes in a scheme of knowledge classification, the corresponding scheme of book classification must add $2^n - n - 2$ extra classes to that array to provide for books of partial comprehension. Such extras must be added in relation to each array. It may be that all the theoretical extras are not required in practice, but some already are. For example, P. V. Seshu Ayyer's *Elementary mathematics* comprehends Arithmetic, Algebra and Geometry, but not Analysis and Trigonometry. Hence, to bring out all partial comprehensions a scheme of book classification must comprise the apparatus necessary to create any number of these extras as and when the need arises. A tall order!

654 A Problem for Research

A tall order indeed! For no scheme of book classification has so far succeeded in satisfying this canon fully. All the existing schemes of classification evade this problem because of the limitations of their notation. Unless some new device is invented any attempt to force the notation, as it is now, to accommodate so many extras of the nature described will lead us to ridiculously cumbersome class-numbers which may prove rather a hindrance than a help. This is a challenge to the library profession, a first-class research problem for gifted students!

655 Library of Congress

The L.C. now and again specifies a class under the name " General special " and this term is defined to denote books of partial comprehension, or " non-comprehensive books "—just one extra class in place of the $2^n - n - 2$ extras required.

656 Universal Decimal Classification

The U.D.C. makes a less trivial attempt to meet the challenge of partial comprehensiveness. Its attempt is within the notational plane. If the partially comprehended foci are all in one array and are consecutive, U.D.C. prescribes that the class number should be made up of (1) the class number of the first focus, (2) an oblique stroke, and (3) the class number of the last focus. For example, 512/514 for Algebra, Geometry and Trigonometry.

If the partially comprehended foci are not consecutive, U.D.C. prescribes the class number to be made up of the class numbers of the respective foci in increasing sequence and added to each in succession by a +. For example, 512 + 514 + 517 for Algebra, Trigonometry and Calculus.

6561 Futility

Neither of the above prescriptions is helpful to the reader. A reader in Trigonometry, for example, will look up 514. He has also to look up 51 for his subject in fully comprehensive books. He would again have to scan the combined numbers beginning with 511 or 512 or 513 to find if any of their combinations contained 514. This is not much less futile a search than looking up all the partially comprehensive books placed with fully comprehensive ones. At any rate it is not as helpful as being guided by cross-reference entries in the catalogue.

657 Present Practice

In the C.C. and other schemes the situation is met in this way. Although the extension of the extra classes required is smaller than that of the all-comprehensive immediate universe, they are all given the class number of the immediate universe. No doubt this is imperfect, and may puzzle users. For, if they pick out at random books bearing the class number of the immediate universe, some will give information

on all the topics expected, whereas others will prove disappointing in
this respect.

6571 A Concrete Example

Let us take a concrete case to show how the aid of the catalogue is
resorted to. Suppose a reader wants a short account of Algebra. Let
us assume that books exclusively devoted to Algebra are all out on
loan at the moment. In such circumstances he would naturally pick
out a book falling within the comprehensive class Pure Mathematics.
Now unless all the books in that class are *actually all-comprehensive,* the
chances are very great of his picking out a book which is only partially
comprehensive and actually omits Algebra altogether. This will
disappoint him.

6572 Bankruptcy

The library profession is at present unable to find a notational
device to represent any partial comprehension satisfactorily without
the class number breaking under its own weight, so to speak. It is not
able to save the disappointment to the reader mentioned in 6571 in the
plane of classification itself.

658 S O S to the Library Catalogue

To tide over this predicament, the library profession sends an S O S
to the catalogue. It has provided the catalogue with what is called the
Cross Reference entry (see rule 2 and its subdivisions). It has adopted
the convention that fully comprehensive books need not be given
cross-reference entries but that partially comprehensive books, on the
other hand, must be cross-referred in the classified part of the catalogue
under the class number of each of the comprehended sub-classes.
When the catalogue is so provided with cross-references the reader
need not depend on chance for his being successful in getting a book
that treats of Algebra from among the books which bear on their
backs the class number of Pure Mathematics, the fully comprehensive
immediate universe. Reference to the catalogue under the heading
Algebra will show him exactly which of these books give information
on Algebra. Chapter 2 of the *Classified catalogue code* of Ranganathan,
third edition (1951), gives detailed rules for such cross-reference entries.

6581 When to Cross-Refer

The following examples will illustrate the value of this cross-
reference convention in the case of partially comprehensive books
which could not be successfully tackled by classification alone.

We do not write cross-references for each of the authors whose
criticism is found in Charles Wells Moulton's *Library of literary criticism,*
8 vols., because it is a fully comprehensive book of reference.

But every author studied in Andre Chevrillon's *Three studies in
English literature: Kipling, Galsworthy, Shakespeare* gives rise to a cross
reference entry. That is because this book is only partially
comprehensive, treating of only three authors.

6582 NEED FOR FURTHER WORK

The above is an over-simplification of the problem. The cross-reference entry no doubt invites the reader to examine the fruitful books of partial comprehension having on their backs the class number of the fully comprehensive immediate universe concerned. But according to the exception made in 6581, he is not asked to examine the fully comprehensive books. This is misleading. At the same time, if this exception is removed the flood-gates will be opened, and the cross-references will smother the substantive main entries and make them invisible. This dilemma may not be acute in literary criticism, but it is in other subjects. There is thus need to keep this problem on the list of those calling for research.

CHAPTER 66

BOOK NUMBER

661 Ultimate Class

An ADDITIONAL CANON IS necessitated in the theory of book classification, arising as follows. In the universe of books, many books and many volumes of a book exist in any given class. In a library many copies of the same book may exist. Let us adopt the following definition: The Ultimate Class of a document is the class of the least extension of the scheme of knowledge classification adopted in which it may be placed.

The documents having the same ultimate class cannot be differentiated among themselves and arranged in a definite sequence by any further subdivision of the universe of knowledge. This is the implication of the definition of the ultimate class. They will therefore have to be subdivided, not on the basis of subject-matter, but on the basis of other appropriate characteristics or trains of characteristics. These characteristics should pertain to the subtle body of the document, such as language, form of exposition or other medium of expression, and to some extent to features of the gross body such as year of publication and number of volumes.

662 The Canon

The following canon may be postulated to implement the conclusion of section 661.

A scheme of book classification should be provided with a scheme of book numbers to individualise the documents having the same class of knowledge as their ultimate class. This is the **Canon of Book Number.**

The book number takes up the individualisation of books at the point where the class number has to leave it as beyond its power. There are different views and different practices with regard to this canon.

663 Common-sense View

There is first the common-sense view recorded by Brown, in his *Subject classification,* third edition, 1937, section 32, in the following words: " Perhaps the most sensible and straightforward way to distinguish books from each other is to rely entirely upon the class number or symbol, plus the lettering on the books themselves. For whatever purpose required it seems much simpler to arrange books on shelves, in charging systems, in catalogues, or anywhere else, in a plain and easy sequence of authors' names in alphabetical order, under each division or subdivision of a class or subject."

As against this, we have the following opinion of Bliss, stated in his *Organisation of knowledge in libraries,* second edition, 1939, page 68. " Some librarians . . . regard internal notation (book number) as unnecessary. On the contrary it appears that the lack of it in one of the great American libraries makes designation and location of its books very difficult, slow and uncertain." My own experience inclines me to uphold the view expressed by Bliss.

Sayers does not appear to express an opinion on this matter. But from the fact that he devotes some pages to the construction of book numbers in both his books, we may, perhaps, infer that the Canon of Book Number has his support.

Assuming the need for book numbers, we may say that two different practices are current. The first practice uses the author's name and the second the date of publication for individualising books having the same ultimate class. The C.C. amplifies the second of these practices elaborately.

664 **Author Marks**

The first form is described by Sayers in his *Introduction to classification,* 1935, page 65, in the following words: " When the whole question of author marks has been considered, we think something may be said for using the first three letters of the author's name, without any further refinements; at least where books are not charged by combined class-marks and author numbers." But it is obvious that this simple type of book number cannot individualise (1) different copies of the same book; (2) different editions of the same book; (3) different volumes of a multi-volumed book; and (4) books by different authors the first three letters of whose names are identical.

6641 AUTHOR NUMBERS

The second method of using the author's name to construct the book number is described by Dewey in his *Decimal classification,* fourteenth edition, 1943, page 32, as consisting of the " Invention of translation systems by which a name is translated by its initial, with remaining letters translated into numbers, e.g. Freeman, F85." This serves hardly any purpose. This is perhaps due to a blind mania for numerals, even when the alphabet serves the purpose equally. Much ingenuity has been wasted over the conversion of letters into numerals. Four attempts are mentioned below.

6642 CUTTER NUMBERS

The most widely used of these translation systems is that of the Cutter-Sanborn numbers. Here are examples of such numbers taken from page 63 of the *Introduction to library classification* of Sayers, 1935.

Ab2	Abbot	Sa1	Saint
A12	Aldridge	Sw1	Swain
G16	Gardiner	Sch51	Schneider
G42	Gilman	Sch86	Schultz
G76	Graham		

6643 MERRILL NUMBERS

Another translation system is that of the Merrill numbers, of which the following are samples, taken from page 64 of the *Introduction to library classification* of Sayers, 1935.

01	A	06	B	11	Bou
02	Agre	07	Ban	12	Brim
03	Als	08	Bax	13	Bum
04	Ap	10	Bix	14	C
				15	Carr

The Jast numbers and the Brown numbers also satisfy the same purpose. But in all these cases, most of the objections already enumerated with regard to the use of the first three letters of authors' names continue to hold good.

665 **Biscoe Numbers**

With regard to the second practice of constructing book numbers, which depends upon the date of publication, the Biscoe numbers were invented in 1885. The Biscoe table is as follows.

A	Before Christ	G	1800-1809	M	1860-1869
B	0-999	H	1810-1819	N	1870-1879
C	1000-1499	I	1820-1829	O	1880-1889
D	1500-1599	J	1830-1839	P	1890-1899
E	1600-1699	K	1840-1849	Q	1900-1909
F	1700-1799	L	1850-1859	R	1910-1919

A book is numbered with the letter and the year number, centuries being ignored. When more than one book in the same class calls for the same number, these numbers are differentiated by adding lower case letters.

This system certainly satisfies the Canon of Book Number more fully than the system of author numbers. But even here there is apparently no provision for individualising the different volumes of a multi-volumed book.

666 **Colon Book Number**

The C.C. goes the whole way in the design of Book Number, by introducing facet analysis here also. It takes all possible characteristics likely to arise in the expression of the thought-content to form the work and just three characteristics of the physical embodiment to form the book.

6661   FACET FORMULA

The facet formula prescribed by the C.C. is as follows. This is a slight modification of the one given in the fourth edition, in anticipation of the fifth.

[L] [F] [Y] [A]; [C].[V]-[S],[R] where

L = Language of exposition. The language number is taken from the language schedule.

F = Form of exposition. The form number is taken from a special schedule, reproduced in section 6662.

Y = Year of publication. The year number is taken from the chronological schedule.

A = Accession part of book number, used to distinguish the different books in the same ultimate class and having the same language and form of exposition. This is serially made beginning from 1 for the second book received in the library or spotted out for inclusion in the bibliography, as the case may be.

C = Copy, other than first copy. The copy number is serially made as for A.

V = Volume. The volume number is taken from the book itself.

S = Supplement. The supplement number is taken from the book itself.

R = Related document. This may be a review article, or a criticism in the case of a pedestrian book, or a sequel which it is more helpful to put along with the original rather than separated from it.

6662   SAMPLE SCHEDULE FOR FORM FACET IN BOOK NUMBER

$a1$ Systematical	$c6$ Chronological	**n Opinion**
$a5$ Alphabetical	$c9$ Other	
$a6$ Chronological	**d Data**	$p1$ Lecture
	$d2$ Pattern	$p2$ Dialogue
b Index	$d3$ Recipe	$p3$ Discussion
$b1$ Systematical		$p5$ Debate
$b5$ Alphabetical	**f Picture**	$p7$ Symposium
$b51$ Title	$f3$ Engraving	
$b55$ Subject	$f5$ Painting	**q Code**
$b57$ Author	$f95$ Photograph	**v Practical**
	g Plan	
c List	$g3$ Relief	$w1$ Verse
$c1$ Systematical		$w2$ Drama
$c2$ Numerical	**h Graph**	$w3$ Fiction
$c3$ Geographical		$w4$ Letter
$c4$ Conventional	**j Parody**	$w6$ Prose
$c5$ Alphabetical	**k Adaptation**	$w7$ Champu
$c51$ Title	**m Catechism**	**x Quotations**
$c55$ Subject	$m1$ Questions	$x2$ Extracts
$c57$ Person	$m5$ Answers	$x5$ Digest

6663   Justification

The schedule given in section 6662 will go some way in convincing readers of the need for the form facet. As a matter of fact, each facet has been introduced only on the basis of actual experience gained by observing the reaction of readers in stack room and noting some of their remarks. The need for indicating volume number and supplement number is inherent. So also the need for distinguishing, by the accession part of book number, the different works with the same class number, language number, form number and year number, will be granted easily.

66631   Language Number

Ordinarily, a reader is able to read only in one or two languages. But a library may have books on a specific subject in several languages; ten languages are not uncommon. It has been observed that readers are irritated to find books in different languages turning up promiscuously while they are scanning the shelf or the catalogue for those documents which they can read in a particular class. On the other hand, they find it helpful if the documents or the entries are separated out into different linguistic groups. It is this experience which led to the prescription of language facet in book number, even in the first edition of C.C.

66632   Form Number

Books in diverse forms of exposition, in one and the same class, were not experienced much in the Madras University Library. Therefore, form facet did not suggest itself for inclusion in the first three editions of the C.C. But in 1950 I had the opportunity to scan the shelves and the catalogues of some of the biggest libraries in the U.S.A. I then found it irritating to find all the forms of exposition or expression promiscuously mixed up. This also made me recall some of the difficulties experienced, back in the days of the Madras University Library, in finding out for readers books in particular forms of exposition such as catechism, dialogue and drama. This led to the recognition of the helpfulness of adding a form facet to the book number.

66633   Copy Number

In the Madras University Library, we had not distinguished a different work on a particular class from a different copy of one and the same book. The earlier editions of the C.C. too did not distinguish them. This had been all along coming to the centre of attention; but, every time, it was brushed aside partly because more serious problems crowded it out and partly because no suitable notational device suggested itself readily. In 1948, I received a letter from P. S. Sundaram. He mentioned that he had used the Madras University Library quite often as an undergraduate, and that his later experience in other libraries in India and abroad made him appreciate the great helpfulness of the shelf-arrangement and the classified part of the catalogue of the Madras University Library. He had then become a

Professor of English, and was put in charge of the College Library. This made him read my books on library science and implement some of the ideas. This made him face a difficulty which had been irritating him during his visits to the Madras University Library as an undergraduate. The book number system in use scattered the different copies of a book on Shakespearean criticism among other works on that subject. As professor in charge of the library, he desired to avert this irritation from his students; he wanted a solution. This made me face this problem and solve it without any further procrastination. The copy number suggested itself. It is only now that it is realised that the connecting symbol for it should be a semicolon, since distinguishing an additional copy is only equivalent to distinguishing another material. This is thus a welcome contribution from a kind reader in the library, who had appreciated and enjoyed the helpfulness of the arrangement secured by C.C. class number and book number.

66634 Edition Problem

But good does not always come in the form of kindness; it need not always arise out of kindly motives; it may arise out of hatred and cynicism too, even as the lotus arises out of mud—indeed one of the names for lotus in Sanskrit literally means " born of mud "! Another reader was a Professor of Law. He would never respect the rules of the library; thereby he brought upon himself the enforcement of rules. He had had to face also the refusal of undemocratic special privileges sought to enhance and assert his prestige. He found an opportunity to avenge his grievances. One day, in the presence of some students, he ridiculed the arrangement secured by the C.C. Some of them, who were shrewd enough to see the motive behind this unusual over-solicitude to make things convenient to them, reported to me that the scattering of different editions of one and the same book on the law of torts amidst other books on the same subject was made much of. This made me go into the unhelpfulness of this scattering. We had been poor in textbooks of law in the Madras University Library. Law students seldom came to us. I had had, therefore, no experience in this matter. On hearing of this unhelpfulness for the first time in 1948, I discussed this difficulty with some other students and teachers of law. It was obvious that the different editions should be brought together. The Canon of Permanence and the Law of Parsimony ruled out bringing them all together at the place of the latest edition. It was therefore decided to bring them all to the place of the first edition available in the library. It was first decided to add the year number of the later edition to that of the first. It has since been found that the copy number itself may be made to look after this.

66635 Differential Application

The prescription about bringing together different editions of a book should not, however, be applied blindly in all cases. Differential treatment is necessary. For example, in medicine, a new edition often incorporates later information, some of which may even deny statements in the earlier edition. In a library for historical research by senior scholars, it may be of help to bring all such contradicting editions together. But in the library of a medical college patronised by students, it may be nearly criminal to take the latest edition far away from its own legitimate place in the year sequence and put it along with a misleading outmoded edition.

66636   Related Document Number

The related-document-facet suggested itself in two ways. Miss Mayo's book *Mother India* stimulated several books criticising it. The need was felt to bring them all next to it. But at that time we could not think of any notational device to bring them together. Of course, the classic device would do it; but the basic book was not a classic book; it was only a pedestrian book. Even earlier, a series of books quickly exchanged between Hilaire Belloc and G. K. Chesterton had raised the same issue. Again a polemical book by Ambedker and the retaliations to it by other books by some others like Santanam raised the same issue. When we began to do documentation work and do bibliographies of the " by and on " type for an author, the problem of bringing a non-classic book and the reviews on it put the book number to a severe test of the same kind. The problem came to be faced seriously in 1950. The first solution sought was to use g as the isolate number in the related-document-facet. This was suggested by the view that the related documents are in essence criticisms of the basic book. But now it is felt that the purpose will be served equally well by the use of mere serial 1, 2, 3, etc., as isolate numbers in that facet.

6664   ECONOMY MEASURES

In spite of the above justification, there is no doubt that the facet formula for book number looks rather formidable. In actuality, however, the Colon book number of the majority of the books is no more formidable than any other book number described in the earlier sections. It is really simple, and this is secured by the following economy measures.

(1) The language facet may be omitted in any class except Literature, if the language of the book is the favoured language of the library.

(2) The language facet may be omitted in the class Literature, if the language of the book is the language of the literature. This implies that a translation will be distinguished from the original by the presence of language number in the book number of the former only.

(3) The form facet may be omitted, if the form of the book is the favoured form of the library. In most libraries, the favoured form will be prose.

(4) Even by the prescription in section 6663, the first book, in the category defined, need not have accession part of book number.

(5) Similarly, the first copy of a book need not have copy number.

(6) The volume number is inevitable; but the occurrence of a multi-volumed book is not very frequent.

(7) The supplement number will occur in a much smaller number of cases than the volume number.

(8) Related-document-facet will be needed very, very rarely in a library collection. But it will be needed more often in an author bibliography of the " by and on " type.

(9) Thus the majority of book numbers will consist only of the year number.

6665 ORGANIC AND NECESSARY

The C.C. book number has been designed in organic relation to the C.C. class number. This becomes particularly useful in the case of linguistic dictionaries and translations. There can be no doubt about the helpfulness and the necessity of an organically designed book number. The B.C. prescribes it as an essential part of the scheme, denoting book number by the term " internal notation."

667 Other Schemes

The U.D.C. also can adopt a book number similar to the one designed by the C.C. Its notational system has most of the necessary apparatus. But it has not yet devoted its thought to it. I commend this problem to the attention of the F.I.D. Committee on U.D.C.

Most of the other schemes do not pay any attention to book number. They seem to be prepared to take on any book number designed, all by itself, without relation to any particular scheme of knowledge classification. This is much like makers of motor-cars not devoting special attention to their own designing of electric equipment, carburetter, or tyre, but taking them over from among those designed by others, without relation to any particular make of car.

CHAPTER 67

COLLECTION NUMBER

671 Definition of Collection

An ADDITIONAL CANON IS necessitated in the Theory of Book Classification. It arises in several ways.

6711 COLLECTION BY UNUSUAL GROSS BODY

The first reason is the physical necessity for grouping and arranging as a different collection, all documents having a similar gross body. For example, collections like the following become necessary: Film roll; Film strip; Microcard; Transparent card; Ceiling book; Gramophone record; Speaking book; and Braille book. None of these can be shelved with ordinary books. Each species must go into a separate collection. Within each such collection, the documents will of course stand arranged parallel to that in the collection of ordinary books. We may call the collection of ordinary books the Main Collection. We may name each of the other collections by the name of the species of materials put into it, say Film Strip Collection.

6712 COLLECTION BY SIZE OR RARITY

Again consider the following:

1 Pamphlet
2 Giant folio
3 Miniature book
4 Roll
5 Book of plates on loaded paper
6 Crumpled and worn-out book, not to be weeded out on account of rarity
7 Rare and costly book
8 Incunabula
9 Manuscript

None of these can be shelved in the main collection. Each species should go into a separate collection of its own. We name such a collection also by the name of the species put into it, such as Incunabula Collection.

6713 COLLECTION FOR PROMPT SERVICE

Apart from collections formed out of physical necessity, a collection may have to be formed for facilitating prompt service to fulfil the Laws of Library Science, particularly the Fourth Law " Save the Time of the Reader." Here are some examples:

(1) Reading room collection, consisting of ready reference documents.

(2) Departmental collection in a public library organised along departmental lines, segregating, for example, the service and the location of Arts books in a separate building or room.

(3) Departmental collection in an academic or industrial research institution, consisting of the materials frequently needed at the elbow, as it were.

(4) Textbook collection in an educational institution, consisting of copies—perhaps several—of the books prescribed for study during a term or a year.

(5) Topical collection, consisting of the documents of topical interest at the moment, such as those bearing on a special course of lectures being delivered.

The exigencies calling for the formation of such sequences have been described fully in chapter 8 of Ranganathan's *Library administration* (1935).

672 Parallel Classified Sequences

Each document in each sequence will get its own class number as determined by its thought-content. It will also get its own book number as determined by its language, form of exposition and other factors. Therefore the documents in each sequence will stand arranged in a classified sequence. The sequences in the various collections will all run parallel.

673 Permanent Collection

Some of the collections will be virtually permanent. The reading room collection and the departmental collection of a public library are examples. To facilitate their replacement after use, there should be some mark provided on the back of the book. To facilitate their being located, the catalogue entries also should have the mark, inserted in them.

674 Quasi Permanent Collection

Some of the collections will be quasi permanent. The departmental collections of an academic or research library and the textbook collection of an educational library are examples. They may stay there for a fairly long time, but not permanently. The departmental collection may have to be disbanded and freshly formed when the subject of pursuit in the department is changed. The textbook collection will have to be changed with change of curriculum. Here also, marks are necessary to denote the collection to which a document belongs.

675 Temporary Collection

The topical collection is by its very purpose and definition strictly temporary. Even then, a mark will be necessary on the document to indicate its collection, in order to facilitate replacement. The mark should also indicate the date on which the topical collection should be dismantled.

676 Definition of Collection Number

The mark added to class number *cum* book number to indicate collection is called the Collection Number. The collection number does not always lie within the sphere of the Classification Section. Often it lies within the sphere of the Maintenance Section. Nor is it wanted in all kinds of bibliographies. Nor can it be permanent in all cases.

6761 NOT WANTED

In a national bibliography published in instalments or in an annual cumulation of it, even book number may not be necessary in full form; for the year number may be omitted; the volume and supplement numbers too may be omitted; because this information will be given in the body of the entry itself. Similarly, the size, collation and the physical make-up in the case of a book of abnormal shape or material, will be described in words in the body of the entry itself. Therefore there will be no need to insert the collection number.

6762 YES AND NO

In a special documentation list, it is helpful to form at least groups corresponding to collections based on physique. Here again, there will be no need to use collection numbers. The nature of the group may be described in words. But such grouping will cut up the sequence of entries into several sequences. This will militate against helpfulness to subject approach. To avoid this, it is desirable to have the entries in a single classified sequence. In this case, the collection number should be added to the class number in the case of an annual bibliography, and to the class number *cum* book number in the case of a retrospective bibliography.

6763 WANTED BUT IMPERMANENT

In a library catalogue and in the documents themselves of a library, collection number is necessary. Location and replacement need it. But in the case of the quasi permanent and temporary collections, the collection number cannot be permanent. For the documents in them will have to be transferred to other sequences from time to time. In their case, the collection number will have to be changed from time to time. Hence, the collection number should be left to the care of the maintenance section.

677 Out of Bounds

For the reasons set forth in section 666 and its subsections, collection number may be deemed out of bounds for a scheme of classification. However, it will facilitate work in libraries and on bibliographies if an illustrative schedule of collection numbers is appended to a scheme of classification. Following is a sample schedule.

It is not worth putting collection number in the catalogue entries of a document in a temporary sequence. It may be sufficient to mark on the date label the date on which the temporary sequence should be

Nature of Collection	Collection Number	Nature of Collection	Collection Number
Pamphlet, i.e. Under-size	Underline book number	Reading Room	RR
Over-size	Overline book number	Textbook	TC
Worn out	Underline and overline book number	Film Strip	FS
Rare Book	RB	Law Department	ZD

dismantled. There is no need for collection number to indicate main collection. In all cases, however, the shelf register cards should be kept in parallel collections. Whenever, a document is changed from one collection to another, its shelf register card also should be moved in a corresponding way. This will involve also change of collection number in some cases. That is why the collection number should be left to the care of the maintenance section. This method of securing mobility for the documents to go from one collection to another, with the least possible amount of work, has been described to conform to the Principle of Parallel Movement, in the *Library administration* (1935) of Ranganathan.

678 Canon of Collection Number

These considerations suggest the following canon of a permissible nature:

A Scheme of Book Classification may be provided with a Schedule of Collection Numbers to individualise the various collections of special documents to be formed on the basis of the peculiarities of their gross bodies, or their rarity, or service exigency to facilitate use by readers. The collection numbers based on physical peculiarity may be of use in bibliographies also.

This is the **Canon of Collection Number.**

CHAPTER 68

CALL NUMBER

681 Definition

WE ARE NOW IN a position to define Call Number. We shall attempt two kinds of definition, one functional, the other structural.

6811 FUNCTIONAL DEFINITION

Call Number is the number denoting the exact relative position of a document in a library and the position of its entry in a library catalogue or a documentation list. In a library without open access, this is the number used by a reader in " calling for " a document. Probably the term owes its origin to this use of it.

6812 STRUCTURAL DEFINITION

Call Number generally consists of three parts: (1) Class Number, (2) Book Number and (3) Collection Number.

6813 WHEN NECESSARY

All these three parts will be necessary in a library and in a library catalogue.

Collection Number may not be necessary in a general documentation list or in a national bibliography cumulated over more than one year. But both class number and book number will be necessary.

In an annual national bibliography, an annual documentation list, an annual abstracting periodical, and an instalment of any of these at shorter intervals, even book number may not be necessary, if the documents listed are all normal books. In any of these only class number will be necessary, and it may also be sufficient. The entries of documents sharing the same ultimate class may be arranged alphabetically by the headings. But if the list includes documents of different languages or forms of exposition the relevant facets of book number will become necessary.

6814 PERSISTENCE

The only part of call number persisting in all cases is the class number. This explains most of the schemes of classification stopping with the prescriptions for class number.

Book number persists in two of the three categories. We may say that it is semi-persistent. This explains the attention paid by the C.C. to prescriptions of book number.

Collection number will be necessary only in library catalogues and libraries. There again the demand for it will vary from library to library, and even in the same library from time to time. This may be said to be non-persistent. This explains the neglect of it in practically all the schemes.

682 Metaphysical Analogy

A metaphysical analogy suggests itself. In certain systems of Indian Philosophy—and perhaps in others too, and certainly in theosophy—every living being is postulated to have three sheaths, viz. soul, subtle body and gross body. All these are separable. Soul can exist by itself; even then it is a being; there is the term, disembodied soul. A combination of soul and subtle body alone is postulated; this too is a being; the eschatology of many religions describe such a being. A combination of soul, subtle body and gross body is a living being; this alone is commonly recognised as a living being; perhaps because this combination alone becomes manifest to the primary senses. The other two are cognisable only as an intellectual or intuitive experience.

6821 HYPOTHESIS

The following hypothesis is common. A soul can get embodied in any number of subtle bodies in succession or even at the same time. A combination of soul and subtle body can get embodied in any number of gross bodies in succession or even at the same time. The *Bhagavad-gita,* for example, emphasises this; The soul puts on and casts off bodies, even as we can put on and cast off clothes. Again according to *Bhagavad-gita*, each individual soul (= *Jivatma*) is but a partial or restricted manifestation, or component, of the Supreme Soul (= *Paramatma*). Other names for it are Brahman and Absolute. It comprehends everything manifest and unmanifest and, in particular, every individual soul. Outside it, there is nothing. It is the universal soul.

6822 EQUATION OF UNIVERSE OF KNOWLEDGE

Applying this analogy to the universe of knowledge, we get the following correspondences:

Soul (Universal)   = Universe of knowledge
Individual soul   = Class of knowledge or subject

6823 EQUATION OF DOCUMENT

Applying the analogy to the universe of books, we get the following correspondences:

Soul   = Thought-content
Subtle body   = Language or other medium, and form of exposition
Soul+Subtle body   = Work
Gross body   = Material in which work is embodied
Soul+Subtle body+Gross body   = Document

683 **Right Classification**

Right classification should distinguish these three constituents of a document. It should recognise each of them, and provide for the classification of each of them. The characteristics used as the basis of the classification of these three components are bound to be different. They should be selected in each case according to the appropriate canons of the general theory of classification. In the notational plane, the classification of each of the constituents should also conform to the special canons to which they are respectively subject. The call number of a document should have, accordingly, the three parts—class number, book number and collection number. They are immiscible. They should be kept distinct from one another.

684 **Wrong Classification**

A scheme of classification is wrong and defective if it fails to recognise the three components of a document. It is defective if it does not prescribe for the classification of each of them. It is unhelpful if it fails to overlook any of the essential and relevant characteristics of any of the three components. It is inconvenient in use if it does not keep the three parts of call number distinct in design and in the way they are written.

685 **Distinctiveness in Call Number**

685 1 Separation in Call Number

The three factors mentioned below stress the helpfulness of separating the class number, book number and collection number, both in the work of designing them and in the mode of writing them all as call number.

(1) The universes classified by the three parts are incommensurable with one another. This is in the idea plane.

(2) The purposes served by the three parts are quite different and distinct from one another. This is also in the idea plane.

(3) As shown in section 681 3, the book number and the collection number do not occur in all bibliographies and in all libraries. This too is in the idea plane.

(4) If all the three parts are integrated into a single number, the length of the call number will exceed the psychological and physiological limits set by the capacity of the mind to hold a number, the requirements of a single breath and of a single comfortable sweep of the eye. This is in the notational plane.

(5) And yet all the three parts become necessary in many cases. This is also in the notational plane.

685 2 Canon of Distinctiveness

To implement the findings in section 685 1, a scheme of library classification should consist of three components, viz. Knowledge classification, Book classification, and Collection classification. Further, its notation should satisfy the following canon:

In a Scheme of Library Classification, the class number, the book number, and the collection number, together forming the call number, should be written quite distinct from one another.

This is the **Canon of Distinctiveness.**

6853 METHOD OF SEPARATION

There are two methods of separating the three parts of a call number while writing.

(1) *Either,* a sufficient, but uniform, space is left between the three parts, when written in in one line;

(2) *Or,* the three parts are written one below the other in different lines.

6854 SEQUENCE OF PARTS

We have next to decide the sequence in which the three parts should be written in the call number. This should be determined by the psychology and the convenience of the reader.

A reader's approach is by subject. Therefore his first interest is in the class number. It names his subject in ordinal numbers. It is this that he will first look for. Therefore the class number should occupy the first position.

After arriving at the class number, his next interest is to choose a particular book or document in that class. Therefore his next search will be for the book number. Hence the book number should occupy the second place.

After getting hold of the class number *cum* book number, which specifies the exact book or document needed, his next interest will be to know the collection containing it. This is his third interest. Therefore the collection number should occupy the third place.

686 Colon Classification

The C.C. does not provide for collection number in its fourth edition; and should deal with it in the next edition. Subject to this shortcoming, the following rules of C.C. implement the Canon of Distinctiveness:

" 013   A double space should separate the Book Number from the Class Number, except in the cases provided for by Rule 0131.

Examples.—B43   F6   C56   113F9   L3   *p*7J2

" 0131   On the spine of the book and on the back of the title-page the Book Number should be written below the Class Number.

Examples.—B43   C56   L3
                        F6   113F9   *p*7J2 "

687 **Bibliographic Classification**

The B.C. too does not provide for collection number. Subject to this shortcoming, the following Principle, stated in section 10 of chapter 3 of the *Organisation of knowledge in libraries,* implements the Canon of Distinctiveness.

" IV   The notation of *classes* (class-marks) should be separated and distinguished from the *internal notation* of the books within the classes."

The following examples are taken from section 8 of the same chapter.

AL, J9   Joseph, *Introduction to Logic.*
AKA, P32   Pearson, *Grammar of Science,* 2nd ed.
IA, J3.2/2   James, *Psychology,* copy 2, v. 2.

PART 7

SCHEMES OF LIBRARY CLASSIFICATION
LOOKING BACK

CHAPTER 71

PRE-HISTORY

711 Mere Grouping

To CLASSIFY IN THE primitive sense is to divide the existents of the universe of discourse into two groups. Perhaps, to the earliest man, classification meant only this simple dichotomy; but he would have soon stepped out of this rut. Sufficiently early in the history of the human race, classification would have meant formation of many groups. The potency of forming many groups would have been increasingly realised with increase in man's power of abstraction—with the evolution of the cortex of the brain.

712 Ranking

Man should have arranged the groups of the same universe of discourse in different sequences at different times. He would have discovered that different sequences were helpful for different purposes. This would have slowly led to his taking classification to be not merely grouping, but also ranking the groups in a way relevant to the purpose on hand. This is classification in the second sense. Children begin to classify in this sense very early in life. Perhaps, this inherent tendency to rank—i.e. to arrange in a specific sequence in space, or in time, or in space-time mesh—is a result of the finiteness of the speed of nervous impulse within the human body. Finite speed gives rise to rank, sequence and structure. To classify, then, in the second sense is probably a neural necessity.

713 System of Knowledge

The neural necessity to classify in the second sense at the material and elementary levels develops into an intellectual necessity when intellectual experience of increasingly abstract nature becomes dominant in the stock of knowledge of the individual or of the community. The communication of knowledge to one another requires the sorting out of the universe of knowledge into ranked groups in space-time mesh. Self-communication too requires such a sorting out. The further development of the universe of knowledge certainly requires such a sorting out. Thus classification in the second sense had, long ago, become essential. The result of such a classification of knowledge may be called a " System of Knowledge."

7131 HISTORIC SYSTEMS OF KNOWLEDGE

Systems of knowledge have been mapped out in different epochs of human history and in different cultural groups. Each system was the result of the tidying up of the universe of knowledge, in the light of what was known of it and of what appeared to be the trend of its further development, in the cultural group and the epoch concerned. Altogether 116 systems of knowledge are enumerated in the appendix in E. C. Richardson's *Classification: Theoretical and practical* (1901). Some of the systems are even described in detail. A critical account of several systems of knowledge forms the subject of R. Flint's *Philosophy as scientia scientiarum and a history of classification of sciences* (1904). H. E. Bliss evaluates, with the aid of his own criteria, a few of these historic systems of knowledge in his *Organisation of knowledge and system of the sciences* (1929). But these do not include the Indian, Chinese, Chaldean, Egyptian or Persian systems. The present renascence in Asia and Africa may lead to the isolation, description and critical estimate of the ancient systems developed in these cultural groups in the different epochs of their history. Just a few systems are described in the succeeding sections of this chapter.

714 Vedic System

A system of knowledge is implied in the *Upanishads* forming the philosophical and the mystic supplements to the different recensions of the four *Vedas* of ancient India. This is perhaps the earliest system known. It was adopted by the later epics, and the encyclopaedias known as *Puranas*. The *Bhagavad-gita* adopted it in its systematic exposition, and so did the later *Tantras*. The Vedic system divided the universe of knowledge into four main classes: *Dharma, Artha, Kama* and *Moksha*. These correspond to the four fundamental values of the same names. In fact any universe whatever—be it of human beings, or animals, or plants, or phenomena, or concepts of any kind, and not merely of knowledge—was classified in the first order array on the basis of these four values. The values themselves and the corresponding classes were usually arranged in the sequence mentioned above. *Dharma* corresponds to the modern classes of law, theology, ethics and sociology. *Artha* includes all applied sciences, natural as well as social. *Kama* comprehends all pure sciences, linguistics, fine arts and literature. *Moksha* covers philosophy, and mystic experience unmediated by the intellect or the primary senses.

7141 SEQUENCE OF MAIN CLASSES

The following sections give the traditional sequence of the main classes of the Vedic System of Knowledge.

7142 DHARMA

The first main class, *Dharma,* is concerned with the preservation of society as a coherent organisation. Evidently, this is regarded as the minimum and primary knowledge with which anybody should start in building his own stock of knowledge, and for his being a useful and participative member of his community. These are, more or less, of a normative nature.

7143 ARTHA

Then came the subjects needed by a welfare state, in the material, economic and political levels. This group forms the main class *Artha*. From the point of view of social well-being and happiness, the applied sciences have to be improved from time to time on the basis of pure sciences. This eventuality takes shape progressively in the measure of the unbalancing of the population pressure on the one side, and the natural and the industrial resources on the other, developing within the community. This is the social motive and pressure for the development of pure sciences.

7144 KAMA

Apart from this, some individuals involuntarily seek joy in the pursuit of pure sciences. Many find joy in the involuntary creation of works of literature and other forms of art. This involuntary pursuit of subjects is inherent in the nature of a few. It is largely an individual necessity backed by individual capacity. It is a matter of one's own will and pleasure, whether to create or merely to enjoy what has been created by others. This is perhaps the reason for denoting the main class comprising these subjects by the term *Kama*—desire, individual desire.

7145 MOKSHA

Subjects involving individualism *par excellence* are put into the last class *Moksha*. It is only a small minority in any community that find competence to develop or even appreciate such subjects. Individualism reaches its very extremity in relation to mystical experiences. It is only one in several millions that feels at home in this region of knowledge. This does not mean that the class of subjects in the main class *Moksha* are anti-social or even a-social. On the contrary, it is extremely beneficial to society. It is the vision concomitant to these subjects that saves humanity in moments of crisis. If normative subjects are necessary for the maintenance of society in a coherent state, if applied subjects are necessary to guarantee well-being of society, if pure sciences are necessary to make applied subjects meet the needs of welfare state, the subjects in the *Moksha* class are necessary to enrich all the other main classes and lift them to the higher pitch needed to meet social needs from time to time; this connection, however, is not immediate or easily perceivable in the view of many. Thus the four main classes in the Vedic system of knowledge are arranged in the sequence of decreasing popular comprehension, decreasing immediacy in social use, and increasing " fundamental " quality and potentiality for social use. It is essentially socio-centred.

7146 CORRELATION WITH D.C.

Guha has made a first attempt in correlating the Vedic system with the system of the D.C. This will be found in a paper published in the *Sarasvati Bhavana studies*. It is rather superficial. Considerable work should be done to get a more or less satisfactory result.

715 European Scholastic System

Plato's philosophy is said to have mentioned logic, physics and ethics as constituting the system of knowledge as understood in his days. This sequence is seen to be the reverse of the one in the Vedic system. Aristotle's system throws the then known major subjects in the sequence: logic, metaphysics, mathematics, physics; ethics, politics, economics; and useful arts. These were formed into a triad in the array of main classes. The first four formed the main class theoretical philosophy; the next three, practical philosophy; and the last, productive arts. Eventually, this led to the scholastic system. In this system, the following sequence of subjects was adopted: Grammar, dialectics and rhetoric; geometry, arithmetic, astronomy and music; theology, metaphysics and ethics. The first group was called the Trivium; the second, the Quadrivium; and the first two together, the seven liberal arts. These were preliminaries to the last triad which formed the substantive group. This system followed the sequence of subjects in the universities of that age. It was the basis of arrangement in the universal bibliography brought out by Konrad Gesner of Zürich in 1548.

716 Bacon's System

In his *Advancement of learning* (1605), Francis Bacon examined the universe of knowledge as it was known in his time. This led him to a new system of knowledge. It had a triad of main classes. These were arranged in the following sequence: History (emanation from memory); Poesy (emanation from imagination); and Philosophy (emanation from reason). This is not socio-centred as the Vedic system; nor was it university-centred as the European scholastic system. It was psychology-centred. The main class Philosophy included all the subjects other than history and literature. Naturally, the subdivisions of this main class were greatest in number. We see the influence of Bacon's system in the array of main classes of D.C. and consequently of U.D.C. also. In the latter systems, history forms the last class; and it is a class by itself. Literature becomes the penultimate class; and it is also a class by itself. These are preceded by the remaining subjects covered by the Baconian main class Philosophy; on account of its vastness, it was shown as seven different classes. This rearrangement is called by Berwick Sayers the Inverted Baconian System. Directly or indirectly, Bacon held sway for a long time.

394

717 Later Systems

During the last three centuries, the development of the universe of knowledge has been steadily accelerating. Its size has been swelling. At present, the interlocking of its parts is on the increase; this baffles any attempt to build a system capable of being singled out as the best. Perhaps this accounts for the nihilistic tone of Bliss's *Organisation of knowledge and system of the sciences*. A few of the endeavours of the last two centuries in portraying a system of knowledge will be mentioned here.

7171 DICHOTOMY STILL

Primitive man's dichotomy dies hard. It still allures many. Some ride it to death, as the saying goes. Kant did it, and here is a picture of his system of knowledge, taken from his *Critique of pure reason* (1781):

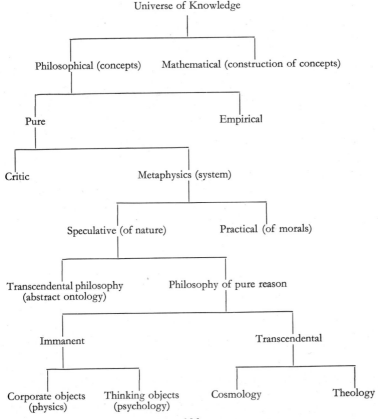

7172 TRICHOTOMY

The Greek triad, like primitive dichotomy, dies hard. Hegel was fascinated by it. Here is a picture of his system of knowledge taken from his *Logic* (1812):

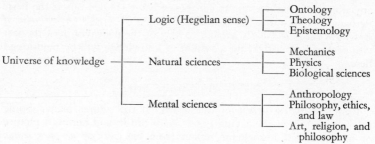

7173 ESCAPE INTO DECIMAL

Dichotomy and trichotomy were the creations of the limited mental capacity of the early man. But it had led to a race-habit. Habits usually outlive their usefulness. Race-habits die out at different rates in different spheres of human activity. For example, dichotomy gave rise to the binary scale of numeration. Binary arithmetic was given up very early as unworkable. Nearly two thousand years ago, India had invented the decimal scale in its place. Probably it was anthropomorphic in its unconscious origin. Whatever it is, this scale has lifted mathematics to very great heights. And yet, that very India is still hugging on to the binary system in its coinage; it is only now that the government has decided to supplant it by the decimal system with the aid of legislation. Similarly, profound thinkers on systems of knowledge surrendered to the race-habit. But the D.C. escaped from it into the decimal system, in setting forth its system of knowledge. It may be of interest to mention here that the binary system is being revived now as the only system that machinery can use in searching for entries in a bibliography.

7174 SERIAL SYSTEM

Another factor began to play an important part in the design of system of knowledge in the nineteenth century. This concerned the sequence of the classes, rather than their number. The socio-centred sequence of the Vedic system, the university-centred sequence of the scholastic system, and the psychology-centred sequence of Bacon were all given up. The pressure of natural sciences led to their abandonment. This led to the concept of serial dependence of subjects. In his *Cours de philosophie positive* (1830), Auguste Comte started off the Serial System of knowledge. He suggested the series: Mathematics, astronomy, physics, chemistry, biology, and social physics. It was claimed that each of these main classes was dependent for its development on the use of the preceding ones. This started a fight over " dependence." Many serial systems were put forth, of course condemning all the predecessors! In his *Classification of sciences* (1864), Herbert Spencer arrived at the series: Logic, mathematics, mechanics, physics, chemistry, astronomy, geology, biology, psychology and sociology. These were all serial systems, of fundamental or nearly pure disciplines only.

7175 APPLIED SCIENCES AND USEFUL ARTS

Another apple of discord in the establishment of the serial system of knowledge was the location of the applied sciences and useful arts in relation to the fundamental disciplines. In his *Leviathan* (1651), Thomas Hobbes had placed them as follows: Engineering, architecture and navigation next to mechanics; and music next to acoustics. In his *Essai sur philosophie des sciences, ou exposition analytique d'une classification naturelle de toutes les connaissances* (1834-1843), Ampère interpolated the useful arts and applied sciences next to the fundamental disciplines on the use of which they were believed to be essentially dependent. His interpolations were as follows: Engineering after physics; mining after geology; agriculture after botany; and animal husbandry and medicine after zoology. The sequence in C.C. had been thus fully anticipated a century earlier. The D.C. continues to be in the grip of Aristotle and Bacon. It segregates all the applied sciences into a single main class and puts it after the main class pure sciences. The only fortuitous feature is medicine following closely after zoology. Perhaps this was the only freedom available; and it has been utilised.

7176 SERIAL SYSTEM OF C.C.

Apart from the interpolation of the applied sciences next to the fundamental disciplines on the use of which they essentially depend, the serial system of the C.C. has certain other features. In bringing them out, the applied sciences may be left out of consideration without any loss of generality.

71761 The Centre

The centre of the serial system is occupied by " Mysticism and Spiritual Experience," the latter half of the Vedic main class *Moksha*. This class accommodates knowledge got trans-intellectually, through intuition. It implies a direct apprehension of " the thing-in-itself," unmediated by intellection or the use of sensory organs. In Indian tradition, the term *Tejas* is used to describe this trans-intellectual, trans-sensory faculty. I have used the term *Intuition* as its equivalent. This gives:

(1) concrete knowledge *par excellence* of the whole entity;
(2) complete knowledge of the relation of the entity to every other entity in the universe; and
(3) pristine knowledge of the entity, quite unaffected by the knower himself, i.e. in its pure native attributes, without any element whatever of man-made artificiality.

In Indian tradition, such a knowledge is said to be *Vastu-tantra* (=thing-dependent). In contradistinction to this, knowledge got by intellection and observation in the usual way is said to be *Kartru-tantra* (=action-dependent, i.e. dependent on the action of the knower). In his book on *Holism*, General Smuts calls this region of knowledge " no-man's zone " for intellection. To go back to Indian tradition, this region of knowledge is ineffable. Speech is an intellectual action. Therefore communication of this knowledge is direct, from intuition to intuition, unmediated by speech. It is described as *Maunam vyak-hanam*, i.e. " exposition through silence." It is real knowledge, though it is beyond intellectuals. It is true knowledge of the concreteness of the entity *par excellence* and of the naturalness of the entity *par excellence*.

71762   The Two Sides

Let us survey the subjects arranged serially on one side of this centre. There is a successive step-down from concreteness towards abstraction. The subjects arranged serially on the other side of the centre show a successive step-down from naturalness towards artificiality. Here it must be remembered that the doublets " natural and artificial " and " concrete and abstract " are only relative. They get defined simultaneously by being used in one and the same sentence. Many doublets like that are in usage. Hot and cold, dark and light, big and small, near and far, and short and tall, are examples. These terms are intelligible only in the context of at least two entities, admitting of the doublet being applicable.

71763   The Side of Abstraction

Let us first examine the serial system of knowledge lying on the side of successive abstraction. We shall begin at the abstract end, and move towards the concrete end.

This serial system begins with mathematics. It is a methodology, made of a set of postulates and axioms and their implications. It is a purely intellectual experience. The entire universe of the knowees is " inside the skin of the knower," so to speak. Mathematics does not concern itself at all with any knowee outside the skin of the knower. Even time, space and matter are only fields for its abstract variables. These do not depend on the existence of these entities outside the skin as " concrete " entities. They are all only " abstract " entities in mathematics.

Next in the series comes physics. It takes time, space and matter as concrete entities outside the skin. These can be observed by the sensory organs directly or indirectly. It studies the properties of matter in the space-time mesh. In doing so, physics does not distinguish between one species of matter and another. It takes any species of matter merely as a representative sample of matter *qua* matter. But the sample has many attributes, which make it a " substance "—say, iron, gold or silver. Physics abstracts from them all the mere " matter-ness " in them for its own universe of discourse. In this sense, it is still abstract, although relative to mathematics it is concrete.

Chemistry is concerned with the study of substances; in this respect, it is more concrete than physics. Yet it is interested only in, say, " iron " in the abstract. The frame of the machine on which I am typing this is *of* iron. For chemistry, it *is* iron. Chemistry is concerned only with the mere iron-ness of the frame. For me, it is essentially a frame, and its being made of iron is only an accident. The useful art of typewriter-making deals with the concrete piece of iron called " frame," making a " concrete commodity " out of the " substance iron." Chemistry deals only with the iron-ness of this frame, so that, relative to the useful arts, chemistry is abstract.

But viewed from the central class "Mysticism and spiritual experience," even the frame—the concrete commodity—of Useful Arts has a shade of abstraction, as it overlooks some at least of the infinity of attributes of the frame-in-itself.

This has taken us through one section of the system of knowledge, on the abstraction side of the centre. The second section is characterised by the taking into consideration the more concrete and individuating quality called " life." This gives the sub-series of " biological sciences." In contradistinction, the earlier sub-series is called " physical sciences." The term " natural sciences " comprehends both of the sub-series, i.e. the entire series on the abstraction side of the centre. The complexity of concreteness increases as we move in the second section from biology, through botany and zoology, to medicine.

Thus there is increasing concreteness as we move from mathematics towards the centre which deals with concreteness *par excellence*.

71764   The Side of Artificiality

Let us next examine the serial system of knowledge lying on the side of successive artificiality or deviation from naturalness, beginning at the natural end and moving towards the artificial end.

This serial system begins with fine arts, and literature, which is itself a fine art using language as the medium. In section 71761, we said that mystical experience is ineffable, yet some mystics are so full of sympathy to the others that they want to communicate to them at least part of the delight of their own experience. Goethe has said so, Ramakrishna Paramahamsa has said so. They have also said that to communicate through words or through any other medium is to take away from the fullness of their experience. It also takes away from the full naturalness of every knowee described. In spite of this, the universe of artists and of poets forms the closest approximation to the fully natural universe of the mystics. It has been vitiated by the element of artificiality to a small extent only. The sacred books of religions also belong to this category. Yet many artificial accretions develop in religion, in the form of creeds and practices, and therefore religion is further removed from the centre of the system. Philosophy is a matter of pure intellect, and is therefore even further away. Moreover, an essential part of philosophy is to tell men how to live. In prescribing a way of life, it does not begin with a dogma based on a partial understanding of the findings of the intuition of another, as religion does, but with " free thinking," and arrives ultimately at a " theory." In working out the details for a way of life based on this " theory," distortion of facts begins, in the interests of the theory, which then becomes a dogma. Thus deliberate, man-made artificiality comes in. Philosophy is thus vitiated by a greater dose of artificiality than the subjects placed earlier in the series. All these subjects, taken together, are denoted by the term " Humanities."

The deviation from naturalness assumes great dimensions as we enter the " Social sciences." Passing over geography and history, which form the basis of the study of social sciences, we pass in succession through political science, economics, sociology and law. In this subseries, the element of artificiality introduced by man increases steadily. In political science, for example, the ultimate decision about right or wrong is left, artificially, in the hands of one man, the king, or in the hands of the Supreme Court. We have fictions like " the king can do no wrong," or " the judiciary can do no wrong." A struggle has now begun between the latter fiction and a new one, " the legislature can do no wrong." In economics, the instrument of credit, called currency, has opened the floodgates of artificiality. With the best will in the world, humanity is unable to escape from the tyranny of this artificial entity created by itself. Sociology is largely descriptive, but its further reaches touch on interference with population, future generations and other factors of society, and in this respect it meddles with the course of nature by the adoption of artificial controls designed by man. Artificiality reaches its zenith in law, which enables man to assert, through the fiat of legislation, for example when time must be changed, whether the hand of the clock should be moved back or forward, quite unmindful of what the sun may be doing.

Thus there is increasing artificiality as we move from the centre towards law at the other end of the serial system.

7177 METHODOLOGY-APPLICATION CYCLE

There is another peculiarity in the serial system of the C.C., incident in the subdivision of each basic class. The serial system within each basic class is as follows: Global account; descriptive account; methodology peculiar to the basic class, given in abstract; application to concrete matter; and application to concrete of a higher order, viz. personality. This internal cycle occurs in other systems of knowledge also, but in C.C. it is conscious, universal and almost mechanised; it is but a reflection of the postulates about fundamental categories set forth in chapter 35. This methodology-application cycle thus persists in all basic classes, and clears off much of the confusion found in the discussions on the helpfulness or otherwise of the sequence of the totality of classes in systems of knowledge. These discussions are often based on oversimplified principles, which are oversimplified to make their application easy. But the universe of knowledge is too turbulent to submit itself to such oversimplifications.

718 Bewildering Number

From the point of view of adoption as a basis for library classification, an important fact of arithmetic should be borne in mind when assessing the sequence of the totality of classes in any system of knowledge. It is the formidable rate of growth of $n!$ (factorial n). It is really the product of the first n integers, which gives the number of possible sequences in which n classes can be arranged. A few examples will show this rate of growth. When the number of classes is five, there are 125 possible sequences; this is of the order of 10^2. When the number of classes is ten, the number of sequences shoots up to 3,628,800—a number of the order of 10^6. When the number of classes is seventeen, the number of sequences flies off to the order of 10^{14}, being actually 355,687,429,086,000. It is by no means a simple matter to select the *most helpful* from among such an enormous number of sequences. Many of them of course will be obviously unhelpful, and no scheme of knowledge worth considering would have such sequences. But a large number will be *more or less equally helpful,* and to assert that one of them is the *most helpful* is hazardous. Indeed, much of the polemical writing on this subject has been purposeless, if not meaningless. It is as futile and pathetic as the fight of two friends over fixing the central point of the surface of the earth. One chose point A. The other went through all the survey operations again, and finally fixed another point B. They quarrelled, each saying that his was the true centre. The distance between A and B was only one foot! There is really no need at all for us to continue this particular battle, although there are various ways in which the mischief of $n!$ causes trouble.

7181 SEQUENCE OF CLASSES IN AN ARRAY

Firstly, the number of classes in each array is large, often more than ten. It is therefore unwise to assert that a particular sequence alone is the most helpful in a particular array. Then, there is a large number of arrays in any scheme of knowledge. This magnifies the unwisdom of assertion, in the measure of the number of arrays.

7182 SEQUENCE OF CLASSES IN A CHAIN

Nor is it worthwhile to decry from a single point of view, the succession of sub-classes preferred by a system of knowledge. Here again, different trains of relevant characteristics will throw the links of the chain in different sequences. Many of these will be obviously unhelpful. No worth-while system will choose them. But a few sequences will be *more or less equally helpful.* To assert that one alone is *the most helpful* can only be a blind adherence to a dogma. Controversy over this serves no purpose.

7183 COLLATERAL CLASSES

The futility of attempting to find out *the most helpful sequence* for a system of knowledge and of controversy over it is seen to be even greater when viewed from the angle of collateral classes. Collateral classes are classes having some affinity to one another and yet not occurring in one and the same array or chain—examples: Chemistry of gold; mining of gold; metallurgy of gold; goldsmithy; gold coinage; trade in gold, sociology of gold; etc. There is no means of bringing them all into a single array or into a single chain, to the satisfaction of one and all. The S.C. attempted it, but thereby it dissatisfied many.

7184 INSOLUBLE PROBLEM

The fact is that the proliferations in the universe of knowledge are too many and are too re-entrant to be arranged in a linear sequence, so as to do equal justice to all the filiations among them. And yet the human mind is still finding comfort only in linear sequences. Therefore every system of knowledge has to be presented at the last stage as a serial system in which the classes stand arranged in a linear sequence. Any linear sequence can only be *more or less helpful*. The problem of *the mos helpful linear sequence* is insoluble.

7185 PANCHA SILA

The fight over *the most helpful* system of knowledge should stop. The library profession at least should propose a vote of thanks to the problem and take leave of it. The Indian policy of *pancha sila* should prevail in the world of systems of knowledge. Peaceful coexistence should be guaranteed to all those interested in portraying systems of knowledge. System-making is inherent in the development of the universe of knowledge. New systems should be evolved from time to time. The purpose for which each is evolved and the explanation for each in the light of the then prevailing stage in the development and structure of the universe of knowledge, should be sought. There should be no heat or extraneous dogma in the matter.

7186 SUITABILITY FOR LIBRARY CLASSIFICATION

This does not mean, however, that any more or less helpful system of knowledge will be equally suitable as the basis of a scheme of library classification. This suitability will have to be determined by the requirements of the notational plane. Work on a system of knowledge can be solely in the idea plane. In fact, it is so in most cases. But a scheme of library classification has to work on three planes. We are here concerned only with two of these planes—idea and notation. It is largely true that the idea plane is the independent variable and that the notational plane is only a dependent variable. And yet, the independence of the former is not absolute. The idea plane can take help from the notational plane in certain situations. There is some element of reciprocity between them. The suitability of a system of knowledge to be used as the basis for a scheme of library classification is in the measure of this element of reciprocity inherent in the system.

71861   Need for Notation

In the first place, for any system of knowledge to be used for arranging documents on shelves and other receptacles, and their entries in bibliographies, catalogues and documentation lists, it should be possible to restore the sequence given by it, whenever any document or entry is pulled out of its place for use. It must be possible to do this without the need to read the document concerned, each time, to find out its specific subject and determine its place among the other subjects, *ab initio*. This is a practical necessity in library classification—indeed, an absolute necessity. An anecdote may illustrate this. Some years ago, I went into a big national central library. The head of the Bibliography Section took me round its collections and showed me the catalogue. It was not alphabetical; it was systematic; and yet there was no notation visible. I asked how the systematic sequence was maintained without the aid of notation. " Very simple. We know which class follows which. There is no difficulty in remembering the sequence," was the naïve reply. But the speaker was the head of the section. The sequence was actually maintained by a junior and not by the head. I realised the futility of pursuing this matter with the head, for it is only the toad beneath the harrow that knows where the pinpoint goes. I therefore asked to be introduced to the assistant in charge of the maintenance of the sequences on the shelf as well as in the catalogue cabinet. I went to the assistant on the next day. She felt proud that I came to her section independently—and that I did not go away, as most librarian-visitors do, after meeting the chief and being " conducted " round. She showed me with some pleasure the region of the catalogue given to my name. I asked her to find out from the systematic part of the catalogue the cards corresponding to certain books and articles. Some, she pulled out readily. She took more time for some others. For some more, she fumbled for a long time and ultimately located them. For a few she could not locate at all. I could see her difficulty. She added that the arrangement of the subject cards in the systematic part of the catalogue was her daily headache. Every time she delved into the catalogue, she found unhelpful placements. " How long are you going to have this headache? " I asked her, " Is there no remedy for this? " By this time she had begun to feel at ease in talking to me. She said with a smile, " You are teasing me. Call number is the Cure, certainly." " But why don't you use it? " I asked. " My chief does not allow it. She insists that I should be able to do without it. Otherwise, I am incompetent! You know what I mean " was the sad reply. It was followed after a pause by the significant words, " These chiefs never insert a single card. They do not know anything of the difficulties. They dictate blindly."

Therefore until a proper system of notation is attached to a system of knowledge, it does not become a scheme of library classification. That is why this chapter on the history of systems of knowledge has been headed Pre-History.

71862   Expansion Without Disturbance

In a library, then, the chosen system of knowledge appears on the documents and in the entries in the form of ordinal numbers. Changing the numbers is a huge task. Therefore a scheme of knowledge should have another essential quality to qualify for use as the basis of a scheme of library classification. The universe of knowledge is ever dynamic. It throws forth new proliferations every now and then. The system of knowledge should absorb the new classes into its serial sequence. In doing so, it should not be obliged to rearrange the already existing classes in a new sequence. When all the new classes are overlooked, the residue should be just the same sequence as was in existence before the introduction of any new class. In other words, each fuller version of the chosen system of knowledge should contain within it every older version without any alteration. Secondly, the newer classes should not be denied independent existence and forced to remain merged in an older, more extensive class, in order to escape the hardship of changing the numbers on the documents and the entries. Otherwise, the need for changing class numbers will arise. This quality in a system of knowledge implies that its suitability for use as basis for a scheme of library classification will be in the measure of the extent of its anticipation of the future trends in the development and structure of the universe of knowledge.

7187   Brunet Scheme

Among the most influential and widely used schemes of library classification, mention is usually made of the Brunet Scheme. It was based on a prior scheme used by Paris booksellers and French bibliographers since the seventeenth century. It was modified and incorporated by J. C. Brunet in his *Manuel du libraire et de l'amateur des livres* (1809). The classification of the Bibliothèque Nationale of France is said to have been based on this scheme. The classification of the British Museum Library also is said to have been influenced by it. In his *Manual of classification*, third edition (1947), Sayers gives a sample of the Brunet call number.

Theology IIAm82 Turkish version of the Holy Bible
where,   Theology IIAm is class number, and
82 is book number, meaning 82nd book in the class.

71871   Sufficiency

The number of classes in the Brunet Scheme is only of the order of 10^4. This was considered sufficient for the number of classes which the universe of knowledge had thrown forth about two centuries ago.

This was all that the literary warrant of those days demanded. Probably, bibliographers seldom descended to the depths of micro-thought, in its application to bibliographies in later days.

71872 Insufficiency

But the capacity of the Brunet notation is no longer sufficient. It cannot take many new classes. Its insufficiency is perhaps due also to the system of knowledge forming its basis, not having in adequate measure the quality mentioned in section 71862. Even the D.C. has proved insufficient for the present-day proliferations of the universe of knowledge, in spite of its capacity being of the order of 10^6. The demand of the depth classification needed for efficient documentation service today is for a capacity of the order of 10^{15}. And it may even reach the order of 10^{20}.

7188 SEVEN SCHEMES

Therefore the first scheme to be treated in the first of the succeeding chapters of this part is the Decimal Classification. The other schemes that have already a large capacity are the U.D.C., L.C., C.C. and B.C. They are even capable of increasing their capacity. They are therefore included with even greater appropriateness. The E.C. and S.C. do not appear to have capacity for increasing their capacity to an equal extent. However, their present capacity is large enough to justify their inclusion. And these are, of course, the seven schemes studied comparatively in the earlier chapters.

CHAPTER 72

(1876) THE DECIMAL CLASSIFICATION

721 Boyhood

THE FOLLOWING ACCOUNT IS taken from Dawe, Grosvenor, *Compiler: Melvil Dewey, seer, inspirer, doer,* 1851-1931 (1932).

Melvil Dewey was the author of the D.C. He was born on December 10th, 1851, at the Adams Center, in Jefferson County, New York. His father ran a general store and made boots. While yet a boy, Melvil learned enough from the shoemakers to make a pair of shoes and boots for himself, " doing every bit of the work, from crimping to the final finish." All kinds of jobs fell to his share—tidying the store, making shoes, cleaning the yard, picking up stones, ploughing the garden, cleaning the cellar and woodshed, spreading ashes on the meadow, splitting and piling wood, chopping up old boards, washing windows and cleaning the sewing machine. These odd jobs were punctuated with reading and chess.

He gradually saved a little over ten dollars, made by running errands, shovelling coal and shoemaking. With this fortune in his pocket, he walked eleven miles, when still under fifteen, to buy Webster's unabridged *Dictionary.* He had set his heart on this book for several years—an early proof of his dogged will.

722 Roman Notation Attacked

At seventeen, he became a teacher on 1.50 dollars a day. His first recorded commitment to Arabic numerals belongs to the pre-Amherst days. On April 13th, 1870, he attacked the Roman Notation in the following words: " The system itself is awkward in construction and almost *incapable of being used* in rapid computations. On the other hand, we have, in the Arabic or Indian notation, a method of writing numbers, accurate, simple, and probably as nearly perfect as man can invent. *That,* awkward and ambiguous, used only enough to compel everyone to be familiar with it; *This,* simple and accurate, in almost universal requisition. Why shall we not use it, then, exclusively? "

723 D.C. Proposed

Shortly after this, he joined Amherst College. His strong subject was Mathematics. From 1872, he began to work in the library as a part-time assistant. His D.C. plan was formally presented to the

Faculty in May, 1873, when he was still a student. After his graduation on July 9th, 1874, he became Assistant Librarian.

724 Career

Leaving Amherst on April 10th, 1876, he settled down in Boston, and during the next seven years loaded himself with too much responsible but unremunerative work. The Spelling Reform Association, the Metric Bureau, the American Library Association and the *Library Journal* were founded in 1876. He also took a leading part in the foundation of the British Library Association (1877), the Readers and Writers Company (1879) and the Library Bureau (1882). These multifarious activities brought him into the limelight. In 1883 he was called to Columbia College, where he stayed until 1888 as Librarian and Professor of Library Economy, trying out all his theories. An incident of the period gives another proof of his will. According to the then-prevailing social prejudices in the U.S.A., the women assistants of the library were not allowed to use the main entrance to the library. As women, they could only come by the narrow wooden staircase for servants at the back of the building. Dewey quietly destroyed the staircase, and the authorities were thus obliged to give equal rights to women, at least in regard to the entrance to the university library. This anecdote was told to me by an old lady, a colleague of Dewey, when I met her in Cleveland in July, 1950.

In January, 1889, he took up the duties of the Secretary of the Board of Regents of the University of the State of New York, and also those of State Librarian at Albany. But the whole Albany period was characterised by a prolonged struggle with the authorities, culminating in his premature resignation in September, 1905. He then retired to Lake Placid Club, where he stayed until his death on December 26th, 1931.

725 Putnam's Estimate

" Mr. Dewey eats, drinks, sleeps and talks library and library work throughout the twenty-four hours, the week, the month and the year. His physical whereabouts at any one time is immaterial. He carries his business with him to his home; he brings it back with him in the evening and in the morning to his office. He is, in effect, as much engaged with it at Lake Placid as he is at Albany; it is as much his play as it is his work. He is the clearest example in our profession of a man who cannot shake off his business. . . . There is no man living today to whom more than to him is due the prodigious activity of the past quarter of a century in the promotion of libraries, and in the diffusion of interest in them. There is no one who has done more to stir with enthusiasm for practical library service competent people who are needed in it. His name is more widely known abroad than that of any other living American librarian, for his contributions to library technique and to the general acceptance of public libraries as a motive force in popular education."

726 **Genesis**

Dewey himself made the following statement in the *Library journal*, Vol. 45, 1920:

" In visiting over 50 libraries, I was astounded to find the lack of efficiency, and waste of time and money in constant recataloguing and reclassifying made necessary by the almost universally used fixt system where a book was numbered according to the particular room, tier and shelf where it chanced to stand on that day, instead of by the class, to which it belonged, today and forever. Then there was the extravagant duplication of work in examining a new book for classification and cataloguing by each of 1,000 libraries instead of doing this once for all at some central point.

" For months I dreamed night and day that there must be somewhere a satisfactory solution. In the future were thousands of libraries, most of them in charge of those with little skill or training. The first essential of the solution must be the greatest possible simplicity. The proverb said ' simple as a, b, c,', but still simpler than that was 1,2, 3. After months of study, one Sunday during a long sermon by Pres. Stears, while I looked steadfastly at him without hearing a word, my mind absorbed in the vital problem, the solution flashed over me so that I jumped in my seat and came very near shouting ' Eureka! ' It was to get absolute simplicity by using the simplest known symbols, the Arabic numerals, as decimals with the ordinary significance of nought, to number a classification of all human knowledge in print."
This was in 1873.

727 **Favourable Factors**

While the D.C. was still in manuscript, John Eaton, Commissioner of Education of the United States, who had a flair for publicity, included it in a special volume on *Public libraries in the United States* as part of his *Annual report* for the Centennial Exposition of 1876.

The Library Conference held at Philadelphia in the same year as a preliminary to the foundation of the American Library Association also very appropriately provided a platform for discussing the scheme and directing attention to it.

728 **Publication**

The D.C. first appeared separately in 1876 as a thin pamphlet of forty-two pages. By 1942, its fourteenth edition had reached very near to 2,000 pages. From the fourth to the tenth edition, the editorial work was shared by Miss May Seymour, one of Dewey's students in 1887 and his chief assistant all through her later life. After her death (June 14th, 1921), her place was taken by Miss Dorcas Fellows, who had been working closely with her for over twenty-five years. The thirteenth edition, though technically posthumous, was as much the result of Dewey's immediate direction as if it had appeared during his lifetime, for the manuscript has been nearly completed before his death.

It was the last edition under his supervision. The fourteenth edition was still further expanded, but the fifteenth edition was greatly reduced in size. It marks a setback in the attempt to meet the demands of the depth classification needed in documentation work. Although during his later years Dewey no longer sat at the desk and actually worked out the expansions himself, to the end of his life he gave effective supervision.

There have also been all along a series of abridged editions of D.C. to suit the needs of small general libraries.

As already described in section 17124, the D.C. numbers now appear on Library of Congress cards, and provision has been made for the perpetual revision of the scheme by an editorial office housed in the Library of Congress.

729 Main Classes, etc.

0 Generalia
1 Philosophy
2 Religion
3 Social Sciences
4 Linguistics
5 Pure Sciences
6 Applied Sciences
7 Fine Arts
8 Literature
9 History

7291 NATURE

1 Enumerative
2 Meagre in auxiliary tables
3 No provision for facet analysis
4 Meagre provision for phase analysis

7292 NOTATION

1 Pure
2 Arabic numerals
3 No octavising
4 Decimal fraction
5 Scheduled mnemonics
6 No seminal mnemonics
7 No classic device
8 No local variation
9 Bias to the West
10 No organic book number

7293 TERMINOLOGY

1 Not too verbose
2 Not suited for chain procedure

CHAPTER 73

(1893) THE EXPANSIVE CLASSIFICATION

731 Boyhood

THIS ACCOUNT IS BASED on Cutter (William Parker): *Charles Ammi Cutter* (American Library Pioneers, 3) 1931.

Charles Ammi Cutter was the author of the E.C. He was born on March 14th, 1837, at Boston. His father was a dealer in fish oils on T Wharf in Boston. His frail body and myopic eyes prevented him from taking part in boyish sports, and all his time was spent in study. He entered Harvard College at the early age of fourteen, and prepared for the Church.

732 Career

After graduation in 1860, Cutter worked for eight years as an assistant in the cataloguing department of the Harvard College Library, then the largest American library. The card catalogue prepared by him for this library is believed to have been the first public card catalogue in America. In 1868 Cutter became the Librarian of the Boston Athenaeum, which was a proprietary library of the best Boston families and a fine collection. This post he held until 1893. The most widely used of his works, the *Rules for a dictionary catalogue,* belongs to this period. On leaving the Boston Athenaeum, Cutter became the first Librarian of the newly established Forbes Library at Northampton, Mass. He had a free hand in everything—book selection, book purchase, classification and cataloguing. He organised it on the most liberal lines and secured a greater daily attendance and a greater circulation *per capita* than any other library. Its books went everywhere. Cutter died on September 6th, 1903, having developed this library for ten years.

In June, 1950, I went to the Boston Athenaeum to see some relic of Cutter. I found it in a living person, his sister-in-law, who was past ninety. She was still in the service of the library, and just a few days earlier the library had honoured her by the celebration of her seventieth year of service there.

733 Genesis

About 1877, soon after the first conference of the American Library Association, Cutter began to rearrange the Boston Athenaeum Library. At first he was attracted by the D.C., published in the preceding year. But he gave it up, saying, "I did not like (and I still do not like) Mr. Dewey's Classification." On the ground that its notation would not afford sufficient minuteness of classification, he started with the twenty-four letters of the Roman alphabet and ten classes with numeral notation. A fellow-librarian criticised it as having a " cabalistic look." Eventually he fixed on a letter notation for his main schedules and numerical notation for form and local lists.

734 Publication

The E.C. was developed in seven stages. The first summary occupied only one page, the second three pages, the fourth six, the fifth twenty-two, the sixth fifty-one. All six expansions were published with an index in one volume of 160 pages in 1893. The seventh expansion was started afterwards and continued until 1903, the year of Cutter's death. It was published in instalments, in folded sheets.

735 Main Classes, etc.

A General Works	M Natural History
B Philosophy	N Botany
C Christianity	O Zoology
D Historical Sciences	R Useful Arts
E Biography	S Constructive Arts
F History	T Fabricative Arts
G Geography	U Art of War
H Social Sciences	V Athletic and Recreative Arts
I Sociology	W Fine Arts
J Civics	X Language
K Legislation	Y Literature
L Science and Arts	Z Book Arts

7351 NATURE

1 Enumerative	3 No provision for facet analysis
2 Meagre in auxiliary tables	4 No provision for phase analysis

7352 NOTATION

1 Mixed	5 Decimal fraction
2 Roman capitals for main classes; Arabic numerals and occasionally Roman smalls for later arrays	6 No scheduled mnemonics, except for geographical subdivisions
	7 No seminal mnemonics
3 Also a dot as connecting symbol for common isolate	8 No classic device
	9 No local variation
	10 Bias to the West
4 No octavising	11 No organic book number

7353 TERMINOLOGY

1 Crisp	3 Full use of Context and Enumeration
2 Precise	

CHAPTER 74

(1896) UNIVERSAL DECIMAL CLASSIFICATION

741 Sponsor

THE I.I.B. (= International Institute of Bibliography) is the sponsor of U.D.C. It is now called F.I.D. (= International Federation for Documentation). A world accumulation of 12 million documents, consisting of books and articles in periodicals—macro-thought and micro-thought! Annual rate of increase, a hundred thousand books and a million articles!! How to keep track of this ever-swelling flood? How to keep every intellectual worker fed exhaustively and expeditiously with just the documents relevant to the work engaging his thought at the moment? To consider this, an International Bibliographical Conference was held in Brussels in 1895. The outcome was the founding of the I.I.B. The Government of Belgium voted the funds. The Palais Mondial became its home.

7411 FEDERAL CONSTITUTION

In 1924 the constitution of the I.I.B. was amended. As a result, I.I.B. became a federal international organisation. It began with five national members. By 1955, thirty-six nations were taking part in its activities, twenty-two of these full members. The remaining fourteen were corresponding members. The assumption of industrial and pure research by several countries, which are just now entering into the ascending phase of the current cycle of their renaissance, leads to their enlistment as members of F.I.D.

7412 I.I.D.

In 1931 the I.I.B. was re-christened I.I.D. (= International Institute of Documentation). It changed from the patronage of a single national government to that of an international organisation. Indirectly, it got affiliated to the Institute for Intellectual Co-operation. In 1937 it made an alliance with the I.S.A. (= International Standards Association). A joint committee called ISA/46 was established to look after standards relating to documentation. After World War II, the I.S.A. was succeeded by I.S.O. (= International Standards Organisation). Accordingly, ISA/46 was re-named ISO/TC46. The I.S.O. itself is a federal body with several national members.

7413 F.I.D.

In 1937 a World Congress of Universal Documentation met in Paris. This led to another change in name. In 1938, the I.I.D. was re-christened F.I.D. The headquarters were also changed to The Hague in Holland. Since then, it is housed in the building of the Dutch Patent Office at 6 Willem Witsenplein. During World War II, the F.I.D. was practically paralysed. But it came back to life with renewed vigour. It now works through several Study Committees. The committee on classification is called FID/C. This works through two Subcommittees, viz. FID/CA on General Theory of Classification, and FID/CC on the U.D.C. The latter Subcommittee has National Committees in nine countries. It has also International Panels for several classes of U.D.C.

742 **Personnel**

The success of an institution depends on the personality of its chief workers—their imagination, outlook, far sight, competence, industry, and the will-to-do even against odds. The I.I.B. was fortunate in its first secretaries. These were Henri La Fontaine (1854-1943) and Paul Otlet (1868-1944), both of Belgium. Neither was of the library profession—one was a senator, and the other an advocate. Their mind was set on international bibliography. They had determination, and they also carried influence with people in power. They continued as secretaries from 1895 to 1938. But in 1924, Donker Duyvis joined them as Secretary-General. They continued thereafter as honorary presidents. In 1938, Donker Duyvis became the sole Secretary-General, and is still holding that office. He was born in Samarang, Java, on April 30th, 1894. He studied chemical engineering at the Delft University. He was for some time industrial consultant to the Government of Holland. In 1929 he entered service in the Dutch Patent Office, and is now its Vice-President.

743 **Genesis**

The primary objective of the I.I.B. was to maintain in cards an ever-up-to-date universal bibliography of all documents—books as well as articles. The arrangement of the cards was naturally a formidable problem. Minutely classified subject arrangement was rightly hit upon. Then came the search for a scheme of classification. The D.C. was then in its fourth edition (1894). It had already extended to 593 pages. Its pure notation of Arabic numerals appears to have appealed to Fontaine and Otlet. Of course, the hospitality of the decimal fraction notation also should have been an important recommendation. There was perhaps no other scheme as widely used as the D.C., and the I.I.B. adopted it. Even in 1895, it began to bring out French versions of D.C. in easy instalments. In 1924, Donker Duyvis became the secretary of the International Committee for U.D.C. The expansion of D.C. into a full-fledged U.D.C. was made in the years 1922 to 1933.

744 **Publication**

The first edition was in French. It came out in 1907 under the title *Manuel du répertoire bibliographique universelle.* The second was also in French, in four volumes. These came out between 1927 and 1933. It had the title *Classification décimale universelle.* The third edition is in German, and is still in print. It is in ten parts, parts 8 to 10 forming the alphabetical index. It has the title *Dezimal Klassifikation.* The first part came out in 1934, and was completed in 1953. The publishing body is the Deutcher Normenausschuss, Berlin. The fourth edition is in English. Its first fascicule came out in 1943, but it has not yet been completed. The publishing body is the British Standards Institution, London. The fifth edition is in French, and began in 1951, but has not yet been completed. It is published by Editiones Mundaneum, Brussels. Proposals for the revision of any class of U.D.C. are first published in *PE Notes.* When finalised in accordance with the rules of procedure laid down for the purpose, the revised version is incorporated in the *Extensions,* published serially and cumulated in each sixth issue.

745 **Main Classes, etc.**

The array of main classes is the same as that of D.C., with the addition of the class oo Prolegomena.

7451 NATURE

1 Considerable analytico-synthetic element

2 Several auxiliary tables

3 Partial facet-analysis, wherever the D.C. core does not stand in the way

4 Phase analysis; but often used to serve the purpose of facet analysis also.

7452 NOTATION

1 Mixed

2 Arabic numerals, and Roman letters in alphabetical device

3 Connecting symbols

4 In all other respects, same as D.C.

7453 TERMINOLOGY

1 Verbose

2 Not taking advantage of the Canons of Context and Enumeration

3 Not fit for use in chain procedure

CHAPTER 75

(1904) LIBRARY OF CONGRESS CLASSIFICATION

751   Library of Congress

UNLIKE ALL OTHER SCHEMES, the L.C. is the creation not of a single person but of a team of workers in the Library of Congress, the National Library of the United States, founded in 1800. During its first sixty-four years it had a very ordinary history. In 1864 Ainsworth Rand Spofford became its Librarian. In 1865 he introduced the card catalogue. By 1870 the library had attracted to itself several other collections, and had taken up the whole copyright business of the United States. It began to grow by leaps and bounds, and a new building was occupied in 1897. Herbert Putnam took charge on April 5th, 1899. The library had then a huge mass of books (750,000), ill arranged on the century-old Jefferson's classification.

Dr. Herbert Putnam (1862-1955), a Harvard man, had already done solid organising work in the Minneapolis Athenaeum Library and Public Library (1884-1892) and reorganisation work in the Boston Public Library (1895-1899).

752   Genesis

One of his first acts was to make a new classification. As a trained administrator, he put himself at the head of a committee with Charles Martel, his classifier, and William Parker Cutter, of the Order Section. This Committee made an extensive tour of libraries using either D.C. or E.C. The Committee met the authors of these schemes and suggested to them certain changes. Cutter agreed to them, but Dewey absolutely refused to make any change on the grounds that it would inconvenience the large number of libraries already using his scheme. On the recommendation of Mr. Martel, the Committee decided to use the layout of E.C. Unfortunately Charles Cutter died soon after this decision.

753   Fate of Decimal Fraction

Martel planned to use two letters for the main divisions and decimal fractions for the subdivisions. But A. R. Spofford, the former librarian, who still continued on the staff as an assistant, bitterly opposed the inclusion of any decimal notation! He carried his point; and the rigid integral notation came in to spoil what would otherwise have been the best scheme in existence, backed by all the prestige, man-power and resource of the most library-minded government in the world.

754 **Publication**

The schedules, which were issued from 1904, are now published in twenty-eight volumes with quarterly supplements; these with the indexes make a total of about 6,000 quarto pages.

755 **Main Classes, etc.**

A	General Works	L	Education
B	Philosophy	M	Music
C	History: Auxiliary Sciences	N	Fine Arts
D	History and Topography (excluding America)	P	Language and Literature
		Q	Science
E	America (General) and U.S. (General)	R	Medicine
		S	Agriculture, Plant and Animal Husbandry
F	United States (Local) and America	T	Technology
G	Geography	U	Military Science
H	Social Sciences	V	Naval Science
J	Political Science	Z	Bibliography and Library Science
K	Law		

7551 Nature

1 Enumerative
2 Some auxiliary schedules
3 No provision for facet analysis
4 No provision for phase analysis

7552 Notation

1 Mixed
2 Roman capitals for first two arrays; Arabic numerals and occasionally Roman smalls in later arrays
3 Also a dot as a connecting symbol
4 Integer, with gaps
5 No scheduled mnemonics
6 No seminal mnemonics
7 No local variation
8 No classic device
9 Severely biased to America
10 No organic book number

7553 Terminology

1 Crisp
2 Precise
3 Good use of Context and Enumeration

CHAPTER 76

(1906) SUBJECT CLASSIFICATION

761 Career

THIS ACCOUNT IS TAKEN from Brown (James Duff) and Sayers (W. C. Berwick): *Manual of Library Economy* (1920).

James Duff Brown was the author of the S.C. He was born on November 6th, 1862, at Edinburgh. He first served in bookshops for about three years, and on Christmas Day, 1878, joined the staff of the Mitchell Library, Glasgow, where he gained his first library experience. In 1888, he assumed charge of the newly established Clerkenwell Public Library in London. The sixteen years he spent in that library were the most productive of his career. He introduced many innovations, one of which was open access. Many others have come to stay. He started the *Library world,* and was one of the first in his country to write systematic books on Library Science. His *Manual of library economy* first came out in 1903. It is encyclopaedic in its range, and still holds the field, thanks to the continuing revision by Berwick Sayers.

In 1904 he became the first Borough Librarian of Islington. The imprint of his personality and genius was still visible in that library when I had the privilege of studying its working in 1924. After a long illness which had set in as early as 1911, Brown died on February 25th, 1914.

762 Discipline of Classification

Apart from designing a new scheme of classification, Brown was one of the first to think of library classification as a discipline, admitting of scientific method. For example, he had anticipated the Principle of Decreasing Concreteness in the facet formula—Personality before Energy—as he wrote on page 79 of his *Library classification and cataloguing* (1912) that the main principle in classification should be to place " subjects under concrete or specific heads. . . . For example, books on the human heart are all together, whether treating of that organ from an anatomical, physiological, or therapeutical point of view." To have said this, and contradicted D.C.'s prescription of the reverse sequence—already in the field for nearly a generation—denotes guidance by basic principles, as in scientific method. Brown's pioneering in thinking out library science was realised by me when I met E. Wyndham Hulme in 1948. There were a handful of librarians fifty years ago interested in developing library science. But the social and academic circles of the time viewed their endeavour almost with

417

ridicule and scorn. On the other hand, the men working in libraries regarded all this theory as too highbrow and mystifying. This small band of librarians, therefore, met and exchanged views under the auspices of an organisation which had to be kept anonymous.

763 Genesis

Although the S.C. took its final shape only in 1906, it had been conceived much earlier. In 1894 Brown placed before the British Library Association a new scheme of classification devised by him in collaboration with John Henry Quinn, Librarian of Chelsea. Its inadequacy was soon discovered, and Brown published a more expanded scheme in 1894 under the title of *Adjustable classification*. He found that even this scheme could not make headway against D.C., which was slowly conquering England, and after all this invented the S.C.

764 Publication

The scheme was first published in 1906. The second edition came out in 1914, the year of Brown's death. In these editions, Brown was helped by his nephew James Douglas Stewart, who brought out the third edition in 1939.

765 Main Classes, etc.

A Generalia	*Mind*
Matter and Force	J to K Philosophy, Religion
B to D Physical Sciences	L Social and Political Science
Life	*Record*
E to F Biological Sciences	M Language, Literature
G to H Ethnology, Medicine	N Literary Forms
I Economic Biology, Domestic Arts	O to W History, Geography
	X Biography

7651 Nature

1 Enumerative
2 One auxiliary schedule called Categorical Table
3 Meagre provision for facet analysis
4 Meagre provision for phase analysis

7652 Notation

1 Mixed
2 Roman capitals for first array, Arabic numerals for all the others
3 A dot as connecting symbol
4 Integer with gaps
5 Categorical Table furnishes scheduled mnemonics
6 No seminal mnemonics
7 No local variation
8 No classic device
9 No bias to any region
10 No organic book number

7653 Terminology

1 Crisp
2 Precise

CHAPTER 77

(1933) COLON CLASSIFICATION

771 Boyhood

S. R. RANGANATHAN IS THE author of the C.C. He was born on August 12th, 1892, at Shiyali, in the Madras State. He had his school education at the Hindu High School, Shiyali. It was interrupted for two years in 1906 by a serious illness. He took his degree course in the Madras Christian College of the University, his first degree in 1913, and his M.A. in Mathematics in 1916. Thereafter, he studied in the Teachers' College, Saidapet, and took his degree in teaching in 1917. He studied in the School of Librarianship in the University of London in 1924-1925.

772 Career

From 1917 to 1923, the author taught Mathematics in three colleges of the University of Madras in succession. On January 4th, 1924, he was appointed the first librarian of the University of Madras. The University sent him to Great Britain for one year to acquaint himself with modern library methods. He first read up the splendid literature on Library Science collected at the School of Librarianship of the University of London, and then did intensive apprentice work in Croydon Public Libraries. After that, he made an extensive tour of Great Britain, visiting all kinds of libraries, and making a comparative study of their practices. This was of considerable educative value, and suggested the formulation of an eclectic system of library economy. As the foundation of the system, he formulated Five Laws of Library Science as the normative principles to guide the development of every kind of library technique and library service. All the books and articles of Ranganathan—there are forty-eight books and about 1,500 articles—are but elucidations and applications of these five normative principles, in each of the branches of library science.

773 Genesis

As for classification, he found the L.C. and S.C. in use in just a few libraries, and spent some time in examining them from the point of view of shelf-arrangement and the reaction to them of classifiers and readers. He found the D.C. extensively used, but considerably mutilated in almost every library. There is nothing more pestering to a librarian than the recurring need to re-adapt a scheme already arbitrarily modified. This was corroborated by Melvil Dewey himself. In referring to the *Five Laws of Library Science,* Dewey wrote to the

author in a letter of September 5th, 1931, " The most praktikal advys
I fynd in the book is paje 401, ' don't mutilate the skeme,' and ending
with ' wyzest thing is to adopt a tryd skeme as it is without modifying
it here and ther'. As the author of the Decimal Classification now mor
wydli used than all others combynd, I have naturali given special
attention to this and I am firmli convinst that 1 of the most serious
mistakes is to waste tym & muni in ' improving ' a classification
skeme." Still, there was the fact that almost every library was " improving " D.C. Why ? There must be some fundamental reason for this.

7731   A Greater Zero Invented

These experiences led Ranganathan to think that a change was
necessary in the basic principles on which schemes of classification
are founded. The first principle hit upon was the synthetic or Meccano
principle. This suggestion came when the author saw for the first
time a demonstration with a Meccano set in one of his early visits to
Selfridge's shop. But notation proved a stumbling-block. One night
an idea struck him. The class numbers were all merely *ordinal* numbers,
not *cardinal* numbers. New ordinal numbers might be invented, though
they would have no cardinal value. This immediately led to the
corollary that the invention of an ordinal number lying between zero
and unity—a greater zero so to speak—was all that was required to
meet the situation. A single dot, the simplest symbol, having been
put to another use in the D.C., the double dot or colon was taken to
represent the new zero. This was late in 1924.

7732   A Warning Acts as Mainspring

With this clue, it was the work of but a few days to design the
layout, and construct the schedules, of a few subjects as samples. At
this stage, Mr. Sayers, whose lectures on Classification were a source
of inspiration to the author, encouraged the construction of a new
scheme. But he also gave a warning that struck home to the author's
mind, and had a steadying effect. He said in effect that schemes of
classification might look all right in the arrays of the lower orders, but
as one penetrated to higher orders—which were the *vital* ones—all
kinds of surprises and insuperable difficulties would appear.

7733   Experimentation

With this warning, the author took an interleaved copy of the
printed catalogue of the Madras University Library—a list of about
30,000 volumes—and experimented with the new scheme. Many
surprises did appear. During the return voyage in June, 1925, he was
the only Indian on board the ship, and found it quite easy to spend the
two weeks of the voyage in complete isolation revolving the " surprises
and insuperable difficulties " in his mind. No books and no notes to
consult and nobody to talk to—an ideal condition to grapple with
ideas—produced the desired result. Some tentative solutions were
made. The moment he landed in Madras and resumed charge of the
library, he began to handle by himself almost all the 30,000 volumes.

In about a year the Colon Device proved its worth. It was made firm, and tentative rules were framed. In those days, fortunately, the author had full freedom to dream, to do, to undo and re-do. The staff also was young and most loyal and participative. Particular mention should be made of C. Sundaram and K. M. Sivaraman, who shared with the author all the pain of this travail of doing, undoing and re-doing. Those were exciting days; they were also glorious days in their own development, for they accustomed them to " work-chastity "—a way of life which has paid well all through later life.

On the basis of the tentative rules, most of the volumes were classified and arranged on the shelves. Then open access was introduced, and for months and months the reaction of the arrangement on the readers was carefully observed. Notes were taken of all untoward reactions and various adjustments were made. The other devices began to appear in the mind in a nebulous form.

7734 SUCCESS OR RUIN

1929 to 1931 were the most important years. " Surprises and insuperable difficulties " did appear at very great depths. They had to be dealt with. Months and months of concentration led to their slow but partial solution. The strain was becoming unbearable. Consciousness of the risk being taken in using the confidence of the Library Committee and committing the University often weighed upon the mind. This strain was further increased by the well-meant and wise advice that Dewey gave in one of his letters. He wrote, " It is much wors to giv the tym and muni which everi librari so urjentli needs to devys still another skeme. None will ever be made that is not justli subject to meni criticisms. The librari that adopts sum 1 skeme in print can blame all its shortcomings on the author. But if it makes a skeme of its own it is almost sure to spend a larj part of the tym needed for the presing work of the librari in devyzing, revyzing, and constantli arguing, and trying to defend the inevitabl mistakes." This made the author say to himself, " Either success or ruin. No halfway hereafter."

7735 CRISIS AND SUCCESS

The crisis came one evening. The library had been closed at 5.30 p.m. It was 8 p.m. Still the author could not leave his seat. Many, many refractory problems began to surge through the mind like phantoms—now utter chaos, now some clearness—and so on. All of a sudden, everything arranged itself. The one Colon Device brought in its train seven other devices. Once this was hit on, everything came to the conscious level and could be handled and manipulated objectively—except the seminal mnemonics and the auto-bias device, which became tractable only after the first edition was printed.

7736 HELPFUL FACTORS

A favourable factor was that the author could count among his personal friends and former colleagues most of the members of the faculties of the University and its colleges. Here special mention must be made of his professor of mathematics, Edward B. Ross, and his colleagues Professor S. Kuppuswamy Sastriar and Professor M. S. Sabesan. These colleagues were experts in their subjects and gave help ungrudgingly in the final shaping of the schedules in the various subjects. There also came another godsend. The Library School was started in 1929. Teaching the subject from year to year led to further clarification, progressive polishing and delicate adjustment of the many details.

774 Further Experience

A good in disguise happened in 1943. Political persecution entered its final phase that year. It was part of an ugly, but perhaps a necessary, stage through which public life had to pass in Madras. This stage had begun, or had been brought about, in 1918. The persecution, which had its roots in this general happening in the land, had sprouted as early as 1924—the year of the author's appointment as the first university librarian. Its thorns had been pricking all the twenty years, and by 1937 its shadow began to cut out light and air. During 1943 and 1944, its poisonous emanations became thick, service to the public was strangled, and the very purpose of staying in the library was thwarted. Emotional and intellectual suffocation intensified. This led to the migration of the author to Banaras, where he stayed for twenty months as librarian and professor of library science of the Banaras Hindu University. That university library had a different kind of collection. It had books and periodicals in several applied sciences, arts and crafts, and professional subjects. The author had had no opportunity to handle such documents in the Madras University Library. This made him learn for the first time the highways and by-ways in these new subjects. Secondly, the collection was largely made of several gifts of a promiscuous nature. In the Madras University Library, on the other hand, the collection was built up systematically, with advanced books and periodicals only, and in a balanced way with direct relation to the studies in progress in the several departments. The junk-shop nature of the collection at Banaras presented many problems at deep levels during its classifying. The author took off his coat, as it were, and classified more than 100,000 volumes within a period of about eighteen months. Continuous work at such high pressure on such a variety of materials gave a remarkable insight into the structure and development of the universe of knowledge. It impressed on him the versatility needed in notation. This was indeed an unusual and unexpected experience of immense richness, and by itself made the migration from Madras a blessing in disguise. But something even more conducive to more concentrated work followed.

775 Sir Maurice Gwyer

The next and perhaps the most productive lap in the development of the C.C. was due to the facilities provided by Sir Maurice Gwyer. He had been Chief Justice of India after the creation of the Supreme

Court under the Government of India Act of 1935. He also became
Vice-Chancellor of the University of Delhi. From then to 1950 he
developed the university from very small beginnings to a great stature.
In this connection he toured India widely to study the organisation of
the other universities. In one of his visits to Madras in 1939 he came
to the Madras University Library, and studied its working with great
concentration for nearly five hours. Here he met the author for the
first time. Since then, their friendship has become closer and closer.
He read the author's *Five laws of library science* and the other five books
that had come out by then, on classification, cataloguing and administration. *Colon classification* was one of them. He was particularly
impressed by *Reference service and bibliography* (1940). From these books
and from close subsequent personal contact, Sir Maurice came to know
intimately the dreams of the author about the future of library service
in India. He learnt of the retirement of the author from the Madras
University Library, and on February 1st, 1945, invited him to the
University of Delhi. But the pressure from Banaras worked its way,
and delayed going to Delhi. This interval was used by Sir Maurice to
get a Department of Library Science established. In June, 1947, he
again wrote an affectionate letter to the author, inviting him to develop
the new Department and fulfil his long-cherished ambition and desires
in respect of library science, and also to discharge his duties as the
" godfather of the Department," as he put it. The author accepted the
invitation, and worked in the University from June 17th, 1947, to
March 15th, 1954. During this period, Sir Maurice provided the
author with the setting for the " *Vana-prastha* stage of life." He had no
administrative duties. He had only to teach, guide research, and do
research himself. Sir Maurice provided residence for all co-students
next to the author's home. Serious and able students came from all
parts of India. The hum of work went on for six years in the calmest
and most helpful atmosphere the author had ever known. Sir Maurice
made ample provision for publishing the chief results of each year in
the form of a treatise, and the Library Science Series of the University
of Delhi was started. He endeavoured to get a chair endowed for
library science, but the liquidation of the Princely states dried up the
source he was tapping. The stimulating national and international
contacts arising out of this setting have been described in section 07
and its subdivisions in the Conspectus. Another of these contacts
was with Unesco. The projects of Insdoc, Delhi Public Library,
Rendering of Asian names, Retrospective Directory of Asian Learned
Periodicals and Union Catalogue of Learned Periodicals in the Libraries
of South Asia grew out of this contact. All these projects enriched
experience.

776 Effect on the C.C.

The events since 1945 helped the further development of the C.C.
The work on the foundations of classification and on the improvement
of C.C. went hand in hand. They were inseparable. Step by step, the
C.C. was equipped with all the features of a full-blown analytico-

synthetic scheme of classification, described in the chapters of parts
3 to 5. The introduction of these new features did not demand any
serious alterations in the various schedules. The only serious change
needed was the adoption of the new connecting symbols. In the
collections of a library, it was found that there were very few books
either with levels of personality facets or with any matter facets. These
occurred mainly in micro-thought. Therefore, there was little need
to change colons into commas or semi-colons, except in the main class
Literature. The only drudgery work needed in a library was the
changing of colons into dots in the case of space and time facets, which
can be done at leisure, and even spread over several years. But the
C.C. has become eminently fit for documentation work, because it has
acquired great versatility to do any degree of depth classification that
may be required for micro-thought, no matter how great its intension.

777 Future Work

This does not mean that the C.C. has stopped growing; far from it.
Stopping of growth always means preparation for death. Moreover,
no scheme can stop growing so long as the universe of knowledge
keeps growing, as it will, so long as humanity continues to exist. The
immediate lines of growth of C.C. have been mentioned in the various
sections of the preceding chapters of this book. In my last class with
the M.Lib.Sc. students, we were led to estimate the number of subjects
in classification on which Ph.D. students may do research and write
their theses. We were able to enumerate some eighty of them offhand.
Apart from this routine kind of research on schedules, a new vista, for
research of a deeper kind, is opened up in the next part of this book.
Each result achieved in this kind of work will call for a re-examination
of schedules in general and of those of the C.C. in particular. It may
be that some of this re-examination will call for trivial changes, or even
drastic changes, to gain in versatility. If the results of research into
Abstract Classification, distilled out of the experience with the C.C.
and U.D.C., ultimately calls for burning our boats and starting all
over again, that would be the final fulfilment of the C.C., even as the
final fulfilment of the flower lies in its fading out in the process of
giving birth to the fruit.

778 Publication

The first edition of the C.C. was published in 1933. The chief
substantial changes in the second edition were the introduction of the
new main class Δ, and the change of sequence of the facets in Law.
This edition was published in 1939, and also contained 3,000 examples
of call numbers in the form of a classified catalogue. This feature had,
however, to be dropped in the two later editions, in order to reduce
the cost of production. The third edition came out in 1948, but did not
have many changes. But partial comprehensions of main classes and
different species of common isolates were introduced in the fourth
edition, which came out in 1952. The forthcoming fifth edition came

out in 1957. It illustrates zone analysis in the schedule for " 9 Labour " in [E[*cum* [2P1[of X Economics. The substance of the earlier edition is given as " V.1. Basic classification." V.2 is proposed to be made of different fascicules for the Depth Classifications of different subjects.

779 Main Classes, etc.

z	Generalia	L	Medicine
1	Universe of knowledge	M	Useful Arts
2	Library science	μ	Humanities and social sciences
3	Book science	△	Mysticism and spiritual experience
4	Standardisation		
5	Communication (general theory)	ν	Humanities
A	Natural sciences	N	Fine Arts
β	Mathematical sciences	O	Literature
B	Mathematics	P	Linguistics
Γ	Physical sciences	Q	Religion
C	Physics	R	Philosophy
D	Engineering	S	Psychology
E	Chemistry	Σ	Social sciences
F	Technology	T	Education
G	Biology	U	Geography
H	Geology	V	History
η	Mining	W	Political science
I	Botany	X	Economics
J	Agriculture	Y	Sociology
K	Zoology	Z	Law
λ	Animal husbandry	(...)	New formations

7791 NATURE

1 Analytico-synthetic
2 Several auxiliary schedules
3 Facet analysis
4 Phase analysis

7792 NOTATION

1 Mixed
2 Roman capitals and smalls, Arabic numerals, Greek letters
3 Connecting symbols
4 Decimal fractional
5 Scheduled mnemonics
6 Seminal mnemonics
7 Local variation
8 Classic device
9 Not biased; but gives schedules of Indian classics in a separate part
10 Organic book number

7793 TERMINOLOGY

1 Only fundamental constituent terms
2 Crisp
3 Brief
4 Fit for use in chain procedure

CHAPTER 78

(1935) **BIBLIOGRAPHIC CLASSIFICATION**

781   Career

HENRY EVELYN BLISS was the author of the B.C. He was born January 20th, 1870, in New York. He had his education in the College of the City of New York, and joined the staff of the library of that very college in 1891. His whole career was in that college. He retired in 1941. He was a keen student of philosophy, and also a poet. Some fifteen years ago, I was delighted to get the volume of his poems. The first edition of my *Colon classification* introduced us to each other. He wrote to me that he happened to glance through a copy of that book in a bookshop in New York in 1933. Along with the letter came a copy of each of his books on *Organisation of knowledge* in anticipatory exchange of my book. Since then, our friendship was kept alive through correspondence. He established contact with many classification specialists, young and old. Some of these have collaborated with him in building up the schedules in particular subjects.

782   **Theory in Advance**

The career of the B.C. appears to have been the opposite of that of the C.C. Theory followed the latter; but it preceded the B.C. The C.C. was brought out without any elaborate prior thought on the grammar of classification, but the B.C. was shaped according to an elaborate grammar worked out through several years. This grammar came out in two volumes. The first volume was *Organisation of knowledge and the system of sciences* (1929). This book traced the history of schemes of knowledge produced at different times. This history was preceded by the author's criteria for evaluating such schemes. The second volume was *Organisation of knowledge in libraries and the subject approach to books* (1933). This book established canons for library classification. Its distinctive feature was concerned with the nature of notation. It was not till 1940 that the first volume of the complete B.C. was published.

783   **Genesis**

But this does not mean that the genesis of the scheme dates only from that year, for the first outline of the scheme was published in the *Library journal* as early as 1910. In the first sentence of the preface to the third volume of the full scheme, Bliss describes it as work " projected to serve a comparatively unimportant local situation." A few lines later, he adds, " It had been originated and imperfectly applied in the Library of the College of the City of New York. . . . A concise publication of the Classification had been planned in 1913." But the war did not allow the plan to be carried out. In the meantime, experiments were made with the scheme in the Library of the College; the books on theory were published; and the scheme was further developed. A three-fold purpose for developing the scheme was enunciated. This was set forth in the preface to the first volume of the complete scheme:

" (1) To demonstrate that a coherent and comprehensive system, based on the logical principles of classification and consistent with the systems of science and education, may be available to services in libraries, to bibliographies, and to documentation.

" (2) To aid revision and reconstruction of long established and more or less antiquated classifications.

" (3) To provide for subject-catalogues an adaptable, efficient, and economical classification, notation, and index."

784 Publication

A condensed, tentative version of the B.C. was published in 1935 under the title *System of bibliographic classification*. The first volume of the complete edition came out in 1940, covering the main classes A to G and the preliminaries. Volume 2 came out in 1947, covering the main classes H to K. The scheme was completed in the third volume in 1953. A fourth volume gave the alphabetical index.

785 Main Classes, etc.

A Philosophy and general science

B Physics including applied physics and special physical technology

C Chemistry including chemical technology and mineralogy

D Astronomy, geology, geography and natural history

E Biology including palaeontology and biogeography

F Botany including bacteriology

G Zoology including zoogeography and economic geology

H Anthropology, general and physical, including medical sciences, eugenics, physical training, recreation

I Psychology

J Education

K Social sciences. Sociology, ethnology and anthropogeography

L History, social, political and economic

M Europe

N America

O Australia, Asia, Africa: Geography, ethnography and history

P Religion, theology, ethics

Q Applied social science and ethics

R Political science, philosophy and ethics and practical politics

S Jurisprudence and law

T Economics

U Useful arts

V Fine arts, recreation and pastime

W Linguistics other than Indo-European

X Indo-European linguistics

Y English or other favoured language and literature

Z Bibliography and libraries

7851 NATURE

1 Some analytico-synthetic element
2 Several auxiliary schedules
3 Not much of facet analysis
4 Phase analysis

7852 NOTATION

1 Mixed
2 Roman capitals and smalls, and Arabic numerals
3 Connecting symbols
4 Decimal fractional
5 Not much of scheduled mnemonics
6 No seminal mnemonics
7 Local variation, even in Context and Enumeration, cf. provision for ethics in three places
8 No classic device
9 Not biased
10 Meagre book number, not individualising

7853 TERMINOLOGY

1 Crisp, in the first specification
2 Brief, in the first specification
3 Not fit for use in chain procedure, because of inclusion of synonyms, alternative explanatory phrases, and names of subclasses without distinct numbers of their own

PART 8

THEORY OF ABSTRACT CLASSIFICATION
LOOKING FORWARDS

CHAPTER 81

INNATENESS OF CLASSIFICATION

811 **Involuntary Arrangement**

IN COMMON USAGE, AS distinct from the technical definition given in chapter 12, classification means what has been denoted by the term "assortment" in section 122, viz. division into groups and arranging them in a definite sequence. In its essence, then, classification means arrangement, as used in popular language. To arrange things in a more or less helpful sequence is an inherent habit of man. A child begins to arrange very early in life. Human species too should have begun to arrange very early in its career. Apart from things, in communicating ideas to others, man mentions them in a more or less helpful sequence. Even in his own thinking, he pursues ideas in a more or less helpful sequence. Perhaps, this inherent tendency to arrange is a concomitant of the finiteness of the speed of nervous impulse within human body. When speed is finite, structure is inevitable. When structure is sensed, sequence is but natural. This gets expressed extra-neurally also. Thus arrangement is a neural necessity. It is instinctive, almost biochemical in nature, and involuntary. The result is involuntary classification.

812 **Deliberate Classification**

The complexity of the universe of things and of ideas has now exceeded the capacity of involuntary, primeval classification. Deliberate classification has become necessary. It becomes necessary even for a child as its sphere of interest and activity widens. The efficiency of a shopkeeper is partly determined by the efficiency of his having classified and arranged his wares. His innate power of classification may be sufficient up to a point, but it has thereafter to be exercised deliberately and with circumspection. Anybody's efficiency, say in packing his personal effects for a long journey, depends on the degree to which his innate power to classify and arrange is deliberately exercised. This is in respect of things. But innateness of classification holds good in respect of ideas too. Sharpness in thinking, clarity in expression, expedition in response, and exactness in communication depend ultimately on the deliberate exercise of the innate power of classification.

813 **Improvement by Training**

In the art of classifying, everything is now left, in many spheres, to the innate flair of the individual. But all are not endowed with adequate flair. This leads to inefficiency and wastage. The smallness of this innate flair in some children leads to their being branded as uneducable. It is not yet realised that deficiency in innate flair for classification can be made up by conscious training. A conscious cultivation of other abilities is happening in the schools of today. It should be extended to the ability to classify also.

814 Classification in Curriculum

Today, classification is assigned to a late and hurried stage in the course on logic, chosen only by a section of the students at the university stage. This amounts to a merely formal recognition of its existence. It is necessary that the rudiments of deliberate classification should be taught to every youth before being discharged from school. The teaching should be mostly through example, punctuated by precepts at suitable stages. Illustrations should be taken from different situations in life and from different subjects, so that every student may be able to follow the subject with interest. Systematic thinking and correct communication will be considerably helped by this.

815 Recognition in Technology

In recent years, engineering and technological workshops have realised the importance of having men with adequate training in the process of deliberate classification, to organise the layout or the plant, the flow of materials, and the distribution of stores, jigs and fixtures. A new branch of engineering has taken shape under the name of " production engineering " for this purpose. In factories, however, it is mostly things and processes that have to be arranged and planned. Classification has thus a concrete setting and intrinsic guidance. In spite of this, a systematic course in the theory of classification will be of much help.

816 Pressure of Knowledge Classification

In knowledge classification it is abstract ideas that have to be arranged and classified. It does not therefore have the advantage of the physical canalisation by the entities classified. The innate classificatory capacity of the classifier is in greater need of being reinforced by systematic training. This is essentially intellectual training. It involves training in the process of abstraction of attributes of entities, selecting the minimum few from among an infinity of them, and finding out a suitable measure of them as the basis for classification. This process of abstraction is something congenial to the human intellect. The practice of it with proper safeguards has been responsible for much of human progress. Classification too must follow the same path.

CHAPTER 82

SCIENTIFIC METHOD

821 Intellection versus Intuition

TAKING ANY DISCIPLINE OR subject through progressive stages of
abstraction with adequate safeguards is itself an intellectual process.
Intellection has to follow an orderly procedure—a method. In this
respect, intellection differs fundamentally from intuition.

8211 INTUITION

In intuition, there is no mediation by the senses. " Man's perceptions
are not bounded by organs of perception; he perceives more than sense
(though ever so acute) can discover," as William Blake put it. The
perception he has in mind is of the " Thing-in-Itself " in its entirety—
in the fullness of its attributes and its relation to the entire universe.
It transcends the space-time matrix. In Indian tradition, this integral,
time-free, space-free realisation is said to be achieved through spiritual
exercise or *tapas*. It speaks of " divine sense "—*divya indriya*. Blake
too speaks of " spiritual sensation." Intuition is spontaneous and
sudden. It shows no stages. It transcends method.

8212 INTELLECT

Intellect cannot apprehend anything in its entirety. It has to understand everything in terms of the space-time matrix. It apprehends but
a tiny fraction of what intuition comprehends. This is the implication
of the opinion that " the more incommensurable, and the more incom-
prehensible to the understanding a poetic production is, the better it
is," communicated by Goethe to Eckermann on May 6th, 1827.
Intellect has to abstract and generalise. Intellection should have
frequent recourse to an empirical check-up with the phenomenal
universe outside " one's skin." In this check-up, it has to anchor
itself on the physical senses, aided if necessary by suitable instruments.
All this makes method essential in intellection. As if to emphasise
this, we reinforce the term and call it " scientific method."

8213 FLAIR

In its partial apprehension and failure to perceive the thing-in-itself,
flair is on the side of intellection. In its apparent spontaneity and

433

suddenness, it is on the side of intuition. In fact, it is the limiting point between intellection and intuition, but belongs to neither. Few among us are endowed with a hundred per cent. of intuition functioning. The small verisimilitude of intuition contained in flair should not lead us to believe that we can get on without method. It is wrong to leave to mere flair the work of designing a scheme of classification in all its details or of classifying. Scientific method is necessary.

822 **Endless Cycle**

Scientific method makes intellection pursue any discipline perpetually round and round a never-ending succession of cycles. Because the cycle is endless, we can begin its description at any of its points. The accompanying diagram is a schematic representation of the endless cycle of scientific method. The terms nadir, zenith, quadrants, lateral points, and semicircles are self-explanatory.

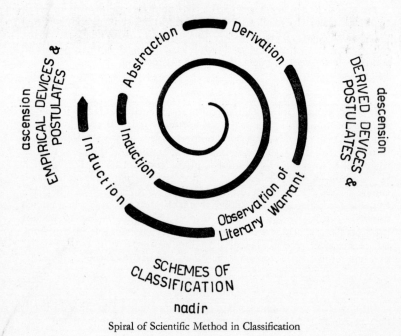

Spiral of Scientific Method in Classification

823 Empirical Phase

We shall start with facts or individual experiences at the nadir. These arise out of apprehension of the phenomenal world through the senses and guided by the intellect. They are far too many to be retained in memory and to be recalled as individual experiences. Therefore, in the progression through the first quadrant, these experiences are boiled together, as it were, with the aid of inductive logic, normal equations and other tools. This may be called the " empirical phase " of the cycle. This phase ends in the distillation of a few " empirical laws," such as Hooke's Law. This is all work through intellect.

824 Hypothesizing Phase

In course of time, the empirical laws themselves become far too many for retention in memory or for recall. There is therefore a jump in the second quadrant from the burdensome number of laws to just a few fundamental principles. These are called " hypotheses " in the field of natural sciences, and " normative principles " in the field of social sciences. Newton's laws of motion form a well-known example of hypotheses. " Sovereignty within a nation is distributed equally among all the adult citizens " is a normative principle now accepted in political science. The jump in the second quadrant may be called the " hypothesizing phase " of the cycle of scientific method. This jump is usually made by one endowed with a large gift of intuition.

825 Deductive Phase

It is implied that all the known empirical laws can be derived out of the hypotheses (or normative principles) by the deductive process. But more laws than the already known empirical laws are usually derivable by deduction. This is because intuition has played a part in the formulation of the hypotheses (or normative principles). They therefore hold in a latent form many laws not hitherto arrived at in the progression through the empirical phase. These are " deduced laws." These are got in the third quadrant of the cycle. Their deduction forms the " deductive phase " of the cycle. Work in this phase is solely through intellection.

826 Verification Phase

The new deduced laws point to facts and experiences, left unnoticed till then. The work in the fourth quadrant consists of verifying them by observation in the phenomenal universe. It may be that more powerful instruments have to be devised to help in the observation. If the observations confirm the indication of the deduced laws, the hypotheses (or normative principles) are continued as valid. Otherwise, more facts of the nature of the contradicting ones are collected, invalidating the current hypotheses (or normative principles). In due course, work is started in the first quadrant and another cycle in the scientific method is also started. New fundamental principles are proposed, etc. Even without prompting from deduced laws, new facts may be found invalidating the current hypotheses (or normative principles) and another cycle may be started. This forms the " verification phase " of the cycle. It is done through the senses and the intellect. It is the verification phase that provides the safeguard mentioned in section 816.

CHAPTER 83

RIPENESS OF LIBRARY CLASSIFICATION

831 Host-Subject

IN TESTING THE ripeness of library classification to enter the cycle of scientific method, we must begin with the testing of its host-subject. The host-subject is of course Library Science. It is concerned with libraries. Libraries are social institutions—institutions established to do some form of social service. The field of library science therefore lies in the region of social sciences. We should therefore expect normative principles, instead of hypotheses, to occur in the cycle of scientific method.

8311 LIBRARY PRACTICES

Looking into the happenings of the past and of the present, we find many facts in library practice. What is more, the practices have been changing through the ages. There have been changes in the location of the library. It was once located in a secluded area far from the madding crowd and haunted only by intellectual aristocrats. It is now located in the very market place, amidst the crowd. Symmetrical buildings, made rigid by a circular or square shape, were put up in the past. Library buildings are now preferred to be asymmetrical and made to conform to elastic modular design and dry construction. In the past, book racks went up to the ceiling and were arranged with but narrow gangways between them. But today the gangways are spacious and the height of a rack is determined by the average height of the readers served. In the past, books were kept in locked cupboards. But today they are mostly kept on open shelves. In the past, the readers were kept outside the barrier. But today open access is the rule. Modern library practice pulls the library staff out of their cloisters and makes them rub shoulders with readers in the stack room. In the past, the library staff had the attitude of saying, as it were, " Here are the books and their catalogue. Take them or leave them." But today they say, " Come, dear reader. These are just the books that will serve your present purpose." There have come many such changes. These changes are experienced at the nadir point of the cycle of scientific method. There have been corresponding changes in the normative principles established at the zenith point of the cycle.

In the past, the library practices were designed,

(1) *as if* books were for preservation;

(2) *as if* books were for the chosen few;

(3) *as if* the time of readers was a matter of no concern; and

(4) *as if* the rate of growth of library was negligibly small.

These were the normative principles guiding the establishment and modification of the library practices found necessary from time to time.

Today, library practices are designed,

(1) *as if* books are for use (even at the risk of their being worn out by use);

(2) *as if* books are for all and every reader should be found his book;

(3) *as if* every book should be found its reader;

(4) *as if* the time of the reader should be saved; and

(5) *as if* a library is a growing organism (either growing by addition as in the case of a child, or growing by replacement as in the case of an adult).

These are the normative principles guiding the establishment and modification of library practices, found to be necessary from time to time.

832   Deduced Laws of Old

The older normative principles did not exert much pressure on the arrangement of entries in the library catalogue or in the arrangement of books on the library shelves. All the potential readers were intellectual aristocrats. They knew the books existing in their respective subjects. They knew their authors and titles. The deduction was, " List the books alphabetically by the names of authors and/or titles." Books were to be picked out not by every reader for himself, but by a semi-literate capable of reading backs of books. The deduction was, " Arrange books on the shelves by their size in the order of accession and give a press mark to each book to facilitate finding."

833   Deduced Laws of Today

The new normative principles exert much pressure on the arrangement of entries in the library catalogue and in the arrangement of books on the library shelves. The books are too many for any reader to know them all. The readers are of all grades and many can only know the subject on which they would like to have books. The entries in a catalogue should therefore be arranged also in a systematic way by subject. Open access indicates the need for so arranging the books on the shelves that a reader pursuing a subject can find all the books directly or indirectly bearing on it, in close proximity, if not consecutively. The deduction is, " Classify the books minutely on the basis of thought-content or subject." Another deduction is, " Give each book a class number, a book number, and a collection number if it does not belong to the main collection, the three together constituting its call number, by which its location can be known."

834 Normative Principles of Classification

The discipline of library classification has itself been drawn by its host-subject into the cycle of scientific method. The practice of classification is now as if certain canons hold good within its own distinctive sphere. They have, of course, to be consistent with the normative principles of the host-subject. Indeed they have to be such as to help the fulfilment of the implications of those principles. The fifth normative principle exerts an additional pressure. The pressure becomes great as there can be no limit to the growth of the number of subjects or of books. It is responsible for many of the canons pertaining to notation. It is also responsible for the suggestion that it is an advantage to develop class numbers as if they constitute an artificial language of ordinal numbers—not of course for conversation or as a medium of literature, but for use in the mechanisation of arrangement.

835 Recent Changes

During the last few decades and particularly since World War II, some new practices are developing in the library field. These are developing under the social pressure set up by the unbalancing coming on between population density and near-natural commodities available. These practices are being designed,

(1) *as if* " documents " should replace " books " wherever the latter occurs in the normative principles of library science and the various deductions from them;

(2) *as if* as much emphasis should be put on micro-documents as on macro-documents; and

(3) *as if* there should be particular emphasis on the needs of research workers.

836 Effect on Classification

These changes in the normative principles of the host-subject have produced some effect on library classification. It may be stated as follows:

(1) Superficial classification is no longer sufficient;

(2) Depth classification is necessary;

(3) It is desirable to have a single scheme to serve both for superficial and depth classification;

(4) Enumerative classification cannot bear the weight of depth classification; and

(5) Analytico-synthetic classification should be preferred.

439

837 Establishment of Cycle

The normative principles of Library Science together with the canons and principles listed in pages 21 and 23 constitute the normative principles of Library Classification. The cycle of scientific method has been formed in the subject. Therefore the designing, the application and the teaching of library classification can follow scientific method. The subject can be approached both empirically from facts of experience and theoretically from normative principles. The former can be enriched by the latent content of the latter. The latter should never be deemed to be final, but should ever be liable to change in the light of the former. New micro-thought, apparently transcending the capacity of an existing scheme and the existing rules of procedure, can in many cases be classified with a proper interpretation of the canons and the rules, and the framing of additional rules. When conscious or unconscious shift in the social purpose of the library calls for an altogether different kind of library service, organisation and technique, and if the current ones stand abandoned by sheer folk force, new normative principles may have to replace the present ones. And the cycle should be started again.

838 Critical Study

The establishment of the cycle of scientific method has made it possible to base critical work in the area of classification on the normative principles. Any scheme of library classification can be evaluated along systematic lines. The faults in a scheme can be rectified. A comparative study of different schemes can be made along impersonal lines. It can now be determined when a scheme of classification is essentially new. It is new only if its system of postulates differs substantially from those of the existing schemes.

CHAPTER 84

GENERALISATION AND ABSTRACTION

841 **Progressive Generalisation**

VIEWED FROM ONE ANGLE, the progression through the quadrants 1 and 2 amounts to progressive generalisation. An empirical law is a generalisation of many observed facts. For example, a wire is suspended from a beam. A weight is attached to it, so that it is straightened. Its length is measured. More weight is added. The elongation is measured. This is done for several weights, several lengths, several cross-sectional areas, several materials. We get quite a number of facts about elongation in this way. By collating all the tabulated data and applying appropriate mathematical methods, we get the generalised relation

$$\text{Elongation} = \frac{\text{weight added, multiplied by length of the wire}}{\text{Area of the cross section of the wire, multiplied by E}}$$

where E is a constant, called Young's modulus, and depending on the material. This is the Hooke's Law, got by generalisation. This generalisation holds within itself an endless number of particular cases. In a similar way, several laws in physics can be generalised into a single fundamental principle and stated as, say, Planck's Quantum Hypothesis.

842 **Progressive Abstraction**

Viewed from another angle, the progression through quadrants 1 and 2 amounts to progressive abstraction. In fact, every step in generalisation is also a step in abstraction. Abstraction is inherent even in the observation of facts through the senses and their formulation through the intellect. For the concrete universe is an integral whole of entities and attributes. But the human senses cannot apprehend them in their entirety. They therefore abstract out only a few entities and a few attributes. The result is called an object by the intellect, say, an orange. Even the orange is not fully apprehended. Only a few attributes are abstracted for selective apprehension. In Hooke's Law, for example, only four attributes are abstracted for formulation, viz. length, cross section, weight and an elastic attribute of the material. The acme of abstraction is reached in the hypothesis (or normative principle) marked at the zenith in the diagram given in chapter 82.

843 **Particularisation and Concretisation**

In the quadrants 3 and 4, the progression is in the opposite direction. It is from the general to the particular and from the abstract to the concrete. This takes place step by step. The acme of the progression is reached at the point marked as facts at the nadir in the diagram.

844 **Danger Spots**

Quadrants 2, 3 and 4, the nadir and the zenith are danger spots in the cycle. The three quadrants correspond to the play of pure intellectual work. The tools are language, logic and mathematics. The tools at the nadir are unaided primary senses, the instruments designed to increase their capacity and range, and the mental set established by race habit and social practices.

845 **Preventive Steps**
8451 Purification of Mathematics

In the nineteenth century considerable work was done on the foundations of mathematics. The silent assumptions were pulled out from their hiding places. The whole number concept was put on a clarified basis. Degrees of approximation were recognised. Boundary conditions were established for the validity of diverse operations. This has amounted to purification of mathematics. The postulational method is proving to be particularly effective in the elimination of dangers.

8452 Purification of Logic

Since the nineteenth century considerable work is being done in logic too. The creation of symbolical calculus by Boole and the initiation of syntactical method by Frege and Hilbert in the study of the logical structure of sentences and relations between signs have been helpful steps in the purification of formal logic. The Polish School has dug up other regions of logic guided by instinct and common sense. As a result, the discipline of semantics is being developed to take charge of meaning, interpretation, and relation as based on meaning, in so far as logical inference is concerned.

8453 Purification of Language

A new discipline called " General Semantics," formulated by Alfred Korzybski, is taking shape. It seeks to expose the fallacies arising out of misunderstandings of the relation between facts and words. It studies the relative values of the intensional and the extensional definitions of terms. Precision in the use of terms is being brought about. This results in the purification of language.

8454 Vigilance in Observation

At the nadir representing the region of collecting facts by observation, vigilance is necessary against the cause of aberration by unconscious or silent assumptions, beliefs and attitudes. Safeguards against them are easier in the natural sciences than in the social sciences. A theory of errors has been developed to estimate the limits of probable error in observation. As man himself is the subject of study in social sciences, as he is allergic to observation, and as his emotional disturbance is unpredictable, the margin of probable error is often so wide as to make generalisation futile.

8455 " As If " Attitude
to Hypotheses and Normative Principles

A great danger at the zenith has been to make hypotheses (or normative principles) authority-centred. History is full of instances of resistance to, and attempts at suppression of, the free pursuit of the cycle of scientific method. These had been in the form of religious inquisitions and political persecutions. A hypothesis (or normative principle) should not be taken to assert, " The phenomenal universe is so and so." It should be taken to say only, " The facts known till now are *as if* the phenomenal universe were so and so."

8456 Boundary Conditions

Another danger in scientific method is overlooking the boundary conditions within which alone a hypothesis (or normative principle) can be taken to be valid. The phenomenal progress of physics during recent years has been due to awareness to boundary conditions. A well-known case is that of the Euclidean hypothesis about parallels, viz. " Through a given point, we can draw one and only one line that will not intersect another given line." It is now known to be invalid in space of astronomical size on the one side and of intra-atomic size on the other. About a century ago, Lobatchevski and Riemann drew attention to these boundary conditions for the Euclidean hypothesis. They also put up alternative hypotheses for the spaces of other sizes, which were commensurable with observed phenomena.

8457 Safeguard

The terms true and false are not applicable to hypotheses (or normative principles). The realm of these is out of bounds to such terms. We can only apply the terms valid and invalid. Validity is to be determined by verification in the phenomenal universe of the new results predicted on their basis and by their commensurability with the new experiences coming to light from time to time.

846 Benefit of Generalisation and Abstraction

Generalisation and abstraction, forming part of scientific method, are helpful intellectual tools, provided the danger spots are under vigilance and safeguards are applied. Without their aid, much of progress would have been impossible. We would not have electricity to do ever so many things at the mere pressing of a button. Atomic power would not have come to meet the situation which will be shortly created by the exhaustion of the conventional sources of power. Indeed, the number and flexibility of the high-level generalisations and abstractions in a community may even be taken as a measure of its potential well-being. We should not develop a cynical aversion to intellectual abstraction in the pursuit of scientific method.

847 Resulting Versatility

Every step in generalisation and abstraction increases the versatility of a subject. This is well demonstrated in the development of mathematics. Let us take the concept of numbers. It began with positive integers. These were generalised to embrace negative numbers, rational numbers, real numbers, imaginary numbers, complex numbers, hyper-complex numbers, and transfinite numbers of different orders. In another direction, arithmetic was generalised and abstracted into algebra and analysis. The operations in these and other branches were then generalised and abstracted into the calculus of operations and the theory of groups. This capacity to abstract and generalise without limit has enabled mathematics to become ubiquitous and make itself serviceable in any field of thought whatever—whether it is in the region of physical, biological or social sciences or in the field of humanities. It is the versatility thus got by it that made Gauss call it the queen of sciences.

CHAPTER 85

TOOLS AND MODELS

851   Analogy between Mathematics and Classification

THERE IS A CONSIDERABLE analogy between mathematics and knowledge classification.

(1) Mathematics is a tool for mechanising inference. Knowledge classification is a tool for mechanising arrangement.

(2) Mathematics uses numbers as its own tools. Classification too uses numbers as its own tools. Classification uses only ordinal numbers, while mathematics uses cardinal numbers largely and also occasionally ordinal numbers.

(3) Mathematics generalises its concept of numbers as and when need arises. This has been already mentioned in section 847. Classification too generalises its concept of ordinal numbers.

(4) In spite of their freedom to create new numbers, both mathematics and classification are parsimonious in exercising this freedom. They both show respect to Ockham's razor.

(5) Mathematics makes an artificial language of its symbolic system. In classification, too, the system of class numbers is equivalent to an artificial language of ordinal numbers.

(6) Mathematics and classification are clear about the sphere of use for their respective artificial languages. In particular, they do not intend them for use as a medium of speech or as a literary medium.

(7) Mathematics separates work in the idea plane from work in the notational plane. When it seizes a problem, it first analyses it into its constituents, selects the relevant ones, and renders them into notation. Then it operates on the notation according to prescribed rules. It retranslates the result in terms of the idea plane. Classification too separates work in the idea plane from work in the notational plane. This has been shown in detail in part 3.

(8) The notational plane of mathematics points out untapped regions in the idea plane. Following its clue, new planets have been discovered, for example Uranus and Neptune. The notational plane of classification points out fallow areas in the universe of knowledge awaiting cultivation. A number like $G11:C5$ given in the notational plane of C.C. suggests a subject like "Radiation of Cells." Actually, the possibility of this subject was examined under the auspices of the Carnegie Institute of Washington; and a volume appeared on "Mitogenetic Radiation." Even the establishment of the impossibility of a

subject implies the concept of the subject and all the negative literature on it have to be given its class number. This is much like a convention in mathematics. To prove that a problem is insoluble is itself deemed its solution!

852 Example Set by Mathematics

Mathematics is one of the oldest disciplines, in point of time. But my Professor Edward B. Ross and Professor V. Ramaswamy Ayyar, the founder of the Indian Mathematical Society, told me quite independently that mathematics was the youngest of disciplines. It is the youngest as it still possesses all the virility and capacity for growth of a new-born baby. Classification is one of the youngest of disciplines in point of time. The several analogies between the two disciplines suggest that it will be profitable for the new-comer to learn from the method of development of the young " old guard " of two thousand years' standing, which is still developing as much as a newborn.

853 Forging New Tools

Forging new tools to solve new problems is a quality of mathematics. It does not deny the existence of a new problem because it has not got in its armoury the tools necessary to solve it. The design of new tools is motivated also to make the solution of a problem more elegant. Classification may benefit by proceeding along analogous lines. A new tool may have to be designed largely in the notational plane or largely in the idea plane. In either case, it will need a new term in the verbal plane.

8531 Condensation by Place Value

Let us take the notational plane first. One mode of forging a new tool is by " Condensation Device." The Dravidian, the Egyptian and the Roman notational systems have been overpowered by large numbers. In Roman notation, for example, a million has to be written as MMM. . . repeated 1,000 times. It is inefficient, as it will take many hours to write it. It is obviously inelegant. The invention of place value as distinct from absolute value has made it possible to represent it by 1,000,000. A number of 1,000 digits has been condensed to one of seven digits only. The notational system of library classification has adopted a condensation device.

8532 Condensation by Index Notation

Even condensation by place value device becomes inelegant and inefficient, when still greater numbers arise in the idea plane. For example, the radius of the universe as explored till now with the telescope is said to be 5,000,000,000,000,000,000,000,000 miles. The number of atoms found within this space is estimated to be 1 followed by 100 zeros. The number of sand grains needed to fill up this space is estimated to be 3 followed by 74 zeros. About 2,000 years ago,

India enriched mathematics with the device of index-notation, though it was not adopted universally for several centuries later. With the new device of condensation by index, the above three numbers can be written as 5.10^{21}; 10^{100}; and 3.10^{74} respectively. This method of condensation does not appear to lend itself for adoption by the notational system of classification. It is in essence planar notation. It needs investigation if class number can stand a planar notation.

8533 CONDENSATION BY OTHER DEVICES

In depth classification, we are now coming across long class numbers. The Canons of Expressiveness and Relativity make them unavoidable. The Canon of Expressiveness creates long class numbers in dealing with micro-thought of great depth. The Canon of Relativity is due really to the absence of effective condensation devices to condense isolate numbers belonging to different levels of facets of different fundamental categories. The device proposed in section 4683 to represent intra-facet relation—that is, relation between isolates within one and the same facet—is a Condensation Device, which will shorten class numbers in certain cases. The table of critical numbers given in section 3686 is also a help to choose appropriate Condensation Device for co-ordinate isolate numbers within an array of the idea plane. Can we find other condensation devices?

8534 HELP FROM VERBAL PLANE

It often happens that the idea plane has created a situation for long numbers, but that the notational plane takes a much longer time to throw forth an appropriate notation. It happened in mathematics. Large numbers of the sizes mentioned in sections 8531 and 8532 had been conceived long before the place-value-device and index-device were invented. The *Ramayana* shows in verses 33 to 37 of chapter 28 of the part on War that help was sought from the verbal plane during the Epic Period in India to denote such large numbers. Archimedes is said to have done similarly in a later age. Here is a table of the verbal aids used:

Epic Period in India				Archimedes Period in Greece	
Number	Verbal Representation	Number	Verbal Representation	Number	Verbal Representation
10^7	*Koti*	..	..	10^4	Myriad
10^{12}	*Sanku*	10^{47}	*Samudram*	10^8	Octade
..	..	10^{52}	*Mahaugham*		

The Verbal Extension of the D.C. number, designed by A. J. Wells for the *British national bibliography* to adapt D.C. provisionally for depth classification, is of a similar kind. This is preferable to the use of nonindividualising class numbers. The primary purpose of classification is lost by the blind imposition of an upper limit to the length of class number as the B.C. does. It would amount to refusing to recognise the fact of the existence of micro-thought of great depth, as it would be to refuse to recognise the fact of the existence of so many atoms in the world. The provisional use of verbal extension to meet the situation will keep the problem ever visible and eventually lead to the invention of a suitable Condensation Device in the notational plane.

8535   ENLARGEMENT OF BASE

Enlargement of the base of the notational system is found in mathematics as well as in classification. But mathematics does not run amuck in this matter. It does not extend the base without satisfying itself that the existing base is truly outwitted. Here is an interesting example: The base of 10, taken along with certain condensation devices, was sufficient to meet many crises. But there are certain entities whose number could not be expressed in these terms. In all cases, the verbal denotation by the general term " Infinity " was used. Cantor showed that the number was not the same in all cases. He called them " Transfinite Numbers," and introduced new digits to differentiate them. He used the Hebrew letter " aleph " with the successive suffixes o, 1, 2, 3, etc. " Aleph zero " represents the number of rational numbers. " Aleph one " represents the number of points in a line, a square, or a cube. " Aleph two " represents the number of possible geometrical curves. The number of atoms in the entire universe even is smaller than " aleph zero." " Aleph one " is greater than " aleph zero " and cannot be expressed in terms of the conventional base and " aleph zero " taken together. So also " aleph two " is greater than " aleph one." We have not yet been able to find any universe in which the number of entities is greater than " aleph two " and needs the introduction of the new digit " aleph three." Classification too should abstain from running amuck in exercising the freedom to create new ordinal digits.

8536   NEW CALCULI

In the idea plane, too, mathematics demonstrates the advantage of new tools to meet increasing complexities. Many problems in geometry made the use of traditional pure methods very arduous. Then the analytical and later the projective methods were designed. For each problem, the most suitable method is chosen. Many calculi too have been designed in addition to the Newtonian one. Calculus of differences, calculus of variation and tensor calculus are examples. A similar thing has happened in classification. Enumeration had proved an adequate tool for macro-thought up to a point. The designing of facet analysis gave better results beyond that point. To deal with micro-thought, even this was inadequate. It was found more comfortable to introduce level and round analysis. These are only the first attempts. Classification should keep continuing its work in designing new tools of analysis in the idea plane.

854 New Models

Mathematics shows the way to classification in yet another way. It is best seen in its relation to the universe of physical phenomena. As far back as the fourth millennium before Christ, the Chaldeans had provided a model to represent the movement of the heavenly bodies. It put the earth in the centre and made the planets, the sun, and the stars move in circles. Certain observed motions did not fit into this model. To fit them in, the model was slightly changed. The circular orbits were changed into epicyclic ones. The observations of Tycho Brahe made this model need too many inconvenient modifications to have the observations fitted. It was therefore abandoned, and another model was set up and improved upon by a series of astronomers— Copernicus, Kepler and Newton. For space of astronomical dimensions, Newton gave a model. When certain later observations did not fit into them easily, Einstein provided another model. At the other extreme of intra-atomic space, several models have been constructed mathematically. Classification too will have to work out several models of classification to meet different grades of depth in the universe of knowledge.

855 Postulational Method

Another valuable feature of mathematics is the Postulational Method adopted in the construction of new tools as well as models. The adoption of this method helps it to keep clear of fallacies likely to make it cross boundary conditions. In this method, one is not bound by any preconceived metaphysical or other ideas, and not even by factual experiences. Certain postulates are assumed, and all the implications are worked out. By varying the postulates, we get different tools and models. In the realm of algebra for example, in addition to the conventional algebra, we now have several algebras. Some of these are non-commutative; some are non-associative; and so on. So it is in every other realm. Here, the whole work takes the form, " If so and so, then so and so." No thought is taken about the existence of any universe of entities, answering the assumed postulates. Mathematics merely sets up several models with several systems of postulates as the basis, quite unmindful of the existence or otherwise of a correlate universe within the realm of experience or facts. It is open to those who deal with any particular universe to choose the particular model whose postulates hold good in the universe. Classification too will gain in its efficiency if the postulational method is adopted. The postulates assumed in the account of analytico-synthetic classification given in parts 3 and 4 have been listed on pages 23-24. The postulates pertaining to the notational plane in the C.C. have been given in its own part 1, consisting of rules. These are only first attempts.

856 Tools and Models in Anticipation

The postulational method admits of forging tools and setting up models in anticipation. Sometimes it takes centuries even to find use of a new tool or a new model. For example, the imaginary and complex numbers were designed by the Italian mathematician Cardan as early as the sixteenth century. No correlate was found for it in the world of experience for nearly two centuries. Thereafter, a French amateur mathematician, Argand, gave it a geometrical interpretation. In the present century, this tool came to help Einstein to combine our ordinary three-dimensional space and time into one four-dimensional space, with which he could set up his new model for the universe. Now that classification has entered the cycle of scientific method, such anticipatory work should become possible. It will be fascinating work.

CHAPTER 86

ABSTRACT CLASSIFICATION

861 What

THE RELATION OF ABSTRACT classification to library classification, or of classification in any other sphere, is like that of pure mathematics to applied mathematics, physics or any other natural science, and social sciences. Mathematics provides a variety of models, constructed according to abstract principles developed for constructing them, without worrying itself whether there are or not actual phenomena answering either to the assumptions at the foundation or to the finished model itself. Our knowledge of the external world, as it is at a particular time, can be correlated or fitted into one or other of these models. At a later time, we may accumulate some more knowledge of the external world, which cannot be fitted into the old model. Then, we choose a more suitable one from among the other models provided by mathematics. So it can be in the realm of classification too. Abstract classification can provide a variety of models, without worrying itself whether the universe of knowledge has put forth or not modes of development or structure answering to each such model. At a particular time, a particular model may closely fit the structure of the universe of knowledge found established at that time. At a later time, it may develop in new ways into a new structure, which cannot be fitted into the old model. Then we look to abstract classification to provide or to have already provided another class-fitting model.

8611 MOULD

A model provided by abstract classification may be looked upon as if it were a mould. By itself, it is an empty shell. The concrete data about the structure and filiation of the universe of knowledge as reflected in recorded knowledge should be poured into it, as it were. Then only, the model yields a meaningful scheme of classification. As the recorded knowledge is poured into it, the schedules for the different subjects take shape, with their distinctive isolate ideas, isolate terms and isolate numbers. Later on more knowledge is recorded; we come to know more of several subjects. Then perhaps some of the unfilled niches in the mould get filled up. Some of the unoccupied places in arrays get occupied. Or some totally empty array gets filled up. Or some further links of a chain get filled up. Or a totally empty chain is filled up. Or it may be that a hitherto empty facet gets filled up. All this will be in the exact measure of what comes to be known and gets recorded and offers itself to be poured into the mould. It may happen also that the mould is unsuited and cracks or even bursts. Then we have to pick out a more suitable mould.

8612 BEFORE WORLD WAR I

Before World War I, the socialised recorded knowledge, sought to be served by a library with the aid of classification and catalogue, consisted virtually of macro-thought embodied in books. Its development was largely through dissection and denudation. Viewed from the idea plane, a model with a single train of arrays proved sufficient. Viewed from the notational plane, a monolithic type of class number proved sufficient. Viewed jointly from both planes, a single schedule proved sufficient and economical. We took from the abstract classification only a model or a mould, which we have named Enumerative. The use of this gave us enumerative schemes such as the D.C. and E.C. They differed from each other only in the sequence of classes preferred in the idea plane and in the species of digits used in the notational plane. Otherwise, they were in essence the same. They conformed to the same model, or they were cast from the same mould, furnished by abstract classification.

8613 BETWEEN WORLD WARS I AND II

Between World Wars I and II, libraries had to handle and serve more of specialised books embodying macro-thought with a larger number of proliferations. The enumerative model or mould was too crude and unsuited for knowledge with such a structure. The structure of many subjects, attracting books, showed a new mode of development which has been called lamination. Viewed from the idea plane, a model with a few independent trains of arrays or facets was found necessary and sufficient. Viewed from the notational plane, a model with at least one digit of an additional species of symbol for use as a non-substantive but connecting symbol was found necessary and sufficient. The class number had to be multipartite. Viewed jointly from both planes, the use of several schedules was found necessary; and enumeration had to be confined to these individual schedules and could not reach the level of class numbers themselves. We were obliged to take from abstract classification a model or a mould, which we had named Analytico-Synthetic. The use of this gave the analytico-synthetic schemes U.D.C. and the C.C. of the first three editions. They were, to a large extent, the same in essence. They conformed more or less to the same model, or they were cast more or less from similar moulds, furnished by abstract classification.

8614 AFTER WORLD WAR II

During World War II, there was pressing need to intensify library service to the point of classifying and cataloguing micro-thought embodied only in articles in periodicals or scientific reports. The benefit of such intensive library service was felt to be profitable for the peaceful improvement of the well-being of humanity, even after the war. Indeed, it became necessary, and it came to be practised. The result was an intensification or sharpening of classification. Taken along with cataloguing, it came to be called Documentation Work. The intensive classification could not be fitted into the analytico-synthetic model as it was used before the war. Viewed from the idea plane, the number of facets was insufficient; many more facets were necessary; and the model or the mould should be capable of mechanising their sequence. Viewed from the notational plane, the number of connecting symbols was too small; more were necessary. Abstract classification should supply a more complex model or mould. Work on it is just in progress. We have named it Depth Model or Mould. As we are now developing it, it appears to be clumsy and difficult of use, for it is only an enlarged analytico-synthetic model, with a few new features. It is much like the epicycles got out of circles by the Chaldeans and the Greeks as a model for the motion of heavenly bodies, referred to in section 854. A model based on a fundamentally different foundation is perhaps necessary and will soon be found by abstract classification.

862 Why

Abstract classification, as a field for study and research, is not a mere creation of fancy. It is no more so than is abstract mathematics. It involves no doubt purely intellectual work at a highly rarefied level of abstraction. But so also is the work in pure mathematics, in the eyes of many. To them, it can be said, as G. H. Hardy said in his inaugural address as Savilian Professor of Geometry at Oxford (published as *Famous problems in mathematics*), that it is at least a harmless occupation. In reality, there are positive reasons why abstract classification should be studied.

8621 Objective Reason

The universe of knowledge is a dynamic continuum, which is ever-increasing in its turbulence. Socialised recorded knowledge also shares this attribute. New modes of development are frequently appearing round the corner. The model in use often gets outmoded. But classification should be done efficiently, if the Five Laws of Library Science are to be fulfilled and the library is to fulfil its function as a social institution. New models can no longer be found easily, unless we have developed a discipline of abstract classification. If this discipline can produce a suitable model or mould, already completed and kept in the show window, it will be ideal. It should at least produce a new design on order. This is the objective and external reason why provision should be made or promoted by universities, the F.I.D., Unesco, and other similar agencies, for the pursuit of abstract classification.

8622 Subjective Reason

As the *Upanishads* pronounced, the essence of man is intellect. The intellect is restless. It cannot help revelling in the pursuit of abstraction at higher and higher levels. This innate urge is irrepressible. It looks for every possible field to feed on. It finds joy in working in abstract fields of every kind. Classification presents one such field in the form of abstract classification. This is the subjective and internal reason why universities should provide for research in abstract classification.

8623 Certainty of Social Use

Provision for work in the abstract field of mathematics is now made willingly, because eventually the fruits grown in that field have always added to social benefit and enrichment. Humanity has learned to act in this matter as if it is guided by the old Indian saw " The world never was and never will be except what it is now." Therefore it makes provision for research in pure mathematics in the full hope of its social use. Provision for research in abstract classification also should be made in a similar spirit. Social use for the fruits of work in that field is certain.

8624 Cynic's Obstruction

The greatest danger is from those within the profession, who lay cynical obstruction in the way. Cynicism may be born in those who do not have the capacity to work in the rarefied atmosphere of abstract classification. Or, it may even be born of sheer idleness in those gifted with the necessary intellectual capacity, in mere self-defence. Mathematics has already overcome the obstruction from both of these types. Abstract classification has still to make its way.

8625 Benign Impatience

The man of full-fledged intuition may occasionally utter words of disapproval of wasting oneself with work in the abstract fields. Blake's disapproval of this sort is typical:

> And this is the manner of the Sons of Albion in their strength;
> They take the Two Contraries which are called Qualities, with which
> Every Substance is clothed; they name them Good and Evil.
> From them make an Abstract, which is a Negation
> Not only of the Substance from which it is derived,
> A murderer of its own Body, but also a murderer
> Of every Divine Member: it is the Reasoning Power,
> An Abstract objecting power that negatives everything.
> This is the Spectre of Man, the Holy Reasoning Power,
> And in its Holiness is closed the Abomination of Desolation.

This is nothing but the impatience of a " Seer "—a man of intuition seeing the entirety in a flash—with the slow process of the man of mere intellect. Blake uses the word " Ratio " to denote the process of abstraction and uses the names of Bacon, Newton and Locke as personifications of the same. However, it is only benevolent impatience. For, the recognition of the right function of the intellect comes. It is realised that the light of unclouded revelation through intuition is far too pure and brilliant to be suitable or bearable to ordinary man. Then, as at the end of *Jerusalem,* Bacon, Newton and Locke are restored to their legitimate eminence. The Upanishadic experience that the essence of ordinary man is intellect is remembered. Work in abstract fields is necessary and unavoidable in the continuous lift of the well-being of society, through the medium of intellect, through the ordinary man's own effort which is out of bounds for miracles.

863 How

To deal with the how of abstract classification, we should refer back to the cycle of scientific method described in chapter 82. At the nadir, we gain experience in the structure of micro-thought and in the filiation in the universe of knowledge. We classify them in several ways, by trial and error. That is, we move through the empirical phase. Empiricism is wrongly believed to belong only to the universe of facts of natural phenomena. This restriction is not necessary. The facts may concern the universe of intellectual constructs and concepts also. This is the positivistic pursuit of classification. All along, we put forth only concrete schemes of classification, while in the empirical phase. Several such attempts make us seize some normative principles and hypotheses. This puts us at the zenith in the cycle. This induces in us an urge for a speculative pursuit of classification. This takes us through the deductive phase.

8631 SPECULATIVE PURSUIT

In this speculative pursuit, we start setting up various alternative sets of postulates about possible modes of development of the universe of knowledge, the structure of micro-thought, and filiatory sequence. These postulates are of an abstract nature such as those about fundamental categories, rounds, levels, zones and phases. These postulates will be in the idea plane. To these are attached some postulates in the notational plane. From all these postulates, rules of procedure are derived for work in the idea plane and for implementing the results in the notational plane. The rules of procedure point to the number and variety of schedules to be put up in advance, how they should be formed, and the extent to which schedules will get created automatically as and when need arises. In due course, lemmas or even more abstract principles are produced to facilitate the putting up of a variety of models-in-abstract.

8632 RELATED SEQUENCE OF MODELS

Experience gained in the construction of models-in-abstract in the realm of mathematics has given us an important principle to be observed in the realm of abstract classification. Models should fall into a related sequence. Of course, several such sequences may be formed. In each related sequence, a later model should contain all the earlier models as degenerate cases. For example, the Einsteinian model contains the Newtonian model within itself as the degenerate case got by making the velocity of light infinite instead of finite. So also it is in the little glimpse got till now into the realm of abstract classification. The enumerative model is contained in the analytico-synthetic model of the simpler kind, as a degenerate case in which the number of facets is one instead of a few. So also, the simpler analytico-synthetic model is contained in the proposed depth model, as a degenerate case in which there is only one fundamental category instead of five, and only one or two rounds and one or two levels instead of many of each of them.

864 Alarm—False and True

Abstract classification may be as empty as a game imagined in a dream. Nothing whatever is in it except the rules of the game. It can get content only when it is applied and a concrete scheme is derived from it in the light of the universe of recorded knowledge. It is therefore not proper to raise an alarm against abstract classification without applying it. It is a false alarm. On the other hand, a true alarm in respect of classification is raised by another party. It is the party engaged in research. It is also the party engaged in the productivity drive in the industrial world. According to them, documentation service is not as efficient as they need. Classification is not as nimble as they need it to be. It is not able to keep pace with the creation of new formations of micro-thought in the universe of knowledge. To meet this true alarm, creation of models by abstract classification should be ever on the move, even as the creation of micro-thought in the traditional regions of the universe of knowledge.

865 Do-All Classification

The complicated structure of micro-thought of deep intension needs a class number with an equally complicated structure. The perfect simplicity of an enumerative scheme is akin to the vacant smile of idiocy described in the *Good earth* of Pearl Buck. Preferring a simple series of arithmetical or alphabetical digits to a complex structure punctuated by connecting symbols is like preferring a circle to an ellipse of which the circle is only a degenerate form. In 1925, a professor of mathematics at St. Andrews gave me a measure of the penetrating power of a mathematical friend of mine in the following words, " Your friend says in his thesis that an ellipse is more symmetrical than a circle! How daring!! And yet how true!!! " Probably, addiction to a simple class number of a few digits of the same species is of the same degenerate kind as addiction to circle—a projection of degenerate and static mentality over the dynamic infinite universe of knowledge. If the principle stated in section 8632 is followed, a good classification-shell furnished by abstract classification to suit micro-thought of great depth, will mould out only simple class number for macro-thought, usually served in schools and public libraries. Abstract classification tells us that a scheme is not worth adoption if it cannot yield with equal ease and certitude a simple class number for huge and simple macro-thought and general book, and an expressive coextensive, though complicated, class number for tiny complex micro-thought and specialised article. It tells us, " Don't go in for a do-little simple scheme. Adopt a do-all elaborate scheme. Like the trunk of an elephant, it can pick up a needle with as much ease and elegance as it can pull out a tree, root and branch."

CHAPTER 87

SYMBOLISATION

871 Formalisation

THE CULMINATION OF CLASSIFICATION schemes and classifying practices in abstract classification is but in keeping with the familiar tendency of all intellectual disciplines increasing formalisation gradually. This has happened in mathematics and logic. Each of them amounts to a calculus. Classification too amounts to a calculus. Formalisation leads to the use of symbols, sooner or later. The *barbara* of Aristotle is an early example. Boole carried it further and made logic safer and more productive. This was on the syntactical side of the sentences used in logic. In recent years, work on the semantic side has found it necessary to have recourse to symbols of its own. Classification too, particularly abstract classification, will have to resort to symbolisation of its own. This is inevitable in any discipline of a high level of abstraction dealing with methodology in abstract. There are reasons for this.

872 Law of Parsimony

In the development of any discipline of great abstraction, several new ideas get created. Many of them are deep composite ideas. They first get expressed in terms of a number of simpler constituent ideas. Therefore the expression or the term for a new depth idea is very long. It has also to be repeated quite often. Its communication therefore requires considerable breath or writing, and time. This triple waste is repugnant to the Law of Parsimony. Brevity, at any cost, is prescribed by it. It recommends the replacement of a long expressive or "intensional" term by a short "extensional" one. Since the practitioners of such abstract disciplines are intellectuals who feel quite at home with *ad hoc* symbols, they prefer a letter, a numeral or any equally short symbol for use as the "extensional" term for each of the ideas to be handled often.

873 Strain of Thinking

Moreover, the expressive multi-worded term denoting an idea often acts as a distraction to the mind. For the constituent elements of the new depth-thought are often not relevant to the further work on it. It is only the integral whole of it that counts. Therefore the strain of thinking—making an inference or arriving at a judgment—becomes great when thinking is done through the medium of long terms made

458

of words in natural language. This happens even if we are using only a well-defined technical jargon, well sterilised and freed from all homonyms and undertones and overtones of suggestion. This amounts to saying that the communication of one's thought, even to oneself, in the building of further thought, becomes arduous. Everybody experiences this occasionally when facing involved thinking. During the last thirty years, I have felt the excruciating pain of this experience in the course of work on classification and cataloguing. In collective thinking and face-to-face communication also, the same experience is felt. This is due to the simultaneous incidence of a new mode of thinking and a new region of thought. Long-drawn-out terms cause strain, slow down the rate of thinking, and even blur thought. This has been frequently experienced by the Library Research Circle in Delhi. Even a small dose of symbolic language has given great relief.

874 Sample of Symbols

The workers on the foundations of mathematics and on the semantic branch of logic have established a more or less universal code of symbols for their use. Workers on the foundations of classification and on abstract classification will gain much by doing similarly. Here is a sample of what the Library Research Circle in Delhi used. It adopted certain conventions before Packet Notation was adopted.

8741 Conventions

(1) No symbol should consist of a bare letter, or numeral, or a combination of them, since the class numbers forming the object of study are so made up.

(2) A symbol got by the contraction of a word to the initial letter or to two or more letters should be enclosed in circular brackets.

(3) To denote a facet, the contraction of the word denoting the fundamental category or the special name of its manifestation should be enclosed in square brackets.

(4) The round to which a facet belongs should be indicated by prefixing the number of the round to the symbol for the fundamental category, within the square brackets.

(5) The level to which a facet belongs should be indicated by suffixing the number of the level to the symbol for the fundamental category, within the square brackets.

(6) The number of the order of an array, or of a zone, or of an octave, or of a focus should be indicated by suffixing the number to the symbol concerned, within the circular brackets.

(7) As in algebra, a generalised number should be indicated by a lower-case letter.

(8) The negative of a concept should be indicated by putting a bar over the top of the symbol indicating it.

(9) When a complex idea has to be indicated by putting the symbols for the constituent ideas, one after another, these symbols

should be put in the decreasing sequence of the extension of the concepts concerned.

8742 ILLUSTRATIONS

Symbol	Term	Symbol	Term
(A)	Array	(L)	Level
(A1)	Array of order 1	(L2)	Level 2
(Aa)	Array of order a	(Lr)	Level r
(C)	Class	(M)	Matter
(CA)	Amplified class	(O)	Octave
(CB)	Basic class	(O2)	Octave 2
(CC)	Canonical class	(OL)	Last octave
(CCD)	Compound class	(OP)	Penultimate octave
(CCX)	Complex class	(P)	Personality
(CH)	Characteristic	(PH)	Phase
(CM)	Main class	(PHB)	Biasing phase
(CN)	Class number	(PHC)	Comparison phase
(CS)	Classification scheme	(PHI)	Influencing phase
(E)	Energy	(PI)	Idea plane
(F)	Facet	(PN)	Notational plane
(FC)	Fundamental category	(PV)	Verbal plane
(FS)	Focus	(R)	Round
(I)	Isolate	(R2)	Round 2
(I3)	Isolate of order 3	(Rr)	Round r
(In)	Isolate or order n	(S)	Space
(II)	Isolate idea	(T)	Time
(IN)	Isolate number	(U)	Universe
(IT)	Isolate term	(Z)	Zone
		(Z3)	Zone 3

8743 COMBINATION OF SYMBOLS

Here are a few examples of combination of symbols:

Symbol	Meaning
[A]	Amplifying facet
[FC]	Facet of any fundamental category
[1E]	Energy facet in round 1
[eE]	Energy facet in round e
[1E] (O1)	Octave 1 in energy facet of round 1
[1E] (OL)	Last octave in energy facet of round 1
[1P1]	Personality facet of level 1 in round 1
[1P3]	Personality facet of level 3 in round 1
[rPp_r]	Personality facet of level p_r in round r
[1P1] (A1)	Array of order 1 in personality facet of level 1 in round 1
[1P1] (A1) (Z1)	Zone 1 of array of order 1 in personality facet of level 1 in round 1
[1P1] (A1) (O2)	Octave 2 of array of order 1 in personality facet of level 1 in round 1
[1P1] (A1) (OL)	Last octave of array of order 1 in personality facet of level 1 in round 1

460

Symbol	Meaning
[1P1] (A1) (Z1) (I)	Isolate in zone 1 of array of order 1 in personality facet of level 1 in round 1
[1P1] (A1) (Z1) (IN)	Isolate number in zone 1 of array of order 1 in personality facet of level 1 in round 1
[rPp_r] (Aa) (Z2) (II)	Isolate idea in zone 2 of array of order a in personality facet of level p_r in round r
[rPp_r] (Aa) (O1) (IQ)	Quasi isolate in octave 1 of array of order 1 in personality facet of level p_r in round r
[S3]	Space facet of level 3
[S3] (A1)	Array of order 1 of space facet of level 3
[S3] (A1) (Z2)	Zone 2 of array of order 1 of space facet of level 3
[T2] (A1) (Z1)	Zone 1 of array of order 1 of time facet of level 2

The above table shows the economy of symbolisation in the discussion of the theory of classification. A long statement like " There can be no first zone in space facet " becomes " [S](Z1) does not exist."

875 Generalised Facet Formula

The use of symbols enables us to set down a generalised facet formula based on the postulates mentioned in part 3. It will be as follows. Though it is spread over several lines due to exigency of space in the printed page, it should be read continuously as if it were in one line.

$$(BC)[A](OL),[A](OP)$$
$$,[1P1],[1P2],\ldots[1Pp_1\text{-}1],[1Pp_1]$$
$$;[1M1];[1M2];\ldots[1Mm_1\text{-}1];[1Mm_1]$$
$$:[IE]$$
$$[2P1],[2P2],\ldots[2Pp_2\text{-}1],[2Pp_2]$$
$$;[2M1];[2M2];\ldots[2Mm_2\text{-}1];[2Mm_2]$$
$$:[2E]$$
$$\ldots \quad \ldots \quad \ldots \quad \ldots$$
$$[rP1],[rP2],\ldots[2Pp_r\text{-}1],[rPp_r]$$
$$;[rM1];[rM2];\ldots[rMm_r\text{-}1];[rMm_r]$$
$$:[rE]$$
$$.[S1].[S2].\ldots[Ss\text{-}1].[Ss]$$
$$.[T1].[T2].\ldots[Tt\text{-}1.].[Tt]$$

where p_1, p_2, $\ldots p_r$, m_1, $m_2 \ldots m_r$, r, s, and t may have any integral value.

The above generalised facet formula is for rounds started by energy foci. A generalised formula can be similarly constructed for rounds started by common isolates. An attempt to state the idea expressed by the above generalised facet formula, in natural language even with technical terminology, will show the need to have recourse to symbolisation in the theory of classification. Even an attempt to make a statement, in natural language, of a facet formula with two rounds and two or three levels of personality, matter, space and time facets, will be sufficiently convincing.

461

876 **Symbolic Meta-language**

However much symbolisation helps to secure economy in expression and communication, and reduces strain in thinking, it is a comparatively trivial use of symbolisation. It should be possible to use symbolic language for the positive purpose of advancing thought. Such a use of symbolisation is being made in mathematics and semantics. In those subjects, symbolic language is used as a meta-language to develop another language—the object-language. In the formulation of postulates in a self-consistent manner, in the making of valid inferences from them, and in being watchful against the unconscious introduction of new assumptions in the course of the development of the theory of classification, the results of semanticists will be of use, because they are designed to help in the making of inferences from propositions. But I have a feeling that an additional type of symbolic meta-language should be designed to help the proper development of the classificatory language of ordinal numbers as an object-language. This object-language is not concerned with the finding out of the implications of a set of propositions. It is only concerned with filiatory relation among concepts. The design of this additional type will help a better exploitation of the potentialities of a language of ordinal numbers. It will enable the setting up of an adequate variety of models in abstract classification. This is necessary to develop depth classification to the pitch of efficiency needed for library service to fulfil its functions in organised research-work-in-series by a far-flung team engaged in the maintenance of social well-being in the world.

CHAPTER 88

PROBLEMS FOR PURSUIT

IT MAY BE HELPFUL to collect together the unsolved problems mentioned in the different sections. Some of these belong exclusively to the domain of the Theory of Abstract Classification. Even many of the others listed below in groups 1 to 3 will perhaps be better pursued with the aid of the methodology to be developed in that theory. The figure given within brackets at the end of an item is the number of the section where the problem is raised and discussed.

881 Problems in Idea Plane

1 Guiding principles for determining the first characteristic for a train of characteristics, and the favoured first characteristic for accommodation in the first octave of the second zone of the array of the first order in a personality or a matter facet (3651).

21 Choice of favoured first characteristic for a facet (3651).

22 Sequence of characteristics in a train of characteristics (3313 and 451).

23 Sequence of facets (3314).

24 Sequence of rounds of energy facets (465).

25 Sequence of facets of matter in a round (466).

26 Sequence of isolates in the application of auto-bias device (323).

31 Guiding principles for determining the correct modulation in fixing the successive links in a chain of isolates within a facet (152).

32 Utilisation of zone 4 of array of order 2 of a main class (3641).

33 Guiding principles for determining the correct modulation in fixing the successive levels of personality facet in a round (467).

41 Number of fundamental characteristics (3502).

42 Number of energy categories (36135).

43 Assignment of characteristics to appropriate fundamental categories (36171).

51 Utilisation of levels of personality in the second and later rounds (462).

52 Utilisation of zones (3624).

61 Isolation of new phase relations (468).

71 Guiding principles for the grouping of the different cultivars of one and the same species of agricultural plant (566 to 5662).

882 **Problems in Notational Plane**

11 Explicit and objective determination of seminal mnemonics (272).

12 Recapturing the traditional seminal mnemonics in Indian, and perhaps also Chaldean, tradition for letters and numerals (272).

13 Establishment of scheduled mnemonics for the penultimate octave used for specials (36723).

21 Need or absence of need to have different connecting symbols for different levels of one and the same fundamental category; and if there is need, the design of the same (36133).

22 Need or absence of need to have different connecting symbols to indicate the round to which a facet belongs; and if there is need, the design of the same (36133).

23 Need or absence of need to have different connecting symbols for the different modes of incidence of energy category; and if there is need, the design of the same (36135).

31 New devices for condensation of notation (8533).

32 Possibility of the use of planar notation instead of linear notation (8532).

41 Mathematical proof of the impossibility of everywhere apupa pattern (445).

42 The possibility or otherwise of the scattering of filiatory isolates in different octaves and in different zones (3242).

51 Fixing the most helpful ordinal value to the starter in packet notation (3623).

883 **Problems in Construction of Schedules**

11 Schedule for zone 4 of the array of main classes (3634 and its subsections and 3635).

21 Schedules for the diverse useful arts and other basic classes in the region of applied sciences (36415).

22 Schedules for complex classes, used as basic classes (472).

23 Schedules for the main classes of zone 1 (3541).

31 Schedules for zone 1 of the first order arrays in personality, matter and energy facets (457, 4561 and 4551 respectively).

32 Schedule for zone 3 of energy facet (4552).

33 Schedule for zone 4 of first order array of matter facet (4562).

884 **Probably Insoluble Problems**

11 Guiding principles for the determination of the most helpful sequence by objective methods, among main classes, canonical classes, and the isolates in certain arrays (7184).

12 Securing everywhere apupa pattern (445).

21 Notational device for every possible partial apprehension of main classes, basic classes, and isolates in arrays or facets (6572).

885 Problems in Abstract Classification

11 Guiding principles for the formulation of a consistent and necessary and sufficient system of postulates (855).

12 Lemmas for working on abstract classification (8631).

21 Forging of new tools for analysis (8536).

31 Establishment of a variety of models in abstract (854).

41 Establishment of a consistent system of symbolisation for universal use to secure brevity and precision in the communication of ideas on classification (874 and its subsections).

42 Establishment of a system of symbolic meta-language to facilitate the study of classificatory language of ordinal numbers as object-language and of the theory of classification (876).

51 The practicability of retaining the postulate that energy facet should have only one array (3536).

886 A Good Augury

The specific problems for pursuit mentioned in this chapter, the theory of abstract classification outlined in this part, and all similar theoretical and abstract problems arising in the practice of depth classification for documentation work, from time to time, should be seized by the Theory of Classification Committee mentioned in section 485. It is a good augury that the F.I.D. has been moving towards this since its Conference in Rome in 1950. A further step was taken by it at its Conference in Brussels in 1955, in the form of two resolutions brought up by the Group Meeting on Classification, General and Special, and adopted by the Plenary Meeting on September 16th, 1955.

8861 Two Resolutions

The following are the two resolutions as given in the F.I.D. document F55-Theme IV-2:

" (1) The F.I.D. recommends that a deeper and more extensive study should be made of the general theory of classification, including facet analysis, and also of their application in the documentation of specific subjects.

" (2) The commission proposes that in liaison with the FID/CA Committee, a permanent Working group be created in order to make mutual exchange of theoreticians' experiences and points of view possible. The rapporteurs shall bring about the creation of such a group and furnish the information and means of work in order that practical results may be obtained in the shortest time, by making mail exchanges easier and more frequent. The scheme proposed by Dr. Ranganathan will serve as the basic document."

8862 STARTING POINT

The starting point for the work outlined in the above two resolutions may well be an International Seminar on the subject. This may be the first of the seminars suggested in section 487. At its meeting held on September 16th, 1955, the Council of the F.I.D. has requested the Bureau to convene an International Seminar on Classification. Let us hope all this to be a good augury for definite advances at national and international levels to help the library profession play its part in a worthy and fruitful way in the global effort to conduct research-in-series for the well-being of humanity and the peaceful coexistence of nations.

INDEX

Note 1: The index number denotes the number of part, chapter, or section, as the case may be. If the entry term is the name of a subject, reference to a particular number includes reference to all its subdivisions also.

Note 2: An index number of one digit denotes a Part, of two digits a chapter, of three digits a section, and of four or more digits a subsection.

Note 3: The following contractions are used, wherever subheadings occur, to indicate the relation between the main heading and the subheading:

a t—applied to *i r t*—in relation to
def—defined *q i r t*—quoted in relation to
desc—described *r i r t*—referred in relation to
illust—illustrated

Classification
  i r t—continued
    Emotional sphere, 3751
    Intellectual sphere, 3753
    Linear arrangement, 313
    Standard procedure, 370
      illust, 57
    Transformer language, 3754
    Trans-intellectual sphere, 3752
  of agriculture, 56
  of mathematics, 52-54
  Schedule, *see* Schedule of classification
  Scheme of, *see* Scheme of classification
  Research Group *r i r t*
    Number of facets, 3313
    Packet notation, 36141
    Prolegomena, 077
Classification and communication r i r t
  International communication, 375
  Prolegomena, 075
*Classification and international documen-
    tation,* 072
Classification of sciences, 7174
*Classification, theoretical and practical
    r i r t*
  Genesis of canons, 12886
  System of knowledge, 7131
Classificationist
  def, 1286
  i r t Intuition, 12883
Classificatory
  Language, 12832
  Terminology, 34
Classified catalogue code
  q i r t Canon of currency, 1713
  r i r t
    Canon of permanence, 135
    Chain procedure, 445
    Composite books, 643
    Sequence of facets, 3317
    Verbal plane, 3333
Classifier
  def, 1286
  i r t
    Analytico-synthetic   classification,
      373
    His autonomy, 281
    His dependence, 282
    Intellection, 12884
    Scheduled mnemonics, 2622
Classifying
  def, 1287
  demonstrated, 57
  Procedure, 370
Closed array, 123
Collateral
  Array, 123
  Class, 123
Collected works, 6233

Collection, 671
  Number, 67
Colon
  Invented as ordinal number, 7731
  Value of, 7731
Colon book number, 666
Colon Classification
  desc, 77
  i r t
  Agriculture, 56
  Alphabetical device, 2234
  Anteriorising common isolate, 45821
  Apparatus for classic device, 623
  Array of canonical classes, 364
  Auto-bias device, 2372
  Autonomy of classifier, 388
  Book number, 6665
  Bounded duration, 4531
  Brown, 762
  Call number, 686
  Canon of
    Classics, 622
    Consistency, 137
    Consistent sequence, 1444
      a t mathematics, 5383
    Enumeration, 1731-1735
      a t Array of
        Main classes, 513
        Mathematics, 526
    Exclusiveness, 537
    Exhaustiveness, 141
    Helpful sequence, 143
      a t mathematics, 528
    Hospitality in array, 223
      a t array of order
        2 in math., 527
        4 in math., 536
    Hospitality in chain
      a t
        Economics, 55
        Mathematics, 542
    by auto-bias device, 2372
    by facet device, 235
    by phase device, 236
  Local variation, 633
  Relativity, 1881
    a t mathematics, 544
  Relevant sequence, 136
  Scheduled mnemonics, 263
  Seminal mnemonics, 272
  Verbal mnemonics, 2521
Canonical class array, 364
Chronological device, 2233
Classic, 6137
  Device, 623
Closed array, 227
Common isolate device, 2235
Connecting symbol *i r t*
  Facet device, 235
  Its number, 36132

ODau-M

23239